Top-To-Bottom
HOME
ORGANIZING

Top-To-Bottom
HOME ORGANIZING

A Complete Guide to Organizing
Every Room in the Home

Caralyn Kempner

Top-To-Bottom Home Organizing
A Complete Guide to Organizing Every Room in the Home

ISBN: 978-1-7323969-0-6

Library of Congress Control Number: 2018907010

Published by:
Yaz Publishing
Sheridan, WY

Contents

PART ONE

Benefits of Organizing

CHAPTER 1

Introduction to Home Organizing

A well-organized home saves you time and money. No more valuable time will be spent looking for things, because an organized home has a definitive place for everything. In a well-organized home, your money isn't wasted on overstock because an organized home stocks what it actually needs, planning only for the near future.

Consider how a cluttered home affects the time you spend cleaning it. More things mean more items for you to dust, wipe, and wash. Too much time is spent clearing, shuffling, and protecting "stuff" before actually getting to clean the base surface.

The organizational process requires time, so you need to be patient. Certainly, don't choose a time to begin organizing your home when life stresses and other commitments are beyond normal. Also be aware that an organizational project doesn't need to be conquered in a given day. In fact, rushing an organizational project can be overwhelming and may force you to make short-sighted decisions that cause mistakes and regret. An organizational plan requires much thought because there are so many aspects involved, such as decluttering, space planning, and shopping for storage essentials. Mulling over an organizational job is important since your best ideas often come to mind after the initial plan is determined. Taking time also allows opportunity for modifications that improve the overall outcome.

Organizing one's home becomes an avoided task for many reasons. Mostly, people don't know where to begin or how to approach organizing. This book helps to guide you through various organizational tasks by breaking down each task into manageable steps that can be spread out over time. Each step is intended to end at a place where your home can still function smoothly. This method makes it easier for most people to fit organizing into their busy schedules.

Many illustrations featured throughout the book are designed to help you understand how to arrange storage spaces. The illustrations display various storage systems and recommended products for a given space. Many different types of storage products are featured that appeal to all kinds of tastes and budgets.

Top Home Organizational Tips

1. Keep your household inventories to a minimum.

The biggest key to successful home organization is downsizing household inventories. Whenever you organize anything, it's essential to keep only the things that you need, use, love, or would buy again tomorrow. Evaluate your belongings with this concept in mind since it's so easy to find reasons to keep things. Often, the excuses we conjure up for holding onto our belongings can wrestle with logic. This creates the common indecision we feel that tends to stifle the organizational process.

Organizing is not about only effectively arranging your belongings; it's equally important to get rid of items that no longer serve a purpose. Carving out time to organize is challenging. Therefore, it's imperative to make good use of your time and declutter with a purpose. Once useless items are out of the way, the home is in the perfect condition to reorganize. Decluttering leads to manageable inventories, which has many advantages. First, fewer storage essentials are needed, which saves both money and space. Also, there's no wasting time making storage arrangements for unnecessary belongings. When you have fewer things, finding what you need usually takes less time.

2. Stick to one organizational project at a time.

Some people start organizing space in one room, and before completing that task, something causes them to get sidetracked with a project in another room. This tends to happen when we shift household inventories from room to room. This is never a good idea because it usually creates a fragmented, overwhelming state by being off task. It's best to keep organizational tasks small and limited until they're finished. Then you can more easily move on to the next task.

3. Don't keep unwanted items just because they *might* have value.

Commonly, people keep unnecessary things because they believe the items hold a significant monetary value. Something kept for this reason should be evaluated for its actual value, which involves a little work. Remember that almost all used items are worth one-half to one-third of their original cost, even when they're in perfect condition, simply because they're not new. Luxury items can be appraised by a certified professional. Most other belongings can be compared with identical items that are being resold.

Resale websites and stores are the best way to determine the monetary value of your used items. In general, the older the item, the less it's worth. Technological devices are a good example of how age can dramatically reduce value. Bear in mind that, in most cases, it's best to sell your things while they're somewhat current because most items depreciate rapidly. This knowledge should assist you in the decluttering process.

4. Be certain you'll use whatever you store.

Many people store items because they think one day they'll be useful. However, before doing so, it's important to visualize the item in use or be able to account for a time when the item will be used—for example, an upcoming vacation or holiday. Make certain that other members of the household are aware of items that are packed away. This way, you can receive feedback about the items and determine if they'll get used. A good way to spread the word to other family members is to place a note on a memo board or connect via digital communication.

5. Items are replaceable.

While decluttering your household inventories, keep in mind that you are dealing with material possessions that are replaceable. When something is not enjoyed or needed, let it go, bearing in mind that it's tangible and not meant to be kept for eternity. Chances are such items will never be missed. Usually, the worst thing that could happen in mistakenly letting go of something is that it needs to be replaced, which is not the end of the world. The replacement usually works out better and receives more use than the one let go. Remember that the space your items occupy is valuable real estate that you may still be paying off and are certainly paying taxes on. This makes it all the more important to use your home space efficiently and wisely.

6. People wear only a small portion of what they own.

The National Association of Professional Organizers reports that we tend to wear only 20 percent of the clothes we own. When you declutter your inventories, remember this statistic. If you continue to buy things and never eliminate useless articles, you'll eventually face stressed and overcrowded storage spaces.

7. Buy organizers after decluttering.

It's common for people to buy organizers first and then organize. This is usually inadvisable since it's easy to misjudge both the number and type of organizers you need before you thoroughly declutter, count inventories, and create a space plan. Returning or adding extra storage organizers is a common chore when we buy organizers before creating the necessary storage space. When you know which organizers you need, purchasing them beforehand is fine, especially when you are able to take advantage of a great sale. However, don't allow prepurchased storage essentials to ultimately influence your storage arrangements at the expense of poorly laid out or inefficient use of space.

Top Home Organizational Tips

→ Keep your household inventories to a minimum.

→ Stick to one organizational project at a time.

→ Don't keep unwanted items just because they might have value.

→ Be certain you'll use whatever you store.

→ Items are replaceable.

→ People wear only a small portion of what they own.

→ Buy organizers after decluttering.

CHAPTER 2

Storage Essentials

Storage systems and organizers are an investment, and proper storage systems and accessories are essential to efficient home organization. Well-planned storage systems help you manage or control household product inventories and save countless hours of looking for things. Additionally, closet organizational systems and built-in storage systems add value to a home.

Everything needs a designated place or storage location. Otherwise, maintaining organization is impossible. If there are no established places for your belongings, then countertops, tables, floors, beds, and seating will be overtaken by clutter. Whenever possible, select storage baskets or containers with handles or pulls. The difference in convenience is noteworthy. Containers housed on lower shelving or in base cabinets should have top handles for easier reach. Likewise, containers stored in upper cabinets or on high shelves function best with side handles.

Top Storage Essentials Tips

1. Multipurpose organizers are your best investment.

Storage essentials, furniture, and accessories that serve more than one storage function are best. End tables with built-in racks for periodicals and remote controllers, or message boards that also store mail and keys, are good examples of multifunctional organizers. One of the keys to successful organization is using your living space efficiently. Storage products that serve more than one storage purpose accomplish this goal.

Use caution when purchasing entertainment centers or designing custom storage arrangements that house televisions, stereos, telephones, intercoms, speaker systems, or any items subject to technological change. Unless the storage center is adjustable, it may have a limited life when storing items that become obsolete.

Don't limit an organizer's purpose only to how it's marketed. Often, it's easy for you to create increased or different uses for just about any organizer. Make a storage spot for retired organizers, and before purchasing new ones, repurpose what you already have by looking for creative uses for them.

2. Organizers are not created equally.

Investigate consumer opinions and ratings about storage products; use your common sense and invest only in the good ones. Products with a confident manufacturer's guarantee are preferable. Stiff return policies on opened packages and the like need consideration. If possible, test a storage product for promising usability before purchasing. Make certain the drawers glide effortlessly. Check that snaps open and close well. Test pulls and handles to be sure they're fastened tightly.

Wood should be thick and sturdy, and plastic unbreakable or strong. Metals should have rounded or smooth edges for safety. Check that painted items are sealed well so they don't chip easily. Don't skimp on quality and buy inferior products in order to save money. It's not worth spending the time and money to repurchase storage items or redesign storage space with new organizers.

Select storage necessities that are easy to clean and require little maintenance. Plastic, nylon, metal, and rubber are good picks. In contrast, fabric storage essentials can rip and stain easily. Wicker can snag and fray. Wood is prone to scratches, cracks, and wear. Use cardboard or paper bags only for temporary storage needs, like garage sale or donation items. Weaker paper-based or flimsy plastic products don't make

good permanent storage essentials since they're never long lasting. Too much energy is given to the organizational process to compromise with short-term storage essentials because rearranging and replacing is challenging and time consuming.

3. Commercial storage essentials are good investments.

Consider commercial storage essentials for your residential storage needs because they're superior in durability and carry large-sized organizers that are hard to find in the retail market. Commercial organizers that transfer well in your home can include recycling bins, garbage cans, buckets, baskets, coatracks, benches, bins, crates, wall racks, shelving, cubbies, garment racks, periodical racks, newspaper stands, television stands, and wall organizational systems.

4. Use over-the-door storage devices sparingly.

Many over-the-door storage items are difficult to secure, so they clank against the door while it's in motion. Such movement also creates scratches on the door. Heavy belongings bound to these organizers increase the volume of the clanking noise and, in some cases, may weaken your door hinges. Articles carelessly placed in over-the-door storage devices run a great chance of falling out simply due to the movement of the door. Over-the-door storage devices located in highly visible home locations tend to be aesthetically unappealing, so place them on the interior side of the door.

Where to Store Your Items

In order to organize your home successfully, store things in convenient places based on how they're needed or their purposes. Logical storage placement and arrangements for things will assist you in finding items more quickly and increase the chance that items will get put back properly.

Acknowledge the purpose and usefulness of everything you choose to store, and locate your storage spaces near where the articles are used. Placing items far away from where they're needed increases the likelihood that the item will not get returned and end up cluttering a counter or in a junk drawer. Sometimes, it will be important to hunt for storage space to accommodate conveniently stored items. There is always a way to find the space, but it may require creativity, such as adding organizers to a wall or floor. Similarly, storing belongings nearby makes it easier to remember where your items are located. It's also logical and helpful to store items that work in conjunction with each together. For example, store your coupons, coupon organizers, scissors, grocery shopping lists, and newspaper sales flyers together.

Don't store mysterious items in a miscellaneous container just because they "appear important." Often, smaller articles like cords, chargers, tools, gadgets, plugs, adapters, and so on get tossed in a container and never seen again since we didn't bother to determine their purpose. Ask people in the house for help in identifying such articles. If an article's purpose is undetermined, throw it away. Also make sure to store these items in the right place. Most mystery items are accessories or parts to things that should be stored with the thing they serve.

More Storage Tips

1. Make your organizers visually simple.

Storage organizers are more likely to be reused when they're plain and consistent. It's best to go with neutral colors, such as black, white, or beige since they match everything. It's common to tire of patterned or bold-colored storage organizers that were bought to match a certain room. Once the room is redecorated, the organizers will look out of place and become harder to repurpose elsewhere. This is often seen with infant and children's organizers in juvenile themes and colors like pastels or primary colors.

There are ways to add uniqueness to neutral storage organizers that are not permanent. For example, you could add decorative pulls on storage drawers or use colorful or patterned drawer liners in baskets or on shelving. Removable animated-character stickers can be added to children's plastic storage containers. Decorate wicker baskets with ribbon, dried flowers, or raffia. Glue ribbon, fabric, wood letters, and the like onto plastic containers.

2. Use professional labels or tags.

Invest in a professional label maker to keep your containers uniform and neat. These labels are easy to remove, so the labeled containers are easy to reuse. Select a high-performance electronic labeling system marketed for commercial use. Many adhesive labels have a tendency to peel off, so choose a labeling system that accepts durable, extra-strength tape cartridges. Printing tape designed with a back slit for easy peeling is also helpful.

In addition to professional tape labels, vinyl letters, tags, magnetic, clip-on, and hook labels are other nonpermanent ways to label storage organizers so you can locate items quickly. Likewise, returning your articles back to their respective containers is easier.

3. Many household items make great organizers.

Many household items and furniture can function as great substitutes for storage essentials. Cookie jars, lidded bowls, armoires, chests, urns, vases, canisters, flower pots, ash trays, and the like have storage potential. Many such items can be stored out in the open for convenient access while being decorative.

4. Use miscellaneous containers sparingly.

Miscellaneous containers can be dangerous because they can easily become convenient catch-all containers. However, miscellaneous containers are still necessary. We usually have many items that serve a sole purpose and cannot be grouped with others. Don't overstuff a miscellaneous container, though. In the case of too many articles, it's best to create multiple miscellaneous containers but divide them in a way that makes sense. Attach a category of items or the name of a room to a miscellaneous container—for example, "Kitchen Miscellaneous" or "Miscellaneous Adapters."

5. Break the junk-drawer habit.

Drawers are valuable storage space and should be reserved for your important inventories. You can prevent forming or adding to a junk drawer by placing clever organizers near where junk drawers tend to form in your home. Decorative organizers that can conceal items are good places to stash common junk-drawer belongings. Countertop organizers, such as cookie jars, urns, soup tureens, canisters, jars, and bowls, are good picks. When these organizers fill, it's time to return the items to their original destinations. Divide the items at the countertop and use baskets to distribute items to where they belong.

6. Keep your unused storage containers for future use.

Storage containers that are no longer used should be stored outside your daily living space. Goods choices would be places like an attic, basement, or extra closet. Always exhaust this collection of storage items first before purchasing new ones.

Top Storage Essential Tips

→ Multipurpose organizers are your best investment.

→ Organizers are not created equally.

→ Commercial storage essentials are good investments.

→ Use over-the-door storage devices sparingly.

CHAPTER 3

Home-Storage Challenges

Sometimes, locating storage spots for certain belongings is challenging. These are household items that are either so universal they can go anywhere or they don't have a logical relationship to any one room in the home, and for this reason it's easy for you to shuffle them into storage spots where they're not well served.

For example, many people have collections, which are best displayed in cases, display stands, card/coin books, and so on. Without these types of organizers, collections are subject to dust and damage and can take over your home. When specialized organizers are outside your budget, substitute with bookcases, wall shelves, china cabinets, or entertainment centers.

The following are household items that can be challenging to locate storage space for. Advice on arranging and containing these items in recommended storage places follows.

1. Stationery and shipping supplies

Items such as notecards, postage stamps, packing tape, Bubble Wrap, bubble envelopes, and greeting cards are generally hard-to-find storage places for in most rooms of the house. Basically, the best setup for storing stationery and shipping supplies is to find a desk, countertop, or table where you can work and have nearby consoles, cabinets, closets, drawers, and shelves to hold supplies. Try to keep all the stationery and shipping supplies in one spot since they relate in nature and are often used together.

2. Gift-wrapping essentials

Gather everything necessary to wrap a gift—from paper to tape—into one location. Gift-wrapping essentials can also be stored near related items like shipping supplies. The long tubes of wrapping or shipping paper are the most challenging for you to store since they cannot fit in most drawers, cabinets, or shelves. Therefore, it's best for you to look to specialized organizers for these groups of items. Fortunately, you can find many gift-wrap organizers. All of these organizers are perfect for closets in a hallway, laundry room, mudroom, kitchen, office, or spare bedroom. Hanging-rod gift-wrap organizers suspend from a hook and have many pockets for various inventories. Alongside these organizers, you can use a zippered garment bag to store gift-wrap tubes. Wheeled gift-wrap organizers are great floor organizers for a closet and can be conveniently rolled out to where they're needed. An over-the-door gift-wrap organizer can face the inside of a closet. One clever spot for these organizers is inside a common armoire. A pullout table added to an armoire makes the perfect place to wrap and prepare packages for shipment.

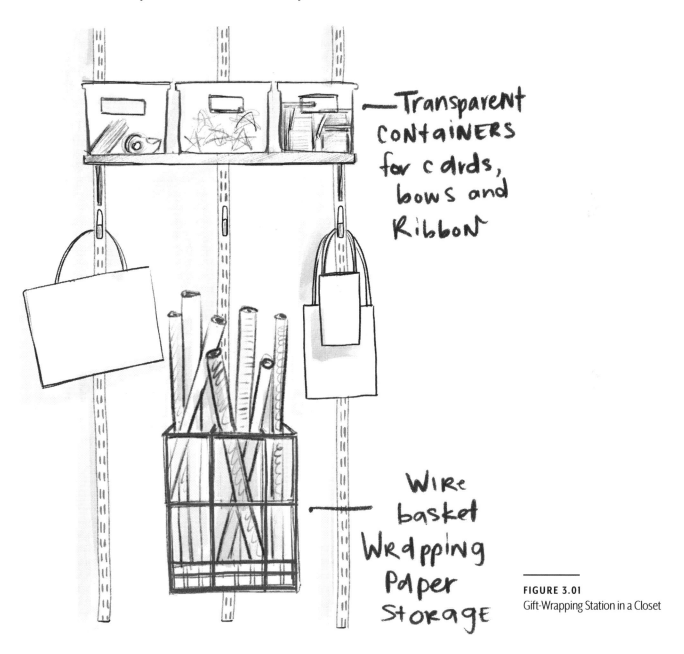

—Transparent containers for cards, bows and Ribbon

Wire basket Wrapping Paper Storage

FIGURE 3.01
Gift-Wrapping Station in a Closet

3. Bulk paper items

Overhead storage is inconvenient for you to access on a daily basis, so it's best to store lightweight items there that are accessed infrequently, such as overstock disposable paper goods such as tissue or toilet paper. Overhead shelves in centrally located closets, pantries, and kitchen cabinets are good places to store these items. Stacking items such as toilet paper, tissue boxes, disposable plates, paper napkins, and so on overhead will make it easy for you to see these items at a distance and if they should fall, they won't cause any injuries.

Also, rolling floor organizers, such a wheeled crates or dolly carts, are other good places for you to store bulk paper products in closets and panties. In the garage, paper products can be stored in labeled, lidded containers where they're protected from moisture, insects, and animals.

4. First aid kit

Every home needs at least one complete first aid kit, which should be stored near where wounds are tended. Most often a bathroom, which offers a sink and a mirror, is the best spot. Store your first aid kit in the bathroom closet, under the sink, or in a nearby hallway linen closet.

Keep your first aid supplies in a portable container, rather than a medicine cabinet, so they can be easily transported to the scene of an accident, if need be. It's easy to make a portable first aid kit in a handled caddy, fishing-tackle box, or sewing box. A container with many compartments keeps first aid inventories, such as tubes of medicine, bandages, tape/gauze, splints, alcohol wipes, muscle creams, aspirin, and the like easy to divide.

5. Flashlights, candles, matches, incense, and lighters

All light- and flame-producing items are related, so it's logical to store together, and it's handy to have them organized together in the event of a power outage. These items can be stored in a set of stackable containers with each holding a different inventory. Such items can also be further subdivided if necessary. For example, one container can hold flameless candles and another votives. Good places for these items are in overhead linen, hallway, kitchen, office, or entertainment room closets. They can also be stored in your consoles, china cabinets, entertainment centers, or kitchen cabinets.

6. Keys and pocket change

One of the easiest belongings to organize in the home is your keys. However, in many homes, no organizers are established for them, and keys are often lost. It takes no time at all to add a wall-mounted key hook or rack next to all the entry points to the home. Since these organizers are visible and simple, they'll receive use. You can also use a special bowl or container that rests on a table by the doorway. In well-secured attached garages, keys can also sit in the automobile cup holder overnight. This works when there is no need to access other keys on the ring overnight.

You also need a place to keep loose change that comes out of coat pockets, pants pockets, automobile cup holders, or the bottom of a purse. A bedroom closet, kitchen, mudroom, laundry room, or an area near a laundry chute are common places where change gets pulled and dumped on countertops or in drawers. At such locations, stash a drawer container, piggy bank, or dish to deposit miscellaneous change. You can go to these organizers when you need coins for the laundromat, car wash, tolls, or whatever need arises.

7. Cellular and electronic devices and household batteries

There are countless ways to keep mobile electronics off floors and countertops while charging. Not only do electronics look messy at these places, but also they're subject to physical and liquid damage. All you need to do is install electric outlets in hidden places, such as inside drawers, cabinets, and closets. Shelving, desktop chargers, outlet chargers, wall-mount chargers, and drawer-tray charging organizers can all hold electronics.

Batteries store best in specialized organizers designed for them, which separate the different types and keep them in order. Battery organizers come wall-mounted for walls or inside cabinets, freestanding for shelving or work benches, and drawer organizers for just about any place in the home. Batteries are convenient to store in places like kitchens, offices, laundry rooms, mudrooms, tool rooms, and storage closets.

8. Backpacks, duffel bags, briefcases, totes, and purses

The best place to house these items is near an entry point to your home. A mudroom or foyer is an ideal spot for storing articles that leave your home on a regular basis. However, many homes don't have mudrooms, and front hall space is often tight. When your home faces space constraints at its entry points, store only the backpacks, duffel bags, and so on that are used daily at these locations.

It's common for your bags and totes to pile up at doorways. Therefore, on a monthly basis, reduce these items to only the currently used to maintain order. You can store the unused backpacks, duffel bags, purses, drawstrings, and the like in other storage locations, such as a spare closet, or separate them according to whom they belong and keep them in their owners' bedrooms.

BACKPACKS: Most backpacks that are hung need heavy-duty hooks. The wall upon which they rest should be lined with a hard surface, such as bead board since surfaces like painted drywall can dent, scratch, and be hard to clean. Shelves and large cubby compartments are other storage solution for backpacks, but make certain they have the proper depth and can bear the weight.

BRIEFCASES AND DUFFELS: Generally, these are wide items with short handles. Resting them on a flat surface like shelving is the best storage arrangements since these items tend to be too wide for hanging storage.

TOTES AND SHOPPING BAGS: Hang these items on coat hooks like pegs along a wall. They can also fold or stack upon one another in a drawer or shelf since they lie even and flat.

9. Cleaning products

It's best to keep the majority of your cleaning supplies in one central location, as opposed to spreading them out in various spots throughout the home. This is the best way to manage inventories and easily recognize which products are running low. A designated closet or cabinet pantry with hooks for holding tools and shelves for keeping cleaners and cleaning tools is the ideal set up. Buckets, especially those that are wheeled, can rest on the closet floor. Use spare buckets to hold hand brushes, rags, toilet-bowl cleaners, and gloves. Steamers, carpet shampoo machines, and vacuums can rest on the closet floor. In cramped situations, bulky machines can move to different locations like a hallway or foyer closet.

It's also convenient to stash a multipurpose cleaner and roll of paper towels for quick cleanups in your hardworking spaces like the laundry room, bathrooms, and mudroom.

Every household needs a well-stocked shoeshine kit with shoe polish, brushes, rags, dyes, and so on. The right storage organizer is necessary to contain these items so they're easy to access and don't leak when tipped over. A plastic basket with handles and multiple compartments, such as a caddy organizer, is ideal. A shoeshine kit's perfect to store with household cleaning supplies in linen closets, mudrooms, kitchen cabinets, utility closets, and laundry rooms.

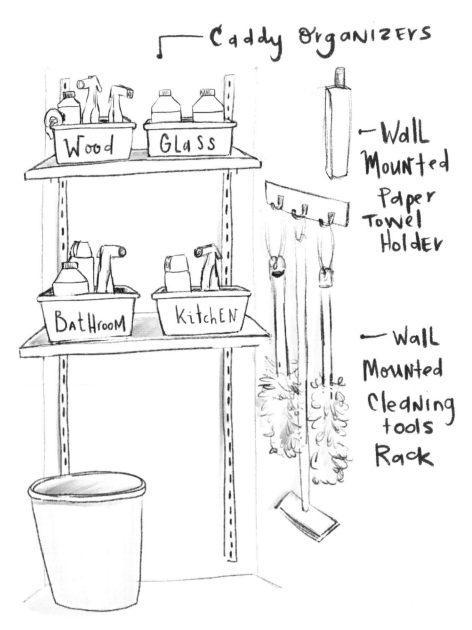

FIGURE 3.02
Cleaning Product Storage

10. Photo albums, keepsakes, and home movies

It's best to store your highly infrequently used items like photo albums, keepsakes, and home movies in areas outside spaces that are used daily. Basements, living rooms, dining rooms, guest bedrooms, and home offices are the best rooms to store these items. Also, front hall closets, bookcases, storage armoires, and entertainment centers can work well.

These items are often irreplaceable and some of the most valuable inventories in your home, so they should receive the best organizers for preservation, which are archival quality. The right type of organizers, plus how safely you stack or file them, are key to keeping them intact for years to come.

11. Calendars

The recommendation is to move your family calendar from the kitchen refrigerator to an electronic calendar option. There are general and specialized family digital calendars. You'll need one that is accessible from both a mobile device and computer through a web app so you can access it from anywhere, which also increases the likelihood that everyone keeps up. Most digital calendars are color-coded to distinguish between schedules like personal or work.

Clear your manual calendars displayed on the refrigerator of items like paper schedules, invitations, appointment cards, tickets, sticky notes, and the like. In order to stop your papers from accumulating onto the refrigerator, get into the habit of immediately replying to events, recording dates onto the calendar, and then filing the paper. Make a "Record & Respond" folder or bin to place invites, schedules, and the like until you can get to them. An accordion file, handled file crate, or plastic eight-by-eleven-inch project case works well and can be stored in a kitchen closet or cabinet.

Since your appointments, schedules, and plans frequently change, erasable calendars will eliminate unsightly scratch outs. Color-code these items with different markers to distinguish people from activities.

12. Newspapers, magazines, and sales flyers

Temporary reading materials need an organizer. Otherwise, such articles find themselves taking over nightstands, bedroom floors, sofas, end tables, kitchen tables, and countertops. Fortunately, there are many types of wall-mounted and freestanding racks specifically designed for such items that are sold in both retail and commercial markets. Many furniture pieces are equipped with racks and shelves for this purpose, as well. You can also use wicker baskets, storage ottomans, or even a trash can to hold them throughout the home until you need them.

13. Coupons and receipts

Coupons need an online filing system or a portable organizer, or both, that can be stashed in a reusable grocery tote or automobile glove box. Attach your shopping list to your coupon organizer so you don't forget to take your coupons to the store. Collecting and organizing coupons does not need to be a tedious chore with countless hours of clipping, filing, sorting, and eliminating the expired ones. Try another couponing method if your old ones never worked successfully. The following two couponing methods are worth a look:

METHOD #1: Digital Couponing

Paperless couponing has never been made more simple than today. Countless online websites offer manufacturer coupons, cash-back offers, rewards programs, and coupon codes for percent-off discounts redeemable with many national and independent retailers. A number of other websites sell discounts for products, services, travel, and entertainment.

Many websites store thousands of unexpired manufacturer product coupons from various places like newspaper circulars and store them in a virtual database. This coupon source is most useful for people who shop for many grocery and toiletry items. Either search by manufacturer or product category. Then view all the available coupons for you to select, click, and print. Although exhausting, it is far more efficient than scanning and clipping paper coupons.

Use mobile apps in conjunction with paper coupons for additional savings. Some apps can also access on a desktop computer. Coupon websites and apps have the capability to link offers to supermarket and drugstore loyalty cards. Simply swipe your loyalty card at checkout to redeem coupons. There are some coupon apps that scan and store loyalty cards so you don't need a physical card. Rebate apps upload your store receipt. You receive your payment in the form of cash, check, gift card, or deposits made directly into your bank or PayPal account. Rewards apps earn points and some exchange them for store gift cards. Some mobile coupon apps have the ability to take pictures of printed coupons and transform them so they become a mobile-ready offer at the register. For the casual couponer, location-driven apps work best. These apps have a "Near-Me" feature that finds offers based on where you are physically present at the moment for unexpected savings. Retailer apps are another great source for coupons. Most grocery stores offer manufacturer coupons on their apps. Many commercial, big-box stores that sell general merchandise or specialty stores offer percentage savings on particular items tracked by a barcode system.

Digital coupon technology is eco-friendly, clutter-free, convenient, and easy to use. There is a wide selection of different types of coupon websites and apps. Collectively, digital coupons can satisfy just about anyone's coupon preference.

METHOD #2: Traditional Couponing

There are a few basic rules that will make your basic clipping and sorting of coupons less work. First, save just coupons for items you'll definitely use. Even if a coupon has a good offer, if it's something you really don't need, chances are you'll end up wasting money and adding clutter to the kitchen cabinets. Dismissing unnecessary coupons cuts down on the time you spend clipping, sorting, searching, and eliminating the expired ones.

Stick with coupons that have at least a 20 percent savings, or they're not worth the time involved. Remove expired coupons when you add new ones to a particular classification. This is important because coupons have short lives, and small piles of coupons are far less time consuming to rifle through. Pick idle times, like when you are waiting for the doctor or watching television, to organize them.

The type of coupon organizer you select plays a big role in maintaining a successful couponing system. It's hard to find the right organizer for coupons since they involve your personal preferences and few effective ones are on the market. The following tips can help you find the right one for your needs:

- Usually two organizers are needed for coupons. One for food, medication, and toiletry articles, and another for discounts and coupons for everything else like entertainment, transportation, dry cleaners, health products, pets, grooming, and the like.

- Organizers should be small so they'll transport easily and the temptation to store too many coupons is eliminated.
- Organizers should have classifications tabs, and dividers need solid borders so creased or torn coupons don't get caught.
- Coupon organizers should be sturdy and have sealed enclosures, like zippers or buttons, to keep everything intact in case they're dropped.
- "Check-file" coupon organizers are good for those who prefer to pull coupons at home against a grocery shopping list.
- Grocery store coupons should be filed by classification, according to how the product is categorized in the food store. For example, "Cereal/Breakfast Food" encompasses oatmeal, granola, cereal bars, and boxed cereal, just like the in the store aisle. You should also have a classification for free, trial offers, and total bill discount coupons.

Receipts can also be placed in coupon organizers with tabs to allow for classifications like dates or stores. Check-file boxes can also categorize your receipts by their built-in tabs. Some people find receipt organization to be too involved. For them, I recommend a simple strategy for holding onto receipts because they're important:

- For your short-term receipts, use a large binder clip and just fill it with typical grocery and retail store receipts that have ninety-day return policies. Fold the receipts neatly and place the most current ones at the top of the pile. When the clip fills, start reducing the pile by discarding the expired ones from the bottom and those for items that have been already worn or eaten.
- For your long-term receipts, place them in an organizer with a filing system, such as a hanging folder.

14. Basic toolbox

Every home needs a basic toolbox that is stored in a central location like a kitchen, pantry, hallway closet, mudroom, laundry room, or under a sink. The idea is to have one nearby to address minor handyman duties, so you don't have to walk to a shed, the garage, or basement where the bulk of the tools are stored. A simple toolbox includes a hammer, screwdriver, tape measure, nails, electrical tape, glue, and picture hooks. You can use an old lunch box, fishing-tackle box, craft box, or any handled carrying bag for this purpose.

15. Automobile odds and ends

Store only your important items that are used regularly inside the car. Necessary items used daily, such as tissues, napkins, antibacterial wipes, gum, hand cream, I-PASS, toll change, sunglasses, and so on, should be within arm's length of the driver's seat. Therefore, use the door storage compartments, center console, visors, and glove compartments for those belongings. Use storage devices like coin purses, eyeglass cases, earphone cases, or zippered pouches for such items so they're easy to find and stay protected and contained. For the visor, use an organizer designed for that space to hold small articles like a pen, gum, tissue, and the like.

Strap-on seat organizers have compartments that face the back seats. Such organizers are usually made of nylon with see-through mesh pockets. There are various designs for these organizers suited to hold umbrellas, beverages, cans, movies, and so on. Other car organizers to consider are compartmentalized nylon tote containers for dividing different belongings. These organizers can sit on your car seat organizer and be moved when other passengers are present or stored in the trunk when the car is full. The idea is to keep your loose articles off the floor and seats where they can be tossed about, broken, or lost beneath the seats. When selecting a car organizer, choose a material like nylon or mesh, which can be shaken or wiped clean. Also, a softer material will not scratch leather or rip upholstery.

It's important to make a special kit in the event of a roadside emergency. Pack a large container with essentials like a blanket, flashlight, flares, water, hats, gloves, towel, cell phone charger, or whatever else is needed, and keep it in the trunk. The container can be lidded or zippered, which makes storing things above it in the trunk easier, as opposed to an open-storage essential.

To keep your car less cluttered with belongings, don't store duplicates, such as two umbrellas, in the car unless they're needed for a regular car passenger. Spares of such items can be housed in a container marked "Car Items," which can go in the garage, mudroom, pantry, or closet. Also, keep seasonal items, such as ice scrapers, sun deflectors, or snow brushes, in this container and place them in the car only during the months they're needed. You can also save car space by opting for travel-size containers. For example, use pocket tissues or travel-size bottles of mouthwash.

16. Insect repellant and sunscreen

Bug spray and sunscreen relate in that they're applied to the skin for a form of protection, so storing them in the same location makes sense. It's a good idea to label all bottles and containers of these products with your name when taking them to beaches, pools, camps, parks, and so on. Also, record the expiration date on the bottle so it's easy to read. Often expiration dates are coded or wear off.

Spray cans or bottles of product are best stored upright in open containers so they don't leak. Wipes and tubes are good to keep in stackable lidded containers. It's best to store insect repellant and sunscreen in separate containers.

In order for you to maintain good inventory control and use up the close-to-expiration items first, purchase removable stickers and place them on the new and unopened products. Remove a sticker only after the opened product is empty and then select the item that has the closest expiration date.

You can store insect repellant and sunscreen in a mudroom cabinet, linen closet, foyer closet, bathroom closet, or kitchen cabinet. Carrying cases, beach bags, purses, camp bags, backpacks, briefcases, and gym bags should stock one small tube of sunscreen lotion and, depending on the climate, insect-repellant wipes.

17. Vitamins and supplements

The number of vitamin and supplement bottles will determine your storage arrangements for them. Some homes stock only one or two bottles of multivitamins, whereas other homes have dozens of individual bottles. It's important to keep vitamins taken daily in a highly visible location. Also, vitamins need to steer clear of heat and humidity since these elements reduce the potency of nutrients.

The best storage places are those you access every day. For example, a nightstand, towel closet, makeup station, coffee cabinet, or near breakfast foods. You can also stash a container of grab-and-go vitamin packets at such locations. Simply create these vitamin packets by filling sandwich baggies with all your daily need vitamins, making them readily available for when you prefer to take them at work or the gym.

Large quantities of supplements need a good organization system in order to keep inventories straight. Arrange many bottles of supplements in single-file rows according to type—like antioxidants or minerals. You can also classify them alphabetically, which is how stores stock them.

In deep drawers, stackable bins can be used to separate the different supplements. Label the tops or lids so things are easy to locate. Stackable open bins on shelves are another method for dividing different types of supplements.

18. Garage sale items

Find an out-of-the-way place to store items being saved for a future garage sale. A basement storage room, shed, attic, or overhead garage space are prime locations for these items. Use strong cardboard boxes that close at the top and stack them to take advantage of vertical space. Organize your boxes so each one holds a certain category of items, such as baby clothes, linens, books, and so on. Label the boxes with their contents, so when it's time for the sale, the job is halfway done.

Home-Storage Challenges

Stationery and shipping supplies
→ assign a workstation and have nearby consoles, cabinets, closets, drawers, or shelves to hold supplies

Gift-wrapping essentials
→ use specialized organizers

Bulk paper items
→ overhead shelves

First aid kit
→ Use a compartmentalized portable container such as a tool, make-up or tackle box

Flashlights, candles, matches, incense, and lighters
→ keep light-and flame-producing items in same vicinity but divide them into different containers by type

Keys and pocket change
→ Wall-mounted key hook/ rack or special bowl/ container at entry points

Cellular and electronic devices
→ hidden places with electrical outlets

Household batteries
→ specialized organizers stored in kitchen, office, laundry room, mudroom, closet, etc.

Backpacks, duffel bags, briefcases, totes, and purses
→ near entry point of home if used daily

Cleaning products
→ one central location

Photo albums, keepsakes, and home movies
→ in areas not used daily such as basement, guest bedroom, etc.

Calendars
→ digital calendar or erasable calendar

Newspapers, magazines, and sales flyers

→ wall-mounted or freestanding organizers

Coupons and receipts
→ portable organizers

Basic toolbox
→ central location like a kitchen, pantry, closet, mudroom, or laundry room

Automobile odds and ends
→ utilize special organizers for important items inside car

Insect repellent
→ store bottles and tubes upright in open containers

Vitamins and supplements
→ separate and store them by type or alphabetize, store away from heat and humidity

Garage sale items
→ out-of-the-way place

CHAPTER 4

How to Maintain an Organized Home

Maintaining organization is easier when your household is straightened on a regular basis and everything is put back where it belongs. Staying in the habit of putting things away immediately or at the end of the day will prevent clutter from forming, and long straightening sessions will be behind you. In homes with many members, it's important for all to do their parts in maintaining order. If fewer members are on board with picking up after themselves, larger piles of clutter will form on a regular basis. Straightening and cleaning simultaneously is daunting; it's much easier to straighten up every day and clean once a week.

Top Organizational Maintenance Tips

1. Don't store questionable items.

As a general rule, discard any household item that hasn't been used in a two-year period. That includes electronics, housewares, clothing, accessories, tools, footwear, eyewear, and so on. After many piles of belongings are sorted and cleared out, you'll end up with much less to organize and store.

2. Scrutinize storing two of the same type of item.

Do away with doubles of anything except for the obvious, such as food, cleaners, and toiletry items. Typically, most appliances, tools, electronics, silverware, glassware, and the like don't require duplicates. For example, your kitchen does not need two toasters or two sets of juice glasses. Select whichever one is better, and eliminate the other. The benefit of additional storage space far outweighs the advantage of owning identical items. Commonly, a spare or double of something is usually the retired item that was replaced by the new one. In those cases, it can be argued that you're probably not going back to using the old one anytime soon.

Consider that the longer you keep a spare item, the older and more obsolete it becomes, to the point that it will be undesirable even if you have a need for it. There must good justification for holding onto a spare, such as an actual instance when you'll need it. For example, when you entertain, you may like to have two coffee pots—one for regular coffee and the other for decaffeinated. A double of an item is acceptable when it holds a sentimental or high monetary value, such as an antique set of dishes. In those cases, make special storage arrangements outside the daily used space for the items when they're not in use.

3. Think through every purchase.

The more items brought into the home, the more organization will be required. Stocking up on sale or clearance items may not always work out favorably, whether they're "good deals." Similarly, purchasing large quantities at bulk warehouse facilities is not always the best solution for saving money.

The downside to stocking up on a given item is that you'll need valuable storage space, and large quantities of items are often separated in a household. As a result, we often lose track of how much we possess and find ourselves purchasing even more of the product on our next shopping venture. Another problem related to bulk inventories of goods is staying on top of the expiration dates. Also, food products purchased in excess lose their appeal simply because people get tired of eating the same thing over and over.

Certainly, there are ways for you to solve some of the problems associated with bulk shopping, such as sharing or splitting bulk inventories with other people, although this process requires the work of dividing, delivering, and exchanging money.

Many times things bought on sale or clearance are not even needed. This is another common reason why our cabinets, closets, and drawers become so cluttered. Never buy anything when you are unsure about your inventory at home. It's better to make a special trip to the store to only buy one particular item than get in the expensive habit of overbuying and wasting storage space. You'll eventually discover that you can get by with fewer things than you think. Shop with a well-thought-out list in order to stay focused. It's almost a guarantee that without a shopping list, you'll forget something, sending you back to the store, which can encourage unnecessary spending.

4. Think like a minimalist.

A minimalist stores only what he or she uses. This is one of the key requirements necessary to achieve and maintain the well-organized home, meaning that useless belongings are always continuously decluttered on a daily basis. Sounds simple and logical, but it's often hard for some people to implement.

In general, it's wiser to purchase the highest quality of belongings that one can afford. Higher-quality products will likely last longer and delay replacement, compared with lower-quality items. Abiding by the quality-over-quantity principle keeps the home stocked with limited high-end products that will be used more, rather than many faulty products that don't receive enough use and turn into clutter.

5. Avoid Detailed Organizing

As a general rule, organize belongings in a general, simple manner and forgo extreme detail. For instance, don't keep soup cans in alphabetical order. Instead, divide by soup variety or just keep all the soup cans in one place since precise

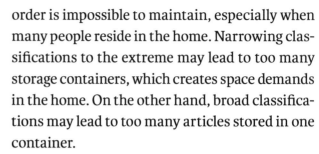

Top Organizational Maintenance Tips

⟶ Don't store questionable items.

⟶ Scrutinize storing two of the same type of item.

⟶ Think through every purchase.

⟶ Think like a minimalist.

⟶ Avoid Detailed Organizing

order is impossible to maintain, especially when many people reside in the home. Narrowing classifications to the extreme may lead to too many storage containers, which creates space demands in the home. On the other hand, broad classifications may lead to too many articles stored in one container.

There are many variables in successful home organization. It's key to understand how buying behavior and attitudes about our possessions greatly influence the organizational process. It's equally important to know where and how to situate our belongings. Selecting the right organizers and efficient placing contribute to perfect order and promote organizational maintenance.

PART TWO

Bedrooms and Closets

CHAPTER 5

Bedrooms

There are many types of bedrooms, including guest, master, children's, and nursery—each with different storage needs. Bedrooms occupied by more than one person have further storage arrangements to consider. One of the most important things to do before organizing a bedroom is to entirely sort out the closet. This is because clothing and related accessories tend to be the majority of the clutter found in most bedrooms. It's easier to add items that are currently taking up bedroom space—such as jewelry, scarves, purses, footwear, and excess clothing—to an organized closet.

There are logical steps designed to guide you through a bedroom organizational process. The following general organizational steps are laid out in a logical order: each one ends at a place that will not leave a bedroom upside down should you need to stop and start up on another day.

Step 1: Obtain organizational containers.

Gets bags, boxes, or containers ready to conquer and divide your piles of clutter. Shoes, clothes, trinkets, electronics, music, books/magazines, toiletries, hair accessories, scarves/ties, purses, and so on are good classifications to create. Also, have containers for trash, donation, recycle, or sale. Additionally, have one for items that belong in other rooms. Label containers accordingly.

Step 2: Work on one area at a time.

Plan to conquer one area of the room at a time, especially when it requires a good amount of time to organize properly. Don't start with belongings that reside in drawers, cabinets, or shelves, because it makes more sense to create order *before* pulling out more.

The Floor

The floor is typically a vulnerable spot and is a good place to begin since there are many open places that invite clutter. Large items, such as backpacks, gym bags, sports equipment, musical instruments, and laundry baskets, commonly dominate this landscape.

Start organizing the floor by removing all the unwanted articles. This may entail sorting through piles of clothes and reducing them to only the ones you'll wear. Then gather all the items that belong in other rooms of the home and return them. Next, place items into a basket or box that has potential to be stored elsewhere in the home. For example, a tennis racket can relocate to the garage and hang from a wall organizer. Lastly, set aside all the articles that need to stay in the bedroom but require a different storage spot. The following are common items that find their way to a bedroom floors, followed by creative ways to store them.

Clothing, Laundry Baskets, and Hampers

People often stack excess clothing in laundry baskets and keep them on bedroom floors when what they should really do is discard the clothes they don't wear to make room for those they do. It's so important to continuously downsize clothing inventories on a daily basis to prevent drawer and closet overflow, rather than wait for a time to tackle the entire wardrobe at once, which is a more daunting task.

Ideally, you want to hide a hamper for dirty clothing in a bedroom closet or disguise it on the bedroom floor. In a bedroom, it's best hide a hamper in a piece of furniture by installing a pullout drawer or basket in a cabinet component. There are also freestanding hampers disguised to look like a piece of furniture in the form of table or nightstand.

Blankets, Throws, and Pillows

Many times, excess blankets and pillows needed at bedtime take over the floor during the day. It's easy to find storage solutions for them, though. End-of-the-bed storage benches, storage ottomans, chests, and under-the-bed containers can house these items and keep them close to the bed where they're needed.

Laptops, Tablets, E-readers, and Cell Phones

Commonly, laptops, tablets, e-readers, and cell phones in bedrooms are laying on the floor plugged into a wall outlet. Such storage arrangements place expensive electronics into a high-risk zone for breakage or liquid damage. Also, dangling cords look messy and are a tripping hazard.

Electronics can be housed in wall-mounted or electrical-outlet dock charging stations to secure them and get them off the floor. Desktop docking stations do the same thing from a counter. Wall shelves and wall-mounted desks can integrate power strips for charging and storing electronics. Electrical outlets placed inside drawers or cabinets can charge, hide, and safely house these items, as well.

Video Gaming Supplies

Without storage organizers, video gaming supplies, such as batteries, video games, headphones, controllers, and the like, will easily scatter all around the television area, including the floor. It's common for these expensive items to be stepped on and broken, which you want to avoid. Also, they're tripping hazards, especially when the cords are not properly contained.

There are many organizers on the market that can easily hold all gaming items in one neat central location. Some can even hold a television or computer. The best ones have hooks, baskets, shelves, and racks to hold everything necessary. You could even use several different organizers, like a wall-mounted organizer for controllers and a storage bench to sit on while playing games. A gaming chair with storage is another option.

Books and Magazines

It's never a good idea to stack books and magazines on the floor where they're hard to see and access. It's easy to find storage organizers because many freestanding and wall-mounted versions are available and empty wall space is common. Wall-mounted shelving comes in many lengths and depths perfect for storing any size book. Track shelf organizers can be arranged with upper shelves and a deep counter-height shelf that can function as a desk.

There are many freestanding organizers for books and magazines, such as bookshelves, that come in all different configurations. Shelves on end tables, benches, and desks can also store books and magazines. Even a storage bench can be outfitted with hanging files and storage compartments to contain books and office supplies.

Footwear

Footwear is often found scattered across the bedroom floor or spilling out from a crowded closet. Before locating space for them, get rid of the shoes and boots you don't need or want. In tight spaces, move off-season shoes outside the bedroom, in overhead closet space, or under the bed.

In the bedroom, use inconspicuous furniture pieces that hide footwear inside a storage bench, cabinet, or drawer. Wheeled under-the-bed footwear storage organizers are easy to access in a convenient location for shoes and boots worn daily.

Trash

When a trash can is missing from the bedroom, food wrappers, crumbled papers, clothing tags, and the like can be everywhere, especially on the floor. Place a trash can in a central location in the

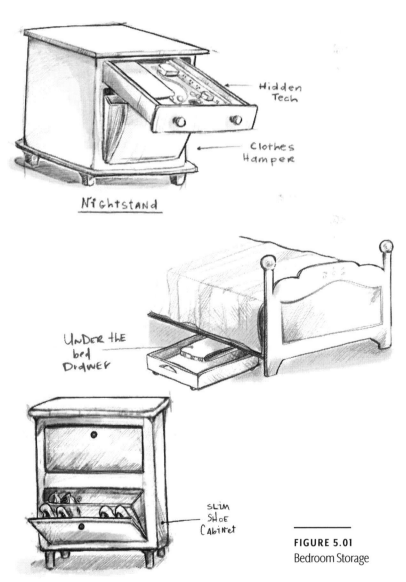

FIGURE 5.01
Bedroom Storage

bedroom or next to the place where trash accumulates, such as near a desk.

Sporting Equipment

Favorite or expensive pieces of sports equipment, like a high-end baseball mitt, can be stored in a person's bedroom. This is especially important considering very hot, cold, and damp garage conditions will degrade many sporting goods made of wood or leather. Similarly, moisture can mildew and rust many types of sports equipment materials.

In a bedroom, keep sporting goods off the floor and in an organizer. Every sport has a specialized organizer; some are wall mounted, and others are freestanding. Single pieces of equipment, like a ball or bat, can be placed on wall-mounted hooks, shelves, and even in a display case. Make certain that wherever you store them in the room, they're kept away from heat sources, such as vents, humidifiers, and sunlight, so they stay at a consistent temperature.

Musical Instruments

In order to pick the ideal storage place for an instrument, it's important to determine where it's played and how often the instrument is taken out of the house. Instruments frequently taken out of the home should be concealed in a carrying case in a freestanding floor rack, closet shelf, or under the bed.

Instruments that seldom leave the home can be displayed on music racks, stands, or wall-mounted organizers specifically designed for the instrument; accompanying cases can be stored in a closet. Most instruments need a temperature-controlled environment. Elements like humidity, sunlight, and extreme cold or heat can damage wood, metal, and electronic instruments. Therefore, store instruments away from windows, HVAC vents, humidifiers, and the like.

Bedroom Organizational Process

STEP ONE
obtain containers for sorting and grouping your bedroom articles into like piles

STEP TWO
Work on one area of the bedroom at a time

CHAPTER 6

Adult/Master Bedroom

An adult's bedroom can look magazine perfect with the right organizers and furniture. Visualizing what your bedroom would look like if you were to sell the house can help in the decluttering and organizing process.

There are places to create storage in a bedroom that are commonly overlooked. The bed area is one of the main areas where clutter forms, and usually storage opportunities are not utilized. There are many ways to gain storage under the bed and surrounding it. The type of furniture selected for the bedroom also plays a significant role in obtaining the best storage for bedroom items. The following covers all the places and ways to capitalize on bedroom storage possibilities.

The Bed

If your bed does not get made every morning because your clothes, laptop, paperwork, books, and the like are permanently residing on the comforter, it's time to find places for those belongings. Organizing the bed should include all the surrounding areas, such as the headboard, nightstands, under-the-bed space, benches and walls since these areas can be used as storage locations for items needed near the bed.

Headboard and Overhead Shelving

A storage headboard or overhead shelving, or both, are key to efficient bedroom storage, but since that area is a focal point of the room, it must stay clutter-free and orderly. Start organizing such spaces by clearing everything out and evaluating the belongings before replacing them. Anything not used at the bed should be relocated to another storage place close to where it's needed.

Items lying loose need containment. Organizers, such as magazine racks, baskets, bookends, canisters, and boxes, both conceal and create order in this space. Take advantage of available outlets or add some for charging laptops, cell phones, and the like, which are convenient to keep near the bed. Items no longer needed or wanted should be donated, sold, or discarded.

Bed Linen Bench

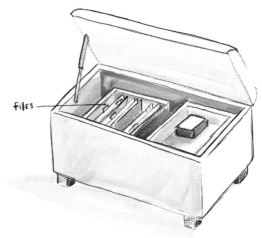

files

office Bench

Bookcase Bench

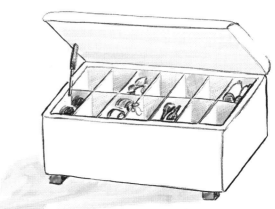

Shoe Storage Bench

FIGURE 6.01
End of Bed Storage Benches

Gaming Bench

Under-the-Bed Storage

One of the best spots to store belongings in the bedroom that is commonly overlooked is under the bed. There are many organizers designed for this space, such as long, shallow, wheeled, lidded containers and footwear organizers, that make storage in this space easy. Besides under-the-bed organizers, there is a type of bed called a *storage bed*, which is designed with built-in drawer compartments below the mattress.

Storage Beds

Beds with built-in drawers below the mattress need to be organized and decluttered one drawer at a time when each one contains separate categories of items. However, empty all disorganized drawers with many categories simultaneously and sort them together. In some cases, dressers and other furniture pieces that hold related items may need to be organized with these drawers. Make certain that the various groups of items are divided by type and decluttered before returning them to the drawer or compartment that best fits the sizes of the inventories. Incorporate drawer organizers to separate different but relatable groups of items in the same drawer, such as underwear and boxers.

Under the Bed

There are endless storage possibilities for under the bed, but arrangements must be compartmentalized and containers should be easy to move in and out. Get started organizing this space by pulling everything out from down under. Sort forming groups of similar items and get rid of things that are not needed and wanted. Decide which items need to stay at this location and whether any can move to a more convenient spot. For example, everyday shoes can be transferred to available space in the bedroom closet or a mudroom shoe organizer. The following are good articles to stash under the bed, along with the best ways to store them.

Footwear

Both off-season and everyday footwear can be housed under the bed. Footwear containers designed just for under-the-bed storage are a good option. Those with a lid or cover keep off-season footwear free of dust. Wheeled open containers are necessary for footwear worn daily for easy accessibility.

Off-Season Clothing

A basic plastic lidded under-the-bed container can easily store off-season clothing. Group like items in the same containers, such as sweaters, pants, shorts, and so on; always label the containers with their contents. Plan to declutter clothing inventories both when you fill and empty containers.

Bedding

The cleverest and most appropriate item to stash under the bed is bedding. All the sheets, pillowcases, and extra blankets are convenient to store at this location. Plus, the linen closet will have more room.

Closet Excess

Under the bed is good for storing bedroom-closet spillover items, such as purses, shoes, belts, clothing, and so on, due to its close proximity to the bed. The long, shallow containers used to store footwear can also hold these items, but use a different one for each category of items.

Headboard Storage

FIGURE 6.02
Storage Headboard

Long-Term Storage Items

When closets and storage areas are jam-packed, the following less-frequently used items are great picks for under-the-bed storage:

- **ARCHIVAL GARMENT STORAGE BOXES** that store bridal gowns, vintage apparel, heirloom linens, fabric keepsakes and the like.
- **ARTWORK**, including works done by artists in your home (i.e., children), can nicely spread out under a big bed. Always contain artwork pieces in professional storage boxes so they stay well preserved.
- **LUGGAGE** always seems to be a big storage problem anywhere it's placed. Wrap suitcases in plastic when stored to keep them dust-free.
- **PERSONAL SPORTING GOODS**, such as skates, rackets, sticks, gloves, cleats, and so on, are good to store in a bedroom where they stay safe and secure away from the extreme garage temperatures. Most under-the-bed storage containers can fit many sporting goods due to their larger sizes.

Built-in Storage

Bed With Storage

FIGURE 6.03
Built-in Shelving around the Bed

FIGURE 6.04
Storage Beds

- **PHOTOS**, **VIDEOS**, **TRADING CARDS**, and **GREETING CARDS** fit nicely in 4.5 x 8 x 11.5 inch-size photo-storage boxes. Many photo-storage boxes have an acid-free, archival construction, which is important for storing these types of items.
- **WRAPPING PAPER STORAGE BOXES** are often difficult to store in a home since they're long and shallow. Oddly shaped thirty-inch rolls of wrapping paper, gift boxes, bags, ribbons, and bows can all be store in specialized gift-wrap boxes that come lidded to keep items dust-free.

The Nightstand

A well-designed nightstand with multiple drawers or cabinets helps keep the bed area tidy. When space allows, use nightstands on either side of the bed to allow for more storage opportunities. When you spend time reading or watching television in bed, it's amazing how many items end up in there with you. However, it's important that nightstand compartments not become the catchall spot for everything. Limit items to those you need and use while in bed. Some of the best items to stock in a nightstand are remote controllers, eyewear, mouth guards, dentures, retainers, eye masks, tissues, nail files, lip balm, hand cream, earplugs, a diary or journal, and writing instruments.

Buy travel-size items or miniature versions for anything stashed in your nightstand since it's a compact space. Figure out how to trim down the bulk in your nightstand drawer—like using pill boxes to store aspirin, sleep aids, or medications instead of the original bottles.

Always create compartments in a nightstand drawer, or the drawer will turn into a junk pile. Shallow desk trays and kitchen, dresser, and bathroom drawer organizers all work for this space. If you have deep drawers, use stacking tray organizers to double your storage capacity. Sometimes a nightstand is just not enough storage. You can also utilize a bedside compartmentalized caddy organizer that attaches to the mattress for nightstand overflow.

Make sure the nightstand remains visually free of clutter so the space looks simple and clean. Good ways to cut down on traditional nightstand items would be to consider ceiling-hung or wall-mounted lighting rather than a table lamp. In place of a traditional alarm clock, use your cell phone alarm or a charging dock with a built-in clock radio. Consider valet docking stations that charge portable electronics and have multiple compartments to hold items like jewelry, watches, wallets, keys, and so on. You can also move all portable electronics to a nightstand drawer and create a safe and hidden charging station by installing an electrical outlet at this location. Replace larger tissue boxes with pocket-size tissues in a small drawer. Use a ring holder or decorative bowl or dish for jewelry, keys, loose change, and pocket items on the nightstand counter.

Bedroom Desk and Entertainment Center

A desk area needs to blend well in a serene room like a bedroom. The best way to accomplish this is by keeping desk items contained in their own spaces for operating convenience, and conceal them as much as possible. A hardworking desk needs a high-performance work zone with plenty of organizers so the space stays organized while looking its best. Note: if your office is in your bedroom, reference the Home Office section of this book to see how to organize this type of space.

A less demanding workspace used for light duties, such as home-related paperwork, needs far less space and can be easily hidden inside a secretary desk; armoire; or foldout, wall-mounted desk.

Start organizing your bedroom desk by removing everything from it. Group like items, such as writing materials, office tools, books, files, reference materials, and so on. Use the trash, shredder, donation, and sale boxes to get rid of things. Computer monitors can be wall-mounted and camouflaged as a picture with a decorative screen-saver photo. Wireless computer peripherals are easy to hide in a deep drawer or a bedroom closet.

An entertainment center in a bedroom is worth the investment in rooms with televisions, audio equipment, or gaming units. Many related items can be neatly stashed out of sight, such as CD/DVD players, computers, portable electronics, charging stations, game stations and accessories, remotes, music, and movies.

The cleanest version is a wall-mounted television in which the cords and cables are run behind the drywall, thus eliminating the need for a stand or center. Cables and cords can be kept in an unseen spot, such as a closet. Since operation can be wireless, DVD/CD players and stereos can also be hidden.

Television or stereo consoles and stands can hold different types of equipment on various shelves or compartments where cords and cables will drop out of the back. Built-in entertainment centers often have many compartments for everything from equipment to music and movies. However, they'll require more work to route and access cables and cords. One of the biggest and most important organizational projects for entertainment centers is cord management, which is worth detailed instruction. See the Home Offices and Armoires chapter for more detailed information about cord management.

Bedroom Storage Furniture

Any piece of bedroom furniture, such as a dresser, chest, highboy, or armoire that contains clothing, lingerie, socks, scarves, belts, and the like, can be organized together. As mentioned, it's important to have the bedroom closet completely decluttered and arranged before you start organizing the bedroom furniture so the contents can be easily transferred to the closet, if need be.

Before you begin dumping drawers and cabinets, have separate bags ready for donation, dry cleaner or tailor, sale or consignment, off-season, trash, closet, or items that belong elsewhere in the home. Also, it's a good idea to have a bag for those articles that you spend too much time deliberating over. Label this bag with a question mark (?) and the date. These items should not go back into the drawer. Rather place them on an overhead shelf or in an under-the-bed storage container. Record a "check-back date" in the calendar when you'll reevaluate them; usually a few months is enough time. Chances are you'll have a more objective viewpoint and be less indecisive the second time around.

If you have not done so already, consider storing off-season articles outside your drawer space. Not only will you create more storage space, but also you will establish a forced decluttering opportunity every season when you empty or place these clothing in storage containers.

Decluttering Drawers
It's best to stick with organizing one drawer at a time when it contains a particular type inventory, such as just sweaters. Otherwise, if all the drawers are in a jumbled mess, empty them out and begin to sort things into like piles. Set aside odds and ends, such as books, makeup, music, journals, and so on. Sort these items into groups, if possible, and

then locate better places for them. For example, journals and diaries belong in a nightstand or a desk. Makeup and grooming supplies can move to the bathroom.

Sometimes we need to create a place for items by adding organizers. For example, you can install a wall-mounted shelf for books and magazines or use an under-the-bed organizer to contain memory items, such as pictures or achievement awards. A spare drawer can also be designated for odds and ends, but make certain to establish division in the drawer with organizers to keep it from becoming a junk pile.

Bedroom Furniture versus Closet Storage

The following reasons are why hanging closet storage is optimal:

- Hung clothing is kept wrinkle-free; folded clothing wrinkles.
- Everything is easy to see at a glance when hung, whereas folded piles conceal.
- Freshly folded laundered clothing usually gets placed on top of an existing stack of clothes. When clothes are accessed, they're usually taken from the top and clothes left at the bottom of a pile are not used. This is a common problem with stacks of folded clothes.
- Folded clothes in a drawer are easy to mess up.

The most important items to move from a drawer to a closet for hanging are those that wrinkle the most when folded in drawers. Items that are harder to arrange in drawer storage, such as bulky sweatshirts, sweaters, jeans, and sweatpants, can be stacked on closet shelves. Many accessories, like belts, ties, and scarves can hang from closet hook organizers. Closet shelves can also store baskets

to hold smaller articles, such as socks, nylons, boxers, underwear, and the like.

Drawer Arrangements

When you are ready to put items back into the drawers, don't revert to old organizing patterns, especially if they were not working. Instead, really think about where to best place certain items. The following are storage suggestions for drawer arrangements:

- Match the item to the size of the drawer: small items in smaller drawers, medium items in medium drawers, and so on.
- Divide inventories by placing a separate category in each drawer, such as T-shirts in one drawer and pajamas in another. However, small inventories can share space in the same drawer, keeping related items together, such as bras and underwear.
- When different categories share the same drawer space, create division by using organizers.

Drawers are great organizers by themselves, but they can also be further compartmentalized with additional organizers. It's always a good idea to look beyond what various drawer organizers are marketed to hold and find new ways to use them. Many kitchen, bathroom, and office drawer organizers can store bedroom items quite well. The following covers the various drawer organizers to use for bedroom belongings:

1. The **SPRING-LOADED BARS** are inexpensive and adjustable and come with separate pieces to divide both vertically and horizontally, thus forming a rectangle or square compartment. They're made in different materials, such as wood, plastic,

and cedar, and also come in adjustable lengths, plus varying heights for shallow, medium, and deep drawers. However, some spring-loaded dividers can lose tension and collapse over time.

2. There are **SLOTTED, THREE-INCH PLASTIC-STRIP KITS** that can snap or be cut apart and interlocked to create customizable drawer compartments. These are limited to shallow drawers since they're only three inches high, but they utilize any dead space.

3. **HONEYCOMB** or **DIAMOND DRAWER ORGANIZERS** contain multiple small compartments good for holding individual pairs of socks, underwear, ties, and the like. The compartments are scaled to fit only one item securely, which prevents shifting. They also keep items easy to see since they're not piled or stacked on top of one another. These organizers are not adjustable

and are limited to shallow drawers and small items.

4. **TRANSPARENT ACRYLIC DRAWER DIVIDERS** are excellent for high visibility. Heavier divider materials, like acrylic, rely on stable holders that mount to the inside of the drawers, making them strong enough to store bulkier items.

5. **INDIVIDUAL REMOVABLE CONTAINERS** or **BASKETS** can separate belongings in a drawer, but measure them to prevent any unused space. These organizers have the benefit of being removable and transportable. Specialized containers for drawers are available to hold items, such as bras and underwear. Some are long and thin and geared toward storing socks or folded boxers in a vertical row. Drawer containers are commonly made with a cardboard

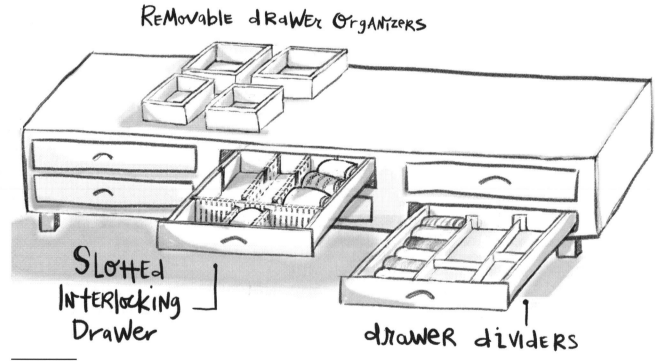

FIGURE 6.05
Drawer Organizers

frame and lined in nylon, linen, canvas, or a soft fabric to complement clothing.

6. Small, thin drawers can benefit from SHALLOW TRAY ORGANIZERS, which are usually only two inches high and anywhere from twelve to twenty inches in both width and length. These organizers have built-in dividers formed into many individual compartments. Some of these organizers are adjustable so you are able to expand the width to fit the drawer.

Storing Clothing in Drawers

There are different ways to store clothing in drawers: folding and stacking, filing, and rolling. These options are a personal preference, and each has both merits and drawbacks.

Folding and Stacking

A traditionally folded item, like they're displayed in stores, fits the length of most drawers. There are organizational tools, commonly referred to as folding boards, that fold clothing this way uniformly, quickly, and easily.

Clothing can be folded in different ways to accommodate space or preference. For example, depending on size, fold shirts and pants over once or twice for varying storage options. Shirts can be folded sideways or face front with the sleeves hidden in the creases. Fold pants so the pockets are seen from the top. This way you can easily identify a pair.

Keep clothing piles limited to three or four pieces each. Clothes will be easier to find and less likely to become jumbled. Place thinner clothing in shallow drawers and thicker items in deep drawers, so piles are scaled to the drawer's height. Certain clothes that don't wrinkle easily, like tanks, tees, leggings, boxers, athletic apparel, and pajamas, can be folded into smaller squares or rectangles to double drawer space.

Stacking folded garments can be neater since rolled clothes can loosen. It's easier to transfer folded garments from place to place in stacks, like from the laundry room to the drawer. No more than three to four folded items should occupy any stack of clothes you create in your closet. This is especially important for drawers that conceal everything but the item on the top of the pile.

Soaring stacks of folded items will inevitably lead to disorganization as you continuously make your way to the bottom or middle of the pile, and a big stack is more work to straighten than a small one. Only load a stack of clothes if they're identical items, like white T-shirts. Then, make sure to rotate these piles by placing laundered clothes at the bottom of the stack.

Rolling

You can roll almost any piece of clothing or accessory, but certain bulky items like sweaters will stack too high in a drawer. Rolling garments has advantages, such as fewer wrinkles. More clothes can fit rolled in a shallow drawer than folded, and they're easier to view and access. In medium or deep drawers, rolled clothing can stack on top and in the crease of two lower rolled garments where they cannot unravel and everything is visible.

Small items, such as ties, socks, and nylons, can be rolled and placed in drawer organizers with many small compartments. With such organizers, you can group certain colors in section so you are able to see at a glance how many you have of each.

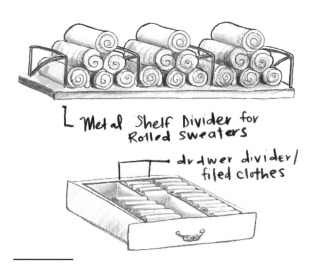

FIGURE 6.06
Rolling & Filing Clothes

Filing

An alternative method to stacking clothes the traditional way is to file your folded clothing. Filing requires that clothing stand in upright stacks with the crease side facing the opening of the drawer; the drawer front becomes the base for the bottom of your stack. This method is space saving and makes clothes easy to access and see.

In order to stabilize filed clothing, it needs to be more compact or folded smaller. For lighter clothing, place a piece of cardboard inside the fold of the shirt to create shape and weight so they file well. Arrange filed clothing in color order. A drawback to filing is that the clothing stack falls over when pieces are depleted.

Whether folding, rolling, stacking, or filing clothing in drawers, use organizers to contain, divide, and secure items in place.

Choose the Right Bedroom Furniture

One of the biggest problems with bedroom organization is ineffective furniture in the room. It's important to be able to spot the pieces that aren't adequately storing your belongings and strongly consider retiring them or make modifications when possible.

Furniture pieces that have too many small or large drawers and not enough middle-sized ones are problematic. Small drawers are shallow and only useful for storing limited articles like socks, scarves, belts, and such. Large drawers are deep, dwarfing the clothing, and they lend themselves to hard-to-manage folded piles.

Certain furniture pieces, like long and low dressers, invite counter clutter and fail to use vertical space effectively. In comparison, highboys, chests, and armoires are better furniture choices because they have many compartments, use vertical space, and take up much less horizontal room, making them easy to arrange in a room.

Armoires or wardrobe cabinets are bulky, but when used effectively, they're great assets in the bedroom. The best contribution these pieces offer is additional hanging storage for closet overflow. In addition, they can be outfitted with drawers, shelves, cubbies, and pullout baskets to accommodate any need. An armoire can also convert into a desk. For more information on repurposing an armoire, reference the Home Office and Armoires section of this book.

Jewelry and lingerie cabinets are smaller, specialized furniture pieces. They typically come with vast amounts of many small compartments to securely store many different types of small belongings. Many jewelry cabinets are designed to be wall mounted and camouflaged in a bedroom. It's best to have just a few efficient furniture pieces in the room that can hold everything. Downsizing wasteful furniture pieces will successfully declutter the bedroom.

CHAPTER 7

Adult-Bedroom Closets

Organizing a bedroom closet is best handled in steps. Which steps you decide to accomplish at any given time are irrelevant, provided you fully complete each one before moving on to the next. Doing so will likely increase your focus and be less overwhelming. Also, establishing steps makes it easier to pick up where you left off, should time lapse in between them.

Reducing Adult Clothing

Probably the most difficult step in organizing any bedroom closet, but particularly an adult's, is decluttering clothing inventories. There are numerous reasons people choose to hang onto clothing even when they don't fit or are no longer in style. It's important to challenge yourself to think in a new way as you review your wardrobe for wearability. Most of us wear only a small fraction of our wardrobe; therefore, a good portion of the remainder should, technically, go. Keep things that currently fit in the closet since that makes finding what to wear easy. Clothing is worth nothing if it isn't worn; rather, it's wasting valuable storage space. Some pointers to consider while decluttering your wardrobe include:

- Remove clothing that does not fit right or makes you feel uncomfortable. Everyone knows which clothes these are, so no matter how much you like them, such issues will keep those articles glued to the hangers.
- Surrender to purchase mistakes, meaning the clothes you regret buying and don't wear. Tags might even still be on them, but because they're so old, you can no longer return them. The thought of wasting money or discarding something you've never worn is daunting. However, most likely, you are never going to change your mind about such clothes, and they're taking up valuable closet space.
- Many times we hold onto clothing that was expensive because we think it holds a high monetary value even when we never wear it. These items are usually out of style or no longer fit. High-end designer brands and clothing made with materials such as silk or leather fit that criteria. It's important to

know that the actual value of pre-owned clothing is usually less than one-third of what it originally cost, because most clothing-material fibers break down and lose shape over time, plus they go out of style. The resale of vintage clothing may not justify the sales effort, and most upscale resale stores don't accept merchandise over two years old.

- Many people congest their closets with clothes that don't currently fit, anticipating the day a weight goal will be met.In order to free space, pack up such clothing and store them elsewhere until they can be worn again. Make certain to first eliminate those you don't truly love. Containerize and label these clothes according to size, type, and season. Record the current date on the label so you establish how long they remain unworn; we often have trouble remembering those important facts. Make a note in your calendar to reevaluate the clothes in six to twelve months and, if they still don't fit, consider donating or selling them.

The Decluttering Process

Before you begin decluttering your clothes, obtain some empty bags for donation, consignment, sale, tailoring, and dry cleaning. Don't put discarded clothes in the trash, because most donation centers, like Goodwill or the Salvation Army, will recycle them, and there's a chance someone else might want them.

Also have a bag for clothes that you waver about keeping; the "maybe" bag is important because if you didn't have it, certain clothes may never leave their hangers. It will function as a holding place for clothes that need to leave the closet but have a viable opportunity to be worn

in the future, so store this bag for a set period of time. Once these clothes have left your personal closet space for several months, hopefully you'll be more objective about them. Pack the clothes in a labeled container and mark the date, size, type, and season. Then record a time in your calendar to review them and make a final decision. You can also take these clothes to a friend's house and ask his or her opinion about whether to keep them.

Another option is to flag questionable wardrobe items with a date-stamped tag or ribbon tied to the hanger and keep them in the closet. When you wear the clothes, remove the tag or ribbon. Then the next time you clean out the closet, remove all the clothes with tags or ribbons still attached. The point is to strategize ways to declutter most effectively and break the habit of avoiding taking action to clear out unnecessary apparel.

Simply trying on your questionable clothing can often help you decide what to do with them. For clothes you decide to keep, look them over closely for snags, tears, spots, stains, or loose buttons. Make sure they're clean and in good condition so you'll wear them. Toss the clothes worth repairing or the dry-cleaning expense into the "maybe" bag. Remember: clothing alterations and repairs can be costly, and there's no guarantee you'll be happy with them afterward.

Decide what to do with off-season items, if you have not already. People with tiny closets or those with several types of clothing—such as career, sports, casual, and dressy—typically need to store off-season clothes elsewhere due to space limitations. If you have plenty of space, it's best to keep off-season clothes in your closet, because packing and moving clothes takes time.

While decluttering, set aside all your off-season items until you are done, and then prioritize key placements for your everyday things and see what space is leftover for off-season items, if any. Those items can be stored in plastic containers above the hanging rod or in a wheeled cart on the floor. Just remember that you'll be rotating the storage essentials with clothes of the opposite season, so your containers need to accommodate the season with the most clothing.

Reducing Footwear

The first step in downsizing footwear is to gather each and every pair, including off-season shoes that are packed away, because you need an accurate count of the number of each type to judge how to actually store them. It's ideal, of course, to keep all your shoes openly displayed in your closet. However, space restrictions may limit the number you can store. In any case, it's best to keep like pairs of footwear stored together.

The bedroom closet should hold shoes in order of their importance: professional or work, business casual, formal, party, street, and then athletic. Store any type of footwear geared toward a certain sport or the outdoors, such as hiking boots or golf cleats, outside the bedroom closet, especially if that footwear gets dirty.

In an open space, sort all your footwear into categories that make the most sense given the type of footwear you own. Start reducing by tackling each group of footwear separately and sort the groups' footwear by color. Notice whether you have similar pairs of a particular boot or shoe, such as several pairs of black pumps or short brown boots. As long as each pair is worn regularly, keep them; otherwise, pare down to one of each type.

People often prefer a certain color, heel size, or comfort feature that draws them to a particular

style of shoe or boot. Therefore, having a few pairs of the same style boot or shoe is acceptable for footwear that is worn daily. As a general rule, when your tastes are limited to a few styles and colors, keep several pairs of a similar shoe or boot. If you have diverse tastes in footwear, try to limit yourself to one boot or shoe per style to keep inventories at a manageable size.

While downsizing, take note of the footwear you don't wear. Perhaps some have been hidden due to disorganization, in which case plan to make such footwear more visible in your new storage arrangements. Discard shoes that are continuously passed over due to discomfort. It's a good idea to always test shoes for comfort before you buy them. Discard shoes that are badly worn. Usually, only newer or well-made, expensive shoes are worth a shoe repair. However, consider that any shoe repair may not meet your expectations, and repairs use money that could otherwise go toward buying a new pair. Donate and recycle unwanted footwear. Only high-end, gently worn footwear is worth your time in resale.

After decluttering your footwear, clean them: wipe off the dust, buff, and work on scuff marks or stains. You'll be happy you took the time to do this since a clean pair of shoes encourages wear. It's convenient to do this now while all your footwear is front and center.

List the pairs of shoes or boots you have of each type; it will be useful when purchasing footwear organizers or installing a new closet system once you are through purging the entire closet. For now, put the shoes back were you normally keep them, but this time in order. Begin to think about how your shoes can be dispersed throughout the home and which storage organizers or closet systems would work best.

Reducing Accessories

Declutter all worn items that accessorize clothing, such as belts, ties, shawls, scarves, hats, gloves, purses, and handbags. These items have a tendency to mount into piles over time. The best way to approach the decluttering process is to focus on sorting one group of belongings at a time.

Belts

Gather all your belts and group them according to color; keep patterned belts in a separate pile, and then go through each pile and eliminate those you no longer like. Chances are if you don't like something today, you'll not like it tomorrow. Bear in mind while decluttering that anything out of style does not typically come back "in" for a decade or more.

Discard all broken and badly worn belts. Your goal should be to wind up with several classic basics in colors like black, brown, navy, and so on. Good belts that don't fit anymore can be packed away in labeled containers until a weight goal is met or you decide to sell them. Note the types of belts you have and whether you are able to hang them since some have buckle plates instead of a loop and cannot hang on a hook. Determine how many you have to plan the best way to store them.

Scarves and Shawls

Lay out your collection of scarves and shawls on an open area, such as a bed. Since there are so many different sizes, materials, and shapes of scarves, place them in piles according to a particular characteristic, such as scarf length or material. You can then subdivide each category by color, keeping plaids and prints separate. Look them over for stains, snags, and the like. Dry-clean, hand wash, or repair the items that you still love and wear.

The number of scarves and shawls to keep depends on how often you wear such accessories. Consider the significance of displaying those worn frequently so they're visible and easy to access. Keep less-frequently worn items in baskets, drawers, or outside the closet.

Neckties

Gather all neckties and sort them by color. Place stripes, plaids, and patterned ties in separate piles and eliminate those you don't like or wear anymore. Check the ties for stains, snags, frays, and loose threads. Donate those in bad shape to a place that recycles, and repair and clean only those that will be worn. Generally, ties made of silk or those that are hand stitched with the same fabric on the inside are considered quality ties and always worth holding onto.

Neckties, as all wardrobe accessories, are classic or trendy. Solids, stripes, diamonds, checks, polka dots, and the like are classic designs. The tie's width, color, and pattern mark a fashion trend. If you're not up to date on current styles, it may be worth your while to catch up before downsizing a tie collection. A fashion magazine or even a clothing catalog can help. You can also match ties against your suits and shirts to help make reducing decisions since some of your ties may be wrong for your current wardrobe. Generally, plain ties go with patterned suits or shirts and vice versa. A tie should stand out and not disappear on a shirt.

Make sure to discard wrong-length ties since a tie too long or short is incorrect. Generally, depending upon how you tie a knot and your collar size, the tie tip should fall just above the belt buckle. Therefore, average-height individuals should only keep standard-length ties, which are fifty-five inches to fifty-seven inches long and three and a half inches to four inches wide. Taller people should only keep long ties, and shorter people, short ties. Reduce inventories accordingly.

Once your neckties are decluttered, record how many you have so you're able to determine an appropriate organizer or storage arrangement. If you regularly wear neckties, a wall or rod-hung organizer in the closet will keep them visible and accessible.

Purses and Handbags

Gather all your purses and handbags, lay them out in an open area, and divide them according to style, such as tote, satchel, clutch, shoulder bags, and the like. Next, go through each grouping of handbags and only keep those you love and use. However, there is an exception to this rule: For example, say you have only one basic black evening clutch that is needed infrequently for special occasions. Even if you don't like it, you may want to keep it in case you need it or until you replace it with another. Think about what your personal needs are from a handbag. Sometimes, things like not enough compartments stops you from using certain bags like a tote style. These are the bags you need to place in a pile to consider whether to sell or donate them.

High-end handbags and purses usually have big price tags. Such items are often hard to part with and should remain, even when not used at the moment. These handbags and purses have long shelf lives when properly stored. For this reason, holding on to them until they're back in style is reasonable. High-end designer handbags and purses also tend to have a strong resale potential. Even vintage bags of this caliber sell

well secondhand. However, you must be willing to accept that, in some cases, they may only be worth half the price you originally paid.

Check all the handbags and purses you want to keep for ripped stitches, torn liners, jammed zippers, broken hardware, and the like. Repair good-quality bags only if they're in decent shape since such repairs are very costly. Any handbags that you're not willing to refurbish can be donated. Take the time to properly clean the bags you keep. It's important to use the right cleaning solutions, brushes, and cloths. You can also outsource to a restoration handbag service that specializes in this type of care.

After decluttering and cleaning your purses and handbags, stuff them with bubble wrap to retain their shape. Don't use tissue paper, because it attracts moths. Undo all removable hardware, like chain straps or handles, and place them inside the bag. This prevents them from marking and scratching the exterior of the bag and any others stacked next to them.

More expensive handbags and purses are sold with protective opaque dust bags for proper storage. Pillowcases made from natural fibers like cotton can make great substitutes for dust bags, if needed. At the enclosure of the dust bag, attach a tag with a string or pin to note the color and type of bag inside. Dust bags certainly do their jobs; however, they're not translucent, so you cannot see their contents at a glance. Concealing the handbags and purses in this manner may cause you to overlook them.

Begin to think about how you want to store your handbags and purses in your closet. Due to their bulk, larger purse and handbag collections may be stored outside a tight closet space. Since handbags and purses are generally not swapped out daily, it's not critical to give them key placement. Under-the-bed storage essentials or bedroom armoires are good alternative storage organizers to bedroom closets.

Hats and Gloves

It's most convenient to store hats and gloves worn daily near the outerwear; a mudroom or in a coat closet off an entranceway to the home is ideal. When storage demands are limited in those locations, however, a bedroom closet is second best. Gather all the hats and gloves belonging to the person(s) who occupy the bedroom and separate the different types. For example, all baseball caps in one pile and sun visors in another.

Next, go through each group one at a time and begin to downsize them. Discard the ripped and badly worn articles and donate the ones that are no longer worn. Seasonal hats and gloves that have not received use in the past two years should exit the closet. Hold on only to the gloves and hats that serve their purpose well. For example, gloves that don't keep you warm and dry need to go. Sometimes we buy certain hats and gloves to match a certain color of jacket. Make sure that you still have or use the jacket since this will help you decide whether you should keep them. There are many ways to store hats and gloves in a bedroom closet. Many wall-mounted mudroom organizers designed to hold hats and gloves also work well in a bedroom or closet.

After Decluttering Your Wardrobe

Once your closet is decluttered, you'll have bags of unwanted clothing ready for their next destinations. Successful organizing is about executing any task in its entirety. Therefore, no bags of clothing should linger in hallways, foyers, or spare closets for very long since you don't want the temptation of keeping them.

Consignment clothes should be clean and in excellent condition, or no place will accept them. Usually, resale shops take clothes for the upcoming season only if they're less than two years old, so separate your clothes accordingly. This is why it's so important to continuously declutter your closets on a regular basis and not let too many years slip by. Immediately schedule an appointment to consign current-season clothing and ask which months of nonseasonal clothing are accepted. Record the dates in case you have other clothes to consign.

Stash your soon-to-be-donated clothing by the door, labeled and ready to go. Plan to drop them off at a donation center within a few days. Garage sale clothing needs to be boxed, labeled, and stored in a common area where other such items are collected.

Compute Closet Inventories

Before you purchase organizers for your various closet inventories and plan out your space, count how much you have of each type. This way, you can purchase the necessary number of organizers in the right sizes without making any mistakes.

A good strategy is to list all your closet inventories and their amounts. For example, record short-sleeve shirts and then their quantity. Keep categories simple, such as long-sleeve tops, jeans, dress pants, sweaters, long dresses, and shirts. Also record how you would like to store each type of clothing. For example, sweaters can be rolled in a basket or folded in a drawer or on a shelf. Preferences matter, so if you like jeans hung on a hanger, write that down, but also record a second storage alternative, such as folded on a shelf. Secondary storage options are necessary to consider because if there are space or budget constraints, it may not be possible to arrange every single inventory the way you'd like.

Closet Planning

Whether you are keeping your current closet system and adding storage components or installing a brand-new closet system, there are some important things to do first. Determine a budget since even a few storage accessories can add up. The budget will define how far you can go with this project.

A do-it-yourself (DIY) approach means that you'll make a space plan by taking detailed depth, width, height, and baseboard measurements first, and then shop for organizers or closet systems, or both, and install them. Conversely, a professional closet company hired to do the job will still require that you get involved by furnishing an accurate record of all your closet inventories, plus they'll need to know exactly how you want them stored or displayed. A closet professional requires direction because they need you to decide which inventories need key placement and access.

Examine your closet in its current state. Estimate whether you think your belongings can fit with easy access and high visibility once you convert your space and given your budget. Remember that inventories should be visible because you might not wear what you don't see. Also think about items that can be transferred elsewhere to save on closet space. Good items to relocate are those that are seldom worn or easy to move and fit elsewhere in the bedroom.

Write down everything that bothers you about your current closet. For example, perhaps you are tight on hanging space so it's hard to view your clothes, or the floors are covered in shoes. Another important area that is commonly overlooked is the closet doors. Pocket-style doors make it tougher to get at things as opposed to bifolds, which allow full access. When you are done with your list of closet annoyances, rate them in order of which ones bother you the most. This is so important, especially when you have a smaller budget that cannot solve all the problems you have with your closet and you need to tackle the list in order of importance until your budget runs out.

Pitfalls of Trading Clothes with Friends and Family

Swapping clothes with friends or family may seem like a great way to pick up some "new" clothes while getting rid of unwanted ones, but be careful. When the other person's clothes turn out to be the kind you would not buy, you may find yourself in an uncomfortable situation. Consider the possibility that you may have better things to bring to the table than they do, which begs the question: Would you be better off selling them?

Before you put yourself in a position to trade clothes with someone, make sure you're the kind of person who can turn down others' clothes without making them feel insulted. If you trade, you position yourself to perhaps feel obligated to wear their clothes when you are around them. Trading clothes with friends and family may turn out to be nothing more than a social time and not productive organizing. Think these factors through before you commit yourself to a clothes-trading opportunity.

CHAPTER 8

The Nursery

The key to organizing a well-appointed nursery is well-structured, efficient furniture pieces that also function as storage. All organizers should be adjustable and versatile so they can adapt to the continuous, ever-changing needs of growing children. Baby furniture is scaled small and is quickly outgrown; eventually, you'll need to replace it with larger pieces, which involves spending more money and reconfiguring everything in the room. It's common to recoup just a small fraction of what you paid for baby furniture, meaning that in the long run it's best to start out a nursery with furniture that can at least convert to the juvenile stage.

Practically speaking, furniture purchased for a nursery should be well made so it can last until the child goes to college, even if they don't use it long. Furniture features to look for are

- many midsized drawers to accommodate most inventories;
- drawers that fully extend for ease of access and viewing;
- adjustable furniture cabinet shelves; and

- furniture pieces that extend above waist level to capture commonly unused lateral space for storage.

Managing Nursery Articles

Clutter chaos is common in a nursery since babies need so many things. To establish order in a nursery, keep only what you'll use *now*; everything else—such as hand-me-downs, bigger clothes, advanced toys, and books—should be containerized, labeled, and stored out of sight.

The following detailed information can help you successfully organize each part of the nursery. Steps are laid out in logical order to help you stay on track while organizing.

Step 1: Organize Baby Clothes
The best but most difficult time to organize your baby's wardrobe is right after birth, which is when you know exactly what fits now and perhaps in the next few months, which is all that needs to be stored in the closet and drawers.

Many people need to prepare the nursery before the baby arrives, and when clothing gifts and hand-me-downs are given beforehand, it makes sense to put them in order. You can always get an accurate estimate of your newborn's birth weight from your obstetrician, which can help you organize the clothes before the baby arrives. Fine-tuning can be accomplished later.

Always keep the tags on everything until you actually use a baby item. Receipts and gift receipts should be well organized. Divide the receipts according to the stores where they were purchased and place them in a labeled folder or envelope. You can also attach the receipt to the tag on the clothing item.

When organizing baby clothes, gather the entire wardrobe and place it on a large, clean surface. Hand-me-downs should be freshly washed. Have bags ready for donation, returns, trash, and items to put away for future use. Sort everything by size. However, keep in mind that there is no size standardization in the clothing industry, so review size charts by clothing brand, which can be found on websites or tags. Then place clothes in their respective size groups.

Within each clothing size, separate the clothes by type (such as pants, sweaters, etc.). Make certain the clothing size matches the season in which they'll most likely be worn. Go through your divided piles and remove all the used clothes with rips, missing buttons, stains, broken zippers, or items that you simply don't like. Check clothes over for safety. Loose buttons, snaps, bows, and appliqués are choking hazards.

It's common to keep too much clothing in each size, because it's hard to judge how quickly a baby will grow. However, it's important to know that babies grow the most in the first year. Layette and newborn sizes typically receive the least amount of use, and newborns don't go many places anyway. At this stage, sleepers are the keepers, so stock less regular clothing—under ten outfits to start. Included in this amount can be one special occasion outfit. Additionally, a single coat, casual jacket, and two pairs of shoes are enough. A typical newborn runs through two to four sleepers and onesies in a day. Therefore, figure out the laundry schedule and stock accordingly.

Keep only clothing that currently fits, plus the next size or two up, in the drawers and closet. Situate clothing by category and use organizers or separate compartments to divide the different sizes. Doing so will make it easy to remove the outgrown sizes and replace them with another size.

Generally, it's best to return new clothes that will not fit until nine months in the future since it's hard to judge a baby's growth rate that far in advance. Store unreturnable and hand-me-down clothing that will not fit the baby until he or she is eighteen months or so in labeled containers separated by type and size. These containers can be stored in overhead compartments in the closet, under the bed, or in a designated storage area.

Hanging clothing is always the best storage option, for many reasons. First, hanging clothes prevents wrinkling. It's easier and faster to flip through hung clothes than hunting through a drawer, bin, basket, or any container. Unlike folded items, you can often judge when clothes are outgrown based on where the garment drops from a hanger as compared to others. Starting in the laundry room, hanging clean clothes is easier than sorting, folding, and stacking them.

Another way to gain additional hanging storage is by investing in an armoire or wardrobe cabinet. Not only do armoires and wardrobe cabinets hide everything away neatly, but also they can hold many belongings. Besides hanging rods, armoires can also be outfitted with shelves, pullouts, and drawers.

Step 2: Organize Baby Linens

The primary baby linens to have are blankets, bibs, burp cloths, and crib sheets. It's necessary to do a diligent job of organizing each of these groups of linens since they're needed, washed, and used on a daily basis. It's important to have the right amount of baby linens on hand so you don't run out; keep them situated in an easy-to-access location near where they're used.

Blankets

The first thing to recognize is that RECEIVING BLANKETS serve more purposes than just swaddling the newborn in a baby's first four months of life. They also make great burp cloths, diaper pads, towels, and privacy drapes for breastfeeding. Down the road, they can be recycled into cleaning rags, pet blankets, and as toy baby doll blankets. Receiving blankets are not all the same size. The smaller

FIGURE 8.01
Wall-mounted & Dresser converted changing table

sizes make swaddling more difficult, and they're quickly outgrown by a baby. It's best to keep the larger ones and return the small ones.

The great thing about receiving blankets is that they're lightweight and easy to pack in a diaper bag, which is where you should always keep a few clean ones. You can roll the receiving blankets, along with some bibs and diapers, and store them upright in an open container or caddy near all the feeding and changing stations in the home. A dozen receiving blankets per baby are adequate, using two receiving blankets per day and allowing a week's turnaround time for laundry.

Usually a baby does not have the motor skills to actually push a blanket away until around age one, which makes them suffocation hazards when left in the sleeping area. Therefore, pack CRIB or LARGER BLANKETS away under the crib or in an overhead closet compartment. Bulky items like these, which need long-term storage, can be stowed in vacuum-compressed bags to dramatically reduce their size for storage conservation. DECORATIVE CRIB COMFORTERS can also be displayed in the nursery, hung on the wall, or draped over a chair.

Burp Cloths and Bibs

Before you tear off the store tags and begin to stockpile bibs and burp cloths, make sure you have the right kind and know how many you actually need. Consider returning or reducing newborn bibs, and use burp cloths as inexpensive substitutes—at least until when the baby is introduced to solid food. Also consider only keeping bibs with Velcro enclosures since strings and snaps are inconvenient.

In order to establish the number of bibs and burp cloths you need, determine how often you replace them on a daily basis multiplied by the number of days between washings. Generally, six to eight should be sufficient; remember: they're quickly outgrown.

Once your baby starts eating solid food, the bibs need to change, along with where they're stored. This is the time when the baby graduates to the high chair, which typically resides in the kitchen. At this time, keep bibs near the baby's food or high chair. A high chair hook or hanging pocketed organizer can store them. You can even stash them in a kitchen drawer, counter canister, or a basket located in the pantry.

Older babies and toddlers have bibs that typically come in two sizes: six to twenty-four months and toddler two to four years. These bibs are typically plastic, so they wipe clean and don't need to be laundered. Therefore, only stock a few.

Crib Sheets

Three to five crib sheets are enough for a nursery, given several changes per week. Babies usually outgrow their cribs between one and three years of age. Therefore, unless you have a crib that converts to a toddler bed, it's unnecessary to invest in more sheets. Many people buy quilted sheet savers to catch drools, leaks, and the like so they don't have to hassle with changing the baby's sheet in the middle of night. However, sheet protectors are not as beneficial as they may seem since they're yet another expense, require storage, and still need to be washed.

Store crib sheets in a separate labeled container inside the linen closet or in the nursery, if they're changed frequently. Under the crib in a wheeled organizer or in a changing table basket are good spots for them in the nursery.

Step 3: Set Up a Changing Table

A designated, central place to change diapers, dress, and groom your baby is necessary.

Otherwise, belongings needed to do these jobs tend scatter everywhere, requiring more steps. Changing tables come in different configurations and dimensions. Make sure that yours is the right height for those caring for the baby.

To save room and money, many people opt to place the changing pad right on top of a low dresser and use the upper drawers to stash diapers, lotions, and wipes. You can purchase a changing table topper for a dresser counter to secure the changing pad. Some even have easy-to-access compartments to store supplies.

A basic, budget-friendly changing table features a top level for the changing pad and two open

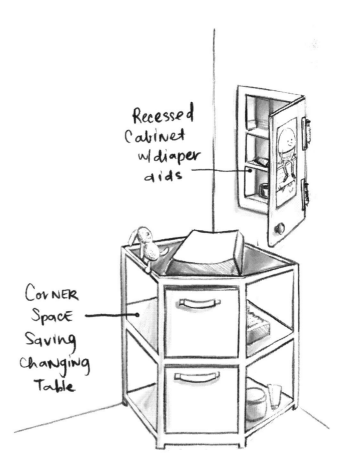

FIGURE 8.02
Diamond shaped changing table &
Hidden Recessed Cabinet with picture front

shelves below. On the shelves, use several open-top baskets or containers to separate items, such as diapers, lotions, and brushes. Place items used daily on the upper shelves, such as wipes and diapers. The lower shelves can hold other items like baby toys. Place items that move to other rooms, such as bathing essentials, in handled organizers like caddies. The lower shelves can also contain larger baskets for laundry and trash.

In small nurseries, use diamond-shaped changing tables designed for corner placement to economize space. Also, foldaway or wall-mounted changing tables also benefit tight spaces.

Changing Table Tips
- Key things to have at a changing station are easy-to-access pullout baskets, drawers, hamper, and trash compartments.
- A good changing table is a safe one. Use overhead shelving sparingly, and don't place daily needed baby-care supplies on it since something will inevitably fall on the baby. Use safety straps on the changing pad. Make sure anything placed around the changing pad cannot break or spill, especially when the baby can grab.
- Plan a smart space since you are dealing with a squirmy baby at this place. Take out diapers, wipes, cotton swabs, receiving blankets, and all toiletries from their original packaging and place them in open, easy-to-access containers. No hard-to-access screw tops, snaps, zippers, or button or clasp enclosures organizers. Avoid deep or big containers since they're too hard to sort through and lift. No breakable or slippery organizers since you are often dealing with wet, greasy hands.
- Limit your inventories so your changing area is never crowded. Excess diapers, wipes, creams, ointments, and so on bought in volume can reside in closets, pantries, or under the crib.

- Prepare the changing table in advance. While the baby is asleep, get ready for the next round of work the baby will bring. If he or she needs medication, have it out, along with a bib, burp cloth, or whatever is necessary by the changing station, so when the baby awakes, things will run more smoothly.

Step 4: Keep Toys and Books Under Control
In the nursery, keep only the toys and books that will be used during the first year of life. Hand-me-down toys or books that are not yet age appropriate need to get packed away in separate containers and divided according to age ranges such as one to three years. Before packing them, donate items you don't like, because they can turn into future clutter. Place storage containers on overhead closet shelves, under the crib, or in a place where they won't be forgotten.

Storage Arrangements for Toys and Books
The key to storing toys and books is to make them easy to access for little people, so when they're old enough to walk, they can help themselves and learn to clean up. Therefore, no high shelves, lidded containers, screw tops, and so on. Also refrain from using large containers that easily become too heavy to move and make belongings hard to find.

Choose safe storage essentials: rounded edges versus sharp square ones, and no unfinished wood that can cause splinters. Storage units should have a stable construction—nothing wobbly. Anything that can tip over from too much weight is dangerous, such as tall shelving units; make sure everything tall is fastened to the wall. Nothing placed overhead should be heavy. Never use tiered storage that is climbable. Toy chests should have two safety-lid supports and cutouts to prevent finger pinching. Chests with top lids, inside which a child can fit, become suffocation hazards.

Use the correct organizers for the right size and weight of items: small toys in little containers and larger toys in bigger containers. Tiered bin storage units are great for dividing small groups of items, such as balls and Matchbox cars. There are bin storage racks that come with slanted shelves for easy access and viewing.

Bulky electronic toys, such as activity centers, sight and sound toys, musical toys, and stacking toys can store in deep shelves, bins, or cubbies. Keep lightweight items like stuffed animals, balls, plush toys, and rubber toys in chests, bins, buckets, and crates on the floor or shelf or in a cubby compartment.

Store books in cubby compartments, bookcases, or wheeled carts, but not on open shelving since small children cannot manage bookends well. Look for bookcases with wall-mounted designs and rails that hold books facing forward so books are easy for children to find. Whenever you invest in a freestanding bookcase, make sure it's not a tipping hazard and purchase a tip-restraint kit for securing it to the wall studs.

Step 5: Create the Perfect Feeding Area

The primary place to nurse or bottle feed your baby should be near the crib for convenient nap and nighttime feedings. A rocker or comfortable chair plus an easy-to-reach table with many drawers, shelves, or cubbies, is the basic arrangement. Add overhead shelves only when you need places for additional belongings because you don't want to clutter the tabletop with too many things and it's important to keep everything necessary nearby.

Other ways to keep your tabletop clutter-free is to use floor lamps or wall-mounted fixtures and wall clocks; place all electronics elsewhere, using remotes to control them from the feeding area. A pocketed chair organizer is a good solution for storing important items close by, and it frees up table space. The tabletop should have only a bottle warmer, electric breast pump, feeding timer, unbreakable water glass, and a place to put a bottle.

Tables with drawers need compartments for separating belongings, such as pocket tissue, over-the-counter (OTC) medications, pacifiers, teething rings, burp cloths, nipple cream, breast milk labels, feeding logs, and writing instruments. Should this area be a breast milk pumping station where idle time needs some productivity, stash packaged snacks, manicure tools, books, magazines, crossword puzzles, and a place for electronics in the drawers to pass the time.

Tables with lower shelving, deep drawers, or cubby compartments can store items like humidifiers, nebulizers, baby bottles, pumping accessories, manual pumps, breast milk coolers, breast milk totes, paper towels, nursing pads and pillows, neck pillows, receiving blankets, and diaper bags.

Bottles, nipples, and all breast-pumping-equipment supplies should be divided and separated in storage. Simply place each group of items in its own compartment or container and keep them next to each other. If there is a secondary place in the home where you feed your baby, fill a handled storage caddy that can easily transport the basics like a bottle, pacifier, burp cloth, or whatever you need for a single feeding. Store this organizer at the main feeding area, where it can easily be replenished with supplies.

Step 6: Prepare a Well-Organized and Safe Sleeping Area

Keep the crib interior free and clear to avoid any suffocation hazards. This also means anything hanging from the crib, such as an activity center or mobile. Consult your pediatrician for safety precautions. Anything placed next the crib should be out of the baby's reach. Make certain that there are no tripping hazards on the floor near the crib. Don't place the crib near a window since it may not be long before the baby can climb. Also, windows are sunny, drafty, and breakable.

Trundles and under-the-crib storage essentials are good investments since they take advantage of dead space. A long crib skirt should be able to hide anything placed there. Some key items to stash under the crib are diaper essentials, toys, off-season clothes, bathing supplies, linens, and breast-pump supplies. Keep your nursing or feeding area close to the crib. Second in importance will be the changing station. You want these places nearest to the crib since they're often used before and after sleeping.

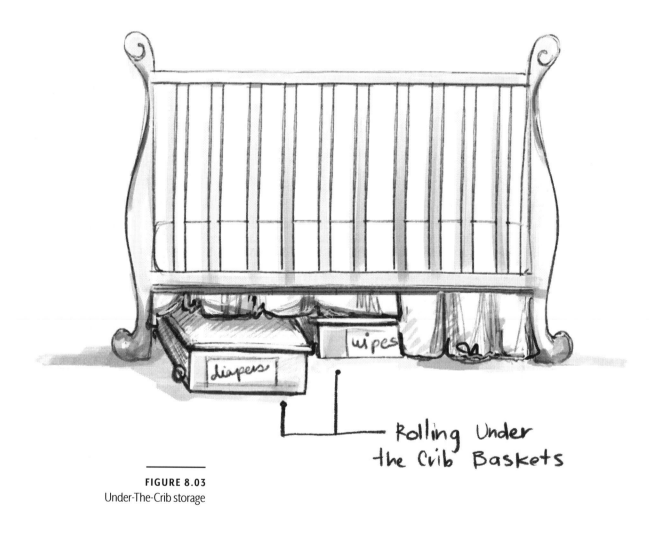

FIGURE 8.03
Under-The-Crib storage

CHAPTER 9

Babies' Closets

Because you need plenty of space in the nursery for changing tables, rockers, monitors, breast pumps, and so on, an efficiently designed closet is all the more important to keep the nursery clutter-free. The more you can neatly store in the closet, the fewer furniture and organizers you'll need in the baby's room. In the long run, it may be better to invest in a well-designed adjustable closet system than to put money into an expensive changing table or baby furniture equipped with storage compartments, because such items have a short life span, even if they're handed down to siblings.

The best way to organize a baby closet is with an adjustable closet system since storage needs from babies to teenagers change dramatically overtime. Since baby clothing is so small, you can begin by doubling or tripling the hanging rods and change the bar heights as the child grows. Stick with medium-size pullout baskets or drawers for a closet system, because this size works best for most clothing and accessories. Small- to medium-size bins are best for shelves since large baskets invite clutter and are hard to go through.

Arranging the Closet

There are two ways to arrange your baby's closet: set up your closet with individual organizers or install a closet system. A closet system is the preferred choice, but it may not fit in every budget. However, there are more and more affordable DIY, off-the-shelf closet organizers that compete well with semicustom closet systems which are found online or in home centers. Many of these systems offer add-on components separate from the original kit, so you don't have to buy everything upfront. This is a perfect alternative for the budget minded who want to slowly build their system overtime. You can always start out with inexpensive plastic containers and incorporate them into a basic structured closet system, and then upgrade on an as-needed basis.

Hanging Organizers

There are different types of closet organizers designed to hang from the closet rod. The most popular one used in a baby's closet are common TIERED, NYLON/CANVAS HANGING "SHELVES" attached by Velcro. Each compartment is typically fifteen by twelve by twelve inches. Hanging tiered closet shelf organizers can accommodate the spillover from crowded dresser drawers or shelves in the nursery and are an affordable storage solution that can easily get reused elsewhere in the home. Ideal belongings to store here are bibs, diaper bags, blankets, crib sheets, clothing, receiving blankets, bath towels, stuffed animals, plush toys, changing-pad covers, and lightweight gadgets.

Some more durable hanging-shelf units come with drawers that create more storage options for holding other belongings, like socks, pajamas, pacifiers, teething toys, breast-pump supplies, bath accessories, bottles, small toys, onesies, hats, gloves, and the like. When selecting a hanging-shelf unit, choose one with sturdy shelving. Many buckle even with light loads. Think about the material of the organizer, as well. Fabric can stain and tear, whereas nylon wipes clean.

Use hanging-shelf organizers in moderation since they take up around a foot of hanging-rod space, which is valuable. However, there are some hanging-shelf organizers designed with shelving only at the base, leaving hanging-rod space above it.

Another hanging storage solution perfect for a baby's closet are **HANGING-ROD DOUBLERS**. This organizer provides an additional hanging rod suspended from the existing closet rod. Look for the adjustable versions of this organizer to change the height of the rod as the baby grows. As his or her clothes get longer, you can simply add space between the two hanging rods. You also want the hanging rod to be strong. Steel construction is more durable than aluminum or wood, which can crack, buckle, or bend. The stronger the hanging rod, the more it can hold.

A double-hung closet rod is an incredibly affordable solution to add hanging space in a closet and is easy to assemble and remove. The downside to this organizer is that it's not mounted at either end, so it can sway back and forth. Hanging space is prime storage because it's hard to replicate elsewhere in the nursery. Hanging clothes is the most convenient way to store them. There is no easier way to find and keep clothes orderly other than a hanging system. Just be certain to use the right size hangers for your baby's clothes.

A **HANGING POCKETED ORGANIZER** is a good organizer for a nursery closet since it holds many small groups of items babies need. These organizers resemble a garment bag and contain several see-through slip pockets to hold small items, like pacifiers, grooming essentials, teething toys, bows, hats, socks, burp cloths, and the like. These organizers also come double sided, which manages space well.

Over-the-Door Organizers

If the nursery closet has standard doors, an over-the-door (OTD) organizer is a good solution. There are many types of over-the-door storage organizers that could suit the needs of a baby's closet, such as **POCKET AND POUCH OVER-THE-DOOR-ORGANIZERS**. The clear plastic pockets are best so everything can be seen at a glance. Depending on the size of the pockets, you can store baby essentials, like diapers, bibs, hats, grooming essentials, socks, hats, toys, pacifiers, toiletries, and medicines.

OVER-THE-DOOR HANGING RODS can instantly increase your hanging space. You can also install **HOOKS** or **PEG-RACK ORGANIZERS** onto the backside of a closet door to hold a number of items, as well as organizers. Many closet organizers designed for a hanging rod can also suspend from a hook. You can even hang a diaper organizer made for a changing table on a door hook to hold diapers, lotions, wipes, and the like, which is especially useful if there's no changing table in the nursery. A hook can also hang a mesh bag that can function as a hamper. A heavy hook can hold your handbag or diaper bag, which always needs a special place.

Another stable door organizer is the **MOUNTED UTILITY DOOR RACK**. This organizer has attachable wire baskets that come in different depths to accommodate various items. The deeper baskets are good for the bottom and can hold bigger items, such as diapers, toys, shoes, first aid kits, receiving blankets, small gadgets, and so on. The

upper baskets should be shallow to hold small to medium items like toiletries, bottles, burp cloths, bibs, and the like.

Floor Organizers

A perfect floor organizer for a baby's closet is a **ROLLING CART WITH TIERED DRAWERS**. Similarly, **STATIONARY FREESTANDING PULLOUT BINS** also work great inside the nursery closet. These units are designed with a shelf top for added storage space. Such organizers come in hard plastic, metal, mesh, or wire.

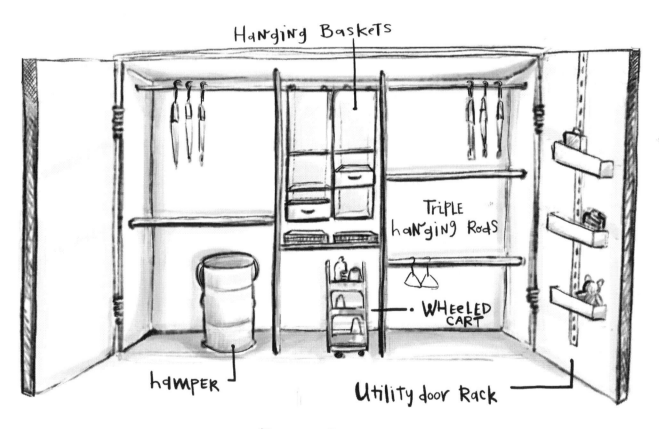

FIGURE 9.01
Baby Closet

Babies' Closet Tip

It's more feasible to opt for neutral-colored, well-constructed storage essentials that can grow with the baby or be repurposed elsewhere.

Moving cart storage organizers like bar carts are perfect for a nursery closet since you can roll them out of the closet and use them near the changing table, crib, or rocking chair. In lieu of a changing table, you could fill a cart with diaper changing essentials that can easily be transported to a diaper changing destination. You can also load a cart with nursing essentials like a pump, bottles, and the like, and move it next to your rocking chair or where you nurse. The tabletop can hold a glass of water or whatever else you need handy while nursing. Some rolling cart organizers allow you to configure drawer sizes into small, medium, or large, whereas others come with varying size drawers.

Modular Cubes

Modular storage components are **CUBED CABINETS AND SHELVING** that rest on the closet floor; some have drawers. Generally, these organizers are stackable, so you can build onto the system when the budget allows or as needs warrant. Depending on the size of a particular unit, they can store just about anything. Drawer- and cabinet-style pieces can hold linens, off-season clothes, everyday clothing, socks, and so on. Shelving units can store toys, books, shoes, humidifiers, music, clothes, or linens. These units are commonly laminate and affordable so they can dress up a closet, making it look customized.

Hampers

A hamper is a necessary organizer in a nursery, and the closet is the perfect location to hide one away. There are numerous lidded floor hampers perfect for the closet. A hamper does not have to be conventional, though. You can use a laundry basket or bin and rest it on a closet shelf. Also, a designated closet drawer or one located in a rolling cart can be used to hold dirty clothes.

CHAPTER 10

A Child's Bedroom

Children learn to put their belongings away and clean up after themselves in preschool, but schools have lockers, cubbies, containers, shelves, and desks marked for designated items. Therefore, children are capable of doing the same at home, provided good organizers are in place so their bedrooms stay tidy and items don't get misplaced.

When organizing a child's bedroom, first decide which articles are best stored there and which items make sense to relocate. In order to determine this, you must decide if other places in the home are available to move things into.

Extracurricular activities and schoolwork will generate a number of personal belongings; perhaps some things are better in the bedroom and other things are more fitting to store in a mudroom, garage, or spare closet near an entrance door. The best way to decide what should go where would be to first ask your child for input and then use this knowledge to figure out your storage possibilities.

There are different activities in a child's life that draw certain belongings and arrangements to their bedrooms. The following items are typically required for children and often need to get arranged and organized in their bedroom. Different ways to accomplish this are discussed.

The Bed

The bed is a personal space where your child may need to keep special dolls, stuffed animals, or blankets. It's important to limit the number of items kept on the child's bed since they'll become a nuisance to remove each night and the next morning when you make the bed. Headboards with storage compartments, nightstands, and under-the-bed organizers are good places to store such items so they're kept nearby.

Storage Headboards
The most commonly unused space in a child's bedroom is surrounding the bed, which is where storage compartments would be useful. Books, music, electronics, games, collections, and so on are convenient to store here. Purchasing a storage headboard in a child's room would be a great investment.

Under the Bed

Don't forget to use the vast space under the bed in a child's bedroom, especially found beneath larger beds, and there are excellent organizers designed for this space. Look for organizers that are wheeled and have a handle for pulling. Key articles to store under the bed are extra bedding, shoes, off-season outerwear, off-season clothing, backpacks, totes, gaming items, electronics, music, toys, sporting goods, and instruments. Extra school supplies and backpacks are good to store under the bed when homework is done in the bedroom.

Children's beds with built-in drawers below the mattress make ideal dresser extensions for items like socks, undergarments, clothes, linens, and so on. Pullout trundle beds are also an asset to a child's room for sleepover guests.

Trundle Bed

FIGURE 10.01
Juvenile Trundle Storage Bed

Foot of the Bed

The foot of the bed in a child's room is the best place for storage benches, ottomans, or chests. Useful items to hold here are extra blankets, sheets, pillows, stuffed animals, footwear, gaming items, back packs, sporting goods, and so on. Wheeled benches and ottomans at this location are convenient to roll near the television for additional or gaming seating.

School Supplies and Computers

A place to do homework or use the computer requires a desk and chair. In order to make the space productive, have good organizers for paperwork, backpacks, books, and other supplies so everything is within reach and easy to find quickly. Backpacks are generally the hardest item to situate in storage due to their bulk. It's best to hang them from a wall or door hook when possible. A cabinet, shelf, and cubby compartment also make good storage locations for them.

Writing materials need a designated desktop holder or drawer compartment so they're at the desk. Children use many different writing tools, such as paper, pencils, pens, colored pencils, crayons, markers, paint pens, and so on. It's best to have these items in open and easy-to-access organizers. Don't store them in stacked or lidded ones, which are hard to access. Some of the best storage essentials to compartmentalize many different types of writing materials are clear-pocketed organizers, rails with individual containers, desktop carousels, and handled caddy organizers.

A bulletin or magnetic board can secure a calendar, papers, photographs, art, and so on. An area to write messages, such as a whiteboard or chalkboard, is handy for homework deadlines and other important reminders. These organizers are perfect for using the often-untapped wall space above the desk.

Wall shelves, bookcases, and desk compartments can hold books. Even desktop organizers or bookends can corral stay-at-home books, such as a dictionary, thesaurus, and the like. Many children's book organizers are designed so the books face forward, making it easiest for small children to find them, as opposed to sideways. When stacking sideways, place them in height order. Children outgrow books quickly, so it's important to downsize collections every six months as their reading levels advance.

Wall systems, including hung organizers that come with attached pockets, bins, and shelves,

can hold a number of small articles just as well as compartmentalized desk drawers can. Items like calculators, erasers, paper clips, rulers, note cards, and staplers are good for these places.

Besides a traditional desk, consider other arrangements that are especially helpful in small spaces. The loft bed and desk combination center, in which the workstation is situated underneath a top bunk bed, is one. A wall-mounted desk or armoire is another way to make room for a workspace in a small bedroom.

Extracurricular Items

Children can be part of many extracurricular activities, most of which come with physical belongings. Items such as sporting goods, dance bags, instruments, and so on may need to occupy a bedroom in lieu of garage, mudroom, or spare hall closet space. For example, messy sporting goods are best stored in a mudroom as opposed to the bedroom. Setting limits, like allowing only favorites, is a way to differentiate among many items that compete for bedroom storage. Or your children may have special items with great value or meaning that they want in their own space. Such items need a designated place in the bedroom.

Toys and Gaming Items

Toys and gaming items are big storage concerns in a household. It's up to you whether they should occupy the bedroom space, where you might not be able to closely regulate how much time is spent playing with them. A child's bedroom can hold many belongings, such as backpacks, homework, gaming systems, clothes, shoes, sporting

Loft Bed

FIGURE 10.02
Juvenile Loft Beds

goods, and so on, so when the bedroom is also the primary place to store toys, it's a good idea to carve out a section of the room, a so-called zone, for them. For this reason, it's important to compartmentalize all their belongings, especially items that can get out of hand, such as toys.

Toys

Store toys in the rooms where they're used. A child's bedroom can store all the toys or just the special ones that find their way there on a regular basis. Organize toys into groups of like items, such as blocks, LEGOs, Matchbox cars, action figures, and so on. Use storage compartments like individual containers, drawers, or bins to divide them. Color-code, label, or use transparent containers for toys. Labels with words and pictures are easy for children to follow. There are pictured toy labels available for sale, as well as free online templates for them.

Short bookcases and low shelving that is properly anchored to the walls to prevent tipping are safe places to store toys in a child's bedroom. Places where toys are kept must be low enough for children to easily reach and return items, making it possible for children to clean up after themselves.

Cubbies with compartments can hold containers for separating different types of toys. These containers should be labeled with their contents and weigh what the child can carry. There are cubby organizers designed to store shoes where the top shelf is used for seating. You can use one like this in a bedroom but store toys inside the cubby

compartments, instead of shoes. Then use the top to display larger toys like dollhouses.

Popular storage organizers for children's toys are tiered shelving units that hold bins. Some come with slanted shelves so the bin contents are easy to identify. Many of these types of organizers come with different colored bins to distinguish different toys.

Open stacking bins are another organizational essential suited to storing medium to small toys in a bedroom. There are stackable bins that rest on the floor and others that glide on casters so they're easy to move. Such organizers can transport to and from the closet where they can remain out of sight.

A floor chest can serve as a gaming bench and open up for toy storage, but use it only to hold bigger lightweight toys, such as plush toys, doll blankets, and larger hollow plastic toys. Likewise, large wire bins and big plastic containers should also only hold larger lightweight items since small items will get lost in a big storage container.

There are dress-up costume organizers for children, and any costumes or dress-up items should be hung. Dress-up accessories like shoes,

Stacking Containers

Plastic Bins

Baskets

Toy Storage

FIGURE 10.03
Toy Storage

belts, and hats need containment. Use shelves, cubbies, baskets, or drawers near where the dress-up clothes are hung to keep accessories. You can also use a pegged coatrack or towel bar and mount it on the wall. Other options are to hang costumes in a special section of the closet or place them on a rolling garment rack.

Gaming Systems and Accessories

There are many storage arrangement options for gaming systems and accessories in a child's bedroom. Entertainment centers, armoires, shelving units, television stands, wheeled carts, and specialized gaming racks are different ways to store these items. Select a storage device that features various compartments or organizers to separate and contain belongings like games, cords, controllers, and the like.

A good organizer for a gaming system should hide and secure all power cords. There should also be good ventilation at the top, front, and back so the console does not overheat. Most gaming organizers are stationary and visible, so it's important to choose one that contains everything neatly. However, a movable wheeled cart organizer can hide everything in a closet while conserving room space when not in use.

Gaming Storage Tips

- Corral the cords so they don't tangle. Use wire ties, Velcro strips, cord covers, and so on so things stay neat. Tag the cords using a separate color tape for each device. This will make it easy to switch cords on the television ports when you change gaming systems.
- When multiple consoles use a single television, invest in a hub so more than one console can hook up to a single television. This will eliminate the inconvenience of having to mess with cords.
- Situate controllers, headphones, and remotes at an easy reach from where the games are played. Hooks can hold headphones or any controller with a cord so they don't tangle. Wireless items like remotes and certain controllers can reside in a seating storage compartment or in handled storage caddy that rests on a shelf near the gaming console.
- Specialized gaming chairs or gaming storage ottomans can be used in the gaming zone. Beanbag chairs are another option. Lightweight chairs like these are easy to move out of the way to clear a narrow walking path when not in use. Ample space allows for more permanent seating like a sofa to welcome guest players.
- Store games near the console in which they're used. Establish a one-in-and-one-out rule with games. Keeping the games right next to the consoles will make it convenient to put them away. A wall-mounted rack or floor organizer placed next to consoles is an ideal arrangement. Disc-style games can be stored on DVD racks inside their jackets. Discs can also be removed and stored in CD books or binders.

CHAPTER 11

A Child's Closet

Children's clothes are relatively easy to reduce since the person in charge of organizing the closet is an objective adult. They're also easy to let go of because they're soon outgrown anyway. It's important to engage children in the decision-making process *if* they're old enough, although some may never care to take part in organizing or concern themselves with their apparel. In those cases, the organizer has free rein. Generally, children over the age of eight can usually tell you whether they'll wear something since this is about the age they start picking out their own clothes.

Reducing Children's Clothing and Footwear

Pull out all the clothes that you know are not being worn. Perhaps these clothes are simply overlooked or forgotten due to disorganization. Decide if this is result of overbuying or not returning enough clothing gifts. For small children, place those clothes in a good spot so you use them. For example, for older children who care about what they wear, set aside twenty minutes for you both to go

through their clothes and determine what should stay and what should go.

Just like when decluttering your own closet, have bags ready for donation, hand-me-downs, repair, and resale or consignment. Hand-me-downs passed on to other household members can be stored in labeled containers with lids. Divide the clothing by sex, size, and season, and record the information on the label. You can also separate clothes by type (pants, shirts, shorts, etc.). The best place to keep hand-me-downs is in the receiver's closet. An upper closet shelf or any place away from daily use storage space is best. Under the child's bed is another key place to store hand-me-downs. There are shallow, lidded containers on rollers designed for under-the-bed storage that are perfect for this purpose.

You may also want to make a separate pile for children's off-season belongings. However, your child will most likely outgrow these clothes by the time the next season rolls around, so only store the clothes that will still fit them. When selecting containers for off-season and hand-me-down clothes, opt for small or medium-size containers, rather than large ones since it's easier to divide different types of clothing in smaller bins. Big containers filled with clothing are too heavy to easily move around and also tend to be too deep, making it hard to dig through them. It's also easier to find storage places for smaller containers.

Sizing

The best way to start reducing a child's wardrobe is to first obtain a pair of jeans, stretch pants, shorts, and a long-sleeve shirt that fit the child perfectly. Use these items as a template to match against the clothes hanging in the closet so you can easily remove those that obviously don't fit. Clothes that are difficult to tell whether they fit or not should be tried on. On a daily basis, keep an empty bag or basket in the closet to hold outgrown clothes as a way to encourage you to take them off the hangers.

Go through the child's wardrobe by tackling one pile, basket, shelf, or hanging rod at a time. If the clothes fit, then decide if the items will get worn. Clothes your child argues about wearing need to go; no one at any age likes to be told what to wear. Next, check over the keepers for stains, tears, missing buttons, and the like. Invest in expensive repairs, like replacing zippers, only if the clothes have a lot of wear left or can be passed down.

Footwear

The same sorting and decluttering principles apply to children's footwear as to adults. The key difference is in the amount of inventory. Generally, no more than a few pairs of shoes or boots of each type are necessary for a child's footwear inventory since everything is quickly outgrown. When decluttering, it's important to make certain that all shoes and boots still fit the child. Organizing children's footwear can reveal our buying habits and allow us to see if we are overbuying.

Designing a Child's Closet

To promote independence in children, design their closets so they can use them. Children need to learn how to choose their own clothing and pick up after themselves. The best way to accomplish this is to move the closet down to their level. Therefore, always invest in an adjustable closet system to keep up with a growing child.

Move hanging rods to the level where children can retrieve the clothes themselves. Depending on ceiling height and the length of the clothing, you may be able to use triple-tier hanging rods. Use the top tier to store off-season, seldom-worn dress clothes and hand-me-downs that don't yet fit.

Strive to provide high visibility and easy access to all parts of the closet. Organizers should be easy to understand and operate. Follow general classifications for filing items like shirts, pants, shoes, and boots. Detailed arrangements may create confusion or lose a child's attention span. Think about the types of organizers at your child's school and replicate them at home. Cubbies, bookcases, and lockers are the main ones.

Toys and Games in the Closet

Prioritize the closet space for all things worn on the body. The following tips can help you decide how to balance toys and other articles in a child's closet.

A child's closet should store only a limited amount of toys. Work with your children to select only certain toys and games. Assure them that you can trade out some for others in the future. Rotate them regularly since most toys and games are bound to hold their interest for a short period of time. For this reason, keep organizers basic to make it easy to change inventories.

The toys and games that do end up being stored in a bedroom closet need to be within the children's reach so they can pick up after themselves. Plus, containers stored out of their reach might encourage dangerous climbing or an avalanche. Floor organizers work great for this purpose. Crates on wheels are good for storing collections of toys, like stuffed animals and balls. Modular cubes or cubby organizers can store single items like an electronic game. Also, the individual compartments for these organizers can keep baskets for holding small, loose articles.

Container Tips for Children

- Avoid lids, screw caps, and the like since they may never make their way back onto the containers.
- Open containers keep things more visible.
- Containers need to be light enough for the child to maneuver with ease.
- Keep containers sized to fit what is stored inside. Place little items in smaller containers and larger belongings in bigger containers. It makes no sense to fill a big container with too many small articles since locating a certain item

would get frustrating for a child and may lead to container dumping.

- Containers should be labeled or have a picture of the contents.
- Don't stack more than two containers on top of one another since this can lead to disorganization once the stack is dismantled.

Closet Safety Tips for Children

- Use rounded-edge children's hangers and blunt-edge hooks—never glass or mirrored containers that break easily.
- Unfinished wood can splinter and be sharp.
- Remove lids on large containers in which small children can fit inside. Avoid hinged chests for the same reason—hinged tops can also crash down on fingers and heads.
- Children often get their fingers trapped in bifold doors.
- Don't space shelving in a way that a child can climb on it like stairs. Children will try to climb if they can get their foot to plant on flat surface and figure a way up; plan accordingly.
- Make sure the child can manage a stool since tiptoeing up one can cause him or her to lose balance and fall. Also, a stool should not have too many steps.

CHAPTER 12

Guest Bedroom

A guest bedroom is a great asset for hosting visitors and can be used for other purposes as well, such as art, sewing, reading, office work, gaming, studying, and child play. A basic guest room is easy to organize. It simply mimics a basic hotel room with a bed, an empty dresser or armoire, nightstands, lighting, television, trash can, and an empty closet with a set of hangers. Additional details could include a luggage stand, desk, alarm clock, robes, stationery, pens, hamper, towels, and basic toiletries.

When you need to incorporate another purpose to a guest room, plan to organize one fluid space. Furniture choices greatly influence the success of using a room for more than one purpose. A multipurpose guest room may need extra pieces of furniture to accommodate the additional functions of the room. Therefore, it's important to go with compact, space-efficient furniture that is marketed for apartment living. Large furniture pieces, such as bulky desks, wide dressers, or an oversized bed that does not scale properly for the space, will make the room harder to organize efficiently.

Furniture Choices

A cohesive look can be achieved by matching all the different elements in the room, such as furniture, organizers, and accessories. The following furniture pieces are worth noting for a guest bedroom.

Space-Efficient Beds

One of the best space-saving pieces of furniture to use in this room is a **MURPHY BED** or **WALL BED**. These beds can be the perfect solution for a multipurpose guest room. Wall beds come hinged at the sides so they lift completely upright and into a frame or encasement that is attached to the wall. The mattress bottom is covered with a furniture front, much like a door to an armoire, that disguises the bed when stored.

Wall beds are designed to stand alone or function in a system of shelves, drawers, or cabinets attached to sides of the bed to complete the look of a full entertainment center or an office workstation. These wall beds serve two or more functions in that they convert into a desk, bookcase, shelf, and so on while the bed is stored.

High-end wall beds are made with superb engineering and hydraulics, making them effortless to operate. Additionally, they're usually far less bulky than conventional Murphy or wall beds.

DAYBEDS are popular guest-room choices that serve other purposes because they also act as a sofa. Opt for a trundle mattress on your daybed if you typically have more than one guest. There are also day-beds with storage drawers below the mattress.

Similar to a daybed, **SOFA BEDS** convert from a couch to a bed in minutes. The advantage of a sofa bed over a daybed is a larger sleeping surface for two guests. A sofa bed can easily transfer to other rooms, if needed, unlike a daybed, which is limited to a bedroom.

In tight quarters, a **COT** or **AIR MATTRESS** may be your only sleep option for a guest room when the room needs to share space with other functions like a home office. A fold-up cot can be rather bulky and heavy, leaving only places like the basement for their storage. An air mattress, which deflates into a smaller size, has more storage options: closet shelves or drawers.

Desks

A desk is a welcomed addition to a guest room because it has multiple functions, such as paying bills, studying, reading, and using the computer with the desk. Also, there is storage potential with

FIGURE 12.01
Murphy wall bed and desk

the use of hutches, overhead shelving, rollout files, and drawers.

There are many types of space-saving desks, such as a **PULLOUT DESK**, which is designed with a retractable, expandable leaf extension for additional workspace. **WALL-MOUNTED, DROP-LEAF FOLDING TABLES** or **FOLDAWAY DESKS** are other space-saving desks for guest rooms. Some of these desks have storage compartments for belongings on the inside, but since the desks fold up and disappear against the wall, nothing permanent can be placed on the table portion. Extra storage compartments can be added around a foldaway table, such as wall shelves, memo boards, wall files, and rolling carts or cabinets. Always locate these wall tables near an outlet.

Guest-Room Closet

A guest-room closet in a sense is a spare storage space when it's utilized for company on an infrequent basis. An underused guest-room closet can be put to good use. When the room is located near other bedrooms, it can house closet overflow from these rooms. Select seldom-needed articles, such as spare backpacks, handbags, formal wear, dress shoes, and off-season clothing, shoes, and outerwear. Even bedroom excess, such as books, school supplies, toys, instruments, movies, music, nursery items, and so on, can be housed in a guest-room closet.

A guest room located near a bathroom can act as a convenient extension to a linen closet. Beach towels, surplus bath towels, seldom-needed medications, sunscreen, and extra toiletries can be stored here.

A more remotely located guest room can house odd and ends, like gift-wrapping and shipping supplies. There are door organizers and wheeled carts designed specially to hold these belongings. Other miscellaneous articles to consider for this closet are decorations, party supplies, photo albums, paper towels, toilet paper, home videos, and audio and video equipment. Make room for more than one overhead shelf to store labeled containers of off-season items. Add additional long-hanging storage when you have a large amount of formal wear that requires this arrangement.

Arrange the closet a little differently than how you would normally lay out a typical bedroom closet and keep it guest ready so you don't have to move things out for company. Establish easy-access hanging-rod storage in the center of the closet for the guests, along with spare hangers. House extra blankets, sheets, and towels for your guests in a visible spot. Keep the floor clear so guests can freely use the space for their footwear, luggage, or travel totes.

CHAPTER 13

Closet Systems

A closet system is an organizational solution that arranges your inventories with shelving, hanging rods, racks, and storage components. An efficient closet system should save you time when looking for things and save you money from purchasing duplicate items that are typically lost in disorganization. A well-designed closet system will utilize every inch of space.

When your closet needs a new closet system, it's a good idea to start the process by getting several estimates from closet designers that sell and install them. A closet professional will see much more than you do and know how to work within your budget, saving you countless hours of research. Get bids for wire, laminate, and even higher-end furniture-grade materials, if possible, so you understand the differences. Ask the closet professional as many questions as possible to learn as much as you can about your potential purchase.

Closet-System Designs

Many closet companies have retail stores, telephone, and online design services so you can visit to receive a drawing and an estimate of their closet system; all you need to do is give them your closet dimensions. Much professional design help is free, although some might charge a nominal fee. Some design teams work with computer-aided design (CAD) drawings, while others engage with you on the phone while you watch them work on your computer screen. Many of these services are quite thorough in helping you create a storage space tailored to your exact needs and specifications. Such closet drawings are ideal for a DIY installation or could be given to a professional closet installer.

The most important thing to ensure when selecting a closet system and storage essentials is that they work well together. They should not be clumsy to operate or inconvenient to use in any way. For this reason, check return policies or manufacturer warranties before buying anything. Take your time and don't make any hurried decisions;

it's inconvenient to return things, and labor will be required to disassemble a closet system once it's installed.

There are three basic closet systems. In order of price from low to high cost, they're wire, laminate, and wood. *Laminate* is an engineered material comprised of multiple-layered particleboard (also called wood composite) overlaid with a plastic outer shell. Laminate is stain and rust resistant, impervious to moisture, and cost effective. Some wire systems also have laminate components. Such systems feature a wire structure with add-on laminate storage pieces. Whether you are installing a new closet system or adding accessories to an existing one, the following information covers all three closet systems, plus the storage accessories that can be used in conjunction with them. This will help you understand how to organize your closet, given your budget and space, even if you only want to add accessories to existing closet system.

Budget-Friendly Wire Closet Systems

Wire closet systems consist of ventilated, wire-based shelving commonly featured in an epoxy-coated, stainless steel, or chrome-plated finish. The thickness of the steel determines the strength. Such systems are commonly sold in easy-to-install, DIY kits that accommodate four to eight feet of closet space—perfect for the typical reach-in closet. A basic kit includes shelves, hanging rods, and all the hardware necessary to install them. These kits are based on a track system that has multiple notches to secure shelving and organizers so accessories can be moved as often as needed. Individual wire shelving, along with mounting supplies, is also sold separately. Most

often, this type of shelving comes with mounting supplies, such as support brackets, that affix the shelving in a permanent, nonadjustable manner. Wire closet-system kits and shelving are easy to find online and at most home centers.

Advantages
By far, a wire-based closet system is the most inexpensive route for both labor and materials. Wire closet systems are easy to install and require basic tools, such a hammer, hacksaw, and screwdriver. The construction allows for good airflow that dramatically minimizes dust and mold buildup. When properly installed, wire is durable, lightweight, and strong in relation to its thickness.

Disadvantages
The disadvantages of a wire closet system are that the shelves have space in between the wires, which can create unstable storage conditions for thin-heeled shoes and tiny objects. Also, wire shelving can create creases on folded garments. There are companies that have created shelves with closely spaced wires, but that does not completely solve all the problems associated with them. The best way to combat these problems is to use the vinyl shelf liners produced by the system's manufacturer.

Many people find that most wire closet systems don't look substantial enough. Several wire-based closet lines lack add-on organizers sufficient enough to conceal belongings, such as drawers or cabinets, thus leading to a more cluttered look and inviting more dust.

Installation
If looking for a wire closet system to self-install, only purchase one that is easy to install and arrange and requires minimal tools. Select a

snag-free and rustproof wire closet system. Look for a wire closet system that has hanging rods that allow the hangers to freely glide without support brackets, which can interrupt movement; they act as obstructions, taking up rod space and making it clumsy to browse through hung clothing.

It's important to become acquainted with the add-on components that come with the closet system you select since they're made to be exclusive and you may need to purchase and install some down the road. For example, only a select group of wire-based shelving systems carry add-on storage organizers comprised of laminate components. This option allows you to upgrade your closet system to look more high end. It's important to like the add-on storage components that come with your chosen system, because they're not interchangeable with other systems.

Wire Closet

FIGURE 13.01
Wire Closet with Laminate Components

Laminate and Melamine Closet Systems

Laminate or melamine closet systems are comprised of storage components made of particleboard or medium-density fiberboard (MDF) center, or substrate, with a veneer overlay on the outer shell. The veneer can be made of real wood or plastic faux wood (called melamine). The real-wood veneer is twice as expensive, but looks like solid wood, and you can use a custom stain.

Sellers of closet systems advertise their laminated products in ways that make it difficult for many consumers to comprehend quality. Many people find the terms used to describe these systems confusing: RTA laminate, melamine laminate, or furniture-grade melamine. As a consumer, the most important things to research when looking at a laminated closet system are the thickness and density of the material and the process by which it's produced.

The process by which the veneer is bonded to the particleboard or fiberboard also determines the quality of the product. Look for a process called "thermofused" melamine or "thermal foil," whereby the veneer is fused under extreme heat and pressure to a core substrate, permanently bonding it together. This process makes the product strong and smooth with a small chance of splitting or chipping seams, which can occur in laminated products.

Thicker shelves hold more weight and are less likely to bow, crack, or fracture. Look for laminated shelves that are three-quarter-inch thick. Many shelves on the market today are five-eighths inch and even half-inch in thickness, so it's important to look into these shelf measurements. Also, the substrate should be a medium- to high-density grade for optimal strength. The manufacturer should be able to tell you how many pounds a shelf can hold, which is the best way to determine shelf strength.

When researching a laminate closet system, find out whether the material is moisture, heat, stain, and scratch resistant. A quality system is usually backed by a reputable company that will guarantee the closet for as long as you own your home. Take time to review opinions about various laminate or melamine closet systems on the internet from people who have purchased them. Consumer reports are also informative and easy to obtain.

Advantages

Laminate or melamine closet systems are more flexible to arrange than most wire-based systems because the drawers, rods, shelves, and so on are easier to move. Laminate or melamine closet systems also have many more add-on organizer options than most wire-based systems; they can include fancy upgrades, such as ironing boards, jewelry drawers, mirrors, and cabinets.

Depending on the laminate or melamine closet system, they also tend to be stronger and more stable than the average wire-based closet system. The most significant advantage to a laminate or melamine closet system, though, is the common

stunning appearance. Made to mimic wood, these closet systems offer warmth and richness to any closet. For all their other advantages, laminate and melamine closet systems also add value to real estate.

Disadvantages

Laminate and melamine closet systems are more expensive than wire systems, and they vary greatly in price. Cost does not always determine value. Also, the parts may not function as well as you'd like, depending on the system's quality, which can be uneven. Make sure you test the functionality of a closet system: the drawers should glide with ease, the doors should close evenly and securely, and the edges should be smooth and not rough so they don't catch on articles of clothes and tear them. See how easy it's to adjust your closet system by moving shelves and the like around. Your closet system should operate well since you'll use it on a daily basis. Again, this is why you need to research the quality of the laminate, because this is what makes up the majority of the closet system.

Installation

There are DIY laminate closet-system kits sold at retail stores and home centers that cost a fraction of what you would pay for a custom system. An off-the-shelf kit may require cutting when it does not fit your closet exactly, although that may not be your priority. Cutting laminated products takes special knowledge and tools so the material does not crack or chip. Therefore, make sure you have the skill or be prepared to hire someone who does. Also, melamine and laminate is heavier to move around than wire, which adds difficulty to the job.

Laminate and melamine DIY closet systems can be found on the internet through companies with live operators or interactive websites to help lay out your closet. The closet system will arrive at your home, ready for installation. If you self-install, you should save at least half of what you would pay a full-service closet company. Closet systems sold in this manner generally come predrilled and with easy-to-follow directions designed with a DIY intent.

Because a custom laminate or melamine closet system is far more expensive than a DIY closet system, it's important to understand quality differences and the cost of labor. If you have to hire a carpenter or handyman to install the closet system, then factor that into your cost. Compare this total with what you would pay for a full-service closet company to do the exact same job and see if it makes sense financially. Also consider return policies if you should order incorrectly. Most reputable closet companies back their product with a warranty that should stretch for as long as you own your home, so don't buy a laminate or melamine closet system that cannot match this offer—even for those you install yourself.

When you choose a full-service closet company, remember that you are also paying design fees for the expertise of the salesperson. Therefore, it's a good idea to shop around and gather as much information as possible. The more closet designers you interview, the more you'll learn and obtain ideas on how to create the right closet for your budget and needs.

High-End Custom Closets

A high-end custom closet is commonly synonymous with one thing: real hardwood. However, many custom closet companies market upscale closet systems using top-notch furniture grade laminate. These closet systems also offer high-end upgrades like glass doors and leather countertops. Usually, walk-in closets are a worthwhile investment for a high-end closet system, especially when they open to places such as sitting rooms or master bedrooms where they're seen. An upscale closet system adds value to any home and may be expected in some. The best part about a custom closet is that it can be designed to your specifications, allocating the perfect room for the amount of clothes, shoes, and accessories you possess.

Advantages

There are many advantages to custom closet systems. They add value to your home and utilize closet space efficiently. Real hardwood adds yet another set of advantages, beginning with the pure aesthetics of its natural beauty. Real wood can stand the test of time since you are able to make it look new or update its color by restaining it. Depending on the species of wood, which is usually selected to be the most durable, it's solid and strong. Custom closets can be handcrafted to the exact specifications of a space. When something is specifically designed for a given space, dead space is eliminated, which isn't the case with fixed laminate or wire closet systems.

Disadvantages

The biggest disadvantage of a high-end solid-wood closet system is the high cost. When spending this much, you need to beware of closet systems that claim to be solid wood when they're merely wood veneer with a plywood core. Wood-veneer closet systems in many cases can cost almost double over a melamine closet system, but you'll still be receiving an engineered wood product. Therefore, it always pays to ask questions about the exact type of material used to manufacture the closet system you are about to purchase.

Solid wood requires maintenance, especially with a hardworking closet system that is ransacked daily. Wood scratches, dents, warps, and chips will happen over time, no matter how well it was stained and varnished. Wood also needs maintenance, such as refinishing and preservation remedies like polishing with proper cleaners. Wood has a list of cautionary measures. For instance, closets near bathroom showers can receive too much humidity fluctuation that will cause the wood to warp. Moisture can also draw insects to wood. It's never good to have a window unprotected from sunlight, which can bleach and degrade a wood finish in the closet. It's also important not to leave cups, plates, perfume bottles, makeup, or plastics on the wood, which can leak onto the surface, causing stains.

Installation

High-end closet systems should be installed by professionals. This is not a DIY project, no matter how skilled you think you are. Materials are simply too expensive to afford a mistake, such as an incorrect measurement. Intricate architectural details in a wood closet system, such as adding cornices or moldings, require more expertise than the average cabinet novice possesses.

Closet Systems

Wire Closets

ADVANTAGES:
- Budget-friendly
- Accumulates minimal dust
- Available in DIY kits
- Durable
- Easy Installation

DISADVANTAGES:
- Articles are highly visible with no hidden storage options
- Cut-rate appearance
- Limited selection of organizational add-on components
- Wire shelving, baskets, etc. are not solid which creates a more unstable surface

Laminate (Melamine) & Custom

ADVANTAGES:
- Tailored & attractive
- Adds to home value
- Hidden storage options
- An extensive line of organizational add-on components available
- Many finishes available
- Some laminate (melamine) are available in DIY kits
- Durable

DISADVANTAGES:
- Certain brands chip and scratch
- Materials such as real wood can buckle, warp, stain, and require costly maintenance
- Expensive
- Laborious cleaning
- Intricate installation required

CHAPTER 14

Hanging Clothes

Ideally, the first thing to do once your closet is decluttered is straighten out the hanging clothes and fix all the items hung incorrectly. This entails closing zippers, buttoning up shirts, and properly aligning waistbands or cuffs onto their clips. Make certain all formal gowns are properly hung. Sometimes, heavy ornamental garments need to be folded over on the right hanger since traditional hanging can ruin their shapes. The best clothes to keep on hangers are those made from linen, rayon, velvet, silk, taffeta, chiffon, and all cotton fabrics, so they stay wrinkle-free.

You may need to remove some clothing or accessories permanently from your closet's hanging rod due to space limitations. Infrequently worn jackets, outerwear, seasonal clothing, and knitwear should go first. Consider moving such belongings to a spare closet or a freestanding rolling garment rack, where they can remain wrinkle-free.

Knitwear needs special attention and must be correctly hung on specific hangers to avoid stretched fabric from hanging tension. Basically, knits should be folded over the top of a nonslip hanger close to the neck where the hook is located.

This is a more tedious hanging task, making alternative storage methods, such as rolling and folding knits, safer and easier.

Off-season clothing can be moved from the hanger and into airtight, labeled containers. Avoid cardboard boxes and plastic bags, which are not recommended for long-term storage. It's important to check over the clothes before they're packed away to make sure they're clean, as stains and spots can set into the fabric over time. Don't store these clothes with mothballs, because they're toxic and unnecessary. Keep clothes from heat, moisture, and sunlight so they don't fade or mildew. Good places to store your off-season apparel outside the closet are under the bed, in a spare closet, or in basement or attic storage.

Remove clothing from plastic dry-cleaning bags and place them on the proper hangers. Clothing requires air circulation, and plastic dry-cleaning bags trap cleaning chemicals, which can destroy fibers. Usually, the hangers from the dry cleaners are meant for temporary use and don't properly store the item well long term. Clothes do need room to breathe in your closet, so space them about quarter inches apart. Tightly packed clothes are hard to go through and can wrinkle when compacted.

Arranging the Hanging Space

When you arrange clothing, always place like items together. For instance, hang pants and trousers in one section and blouses in another. Some clothing categories are shirts, skirts, pants, dresses, suits, athletic apparel, sweaters, vests, tanks, camisoles, sweatshirts, and zippered

Partition

FIGURE 14.01
Partitioned hanging rods

hoodies. It's best to separate your clothes into broad categories when hanging them. Otherwise, it's hard to keep them in order.

Don't divide your clothes by career, casual, formal, and the like since so many clothes are versatile and can go from business to casual when paired with the right separate or accessory. Additionally, it will look much neater when all the shirts, pants, and jackets are divided and located in the same region of the closet. It's also a good idea to organize your clothing groups by color. From left to right, organize light to dark: white, yellow, tan, sky blue, turquoise, dark blue, and so on. Group stripes and prints into their own category. This type of order helps you locate clothes first and allows you to quickly see how much you have in each color, which is helpful when shopping for new clothes.

It also looks neatest to hang clothes from shortest to longest, left to right. For example, shorts, capris, pants, and then leggings. For shirts, use the sleeve length to determine order, such as camisoles, tank tops, cap sleeves, short sleeves, and then long sleeves. By keeping garment lengths divided, you can design your space efficiently and avoid dead space. For example, arrange just enough space for a certain group of belongings to fit exactly into a designated compartment, leaving little room at the sides, top and bottom.

There are partitioned closet systems in which several hanging rods are divided and contained within individual compartments, as opposed to one hanging rod stretching across a long space. In other words, a closet system is comprised of many separate boxed structures, each containing its own hanging rod. Partitioned closet systems do the wardrobe dividing for you.

Place all clothing in the same direction. The front of the garment should face the direction that is easiest to view. Swivel-hook hangers keep this order simple since you only need to turn the hook instead of taking the clothes off the hangers to change the way the garment faces. This type of order may seem particular, but it will make a difference in how organized the closet looks, and it will make finding things much easier.

Double Hanging Rods

Prioritize your limited hanging-rod space for clothing that must be hung, such as items that wrinkle easily. Make sure you know how many feet of both horizontal and vertical space you need for your short-, medium-, and longer-length clothes items in order to plan your space. It's best to double hang your rods, one on top of another, for short items. You can accomplish this in two ways. First, the quicker and less expensive route to take is to use a double-hung closet organizer that attaches to the existing rod. The advantage is that it's easy to move around since it's not mounted with screws. The drawback is that it's not stationary and bobs back and forth. Also, they come in fixed lengths, so you may not get the custom measurement you need.

The second option is to mount two separate hanging rods on top of one another. Generally, allow around eighty-four inches for the top rod and forty-two inches for the bottom one to hang average-size short items. You should have twenty-four inches of closet depth for hanging clothes so they don't hit the back wall of the closet. The hanging rod should also be stationed so clothes have at least fourteen inches of room to freely exit the space. To create more short items, use suit and pant hangers that fold slacks in half. Look for those specially designed to hold pants in place and minimize creases.

It's important to decide how to hang your pants, especially when double hanging rods are available. Full length by the waistband or cuffs offers the best chance they'll remain wrinkle-free, but that may only be possible in large closets where ample long-storage space is available. In small closets, you may need to consider placing hanging rods on top of one another to gain enough storage space for everything. Some closet systems have storage devices, commonly referred to as *sliding pants racks*, that hang pants folded over and suspended on individual rods. The pant rack glides out to easily see, put away, and remove pants. There is also a fan rack that allows you to flip through pants easily. Generally, these organizers are good to mount low with a hanging rod above them.

Utilizing Closet Dead Space

Consider all the ways in which a closet system can offer additional hanging space. There is a unique spiral-shaped 360-degree spinning clothing rack that is perfect for capturing awkward, hard-to-arrange corners.

Examine your existing hanging-rod space to figure out ways to gain more room. Besides removing all the unwanted items, use slim velvet hangers, S clips, single-clip hangers, and cascading or tiered hangers in place of bulky plastic or wooden hangers. Cascading and tiered hangers vertically store multiple garments from a single rod hook. Tiered hangers have multiple hanging rods each used to hold a separate garment. Cascading hangers have multiple hooks each used to hold an individual clothes hanger. The best cascading and tiered hangers are designed to keep clothing wrinkle-free and secure the garment in place. Use a tie hanger to store multiple tank tops, camisoles, or spaghetti strap shirts by the sleeves.

You can move certain items off the main hanging rod by storing them on the backside of the closet door. Simply install a short drapery rod or towel bar and use S clips or single-hook hangers to hold items like scarves, baseball caps, ties, belts, small handbags, tanks, pajamas, and any light-weight articles that currently reside on the main hanging rod. Remove any bulky hanging organizers if you're short on hanging-rod space. Organizers like chunky belt or scarf hangers are good to remove when it's easy to transfer these articles into drawer, wall, or door organizers. Popular hanging-shelf organizers that are arranged with multiple tiered shelf compartments occupy a foot of horizontal room. It's best to move articles that are stored in them to other spots given limited hanging space.

In order to capture dead space, look to closet systems that offer shelving, drawers, or shoe-cubby compartments that can be placed in between a pair of tiered hanging rods. Use this space to hold bulky sweat-shirts, sweatpants, folded jeans, exercise clothes, shorts, and sweaters that were tak-ing up space on the hanging rod.

Hanging Women's Clothing

How clothes are arranged on a closet's hanging rod plays a major role in the ease of finding what you need fast. Also, properly storing clothing on a hanging rod contributes to precise knowledge of what you own at a glance, such as the number shirts and colors of each type. The following are suggestions on how to organize the different hung items in a typical closet.

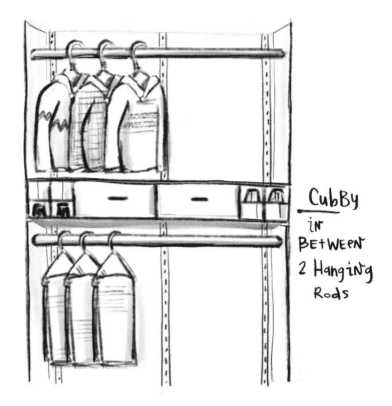

CubBy in BEtWEEN 2 HangiNg Rods

Track Rail Supports HangiNG rail & cubby orgaNizEr

FIGURE 14.02
Organizer in between 2 hanging rods

Tops

Place tops in order by sleeve length: camisoles and straps, tanks and sleeveless, cap, short, three-quarter, and long. You can further divide tops by sorting each shirt length by type. For example, within your group of long-sleeve shirts, keep all your blouses, button-down shirts, knits, and the like together. Then file tops in color order within each group.

Long tops like tunics may need to hang in a separate location if you use double hanging rods, as they'll not fit lengthwise, so long tops can be hung with dresses or jackets. Long jackets or pon-chos can also be stored with dresses.

Suits and Separates

Place suit sets on a single suit hanger. This type of hanger is thick and wide enough to hold a heavy suit jacket with an attached hanging bar that comes with either two clips or is made of nonslip material to hold pants and skirts firmly in place.

Then file suits in color order. Next to the suits, keep separate jackets and blazers also sorted by color. Vests that are paired with a suit jacket or pants should be hung on the same hanger. Hang vest separates together and by color. Group separate skirts by length: short, medium, and long, and divide them by color within each length.

Dresses, Jumpsuits, and Rompers

Sort and store dresses by type, such as sundress, party, office, and evening. Within each subgroup, file by color and length. Separate jumpsuits from rompers and store them next to dresses due to the similar lengths.

Pants, Leggings, and Shorts

Separate your pants by fabric since, in most cases, this places them by season as well as type, such as casual or dress. For example, corduroy, denim, polyester blends, wools, and the like. Then sort by color within each fabric group.

Sort leggings by color and hang with pants or fold them and store near lingerie items in a dresser, if you are short on hanging space. Store all capris and longer shorts, such as Bermudas, in the same section. Generally, it's best to hang any length of shorts when they're made of a material that wrinkles easily, such as linen, rayon, silk, and even certain cotton blends, provided there is space. Carving out a section of the closet to install three hanging rods, one on top of another with enough room for the length of your shorts, is a good way to gain desirable hung storage. Otherwise, move all or certain pairs of shorts into drawer storage and keep only the cropped capris and longer shorts on the hanging rod. Then divide shorts by color and length.

Loungewear

Keep all your sweats, hoodies, flannels, fleece, velour, terry cloth, and other comfy clothes together. Divide them by type of clothing and keep everything in color order. This type of clothing tends to be bulky and hogs hanger space. In most cases, loungewear clothing is folded on closet shelves or in drawers, but if you have the space, store them on the hanging rod. Some double-hung rods may work well, depending on the length.

Since hanging-rod space is usually tight, store bulky long items like robes from a heavy-duty hook on a closet door or wall.

Activewear

Keep activewear in your closet next to the loungewear. Separate the sport shorts, running pants, yoga pants, jerseys, pullovers, and so on. Arrange them in color order within each group. Divide sport tops by sleeve length, such as straps, short, and long. Divide any warm-up suits by color and store them next to your activewear and loungewear.

Hanging Men's Clothing

Much like women's clothing, men's clothing that needs to be hung should be arranged in a particular way, so everything is grouped by type and in color order. The bulk of male clothing is comprised of suits, jackets, sweaters, shirts, shorts, and pants. However, it's not recommended to hang sweaters, especially wool, cashmere, and angora since they'll stretch out. Hanging them safely is possible by folding the sweater lengthwise and then draping it over the top of the hanger so that the armpit rests in between the hanger hook. Then the sleeves go across one side and the body of the sweater on the other. One or two sweaters is acceptable to hang when hung properly, but it's not recommended to hang many sweaters due to their common bulk, which crowds valuable hanger space.

Since men's clothing classifications are broad, it's best to break them down by distinguishing them according to level of dress, such as casual or work. Categories such as dress, work, casual, gym, and formal are good. Among such classifications, further divide them by sleeve length, color, or even fabric in certain cases. The following classifications detail the best ways to handle organizing men's clothing in regard to hanger storage.

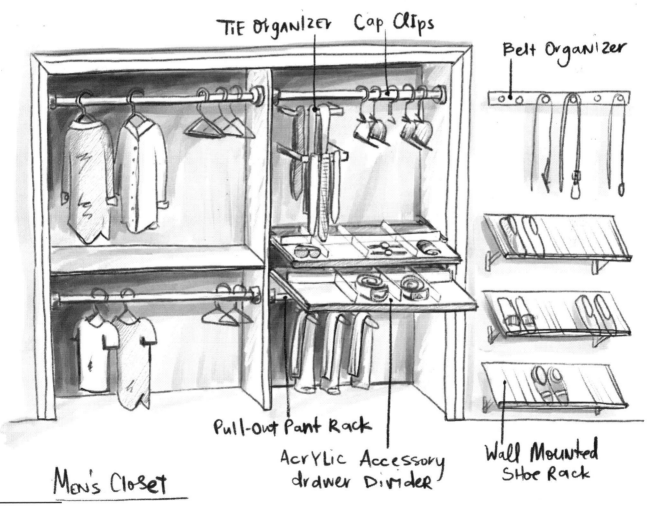

FIGURE 14.03
Men's Closet

Shirts

Divide different types of shirts into categories, such as button-downs, polos, crew neck, knits, and so on. Then separate the short from the long sleeves in each group and organize in color order.

Pants and Shorts

Separate pants by fabric, like denim, wool, linen, polyester blends, and the like. Divide each group by color and keep patterned or plaids separate. Then divide shorts by fabric and separate in the same way: by color and patterns.

Suits and Jackets

Suits and jacket separates should hang next to pants. Suit components should stay together on a single suit hanger. Store jacket separates next to suits. Keep them in color order.

Loungewear

Divide sweats and comfy clothes made from fleece, cotton, velour, flannel, and terry cloth by type and color. Situate them next to your athletic apparel. Keep this type of clothing on the hanging rod only when there is ample space since these items can be bulky. Drawers, shelves, and closet floor organizers, such as tiered pullout basket organizers, are good spots to contain loungewear if folded.

Athletic Apparel

Separate athletic pants, shirts and tops, jackets, and warm-ups and hang them next to one another. Divide shirts by sleeve length and store accordingly. Divide each group by color. Store your athletic apparel next to loungewear.

Hanging Children's Clothes

The key to hanging children's clothing successfully is to make everything in the closet kid friendly. Lowering the hanging bar to their level and using appropriate size hangers will make it possible for children to successfully participate in retrieving and putting away hung garments.

When your child is half your size, you can double hang almost everything in their closet. Keep infrequently needed and some off-season clothing, such as a heavy sweatshirt during the summer for a cool night, on the upper hanging rod and all items worn on a daily basis on the lower hanging rod for easy access. A sturdy stool could help some children out when the hanging rod is a stretch for them.

Follow the same storage arrangements for children's clothing as you would for adult clothing. For example: girls' clothing would be arranged similarly to the advice given in the previous women's section and boys' clothing would mimic how men's clothing is arranged.

CHAPTER 15

Hangers

The right hangers will save you money in the long run by extending the life of your garments since the correct hangers protect clothes and keep them in optimal shape. When garments hang vertically, there is actual tension taking place on the fabric seams. Therefore, the proper hangers used for specific types of clothing reduce this problem. Knowing how to choose the ideal hanger can help you stay organized, protect clothing, and make your closets beautiful.

You may have plenty of extra hangers after downsizing your clothing. Sort through them and discard the broken and bent ones. Decide if you can invest in a new set of hangers should you have a mismatched set containing some wire ones from the dry cleaners and flimsy plastic ones that were included with your clothing purchases, or if you need the correct hangers to protect different types of clothing made of different fabrics.

Besides clothing care, a cohesive set of hangers will make a huge difference in the overall neatness appearance of your closet since hangers will be the same color or material and clothes will line up perfectly. Hanger thickness plays a major role in hanging-rod storage room. Thick bulky hangers take up almost double the room as thin hangers. It's important to take hanger size into consideration when outfitting a hanging rod.

Different Hangers for Different Functions

It's important to note that because hangers serve different functions, it's not possible to use the same type of hanger for everything, which would be visually perfect, but you should use identical hangers for the same *types* of clothing. For example, when you use the same hanger for all your pants, such as the clip-style version, the waistbands will line up and drop at the same spot, offering a uniform, sleek appearance. The best way to tie different types of hangers together is to keep them in the same material or color or both. One common feature to look for in most hangers is the ability for the hook to swivel 360 degrees. This feature makes it easy to face clothes in same direction on the hanging rod without having to take the garment off the hanger.

Analyze your clothing carefully and think about the different types of hangers you'll need to properly care for garments. Basically, every type of clothing will require a hanger that has a particular size, shape, purpose, and possibly material. It's important to note that hangers are a personal decision and there is more than one way to hang an article of clothing. Although some recommendations are in order, personal preferences matter most. Choosing the right hangers can be confusing. This guide can get used to help you decide which clothes hangers will best suit your needs.

Hanger Sizes

It's important that the hanger is sized correctly for the garment. A hanger that is too wide for a shirt will inevitably stretch the sleeves until they develop a transparent shoulder "points" in the material. Alternatively, a hanger that is too short for a shirt will cause the sleeves to droop and create creases.

Hangers can be purchased in a particular size in order to maintain the original shape of your clothing. The following guidelines correlate the age of the person in relation to hanger size:

INFANT: Newborn to three years of age— ten-inch hangers

CHILDREN: Toddler through eight years of age—twelve-inch hangers

ADOLESCENTS: Ages nine through twelve— fourteen-inch hangers

PETITE ADULTS, LARGER CHILDREN, AND OLDER TEENS: fifteen-inch to sixteen-and-a-half- inch hangers

ADULTS: generally, sixteen-and-a-half-inch to seventeen-inch hangers

EXTRA-LARGE ADULTS: eighteen-and-a-half- inch hangers

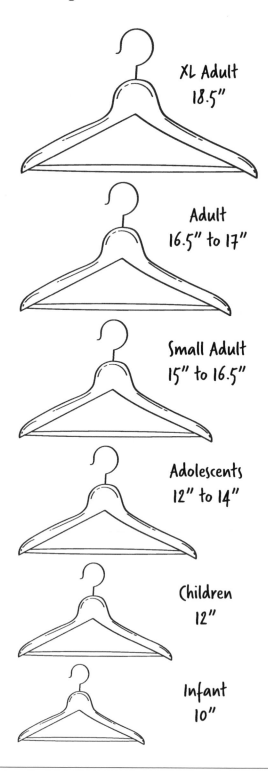

XL Adult 18.5"

Adult 16.5" to 17"

Small Adult 15" to 16.5"

Adolescents 12" to 14"

Children 12"

Infant 10"

Another variable to consider is hanger thickness. A standard hanger is about half-inch in thickness and holds most clothing. Heavier coats, robes, and jackets need the strength of a hanger that is one-inch thick.

Hanger Shapes

FLAT HANGERS are designed to have a slim profile so they take up less hanging space. Mostly, the popular velvet hangers are flat and marketed to conserve room. You don't want to use ultra-thin flat hangers, though, because they can easily break and compact clothing too tightly, causing creases. It's best to look for flat hangers that are marketed as heavy duty.

CASCADING or TIERED HANGERS are designed to hang multiple slacks or shirts from a single hook and are considerable space savers. There are many of these products on the market but not all are made well. Seek well designed tiered or cascading hangers that separate the clothes enough so they do not compress clothing too tightly, which can wrinkle them. Surfaces should also secure garments well since such hangers involve maneuvering.

CONTOURED HANGERS are formed to match the curvature of the shoulders to offer the ultimate guarantee that your garment will stay in its original shape. These hangers can be used for suits, coats, and dresses. The downside is that because these hangers curve, they take up more horizontal space on the hanging rod than most hangers.

Hangers by Purpose

Using different hangers for their intended purposes will help protect the clothing from wrinkling, slipping, and damage. The following hangers are specifically made for certain clothing.

Skirt and Pant Hangers

CLIP-TOP HANGERS: These hangers are designed with two adjustable clips that slide along a straight bar to hold almost any bottom piece of clothing. Some clips are stationary, but these types of hangers are rare and not recommended since they limit which types of garments can be hung. Some metal clips can stain and also leave an indentation in the garment, so make certain they're coated to prevent this from happening. Certain shirt hangers come with either a removable hanging bar or removable clips. These hangers are good since they encourage use.

There are two ways to hang bottoms from clips. They can hang open-faced from the waistline or folded. Generally, pants and shorts commonly fold in half and hang upside down suspended by the clips. It looks neatest when the back of the pants is facing front.

CLAMP HANGERS: These hangers are designed with two straight bars that press together to hold the garment in place. It's best to choose clamp hangers that are lined in felt to securely grip delicate garments made of silk and the like. The downside to clamp hangers is that they're cumbersome to operate.

OPEN-ENDED SLACKS HANGERS: These hangers are marketed for pants, but they can also hang tablecloths, throws, towels, blankets, drapes, and folded sweaters. They're comprised of a single bar with an open side so the garments are easy to remove without the hanger leaving the rod. Typically, the hanging bar is coated with foam to protect delicate items and provide a nonslip surface to keep clothes in place.

SUIT HANGERS: These hangers are designed to hold both the jacket and pants belonging to a suit. For this reason, a suit hanger is usually heavy duty and thicker than most. Flat suit hangers are designed to take up less hanging space, but they omit the curved design that keeps the natural shape of the jacket. Some suit hangers include notched shoulders for hanging the straps and security loops found in certain women's suits. Suit hangers also have a trouser bar for the bottoms. Some bars are locking, whereas others have adjustable clips to secure pants or skirts. Any hanging bar should have a nonslip surface to hold delicate or slippery suit fabrics. Many suit hangers come in solid wood, which can get pricey, but they also come in more budget-friendly heavy-duty plastic.

PADDED HANGERS FOR DELICATES: A padded hanger is filled with quilt batting, a cotton wadding, which makes it soft and cushion-like. The batting is concealed in a fabric like canvas, linen, or satin. Padded hangers are marketed to hold delicate silks, satin, and lace garments. However, they can hold just about any garment, such as knits, evening wear, costumes, jackets, blouses, shirts, and so on. Padded hangers safeguard against snags and look elegant lined in any closet. They also hold garments in place well.

COAT HANGERS: These hangers tend to be thicker and wider in the shoulder in order to bear the weight of a coat or heavy jacket. Heavy-duty plastic or wood are the common materials used for them. They're also good for holding larger size shirts, such as double extra-large and bigger.

Hanger Materials

When refitting your closet with new hangers, remember that most types of hangers, such as shirt, pants, or skirt, come in various materials: metal, plastic, acrylic, velvet, and wood. Therefore, it can be possible to create a cohesive look among your hangers by selecting the same material for all your hangers, even if they're from different manufacturers. The following information covers the various materials from which hangers are manufactured, along with their pros or cons.

Wire

Wire hangers are the least expensive hangers and preferred by dry cleaners for that reason. Wire hangers are good for travelers since they're unbreakable and lightweight; however, they're bendable, flimsy, thin, slippery, and usually not wide enough to properly hold many clothes.

Wire hangers cannot support heavy garments, which is why they buckle. Since wire hangers are thin, they can compact a wardrobe too tightly, causing creases in the clothes. Depending on the material, some wire hangers can rust or discolor garments. Dry cleaners cover wire hangers in paper sleeves to prevent garments from slipping off and discourage rust from getting on clothing. Wire hangers are twisted around the hook with a sharp end, which can snag delicate knits, woven, cottons and the like.

Heavier metal hangers, containing a high thickness gauge of at least four millimeters, are strong and durable. Find the ones with notches to expand their use that are also made of anti-rust stainless steel. Metal hangers offer a slim profile and use less space than most plastic hangers. The larger metal hangers can hold jackets and conserve room in a coat closet.

Wood

Wooden hangers are sturdy and handsome in any closet. They're made for every type of clothing.

The finishes used to protect the wood can become slippery, though. Therefore, they can require non-slip areas in certain places of the hanger. Wood can be bulky and get expensive to furnish for an entire wardrobe with them. Matching different types of wood hangers can be hard to do, even when pulling together those pertaining to the same wood family such as cherry or maple since stain colors can be different. Red cedarwood hangers safely and naturally absorb moisture, mold, and mildew. Red cedarwood is a natural insect repellant.

Plastic

Plastic hangers come in a variety of shapes, styles, sizes, thicknesses, and weights. Some found at discount retailers can be skimpy and break easily, and the cheap versions have jagged seams that can tear clothing. Plastic skirt or pant hanger clips should lock in place and not slide too easily along the bar so clothes don't bunch. Look for heavy plastic hangers with a smooth, continuous tubular frame. Notches also expand their use. Plastic hangers are generally the most economical choice.

Acrylic is considered a high-end plastic; acrylic hangers are glamorous and showcase nicely in a master bedroom walk-in closet. Shirt, coat, skirt, and pants hangers can be found in acrylic.

Velvet

Velvet hangers are designed to be flat and thin to conserve hanging-rod space. The flocked velvet surface of the hanger covers a plastic interior; its thickness determines strength. The velvet surface is made to prevent clothing from slipping. The shape of most velvet hangers has a slight notch along the frame to secure thin straps and sleeveless tanks. Velvet hangers are competitively priced and receive good reviews, accounting for their popularity.

CHAPTER 16

Hanging-Rod Storage Organizers

A handful of organizers are made to suspend from closet hanging rods, primarily by hooks. These organizers typically require no installation with an easy-to-hang design. Hanging organizers make closet belongings easy to access and find.

The valet rod organizer is a separate hanging rod that complements a closet's central hanging rod. Most hanging-rod organizers are highly visible with clear pockets or open shelf features for holding shoes, purses, sweaters, scarves, hats, jewelry, and just about anything that is expected to store in a bedroom closet. The following covers the most popular bedroom hanging organizers.

Valet Rod

A valet rod is a telescopic hanging pole that pulls out from a casing when in use and slides back in where it's out of view. Most extend to around a foot and can hold anywhere from thirty to fifty pounds. These devices are commonly mounted onto closet partitions or the underside of a closet shelf. Although a valet rod is not a storage accessory designed for the hanging rod, it functions in the same manner in that it holds garments by the hanger.

Valet rods can be an accessory to a closet system or sold separately. They're inexpensive, easy to install, and come in various colors, such as bronze, nickel, or brass to match existing closet systems. These storage organizers are great holding places for clothing that needs to enter or exit the hanging rods in a closet. They can temporarily hang dry cleaning, outfits picked out for the next day, clothes for packing, and so on.

Tie, Belt, and Scarf Hangers

Specialized hangers with hooks, holes, or clamps are designed to store ties, belts, and scarves. These are affordable and efficient organizers if you don't have any wall or drawer space in your closet to store these articles. The downside to using these organizers is that they're bulky and take up valuable hanging-rod space. These hangers can be clumsy and tip to one side when the load is unbalanced. They also don't store well in tightly packed closets where belt hooks or hardware can become caught on certain fabrics.

A revolving tie rack is a motorized device that rotates the ties around so you can easily find the one you need. These organizers attach to the hanging rod. Ties file in a row, where each one occupies its own rack, so it's easy to organize them by color or style.

Hanging Modular, Tiered Open Shelves and Hanging Pocket Organizers

There are **HANGING-SHELF ORGANIZERS WITH MULTIPLE POCKETS** that attach to a closet rod by hooks or Velcro fasteners. Pocket organizers resemble a short garment bag and have several see-through compartments designed to hold small articles like jewelry, scarves, hair accessories, gloves, nylons, socks, and the like.

In contrast, **MULTIPLE-SHELF HANGING ORGANIZERS** are designed to store larger articles with twelve-inch openings and equal depths. Items like sweaters, shoes, jeans, leggings, handbags, and the like are suitable for these organizers. Although seemingly effective, these organizers can take up too much space in small closets. When these organizers are improperly weighted down, they may buckle or sag from the center. The shelves are not adjustable, so if they're not filled, they waste space. However, these organizers are budget friendly and useful when your shelving and drawer space is limited. Shelf organizers are popular in children's closets because they're open, making it easy for them see and access their belongings.

SPINNING or **CAROUSEL HANGING ORGANIZERS** are circular in design and all sides have compartments to hold footwear, clothing, and handbags. These organizers suspend from a hanging-rod hook and rotate a full 360 degrees. Carousel organizers can become weighted down, which makes them hard to maneuver, so be careful not to overload them.

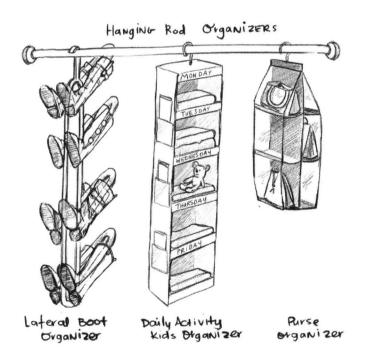

FIGURE 16.01
Hanging Rod Organizers

CHAPTER 17

Closet Shelves

The most versatile closet organizer is a shelf, which can hold just about any closet item except for clothes that require hanging. Shelves are a less expensive storage solution than drawers and cabinets. Another advantage of shelves is they visibly display closet articles to lessen the risk of them being forgotten. There are a number of ways to arrange closet shelving. Open-storage shelving can hold just about any small organizer and also stack, file, or pile many types of articles.

Shelves should correlate in size to the items stored on them. It's not a good idea to place smaller items on deep shelves, because they can get lost in the back where they're hard to see and access. Also, shelves are more likely to become messy with more room to spread things around. Alternatively, it's unsafe to place large items on shallow shelves where they can fall off. Bigger, weighted items can also cause slim shelving to buckle.

Generally, a fourteen-inch-deep shelf can hold the average bedroom-closet items like purses, footwear, or folded garments. Deeper shelves,

seventeen inches and up, should be placed closer to ground level, where they can hold bulky items like blankets, sleeping bags, pillows, gym bags, suitcases, large totes, large handbags, and so on. Lower shelves are good for stocking bigger, heavier items that are safer and easier to lift from this location than if placed overhead.

Most shelves are sold in widths of twenty-four inches, thirty-six inches, and forty-eight inches. This information will help you determine how many articles can fit together on one shelf. For example, a folded shirt or pair of shoes is about twelve inches wide. Therefore, you can store three stacks of folded sweaters on a thirty-six-inch shelf or four pairs of shoes on a forty-eight-inch shelf, and so on.

The amount of space in between the height of your shelves is another important factor to consider when arranging your closet space. Generally, eight to ten inches apart is sufficient since that gives you enough room to retrieve a single pair of shoes or stack a few sweaters.

Shelf Organizers

With so many different types of storage essentials designed for shelves, almost anything can look tidy on a shelf. It's important to first decide which belongings need to go on shelves by understanding their purposes and whether another alternative storage location is better suited for them. Then decide whether to contain them in an organizer. Sometimes an organizer can hide the item or actually make it more difficult to retrieve. For example, baskets can separate different styles of handbags. For certain people, though, taking them out and putting them back into their baskets is too much effort.

Some people like their handbags, shoes, sweaters, belts, scarves, or jewelry highly visible, which might mean lining all their shoes in a row across a shelf. Although they'll get dusty, this is an esthetic preference. It's important to achieve a balance between storage function and artistic display in a closet, as both can be important to an individual.

Dividers

Shelf dividers nicely separate closet inventories, such as purses, pillows, blankets, toys, photo albums and the like, while keeping them visible. Use shelf dividers to separate clothes according to material, pant length, sleeve length, and so on. Similarly, use them to separate handbags by style, such as shoulder, clutch, satchel, and the like.

Containers and Baskets

Using the right containers makes a big difference in a closet. It's important to select storage containers for your belongings that fit the size of your items. Therefore, use smaller ones for smaller items and bigger ones for larger items. The idea is never to have too many articles in one container so they don't become work to dig through and too heavy to lift. Typically, lidded and stacked containers are a nuisance to use on a regular basis.

If there is excess lateral space on a shelf, use stacking bins with easy-access openings. See-through containers, like wire or mesh, are better than opaque ones for ease of viewing. Opaque baskets or containers that are below and above waist level will need labels to easily identify their contents. Look for bins with a tall back and short front that can hold a pile of folded clothes securely and visibly.

A basket should fit just right on a shelf with little room surrounding it—otherwise you are not maximizing storage space. Baskets can fit snugly together on a shelf since you don't need much room in between to move them. Measure the shelf

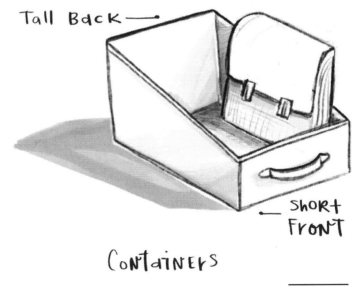

FIGURE 17.01
Tall Back/Short front Bins

depth and width before purchasing baskets or bins to buy the right size and number to fit the shelf perfectly. Using identical storage containers will look best, offering a neat appearance in your closet.

Under-Shelf Organizers

Under-shelf baskets are great storage solutions for capturing dead space found in between fixed shelves. These devices simply slide onto the shelf without the need for installation. Under-shelf baskets are also inexpensive and easy to remove when storage needs change. They're ideal for storing odds and ends or smaller items, such as portable electronics, journals, slippers, neck wraps, and the like.

Like under-shelf baskets, freestanding portable "helper" shelves capture the lateral dead space on fixed shelves. This type of shelf simply rests on top of a shelf's surface to create another platform for additional belongings; they're not permanent and easy to move around. Look for jumbo shelf helpers that are big enough to hold folded clothing and footwear.

Overhead Storage Organizers

Shelves above the hanging rods are commonly not outfitted with organizers and can therefore become a breeding ground for clutter. This space is valuable, and organizing it properly will have many benefits.

Since this location is not necessarily the easiest place to access, a sturdy stepladder is a good investment. Overhead storage works best for infrequently used handbags, formal shoes, blankets, pillows, sheet sets, photo albums, suitcases, fans, humidifiers, audio/video equipment, sewing kits, and off-season clothing. Handled or easy-to-grip containers will be necessary to divide such belongings.

Keep storage containers labeled and don't use large containers, which are clumsy and dangerous to move from overhead spaces. For example, separate off-season clothing into several medium-size containers to narrow the categories to specific groups of clothing, such as cardigans,

FIGURE 17.02
Overhead Cubby Compartments

rather than a broad category like sweaters. You can also store frequently worn bulkier items overhead to keep them from cluttering the closet floor. Easy grab-and-go items, such as gym bags, briefcases, backpacks, exercise mats, personal picnic baskets, and the like are good items to store here, as well, if there is room.

Besides removable containers, stationary cubby organizers work well in overhead shelving to create compartments. They can separate shoes, handbags, clothes, hats, and so on. You can insert small containers into individual cubby compartments to store loose articles like scarves and gloves.

Pulldown hanging rods make hanging clothes easy to reach when rods are in two or three tiers. If you are short on hanging space or prefer to hang clothes, it's best to occupy overhead space with pulldown hanging rods.

Closet Storage

FIGURE 17.03
Pulldown hanging rod

CHAPTER 18

Closet Wall Storage

The great thing about using your walls for storage is the endless possibilities of how you can configure them. Many wall organizers serve multiple purposes beyond their intended uses. Therefore, it's important to look at many different types of wall organizers and decide which ones fit your inventories the best.

A bedroom closet wall should prioritize storage for items worn on the body, like handbags, clothing, footwear, scarves, ties, and so on. Leftover room can hold personal odds and ends, such as photo albums, audio/video equipment, media, personal electronics, and keepsakes. Any amount of spare closet wall and corner space can be put to use. Creating a storage place for something that is otherwise cluttering another spot in the home is solving a storage problem. Even something as simple as a mirror or clock adds value to a blank wall.

Wall-Mounted Organizers

Any available wall space in a closet needs to be considered for storage. There are many creative ways to capture additional storage from even the tiniest section of a closet wall. Something as simple as a single hook can get an article off the closet floor. The following covers good ways to store common bedroom belongings on wall organizers.

Coatracks

Wall-mounted coatracks or a single-mounted coat hook can be used in closets for storing not only jackets, but also handbags, belts, scarves, back packs, robes, jewelry, umbrellas, ties, totes, laundry bags, and the like. Anything with a loop at the end can be stored on a hook.

Towel Bars

A common bathroom towel bar can be put to good use on a bedroom-closet wall. Rod hooks formed in the shape of an S can be added to individually hold a number of closet inventories, such as scarves or jewelry. You can drape items over the rods instead of using hooks. There are also wall-mounted rod organizers with specific purposes. A favorite is the tie rack that includes necktie hangers, so items are individually hung.

Pegboard, Slatwall, and Gridwall Systems

The storage possibilities are endless with a pegboard, slatwall, or gridwall system in a closet. These systems make it easy to locate belongings and help keep drawers and counters clutter-free.

A pegboard wall is a great closet organizer because it can store so many different items; plus, it's easy to reorganize when needs change. Pegboard walls come in tempered hardboard, plastic, and steel. They're generally sold in square or rectangle sheets in sizes like two-by-four feet or four-by-four feet; it's also sold in strips. Pegboard systems typically come with attachable organizing accessories, like hooks, baskets, shelves, and bins.

Although inexpensive, pegboard made of tempered hardboard is a wood product, so the fastening holes enlarge with wear and cause the hooks to fall out. Consider this product only if you plan to store just one item per hook or lightweight items. The advantage to the tempered hardboard is that you can get it in a paintable finish and customize the color to match the closet. It's the easiest pegboard material to cut, so it can be wrapped around tight spaces.

Although costlier, a steel-and-plastic pegboard is your best bet for hook stability. You can find such pegboard designed so the peg hooks lock in place, which dramatically improves hook stability.

Gridwall and slatwall storage systems are sold through both retail and commercial companies. The commercial outfits sell their systems to businesses as store fixtures to display retail merchandise. These systems are designed to hold items such as clothing, scarves, handbags, hats, and all bedroom-closet inventories, which make them worthwhile to look into for your closet. Another benefit of commercial wall systems is their durability since they're designed for a high-traffic retail

Slatwell Organizer

FIGURE 18.01
Slatwall storage in a closet

store. They're also maintenance-free and require minimal cleaning.

There are storage accessories, such as face-out tubes, trays, baskets, bins, shelves, hooks, and so on, that come with these systems. Baskets and bins are great for corralling all those small essentials that are convenient to have in a closet, such as combs, lint removers, sewing supplies, shoe polish, lip balm, and scissors. Shelves can store items like perfume, deodorant and anti-wrinkle and antistatic spray. Hooks can store belts, scarves, handbags, totes, umbrellas, any item that has a loop. Face-out waterfall tubes have multiple hooks for storing inventories of handbags, scarves, ties, and belts.

Magazine Racks and Tiered Storage Baskets

Wall-mounted organizers with basket or pouch-like compartments are ideal for taking care of the overflow from drawers. Items like socks, underwear, leotards, nylons, tights, boxers, T-shirts, pajamas, and leggings are good items to stash in these organizers. Also, hair accessories, magazines, journals, hats, gloves, scarves, water bottles, cellular accessories, and all those little odds and ends that wind up cluttering a bedroom dresser countertop are also perfect picks for these organizers.

Shoe Racks

Wall-mounted shoe racks are great for managing footwear that usually winds up covering the closet floor. Utilizing any untapped wall space for shoe racks is so important since there never seems to be enough storage space for footwear in the average closet.

CHAPTER 19

Freestanding Closet Organizers

An economical way to organize a closet is with basic stand-alone organizers that reside on the closet floor, which is commonly unused space anyway. There are many freestanding organizers on the market, but the key is finding less bulky ones that use floor space wisely. Also, there is a good chance that no matter what organizer you find, a wheeled, freestanding version also exists. Wheeled floor organizers are easily accessible and movable when it's time to clean. The most popular freestanding organizers are tiered-shelf shoe organizers, cubby organizers, hampers, and rolling shelves and carts with multiple drawers. The following covers detailed information on the most popular freestanding organizers.

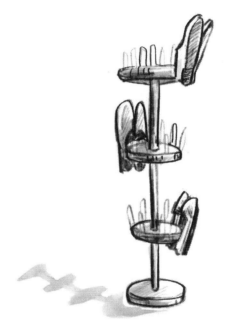

Spinning Shoe Rack

FIGURE 19.01
Spinning tiered shoe rack

Freestanding Shoe Organizers

Shoe racks should accomplish several goals: display shoes in an easy-to-view and accessible manner, hold footwear in place well, and maintain their shapes.

There are two types of freestanding shoe racks: the spinning or tiered-shelf racks and the cubby organizer. Shoe racks can be found in different levels and widths. Some have a wire construction, whereas others are solid shelves. Wire versions are made of nonslip aluminum and polymer tubes that grip shoes quite well. Adjustable tiers are best to accommodate chunky shoes or boots. Also, shoe organizers with angled shelves are best for viewing. Spinning tiered racks hold footwear along the circumference of a circle that rotates 360 degrees, making them good organizers for closet corners.

Cubby organizers are either square or rectangular open-front boxes divided into several smaller compartments to store single pairs of shoes. Look for those that have a large enough cubby compartment so the shoes' soles all face down and are not squeezed in sideways, which scuffs and misshapes them.

Freestanding Hampers

A hamper is a great closet storage item because it's better left unseen. There are many different types and styles on the market today, so finding one to fit your space should be easy. A wheeled hamper is worth consideration since it can conveniently be moved to a laundry room. You can have more than one hamper for other purposes, as well, such as laundry separation, dry cleaning, tailor, donations, and so on.

In order to maintain organization in your closet, permanently keep a basket, hamper, or bag there to toss unwanted clothes and accessories. To stay on top of closet decluttering and prevent it from becoming a monumental task, continuously add items you no longer want to the pile.

Some items stay on their hangers or hooks because we are undecided about getting rid of them. Everyone has these items in their closets. A good strategy for taking some action is to create a hamper or bag for these items, marked with a question mark (?) for an "indecision bag," so this bag does not go to donation. This will at least encourage you to get questionable articles off the hangers, where they may just hang forever.

Once this indecision bag or hamper fills, move some of the pile to the "donation hamper" and then store the remainder. Mark a date in your calendar to review and reduce the articles in the container—for instance, a month. Once these items have been removed from your personal space, you may develop a more objective opinion about them. Methods like this are ways to reduce inventory while not producing the kind of pressure that leads to feeling overwhelmed or anxious.

Rolling Shelves and Modular Cubes

A rollout shelf resembles a workman dolly cart, but has four shallow sides so belongings don't fall off. It's a low-to-the-ground platform mounted on four rolling wheels with a front handle for easy access. These organizers can hold heavy-duty loads or just large items. Some good bedroom-closet items to store on them are blankets, backpacks, books, laundry baskets, purses, briefcases, and folded clothes.

An inexpensive alternative to a laminate closet system is to incorporate a modular storage system comprised of individual cubes that can stack together in a vertical or horizontal arrangement. Storage cubes can also contain baskets or containers to hold loose articles.

Pullout Baskets and Drawers in Closets

There are many advantages to having pullout baskets or drawers in a closet. Primarily, they can take care of bedroom spillover or at least lessen the demand for highly functional furniture pieces to accommodate drawer storage for

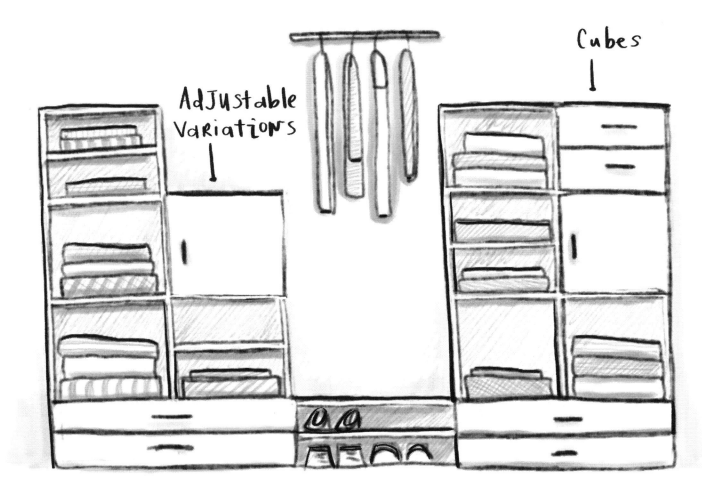

Adjustable Variations

Cubes

Freestanding Modular Cubes

FIGURE 19.02
Modular storage units

pajamas, underwear, boxers, tanks, tees, and so on. Drawers or pullout baskets are convenient and highly accessible, making both retrieving and putting things away simple. Pullout baskets and drawers are prime storage organizers because they easily conceal and divide items.

Both pullout baskets and drawers come in different sizes, making them easy to fit almost any group of articles. Most wire closet systems offer ventilated, grid-patterned pullout baskets. Some wire-based closet systems and most

laminate closet systems have solid drawer organizer options.

There is also a good assortment of freestanding tiered-drawer cart organizers in all different materials, such as wire, laminate, steel, or plastic, that can be incorporated into an existing closet system or stand alone on the closet floor. Many add-on kitchen organizers have pullout basket and drawer organizers that can be purchased separately and installed on secure closet shelves.

Pullout Baskets versus Traditional Drawers

Pullout wire baskets are an inexpensive alternative to traditional, solid drawers. For the most part, wire baskets are easy to see through, so labeling their contents may not be necessary. However, a label may offer additional guidance for small children.

Wire baskets are well ventilated, making them ideal for storing spare blankets, bed sheets, and pillows that can smell musty in closed storage. A pullout wire basket can also serve as a clothes hamper and benefit from such ventilation. The downside to wire baskets is that their grid structure leaves indentations on clothing, and the gaps in between the wires allow small items to fall through. Although a simple piece of cardboard or liner can fix the bottom, the basket sides are exposed to this problem. Wire baskets can also look less tidy, especially when their contents don't remain organized.

Drawers that come with traditional closet systems are mostly laminate or wood, and they tend to be an expensive upgrade. Transparent acrylic drawer fronts are becoming a more popular feature. Translucent drawer fronts are glamorous and allow you to easily see the contents at a glance, but they do advertise a disorganized drawer. Acrylic can scratch, and regular cleaning is necessary to keep fingerprints and dust at bay.

It's important to note that over time, we will automatically know which drawers hold certain belongings, so transparent, wire, or even labeled drawers eventually become unnecessary.

Unique Storage Essentials for Closets

It's important to consider that there are other ways to organize a closet besides expensive closet systems and storage essentials. The average home may have spare furniture or unused organizers elsewhere that can be repurposed in a closet. The following covers several ways to accomplish organization by using belongings that are not typical for the space.

Adding Furniture

New or recycled furniture pieces—like dressers, desks, armoires, and bookcases—can become great storage essentials for a closet. Certain furniture pieces can also inexpensively add an upscale look similar to that of a custom closet. The furniture should fit efficiently in the space, so it cannot be too bulky. It also needs to operate well. For example, drawers and doors should be able to fully extend without obstruction. It's also important that the furniture mimics a good storage organizer. For example, it should offer adjustable components or ample drawer space.

Tall, slim armoires or bookcases outfitted with shelves can hold many different types of inventories. They can house baskets, bins, folded clothes, valet boxes, jewelry boxes, humidors, pillows, covers, sheets, handbags, books, perfume, cologne, makeup, toiletries, fans, humidifiers, and all personal articles.

A clothing rod can be installed in an armoire in order to add extra hanging space. Glass doors can be added to showcase footwear, handbags, trophies, and so on. Adding vanity mirrors to the front to the doors is a good option when you dress in or near your closet. Doors also eliminate much of the dust that shelves attract.

A sitting bench is an added bonus to any walk-in closet. It's best to utilize space beneath the bench for storage. There are benches with cubby compartments, drawers, and racks for holding many types of belongings below the seating area.

Freestanding Coat, Scarf, and Handbag Racks

A common coat-tree rack is a useful organizer in a bedroom closet. One with many hooks placed at different levels can hold a number of closet inventories, such as scarves, handbags, ties, necklaces, totes, backpacks, gym bags, umbrellas, yoga mats, and outerwear. These organizers take up only vertical space and are perfect for occupying a dead corner or anywhere there is free space.

Hand Bag Rack

FIGURE 19.03
Freestanding handbag rack

CHAPTER 20

Over-the-Door Closet Organizers

A number of storage organizers are designed for the standard residential, full-swing closet door, as opposed to bifold or pocket doors. The majority are referred to as OTD organizers. This means that they have a hook attachment that simply slips over the top of the door; thus, no assembly is required. Make sure the hook is covered in a rubber coating so it does not scratch the door.

Only some types of door organizers are made with both over-the-door hooks and a mounting option. Even fewer door organizers only offer the mounted option. Typically, mounted door organizers are marketed for kitchen dry goods and supplies. However, they can be used in more closets throughout home. The most popular mounted door organizer is tiered wire baskets which attach to a long vertical rail that is screwed into the door. Clearly, mounting an organizer to a door is a highly stable option, but the door should have a solid core for stability. Mounted door organizers are less in demand because not all doors have a solid core. Another option for a door organizer is a simple hook to hold different types of items, from clothing to bags.

When selecting a door organizer, make sure that there is enough depth available for your organizer when it's filled with belongings so the door can properly close or open, depending upon which side of the door it's installed on. The following over-the-door organizers are easy to find at most home stores and online.

Over-the-Door Shoe Organizers

There are different types of OTD shoe organizers, but remember that you'll still need a place for your boots. Since it's usually best to store all footwear in one location, think about how this arrangement will work in your closet. Shoe-rack door organizers are usually made of epoxy-coated metal and can hold anywhere from twelve to thirty-six pairs of shoes. These racks are commonly slanted toward the door so the shoes' tips all face the door, not offering the best view.

Other rack-style organizers are designed with a series of wire arched-loops in the shape of a single shoe. The base of the shoe faces the door, and the body of the shoe faces outward, offering a good view of the shoe. These organizers secure the shoe well from shaking loose from door movement.

There are also pocket- and cubby-style over-the-door shoe organizers. Avoid the ones that are opaque, so shoes are easy to see at a glance.

Over-the-door Shoe Rack

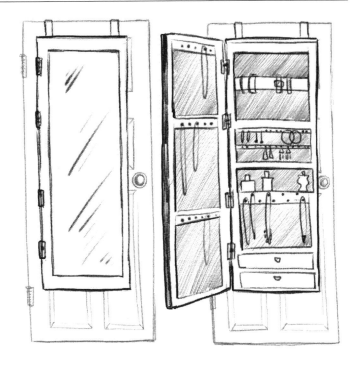

Over the Door Jewelry Organizer

FIGURE 20.01
Over-the-door shoe organizer

FIGURE 20.02
Over-the-door jewelry storage

It's best to invest in shoe organizers that you can wipe clean since shoes attract dirt. Some of the drawbacks to using over-the-door shoe-cubby organizers are that they tend to be harder to clean deep inside the pockets. They also are prone to sag when weighted down.

Over-the-Door Hanging Rods and Racks

There are different types of OTD storage devices for hanging garments on the inside of a closet door. Over-the-door hanging rods are designed to hold garments with a hanger. This can be a great place to store temporary items, such as dry cleaning or a specially planned outfit for an upcoming event. Some people also like to pick out their outfit for the next day, which makes this a neat place to keep this clothing. An additional hanging rod like this can also be a great place to store bulky robes, outerwear, jackets, and sweatshirts that can hog your hanging rod.

Another OTD storage device for hanging garments is a hook-style coatrack that can hold belongings by the collar or loop. Items like outerwear, umbrellas, tennis rackets, robes, scarves, and clothing that does not wrinkle easily are good to store on this organizer. Some over-the-door coatracks have staggered hooks so items can hang at different levels.

Over-the-Door Jewelry Storage

There are a couple popular OTD jewelry organizers. The rack-style, over-the door jewelry organizers openly display everything from hooks or wire rods. Different sections of these organizers can hold a particular type of jewelry. The downside to this type of jewelry organizer is the rattling and clanking that occurs from door movement. Also, pieces not securely fastened are prone to fall off and get lost on the closet floor since the rack is not contained in a box.

There are also cabinet-style over-the-door jewelry organizers that are often featured with a mirrored door. These organizers are usually pricey, but they're worth it. Many can also be mounted with hardware, so they're transferable to a wall if your needs change. These organizers are roomy inside, and the compartments are well laid out so jewelry is easy to view. The door hides the contents and provides a clean look.

Over-the-Door Pocket Organizers

Probably the most popular OTD organizers are the pocket-style varieties. These organizers are comprised of large flat sheets of canvas or nylon

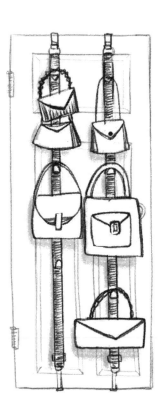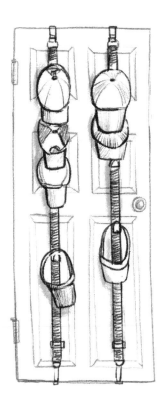

Over The Door
Band Organizers
(with Adjustable Hooks)

FIGURE 20.03
Over-the-door band organizers

sized to fit on a door with several attached storage pockets. Some pockets are clear plastic for easy viewing, whereas others are made of breathable mesh material that is somewhat transparent. Pockets that are solid canvas or opaque plastic will need content labels.

Pocket organizers with several small pockets are good for storing jewelry, remotes, sunglasses, socks, hair accessories, makeup, brushes, keys, wallets, or any small bedroom item. There are also large pocket organizers that fit a good portion of the door's width. These pockets are usually lined with a metal frame to support the weight of larger articles, such as magazines, journals, throws, and so on.

Specially designed pocket organizers for shoes and jewelry with tailored compartments are also available.

Over-the-Door Basket Organizers

There is a large assortment of OTD basket organizers. Most of these organizers come with multiple tiered baskets attached to bars with hooks that go over the top of the door. Baskets can be found in shallow or deep sizes. These organizers are mostly adjustable.

Over-the-Door Hook Organizers

The least common OTD organizers are two types of hook organizers. One consists of a single slim metal bar with a dozen attached hanging hooks. It's designed to hold lightweight accessories, such as jewelry and scarves. The other OTD hook organizer is made from a thick nylon band that has adjustable hooks attached to it. The band is designed with elastic inserts at either end so it can stretch vertically across the door and hook in place over the edges. Both these organizers are slim enough so more than one can attach to the closet door; they're also the most economical of all the over-the-door organizers.

Over-the-Door Gaming and Media Storage

Bedrooms that have televisions with attached gaming and video equipment can benefit from a hidden location like behind a closet door for storing all the headsets, games, movies, and the like. You want an organizer that is adjustable so it can respond to the rapid advances in technology. Organizers that offer several width and depth components serve these inventories best.

Over-the-Door Laundry Organizers

A clever item to add behind a closet door is a well-ventilated, over-the-door laundry bag. This frees up closet space or floor space by eliminating a traditional hamper. A removable bag can be easily moved back and forth to the laundry machine. An over-the-door-ironing board is also a good organizer to install on a closet door for convenience and space efficiency.

CHAPTER 21

Linen Closets

A linen closet traditionally stores all household cloth goods. It's an important closet since it can hold so many different items. If your home does not have a special closet for linens, it can be easy to convert a less important closet into one or use a storage organizer, such as an armoire, hutch, buffet, cabinet, or shelving unit to contain linens.

A linen closet is typically found off a hallway near bedrooms and can also be found in full bathrooms. What you store in a linen closet depends on where it's located in the house. For example, a hallway linen closet by bedrooms can prioritize storage for sheets, blankets, sleeping bags, beach towels, pillows, and guest towels. Full baths can prioritize storage for bath towels, wash clothes, and toiletries. Second-floor linen closets don't necessarily need to store items that are used on the main level, like table or powder room linens. These items are better stored in places like a china cabinet, buffet, bathroom vanity, or kitchen pantry for convenient access.

Commonly, a linen closet becomes the catchall clutter trap, similar to a kitchen junk drawer. The best way to combat the clutter problem is to fit all the closet areas with organizers for every stored inventory, making it less possible to just stuff something anywhere.

In lieu of a built-in linen closet, there are many substitutes on the market because they're so important in a home. There are over-the-toilet cabinets and many freestanding cabinets that are specifically designed for linen storage. An armoire is also another option for linen storage.

Decluttering and Storage Tips for Linen Closets

Now is the time to permanently remove the children's outgrown character sheet sets, out-of-style patterned sheet sets, or sheet sets that no longer match a newly redecorated bedroom. Don't forget about getting rid of the sheets that don't fit the bed for any reason. Any sheets that are continuously passed over and just sit in the closet are the ones to eliminate now. Also consider eliminating all the flat sheets you don't use. Many people prefer just making the bed with a fitted sheet and use a duvet cover in lieu of a flat sheet. If you are one of these people, you'll save a ton of room getting rid of the flat sheets.

Follow the same procedure when reducing pillowcases. Separate the standard, euro, king, and shams. Pair the matching pillowcases; if one of the pair is in bad shape, perhaps the other one can match the sheets being used for a twin bed, cot, or pullout sleeper before discarding or recycling. Keep no more than two to three sheet sets for each bed in the home; the remainder is excess that is taking up valuable storage space.

Bedding Storage

Locate all bedding, such as sheets, pillows, mattress covers, blankets, and the like, and divide them into like groups. Next, separate out all guest bedding and seasonal items, such as flannel sheet sets, and then tackle your everyday bedding.

Guest Bedding

Start with the bedding reserved for your guests. First, get rid of anything that is unworthy to present to a guest. Make sure to look closely for tears, stains, yellowing, and the like. Anything that has yellowed or stained needs to be tossed into a laundry basket. Chances are you can improve or even correct these problems with the right cleaning agent or process. Work on this before storing these items away since set-in stains and yellowing only become harder to remove over time. Put aside any tears that can be mended and repair them before returning to storage. Recycle or donate anything beyond repair to an animal shelter.

How many sheet sets to have on hand for guests would be determined by how many guests you host and how long they stay. One sheet set per bed is usually sufficient unless your guests stay for more than one week. This would increase the number to two sets per bed, figuring on weekly washings. Blankets don't need as much cleaning, so guests need only one per bed—two if they're thin.

Even though bedding is expensive, second-hand sheets and blankets hold little value, so part with some of your surplus, especially those not receiving use. Donate them to a homeless or animal shelter. There are also other countless ways to recycle them, such as using them as rags, plant covers, pet bedding, painting tarps, children's forts, and beach/picnic blankets.

Since guest bedding is used much less frequently, pack it away so it stays fresh. The best way to protect bedding and save space at the same time is to use vacuum-sealed bags. These airtight bags compress the articles to one-third of their size by sucking out all the air from the bag with a vacuum hose. The bags are easy to use and lock out dirt, bugs, and moisture, so they're safe to store anywhere. The bags are transparent, so the articles stored inside are visible, but you still should use a label on the outside to record the contents. Stackable, lidded containers are also fine to use. Guest bedding can be stored in the overhead space of the linen closet. You can also transfer it to a guest-room closet or underneath the guest bed.

Off-Season Bedding

First, consider which bedding items were not actually used during their previous season. If it takes surveying household members, you'll get your answers and perhaps additional information that could help with buying future bedding. For example, you may discover that the wool blankets you thought were being used are being avoided because they're itchy. Anything your household members don't use is unnecessary surplus and should be donated.

Evaluate your off-season items to see if it's possible to use them throughout the year before you store them away. Again, get your household members' opinions about using certain off-season items all year round. For instance, many people prefer cold-weather bedding items in a well air-conditioned home. Likewise, lightweight cotton blankets can be used in the winter by individuals who are always hot at night.

Generally, one off-season sheet set, comforter, or blanket per bed is enough since you have others that are used throughout the year. Off-season bedding items can be stored in vacuum bags to conserve space and keep articles fresh. They're also fine to containerize. Keep off-season bedding stored alongside guest bedding on an overhead linen closet shelf. They can also be tucked away in a storage room, under the bed, or in a bedroom closet.

Everyday Sheet Sets

Separate the current-season sheets by flat and fitted. Then form groups for the different sizes, like king, queen, and so on. Sometimes, sheet labels fade from bleaching, so make sure to record the size on the sheet with a laundry marker if the label is unreadable. You can also attach laundry stickers, marking them with the sheet size.

Look over your sheets for stains, tears, and yellowing. Try to successfully treat them with the right cleaning agents before storing. Stubborn stains and dingy sheets that don't respond to treatment can be donated to an animal shelter or recycled. Mend any tears and rips, when feasible.

Open Storage for Sheets

If arranging sheets on open shelving, stack them as neatly as possible. Keep same-size sheets together,

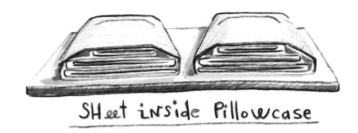

FIGURE 21.01
Sheets contained in a pillowcase

and position them so the folded sides face outward. On solid shelves, consider using shelf dividers to separate the different types of sheets, and then label the shelf edge with the type of sheet. Note that unfinished wood shelves may stain sheets. You can do the same for wire shelving and label the type of sheet with a tag that hangs from the wire.

A popular idea for storing sheets is placing a complete folded set inside one of the corresponding pillowcases. You can also wrap the pillowcase around the flat and fitted sheet. The sheet set becomes easy to stack with others on a shelf, or it can be contained in an organizer more easily.

Container Storage for Sheets

Containers are the best way to keep your sheets from scrambling over the closet. Different sheet-set sizes are easier to find when separated and labeled in different containers. Also, the burden of having to perfectly fold sheets for neat stacking is eliminated when you conceal them in containers.

To maintain your sheets' freshness, store them in breathable, well-ventilated containers. This is especially important if your linens are stored in a moist location like a bathroom with a shower. Sachets, cedar blocks, linen sprays, and air fresheners help revive the stagnant closet air. You can also stash laundry dryer sheets in between bedding. Yellowing of sheets is a common problem that can occurs for a number of reasons. Acid-free tissue paper stored in between sheets can prevent some of the problem. When laundered sheets are returned back to the linen closet, place them at the bottom of the stack to ensure even rotation and optimal freshness.

Another good container for sheets are those with a high back and low front so you get a full view, good support, and proper ventilation. The sides descend down from high in the back to low in the front.

Pillows, Mattress Covers, and Bed Skirts

Scrutinize the seldom-needed linen closet items, such as mattress pads, pillows and pillow protectors, bed skirts, and so on. These items are not replaced often and are usually purchased on an as-needed basis. For example, a bed skirt stays on the bed until it rips or the room is redecorated. Store these items overhead or at the base of the closet. In tightly packed closets, consider moving them to other places like the under the bed or in a bedroom storage bench.

It's common for people to keep these items even when they're replaced with a better one, which makes the chances of using the old one unlikely. Unless these items were purchased new in anticipation of future use, it could very well be time to remove them from the linen closet.

Everyday Blankets and Comforters

Keep extra blankets and comforters in the room they're used. They can be concealed in a bedroom chest, storage ottoman, closet, or in an under-the-bed organizer. A linen closet should be a last resort for storage since these bulky items can quickly crowd a smaller linen closet, and it's not the most convenient place for them. When blankets and comforters need to be placed in a linen closet, use the less accessible spots like overhead compartments or shelves.

Towel Storage

First, make sure that your laundry is up to date in order to obtain an accurate count of the number of towels you have before eliminating any in the reducing process. Remove your bath, hand, face, guest, and wash towels out of the linen closet. If your beach, kitchen, holiday, and cleaning rags are there, take them out as well. Separate them accordingly. Have a bag ready to toss the tattered and badly stained towels that should now become cleaning rags. Also, have bags for donation or sale items.

Start with one pile at a time, unfold them completely, and look for stains, yellowing, bleach damage, tears, and any wear. At the same time, get rid of the towels you don't like or use anymore. Some towels may no longer match a newly remodeled bathroom or are in a length you don't prefer.

After you are through reducing, sort the towels into similar groups, such as washcloths, hand, bath, guest, holiday, and so on. Keep towels unfolded during the process to see their lengths or sizes while sorting. Also, divide towels by color when different bathrooms use certain colored towels. Generally, keep enough bath, wash, and hand towels to accommodate the household members. Two to three of each towel type per person should cover household members in between laundering.

Now is the time to decide if certain towels are better stored outside of the linen closet for convenience or as a means to help free up a congested closet. For example, holiday towels can be packed away with holiday decorations. Beach towels can be moved to a mudroom cabinet. Cleaning rags can rest in a container or bucket where the cleaning products are stored.

There are ways to store towels outside a linen closet with the use of organizers; they're especially worth the expense and effort if your linen closet is full. In the bathrooms where the towels are used, you can install wall organizers or freestanding organizers, or use vanity cabinet space. Towel racks can be installed behind the door, or an over-the-door towel rack can hold them.

Open Storage for Towels

To make your towel stacks look their best, copy how spas and stores display them. First fold the towel lengthwise so their edges meet. Then fold the towel over twice, forming a stable, tight fit. Face the folded side forward on the shelf, making a neat appearance. Many organizers call for rolling the towels, which is a commonly done in spas and is perfect for an open-storage arrangement.

In a linen closet, fold and stack towels in piles on an open wire or solid shelf. You can incorporate shelf dividers to separate different types of towels. Label the edge of a solid shelf or hang a tag from a wire shelf to identify individual towel stacks.

Try to balance the shelves by keeping towel stacks close to the same height. This eliminates dead space that can form in between shelves. Adjust height differences between stacks of towels by using a platformed shelving unit called a *helper shelf*. This organizer is a freestanding shelf that sits on top of the existing shelf with leg supports, thus adding another level of storage space. These organizers are great for dividing and storing small towels like washcloths or hand towels that cannot stack very high.

Containerized Storage for Towels

Containerizing towels in the linen closet guarantees that the stacks stay corralled. Containers keep the closet looking its neatest since piles of towels can sometimes become jumbled and stray from the stack. Use containers that have label inserts or are easy to label. Always use well-ventilated containers or baskets for towel storage.

Towels can also be rolled or folded in containers. Ventilated wire pullout baskets are great for storing towels—or any linens, for that matter. Some pullout baskets come with closet systems, and freestanding versions are also available.

Table Linens Storage

Begin organizing your household table linens by dividing them into similar groups, such as kitchen tablecloths, cloth napkins, holiday linens, and so on. Have bags ready for repair, cleaning, recycling, donation, or sale. Unfold all your linens and look for stains, tears, and any wear. Put aside napkins and placemat sets, and count them to make sure they're complete before cleaning, repairing, or storing them. See if you can still use an incomplete set or whether it's feasible to replace the missing pieces, if you really like them.

Determine how much of each type of table linen to stock according to how frequently they're used. For example, if you entertain several times a year in a more formal setting like the dining room, several sets of dressy table linens are necessary. You may prefer light colors for spring occasions, autumn colors for fall gatherings, and specialized holiday table linens; one for each occasion is sufficient. In general, two sets of table linens are all you need for infrequently used table linens.

Three sets of table linens may be necessary for regularly used linens, like those used a kitchen. Reevaluate any sets that have not been used in the past year and determine why they weren't used. If you think they no longer match the decor or you simply no longer like them, indicate this by moving them to the donation or sale pile. If you can repair or clean linens yourself, move them to your laundry area; otherwise, investigate professional cleaning options to see if they're feasible. Antique and some luxury linens that need attention can be restored at a fine table linen service or dry cleaners. These items are best professionally cleaned and boxed by a restoration service specializing in delicate linens. Cleaned pieces can be lined in acid-free paper to prevent yellowing and then either hung, bagged, boxed, or containerized the proper way.

After making your final decisions about your table linens, decide where to place them. If short on linen closet space, keep them in a dining room buffet, kitchen hutch, or pantry near where they're used. There may also be other good places to store table linens, so before putting them back in linen closet, consider possible alternative arrangements.

Tablecloths and Runners

Label each tablecloth or runner individually with its size to make finding what you need easy. Use pins to attach a label to the fabric or mark delicate tape, like painter's tape, with size information.

Towel bars hung on the inside of a linen closet or an over-the-door towel rack keep table clothes and runners in good shape and free up shelf space.

A pullout pant rack installed in a linen closet can also hold tablecloths and runners. Install it near the floor to avoid any key eye-level storage space that needs to be reserved for sheets and towels.

Desktop paper sorters or racks that hold file folders/papers are good organizers for separating folded tablecloths and runners, as well. These organizers can reside on a closet shelf. Containerize tablecloths and label them according to size, such as sixty-inch round tablecloths or 108-inch runners, or divide them by type: kitchen, dining room, holiday, and outdoors.

A clothing rod installed in the linen closet holds tablecloths and runners by hangers. Use velvet or gripping pant hangers that can hold the material in place, versus plastic or wire hangers that create creases.

Napkins and Placemats

Everyday cloth napkins and placemats that are used in the kitchen should store in a drawer, cabinet, pantry, or closet belonging to this room. Infrequently used holiday or formal sets can store in a dining room buffet, chest, or cabinet where they're used. Try and use the linen closet as a last resort unless you have ample space.

Napkins

Cloth napkins can be store individually secured in napkin rings and placed in a storage bin or container. Sets of napkins could also be bound together by a clip or in separate bags in shallow drawers or pullout baskets. Stacks of cloth napkins are hard to keep neat, so it's best to make the piles low and store them in shallow drawers.

Placemats

Store placemats together in sets. In a linen closet, placements can be rolled and stored in shallow organizers, such as a drawer, a pullout basket, or a tiered file paper sorter. Rolled placements may also stand in a basket or container.

Placemats can lay flat, stacked on a closet shelf. However, many different sets stacked on top of one another can be hard to access; it may be a good idea to add extra shelves so only a few sets rest on each shelf. Under-shelf placement holders are great for capturing common dead space in between shelves.

Slanted shoe shelves are angled shelves which have a securing front shoe fence making them ideal to install in a linen closet for placemat storage. In these organizers, sets of placemats can lay flat and overlap another so many different sets are seen at a glance. There are also freestanding, wheeled, slanted-shelf shoe carts that could hold placemats. This wheeled organizer is easy to access when placed on a linen closet floor.

Throws and Slipcovers Storage

Throws adorn bedding, sofas, couches, chairs, and so on; they're also used for warmth. Keep throws near where they're used in places like a storage ottoman by the sofa, not the linen closet. However, seasonal throws can be stored in a linen closet alongside other seasonal items.

When examining throws that somehow ended up in your linen closet, answers to how they got there in the first place may help you in the reducing process. For example, you may have stuffed one there when you decided it didn't look good on a sofa. In such cases, donate or sell it since it's unlikely it will leave the linen closet otherwise.

When downsizing your furniture slipcovers, first group them according to the piece of furniture they protect (for example, bar stool, dining chairs, sofas, and so on). Next, unfold each piece to check for stains and needed repairs. Make one pile for repair and another for cleaning or both. Move any pieces you can personally repair or clean to laundry or sewing areas. Bag and label everything that needs professional assistance.

Make sure you are using your slipcovers for their intended purpose, which is why you purchased them; when you are not, it's most likely time to donate or sell them. For example, those bought to protect furniture while entertaining should be taken out for parties. Slipcovers that were purchased to change the look of your interiors but are now hiding buried in the linen closet could be purchase mistakes. Slipcovers that don't fit correctly will never be used. When slipcovers

are used seasonally, light colors in the warm months and dark colors in cool weather are best; make sure these are rotated accordingly.

When slipcovers are used on a daily basis to protect furniture from pets or children, a second set is needed while the other is being repaired or cleaned. These slipcovers can be stored on an upper or lower linen closet shelf when not in use. Rolling carts on the closet floor make great organizers for these bulky items. Deep pullout baskets are also good storage choices for them. Be careful not to overload containers with bulky slipcovers when stored overhead; instead, use many small containers so they're easy to move around.

Bathroom Items Storage

A linen closet located in a bathroom can store items used in that and other bathrooms on the same floor. You can also keep these items in various convenient places throughout a bathroom and reserve overstock for the bathroom linen closet. Linen closets located in a hallway can store excess toiletries, paper products, and decorative items. It's important to keep opened packages and bottles of toiletries separate from the unopened surplus. This strategy can eliminate having too much of the same product open simultaneously and possibly wasted.

Toiletries
A good storage strategy is to separate toiletries by type into labeled containers. If you don't divide your items in this manner, it's easy to lose track of quantities, which is why many people purchase more that they need.

Some useful classifications for toiletries include the following:

- acne treatments
- allergy and asthma
- body soaps and powders
- bronzers and sunscreen lotions
- children's medicine
- cough, cold, and flu
- digestive health
- face cleansers and moisturizer
- first aid
- hairstyling products
- hand soap and sanitizers
- heated styling tools
- linen spray and air fresheners
- lip balm and cold sore medicine
- makeup
- manicure and pedicure
- men's skincare
- oral care
- pain and fever
- shaving and razors
- sleep and snoring aids
- vitamins

The best containers for toiletries are see-through, such as those that are translucent, mesh, or ventilated. It's also helpful for a container to have a gripped or carry handle. Popular stacking shoebox-style containers are inexpensive, but they have a few drawbacks for toiletries storage. Lidded, stacked containers are hard to access, especially those at the bottom. Many toiletry items placed sideways in a shoebox will leak. It's also harder to create order in shoeboxes because they're hard to compartmentalize.

Toiletries can also be filed without an organizer on a linen closet shelf, where each row consists of a separate category, or placed on a staircase-style tiered shelf. Mounted storage racks that come with different sizes of attachable

Vented Plastic Containers With handles

FIGURE 21.02
Handled vented plastic toiletry container

baskets are good organizers for storing toiletries. They can be mounted on a door or attached to a closet wall. Clear-pocketed organizers can store many odds and ends, such as travel-size toiletries that are always hard to organize. These organizers can mount to the closet door or wall.

Paper Products

Excess facial tissue, guest napkins, paper towels, and toilet paper are perfect bathroom items to store in a centrally located hallway linen closet, because a single bathroom can just stock enough paper products to accommodate that room.

An overhead closet shelf, bottom shelf, or floor organizer are good places to store your paper goods. Remove bulk packaging, like cardboard boxes or plastic, before storing, and stack your items in neat piles, as this saves space and makes things easier to retrieve.

Decorative Bathroom Items

When we redecorate or replace a decorative bathroom item, like a bath rug or shower curtain, many of us tend to hang onto the old one. These items are often stuffed into the linen closet "just in case." However, we typically don't reuse these items simply because we replaced them in the first place for a good reason. Most often, these items should be donated or sold unless there is a good reason to keep them, such as saving them for a child's college dorm room. In such cases, move the items into long-term storage, such as a closet.

Extra Storage Space in a Linen Closet

Don't let valuable extra linen closet space—or any closet space, for that matter—go unused, because closets are prime storage space. Every home has belongings that could use a better storage spot if the current one is visible, inconvenient, or congested. For the most part, items that are in a class by themselves and don't specifically relate to a given room—such as board games or wrapping paper—are good to store in any spare space a linen closet may offer. Some of the most logical items for the extra space in a linen closet are cleaning and ironing tools/products, sewing/knitting supplies, audio/video equipment, and household appliances and electronics. The following addresses storage recommendations for these items.

Cleaning and Ironing Tools/Products

It makes sense to use this closet for all your cleaning and ironing products if it's centrally located in the home. A bathroom linen closet can just hold one handled caddy filled with all the tools and cleaners necessary for cleaning that room. A good system for arranging cleaning products in the linen closet is to house them on a lower shelf, thus preventing products from spilling over onto items that can stain, such as linens, or consumables like medications.

When storing cleaning agents on a shelf, use a plastic lining with curved edges, such as a boot tray, to contain spills. Divide products by type and place them in single-file rows to keep tabs on your inventories. For example, all glass cleaners in one row and wood cleaners in another. Also, this type of order promotes using up what is first in line so you don't wind up with several open bottles of the same cleaner.

You can also containerize cleaning agents by grouping them in categories, such as glass, wood, stone cleaners, floor cleaners, and so on. You also want to have plastic, handled containers like a caddy to transport your cleaning products from room to room. Cleaning buckets and caddies can nest inside one another on the linen closet floor. Cleaning accessories, such as brushes and rags, can be placed in a dish tub or bucket on the floor. Cleaning tools can hang from wall or door-mounted hooks, placing a tray beneath them to catch drips.

An iron and spray starch can rest alongside cleaning products. The ironing board can be mounted onto the inside of the linen closet door.

Sewing and Knitting Supplies

Many people have a well-stocked sewing basket in lieu of a sewing machine or have a small one that supplements their sewing machine. It's fitting to house a sewing basket in a linen closet. Similarly, knitting supplies are suitable to store in a linen closet. Knitting supplies should be stored in a handled container so they're easily transported when needed. Both sewing and knitting containers can fit on a linen closet shelf.

Household Appliances and Electronics

There are certain household items that are logical to store in a linen closet, especially when it's in a central location. Items like humidifiers, massagers, weight scales, fans, hampers, wastebaskets, foot baths, vacuum cleaners, facial steamers, and the like are perfect to tuck away in a linen closet.

Hampers are a great asset to a linen closet in lieu of a laundry chute. Most closet systems have a wire-based hamper accessory or a freestanding floor version that works well.

It's advisable to always keep your midsize appliance items in their original boxes to contain their cords and parts. If you no longer have the original box, look for a well-constructed cardboard box and attach a photo of the item to the outside of the box. Neatly line your upper or lower shelves with your appliance boxes. Try not to stack boxes behind one another, but if you need to, place the taller boxes in back. Rectangular boxes should face sideways, when possible, so they occupy less width.

It can be too hard to find good storage places for many electronics, like cameras, radios, and mobile technology, and their parts. Usually, it's best to keep the items' original boxes for warranty and resale purposes. Therefore, such boxes can house parts, manuals, and accessories for these articles and reside on an upper linen closet shelf.

However, use caution when storing actual electronics, such as a camera, if the linen closet is in a high-humidity part of the house, because condensation can lead to corrosion. Some electronics have built-in safeguards for such climatic conditions, so it's best to investigate your electronics before subjecting them to humidity.

Electrical Outlets

Bathroom linen closets can certainly benefit from an electrical outlet. They're great places to hide or charge electric toothbrushes, water picks, mobile phones, radios, massagers, and the like. Heated styling utensils can be plugged in and used from the linen closet. This is a good solution for freeing up congested bathroom vanities. Specialized organizers can hold these tools even while in use, so electric items are not near dangerous water spots like the toilet, tub, or sink. Wall-mounted or freestanding organizers for heated styling tools can easily be added to a linen closet shelf or door.

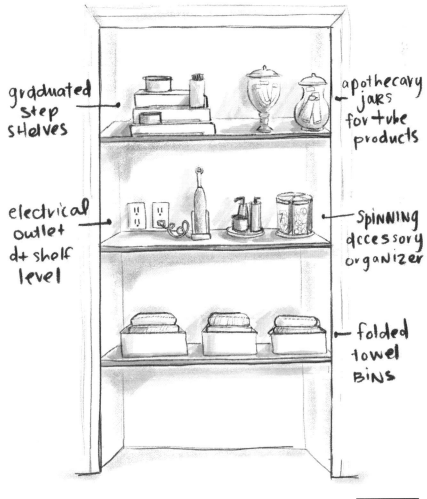

graduated step shelves

electrical outlet at shelf level

apothecary jars for tube products

spinning accessory organizer

folded towel bins

FIGURE 21.03
Linen closet

CHAPTER 22

Front Hall or Coat Closet: Priority Items

Many front hall closets are also considered coat closets and offer little depth. These closets typically are straightforward to design with all the organizational components facing forward.

However, for deeper closets, a walk-in closet system can be installed that dramatically expands design options. Just a little more depth allows you to separate inventories better by arranging certain organizational components on different walls. For instance, a deep-enough side wall can hold hanging rods or shelves. Then the back wall can store another organizational component, such as shelves for storing another category like shoes. A deeper closet offers many arrangement options, so it's important to look at all the possibilities when designing these spaces.

The front hall closet is often times over-stuffed with many odds and ends, but outerwear, footwear, gloves, scarves, and hats take storage precedence in the front hall closet. It needs to be decluttered a few times a year, especially between seasons. You may need to clear an area around the closet, such as an entry hall, to place belongings while you sort and downsize. Have bags or boxes ready for off-season, sale, trash, recycle, donation, and items to transfer elsewhere.

When your coat closet is filled to the brim, you may need to seek alternative locations for some of the items. In such cases, determine which things can logically go elsewhere. For example, shoes, hats, and gloves can be separated by individual household members and placed in their individual bedrooms. You should also look just outside the closet door to create places to store items that are traditionally placed in a coat closet. A foyer chest, bench, armoire, dresser, or wall organizer can hold countless items.

Leaving a front hall closet half full to save room for guest coats is an antiquated concept. A portable coatrack that can be broken down and stored away is good for guests' outerwear and can also be repurposed as a garment rack for a garage sale. This way, you can make permanent use of your closet space all year long.

Organizing the Front Hall Closet

Start by first emptying out all the contents currently in the front hall closet. Next, sort belongings into like groups and then split the pile by household member. For example, place all your winter coats in a pile and then subdivide them by family member. This is important to do since you may need to console some individuals about reducing their things. Downsize any inventories you have control over first; those that need another person can be placed aside until they're ready to help.

You want to establish rules to control closet clutter. For example, allow no more than two in-season jackets, gloves, hats, scarves, shoes, boots, and the like per person. Plan to remove the excess by relocating, donating, selling, and so on. Now is the time to make good decisions about what should stay in the front hall closet and what should be relocated. Even if the front hall closet has the room for certain items, it still may be better to move certain items into other closets, rooms, or different home entry points if they're the more convenient places for easy access.

If not already in place, begin a system so off-season articles are removed from the coat closet and held at another location. You should have a set of storage containers labeled off-season coat closet or labeled with the name of the articles.

Downsizing Outerwear, Footwear, and Accessories

When downsizing wearable items like coats, hats, gloves, and shoes, look them over closely to ensure sure all buttons are present and not loose. Test zippers and snaps. Check for stains, rips, and tears. On footwear, look over both heels and soles.

Generally, wearable items that are in good condition but have not been worn in the past two years are likely to never be worn. Find out why the item is not worn and see if it's correctable. Perhaps a minor

detail, like changing the buttons, is in order. This is your opportunity to take charge and fix the problem, rather than procrastinating. If the work or expense is too much effort for the return, it's time to donate or sell the items.

Bag all articles that need special attention like fur storage, shoe repair, and cleaning. Make sure that you really want to keep things before making the effort to preserve or properly care for them, because doing so is time consuming and expensive. Have household members choose the coats and shoes *they* want hanging in the front hall closet. Again, limit to only a few coats, shoes, and so on per person.

You should end your decluttering session with bags of items to donate, sell, repair, alter, and clean on their way to their next destination. For example, donation bags should be loaded in the car or

Sidewall Entryway Closet

FIGURE 22.01
Entry closet with side shelving and hanging rods

115

a call should have been made for a pickup. Items to sell should be boxed, labeled, and placed in a designated storage place for them.

Outerwear Storage

Most outerwear should be hung on a rod for jackets and coats to maintain their shape. However, it may be more convenient to use hooks for children's jackets so they're more easily accessible. Over-the-door or door-mounted coatracks with hooks can also be used. These organizers free up valuable hanging-rod space. Double-hung hanging rods are perfect for closets short on space. However, there should also be enough room to have a rod for long coats.

In very shallow front closets, hanging rods can be mounted on the sides of the closet,

SidE-Hanging Rods

FIGURE 22.02
Hang rods from sidewalls in shallow closets

perpendicular to the door and facing each other, instead of the conventional way. This is a good solution when thick coats and jackets don't clear a closed door.

Footwear Storage

The most important thing to accomplish with footwear storage design is not to end up storing any loose shoes on the floor, no matter how well they're initially lined up. Inevitably, order will be lost, and the closet floor will become a mess. Footwear can be stored in a number of organizers. All closet systems have footwear storage components, such as slanted shelving, pullout shoe racks, and cubby organizers. These footwear organizers are best placed at eye level and below, so everything is easy to see and reach.

The most common footwear organizers to add to an existing closet are shoe-cubby pocket organizers that suspend from a hanging rod. However, these organizers are prone to sag when weighted down with too many shoes, so keep loads light. These organizers are commonly found in canvas, but they're made in plastic, as well, for easier cleaning. Make sure that you are still able to share the hanging-rod space, so jackets and coats can move freely.

Door-mounted or over-the-door shoe organizers free closet space. Door organizers that use wire arch-shaped loops in the shape of a shoe or upright prongs to secure footwear are stable and vent the footwear. Over-the-door pocketed shoe organizers tend to have tighter pockets, making them suitable only for slim footwear.

Freestanding cubby or tiered-shelf shoe organizers designed for floor storage come in many sizes and materials. Some are even movable and have casters for optimal access. Be careful when selecting cubby organizers, because they're generally not adjustable and many have small compartments that cannot fit boots or even chunky shoes.

The bottom shelf of a floor-based shoe organizer should almost touch the ground so you are not wasting any space. Doing so will cover the floor and avoid the chance that shoes wind up lying on the ground, which leads to disorder.

Scarves, Hats, and Gloves

Gather all outwear accessories throughout the home and sort them into different groups, such as dress gloves, ski gloves, fleece gloves, mittens, ear muffs, ski hats, headbands, scarves, and so on. Match up pairs of gloves or mittens. Place single gloves missing their mates in the same place you keep single socks that are not paired. Pin a note with the current date to the glove or mitten so you are able to keep track of how much time passes, so you're not keeping them forever. Discard such socks or gloves in a month's time after making an earnest search for the mate.

Check your outerwear accessories for rips, stains, and wear. Anything outgrown or not worn in the past two seasons should be donated or sold. Each household member may need two pairs of casual hats, gloves, and scarves. It may be necessary to have a number of pairs of each to accommodate extensive collections of outerwear involving many colors, but think conservatively and stick with what is actually worn. Additionally,

dress or work outerwear accessories, or both, may require another set.

Outerwear accessories can be divided and stored in separate bins, containers, or baskets. Each group can store a single person's accessories or hold a separate category like gloves. Label containers with their contents. Use glove clips to keep pairs together in a storage container so they're easy to locate. Over-the-door or wall-mounted clear, pocketed organizers easily divide individual pairs of gloves and keep them visible and accessible. Towel bars mounted onto the backside of a closet door can hold gloves and hats with rod clips. Scarves can hang over rods tied in place.

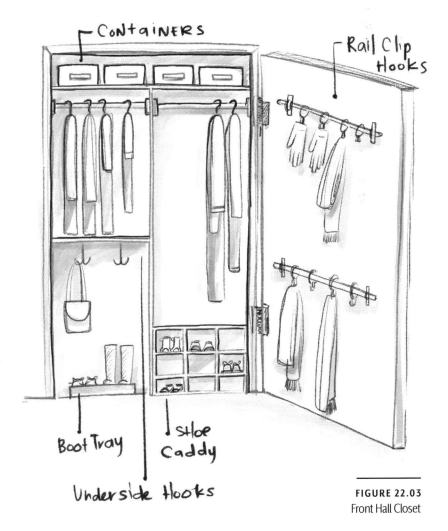

FIGURE 22.03
Front Hall Closet

CHAPTER 23

Front Hall or Coat Closet: Miscellaneous Items

The next things to consider for storage in a front hall closet are those items not needed in any particular room, making them logical to store there. When such articles already reside in the front hall closet or you desire them at this location, they'll need to go through a downsizing process. The following covers belongings good to house in a front hall closet, along with how to declutter and arrange them in this space.

Photos and Home Films/Videos

First, make sure your front hall closet is a safe place to store your photos, discs, home videos/films, and the like; they require a cool, dry, and dark storage place or are subject to damage. Now is a good time to replace tattered photo albums or the containers holding photos, negatives, or videos.

If you are certain about updating everything into a newer technological format, don't bother arranging space in your front hall closet for these items right now. Box everything up and place them aside. Continue organizing the closet without these items, and leave space for the newly

converted items. After conversion, save all the tapes or videos and relocate them outside the front hall closet in a space safe from damaging elements like heat, sun, and humidity.

Now is not the time to pull out all your printed photos and work on placing them in chronological order, especially if your pictures are in a state of chaos, as these projects can take weeks or even months. Concentrate primarily on storing photos, discs, videos, and negatives in storage essentials designed especially for them, so they're well preserved. For example, loose photos can be shuffled into neat piles and placed inside archival photo boxes or matching albums. Matching photo organizers look neat stacked or filed on a shelf. When organizing printed photos, label the boxes or albums with the year(s) they were taken and use the inside pages or dividers for event details.

For loose photo discs outside protective jewel cases, place them into a ring binder with pocketed pages to secure them or buy new jewel cases. These albums are portable and can stack in a basket or rest like books on a shelf. There are many different types of organizers designed to store CDs, such as wall-mounted, desktop, album, freestanding, carousel, and suitcase-style versions, and you'll have no problem finding a good arrangement for them in your front hall closet.

Print Photos: Plan For Extra Organizing Time

If you have not tried to organize your photos for many years, trying to place pictures in a chronological order and putting like events together can take months. But you owe it to future generations to organize them now, so they can be cherished. Consider the possibility that you may only have limited time to ask elders in the family who are in certain pictures and in what year they were taken. Pictures of nameless faces or with unrecorded dates may be discarded one day since they may be viewed as worthless.

The first thing to understand before organizing your printed photos is that almost any state of disorganization will most likely require more than just one sitting. Therefore, find a big space where you can spread out and divide your photos; an uninterrupted place like an unused dining room is perfect. You could also set up cardboard tables in a remote spot. Carve out time in your calendar for organizing photos, but don't make the sessions too long.

Gather all the printed photos from around the house and empty any disorganized photo boxes and albums. Place all your pictures next to your workspace, but not on the tabletop area. In batches, move printed photos onto the workspace and separate them into containers marked according to photo size, such as eight-by-ten inches, five-by-seven inches, four-by-six inches, and so on.

When finished, move containers aside and organize one at a time. Sort printed photos by placing them into piles according to the year they were taken. Many photos are already date-stamped,

but those that are not need your best guess or the help of a friend or other family members. People in the pictures are usually the best ones to contact if you need help with dates and places. When you cannot determine the year a picture or set of prints were taken, stuff them in an envelope and pin it onto your memo board. In your spare time, see if you can contact someone that could help you determine the time period.

After sorting photos by year, sort them by season or month. It's usually easy to tell approximately what time of year a photo was taken since certain events like holidays giveaway the month. Also, in seasonal climates, how people are dressed in the photos pinpoints the season. Finally, group them by an event or the day the pictures were shot. You can usually put together photos that were taken at the same time because people in the photos would be wearing the same clothes.

At this stage, you'll be able to notice any duplicate photos, which can be given away or discarded. If you choose to hold onto them, use a photo-safe marker and label the backside of each duplicate with the date, event, and people in the photograph. Photo-safe storage boxes are good containers for duplicates. Consider discarding the photos that are blurry or meaningless; don't make the common mistake of keeping every single photograph.

Pictures can be arranged in different ways, but chronologically by year is logical and prevents confusion. For example, categorizing your photos in classifications like friends and family can lead to overlap since a friend could also be in a family photo, making it impossible to divide a picture between two categories.

Photo Albums

Ideally, you want archival-quality photo-safe albums that contain both acid-free and lignin-free paper. Otherwise, your photos will be prone to fade or discolor over time. Additionally, the plastic slip should be made from polyester or polypropylene materials, not PVC that is found in older albums since this can also degrade photo quality. Definitely discard any older magnetic-style photo albums with the sticky pages since they contain damaging chemicals that will harm photos over time. Also, the adhesive tends to dry up, which causes the photos to fall out. Photo albums should have a contents label on the spine. Photo pages should notate the date, people, and event of the pictures.

The easiest photo albums to use are those with slip-in pockets:

- Book-bound albums with slip-in pages have a fixed number of photo pockets. You could control the number of photos contained in these albums to a degree by simply not using all the pages and finishing the album where a group of pictures end.
- Ring-binder albums come with refillable slip-in photo sheets, and you decide how many to use.
- Photo albums that contain blank pages, which are used for scrapbooking, require the most imagination and work to lay out. When incorporating decorative scrapbooking essentials, make sure they're acid-free and lignin-free for optimal photo preservation. A benefit to a blank-page photo album is that you can store both large and small photos inside the same album.

Photo-Storage Boxes

Photo-storage boxes are commonly formed in a shoebox style and do have some advantages. Typically, they have divider index cards and metal identification holders on the outside for labels. It's easy to divide photo boxes since you can control the number of pictures contained in each box, including adding new ones.

Photo-storage boxes should be made of an acid-free board construction. They're primarily designed for shelf storage, as they're stackable. They come in many decorative styles and are attractive to display openly. Photo boxes are reusable, and they can store a countless number of other household items, should needs change.

Once all your photos are in order, it's time to count them. Record the number of all the photos you have in a particular year and month, as well as the names of the events. This will allow you to know how many albums or boxes you'll need for a given set of photos since these organizers have predetermined capacities.

Photo Albums versus Boxes

It's generally best to keep all your photos in either photo boxes or albums, not both, for the sake of consistency. It also keeps storage arrangements uniform and easier to configure. Photo album storage may be a safer bet over photo-storage boxes, because when photos are taken out of a storage box they're subject to fingerprints, tears, and loss. Also, when viewing photos, you must be careful to put them back in the right order since photos pulled from many categories are easy to mix up.

When you start to fill up your photo albums or storage boxes, begin the process with your earliest photos first. It's important to have your photo organizers finish with a particular set of photos, as to not carry them into another album or box, even if this involves not filling an organizer to capacity.

Negatives

Photo negatives, which can make a perfect copy of a photo, need the same type of preservation requirements as the photos themselves. However, photo labs now use PVC-free photo sleeves to wrap around the negatives. You can purchase archival negative sleeves and place any unprotected negatives inside. Store negative sleeves inside archival boxes in order by month and year, using index card dividers.

You can also store negatives in archival-quality pocketed sheets in three-ring binders. Label the sheets with the month, year, and event. It's a good idea to switch over your old 35mm negatives and photo slides into a digital format. The photo negatives and slides are scanned and transferred. Since physical negatives and slides have a limited life, it's important to transfer them as soon as possible. Some people like to discard outdated negatives and slides once they have been transferred to digital, but it may not be a bad idea to hold onto them and wait for technology to advance to the point where you can possibly scan with higher resolution.

Home Movies

All home movies, including film reels, VHS, Betamax, mini DV, DVDs, and movie slides can be organized at the same time. Recognize that anything recorded onto magnetic tape has only a ten- to thirty-year maximum shelf life. Improper storage or simply playing and rewinding magnetic tapes creates wear. The longer you wait to digitize, the more your tapes will degrade and no longer be watchable.

Standard 8mm, Super 8mm, and 16mm require such demanding storage requirements that it's best to consult a professional film archivist so your film does not disintegrate to the point of permanent damage. Use a professional to transfer footage into a digital format since the equipment is expensive and technical. Other types of data transferring, like VHS to DVD or digital file, can be done on a purchased or rented equipment. Alternatively, you can use a service to transfer this type of data, and until this technology becomes more obsolete, many of these services are competitively priced and relatively affordable. Generally, the older the format, the fewer people with data-transfer knowledge and the proper equipment will be available to help.

Digital Storage Options

Digital storage is the optimal storage method because all the alternatives are subject to physical degradation and are becoming so antiquated that they're no longer viewable or transferable to new technology. It's fine to keep and use the latest hard-copy technology, but also make backups of your collections. For example, convert your movie library to cloud-friendly digital files so you can store those files on a server and stream them to a viewing platform of your choice from anywhere, anytime.

Think about transferring films, tapes, and printed photos into a digital format, if you have not already done so. In many cases, the newer technology is necessary for extending the life of your memories and will take up less space. Computer and cloud-based storage eliminate physical storage altogether.

When you digitize your CD and DVD libraries, you can watch movies and listen to music on electronics that don't have a CD/DVD disc drive, such as your tablet, smartphone, laptop, gaming console, and smart TV. There is no need to worry about disc damage from loss, fire, scratches, and so on. You can also upgrade to high definition. Another major advantage is the ease in retrieving and deleting movies and music, once digitized.

Data is also permanently saved in cloud storage. Remember, though, that not every copyrighted movie can go from disc to digital—only those that support a licensed digital copy.

Computer Hard Drives/ External Hard Drives

Backing up photos and videos onto a computer's hard drive can hog RAM, and it's not foolproof because computers can crash. People are turning to other avenues now—an external hard drive is one solution. These devices last longer than your computer's hard drive since they're not constantly running. An external hard drive is compact and portable, so you can carry your pictures with you to share with others. They also have a larger storage capacity over both computers and discs. Keep your external hard drives in a special case when not in use, to safeguard against fire, floods, and theft.

Online Cloud Storage Service

There are many online cloud storage services to choose from for your digital data, each one offering different features, services, and pricing; some are even free. These services take a portion of your hard drive and synchronize it with the company's online storage. When changes are made to a computer's hard drive, they're replicated on the cloud storage and backed up. Apple's iCloud is a well-known one.

These companies maintain a network of servers in various locations so if one crashes, another will have your memories saved. For these reasons, cloud storage is considered the safest and most secure place to store and backup digital data. Another benefit to online cloud storage is the ability to share your videos and photos via social networks, email, and text. Online digital data in the cloud can also be accessed from multiple connected sources, like a television, smartphone, tablet, and so on.

Disc Storage

When saving photos into a disc format first originated, it was a big step from tape storage. The shelf life for them ranges from seventy to one hundred years. The storage capacity per disc will depend upon the type of disc used, such as CD or DVD. Although strong, discs can break and should always be stored properly. A paper sleeve is better storage choice than a spindle device, which causes scratches, but nothing compares to jewel cases for optimal protection. Always keep discs out of the sunlight and away from excessive temperatures.

Consider digitizing your CD and DVDs as more storage space is available since there is no reason to keep your hard copies. Reselling DVD and CD discs offers a small return for time. You can always recycle discs and cases.

CD and DVD Media Storage

Think about the rapid changes in technology that will make your current media storage organization obsolete one day. Therefore, don't make too big of an investment in storage essentials. The following lists the pros and cons of various disc-storage methods.

DVD and CD Jewel Cases

While the most protective, individual jewel cases do add extra mass to disc storage, which is something to consider if you have big collections of CDs and DVDs and limited space. Cases are strong, so there are many storage options: boxes, drawers, or filed on a shelf. There are wall, floor, and portable organizers designed to hold them. Cases are easy to label and identify at a glance, and it's easy to replace or create a new cover. Explore CD/DVD-cover websites that archive custom-made, professional jacket covers. You can also create labels with a graphics editing program.

Consider how you want to categorize your music or movies when your libraries are extensive. Arrange in an order that makes things easy to locate quickly and maintain. Large collections of diverse music can be sorted by genre and then artist. Movies are best stored by title; only big libraries would be sorted by genre and then title.

Multimedia Storage Units

Organizers made specifically to hold individual jewel cases come in different sizes and shapes and can be added to a front hall closet. The best ones to invest in are those with adjustable shelves to change them when technology alters the shape and size of your music. The advantage to these organizers is that they hold music in their protective cases. The problem is the huge space demand. They also get dusty and are not portable.

Crate-Style and Lidded Box Media Storage

Containing jewel cases in box organizers has the benefit of mobility. Many media storage containers are stackable. Some media organizers can divide different genres or artists with tab inserts to color-code categories. Select containers that have grip handles.

Megastorage CD Players/Changers

It's convenient for your audio player store all your CDs. There are CD players that can store several hundred CD and play any one you choose with the flip of a remote control, similar to an old-time jukebox. A menu displays on a screen to show all your CD choices. You could have a spreadsheet in numeric order of all your CDs to correspond with your CD player.

If you have the space, these devices can reside on a front hall closet shelf with the speakers wired to your living space so your equipment remains out of sight. The downside to this CD storage arrangement is that your CDs are not easily mobile. However, you can place a stack of jewel cases next to your CD player and eject those you want to transport at any given time.

Wallet Cases

Wallet cases store discs outside their protective cases. Wallet cases are ring-style binders that have slip pages for discs, eliminating individual cases and dramatically reducing storage space, which is their biggest asset. Wallet cases can be filed on a shelf or in a drawer or basket. These binders save the hassle of having to locate and return music to a particular case, which is usually why there is so much disorder among them. The binders are conveniently portable and make classifying music easy. You can color-code binders by genre. For example, put classical music in the red wallet case. It's easy to alphabetize artists or bands because the first page can start with *A* and descend from that point.

The downside to wallet cases is that you are more apt to fingerprint the front and back of your discs. Sliding discs in and out of plastic could possibly scratch them, especially if debris becomes caught in the pockets.

Carrying Cases

A carrying case is a good organizer should you need to transport your music. However, be cautious when handling carrying cases because even though they have secure shoulder straps or handles, disc damage could occur if the case drops or music falls out while in transport. You also have to be more careful about avoiding extreme temperatures and sunlight while transporting discs from place to place. Carrying cases are easy to store on closet shelves or even off a hook since they have straps and handles.

Over-the-Door Racks

There are door racks specifically designed to store DVDs, CDs and video games to their exact dimensions. These devices are typically made of a wire construction and consist of a single-mounted track in which storage baskets attach. The downside to these organizers are that they're hard to reuse should needs change.

Closet Shelves

The most versatile organizer for a closet is shelving, which can house discs in a number of ways. Any desktop media storage organizer can rest on a shelf, or individual CD and DVD cases can stack or file on a shelf. It's best for a shelf's depth to correspond to the size of the organizer or article stored on it, for more efficient storage.

Audio and Video (AV) Equipment

Cameras, camcorders, projectors, headphones, cables, and the like are often stored in a front hall closet. It's important to first sort all these items into like groups. Tally how many items of each type of equipment and acknowledge who they belong to in the home. Decide if household members want their personal AV equipment in the own spaces before making the decision to keep them in one central place.

Each and every device must actually be used to warrant taking up valuable closet space. Many times we advance to new technology and keep the older equipment for backup. Of course, what ends up usually happening is that the older models sit for eternity when they could have been sold when you first retired them to the shelf. Remember that technology moves at a rapid pace, so you are always better off selling them as soon as possible to receive top dollar.

Check to make sure that all your equipment works properly, as some items may not be functional and should be either repaired or reduced. A simple telephone call to a repair technician can usually generate a ballpark estimate of what a repair may cost, when given the description of the problem. Expensive equipment and anything still under warranty should get to a service center immediately.

AV equipment can remain in their original boxes with a picture and description of the contents. Also, it's good to keep the original box for warranty and resale purposes. Specialized carrying cases are another ideal storage essential for audio and video equipment since they're easy to identify with a brand name tag. Additionally, they're designed with compartments to store the accessories.

Audio and video cables, connectors, and cords are so important to separate, label, and bind individually with ties. It may take some investigative work, but you must find the purpose of all of them, so they don't just sit in a container unused and you're not buying unneeded duplicates. Discard any mystery cables, cords, and connectors, because they'll never receive use. Don't be tempted to keep them, thinking one day someone will figure out their purpose, because if you cannot do so today, you most likely never will. Get rid of cables and cords that are obsolete or appear faulty in any way.

Extension Cords and Power Strips

It's sometimes tricky to find storage for extension cords, power strips, surge protectors, and wire-carry systems. A hall closet is a convenient location since these items are used for so many purposes throughout a home. First, gather all these items together, which may entail going through each room and removing the unnecessary ones found lying on the floor near outlets. Next, separate into groups according to type. For example, extension cords in one pile and power strips in another. Also, separate the outdoor extension cords from the indoor ones and store the outdoor cords in the garage or tool shed.

Inspect them all and make sure they're safe to use by looking for any cracks, gouges, wear, splits, burn marks, or missing prongs since this would make them faulty and could lead to serious injuries, fires, and equipment damage. Discard any that are unsafe or even questionable. Also consider getting rid of surplus amounts of these items. A typical household should stock no more three of each type: outdoor extension cords, indoor extension cords, power strips, and surge protectors.

Since indoor extension cords tend to be thinner and lighter, you can use one bin for everything as long as your inventories are small so the container is not too heavy to lift. Another idea is to use several smaller containers and divide extension cords according to use, size, and wattage. You may also want to label the number of prongs like two, three, or specialty types. Bind cords with Velcro strips, twist ties, or cord clips, and use a tag to label the lengths of the cords. Also, you could separate cords using individual baggies and label them.

Pet Supplies

A front hall closet near the door where your pet exits the home is an ideal place to situate certain pet belongings, such as leashes, collars, toys, plastic bags, strollers, muzzles, and carriers. Many pet items with loops, like leashes, can be hung on wall hooks or coatracks installed on the closet wall. You can also hang nylon bags to hold batches of plastic bags, clothes, and toys from hooks. Many pet accessories can be stored in wall-mounted baskets or bins or in shelf containers like open baskets. Store seldom-needed pet items, like carriers, strollers, and pens, on overhead shelves.

Cleaning Machines

It's better to contain your household cleaning machines in the same closet as your cleaning supplies. However, this is not always possible in many homes. When there is spare floor space in a front hall closet, it can be a good home for a vacuum cleaner or floor steamer, provided they receive regular use. Infrequently used cleaning machines, like a carpet cleaner, should be contained in box and placed in a remote spot or on an upper closet shelf.

Sewing Kits and Board Games

A small-scale sewing kit filled with just basics to perform a quick repair is good to have around the home in an easy-to-access place like the front hall closet. You can use a specialized sewing box or an inexpensive, compartmentalized fishing-tackle box to separate small items, like thread, needles, and scissors. An overhead shelf is a good spot for a sewing kit in a front hall closet.

It's hard to find good storage places for items like board games; a front hall closet can be a good place when the games are used in a nearby room. Shelves or hanging-shelf-cubby organizers can keep board games visible and easy to access.

PART THREE

Kitchens

CHAPTER 24

Kitchen Organization Overview

Organizing a kitchen covers sorting, reducing, and arranging three primary areas: First, kitchen utensils, appliances, dishes, cookware, and so on need to be thoroughly decluttered and properly arranged. Then all foods, such as dry goods and perishables, should be reduced and situated in kitchen cabinets, pantries, and the refrigerator. And third since a great deal of cleaning takes place in the kitchen, the cleaning tools, appliances, and entire sink area also need to be well organized. This chapter discusses how to successfully sort, reduce, and arrange the three components of a kitchen.

The kitchen, traditionally a place to cook, bake, and eat, has increasingly become the hub of family life. It's no wonder that hordes of clutter make their way to the kitchen countertops, floors, tables, and chairs. The more disorganized a kitchen becomes, the more likely additional clutter will form because the new clutter will not look out of place.

Kitchen belongings alone make the room challenging to organize. When factoring in other articles that often find themselves in the kitchen, we can find ourselves confused about what actually belongs in this space. Since so many things compete for kitchen space, it's important to pick the most important items and then determine the best storage locations for them.

It's a good idea to get mentally ready to pursue your kitchen organizational project since it's usually the most challenging home space to successfully organize. At your leisure, purchase decorator kitchen magazines for inspiration, or locate magazines that feature organizational tips for kitchens. Clip and save the articles that interest you and take note of ideas you would like to copy in your kitchen.

There are so many aspects to kitchen organization—such as planning, sorting, decluttering, purchasing, installing, and cleaning—that spreading the project over time makes the most sense. Organizing your kitchen over a period of time will afford you the opportunity to plan well and think through your decisions. The best strategy for managing an organizational project is to create a schedule in your calendar, as you would for any important appointment, to plan time for uninterrupted organizational sessions. A kitchen put in proper order will save you money at the grocery store and time searching for things; it only makes sense to invest quality time to organize this space.

Be true to your decorative tastes when it comes to selecting organizational arrangements and choosing storage organizers since they relate to each other. Decide whether you desire a showpiece kitchen (where articles are hidden out of sight), or if you prefer the look of open storage. It's also necessary to establish realistic expectations about your kitchen, based on your budget and your kitchen's actual potential, when it comes to outfitting it with organizational systems and organizers.

Popular Organizational Strategies for Kitchens

There are several ways to organize a kitchen, and it's important to select the approach that fits your personality and lifestyle. How you organize your kitchen will be different from anyone else, because your kitchen space and household members' needs are unique. Getting started with any organizational project is the hardest part for most people, which is why scheduling organizational time is essential to initiate action. There are a number of popular practices designed to assist in the creation of an organized kitchen.

Sort, Reduce, and Arrange

One practice taught by organizational professionals is to first empty all the articles from their current kitchen locations, such as cabinets, pantries, and closets. Then sort, reduce, and arrange them back into storage. When you empty out all the kitchen inventories from their storage locations at the same time, everything usually winds up spread out all over the kitchen counters and tables. This can be chaotic and may cause the

organizer to feel pressured and rushed, which may lead to poor decisions and results. Therefore, in most cases, it's more manageable for people to spread out this organizational project with a planned schedule in place.

Zoning

Another popular method is establishing certain work zones where the kitchen space is divided according to a specific function, such as baking or cooking. Each zone is located in the best location for its function and is equipped with all the essentials to perform the tasks. For instance, a cooking zone is placed next to the stove. Although kitchen work zones are logical and convenient, there can be problems with establishing and using them. For a few specialized workstations, a kitchen would need ample counter space typically not found in the average home.

Zoning involves dividing and storing the proper utensils, bowls, pots, pans, and ingredients within a specific area, as opposed to a more general arrangement, which could be too detailed to maintain. Kitchen zones can also be confusing for household members with little culinary knowledge, which makes finding things more difficult. And what to do with multipurpose articles that can go in more than one zone? This may require the need for duplicate items, which would not be necessary if things where arranged in a more general manner.

Kitchen zoning is a useful concept in the right home but not critical for effective organization. A zone-free kitchen requires only that you take more steps when you gather your kitchen belongings from various locations before preparing to bake or cook. Remember: the most time-consuming thing to do in the kitchen is to clean it, not round up items used to prepare a meal.

Organize in Manageable Steps

The best approach to organizing your kitchen which is particularly useful when dealing with large quantities of items or kitchens: turn the job into manageable parts or steps. In fact, the easiest way to put any room—but particularly a kitchen—in order is to do so in stages. Kitchens have many different groups of items and areas that are easy to divide, such as dry goods, dishes, closets, or refrigerator. For this reason, it's easy to declutter, arrange, and plan for new storage essentials or bigger items like closet systems on one such group of items or area at a time.

An individual step can address a specific task, such as reducing dry goods from a pantry or decluttering the sink area. It's necessary to estimate the amount of time it may take to complete each step in order to figure out how many steps you can handle in a given amount of time. Then schedule that organizational time in your calendar.

Have a budget in place for the kitchen storage organizers or systems. Don't purchase any organizers until after you have completely sorted and reduced all your kitchen inventories. Only at this time would you know how much you have of each inventory, which is necessary information when selecting the various organizers.

The following steps are designed to end at a place where the organizer can stop and still maintain order in the room. When you organize in steps, it's important to never start another step when tired. Always plan a generous amount of time for each step. You never want to feel rushed or leave a step unfinished in the organizational process.

Optional Step One: Create a
Kitchen Inventory List

Purchase a binder or notebook with pockets to record and store pertinent information about your kitchen organizational project. Use this notebook to record all the useful information, such as storage dimensions, ideas, and desired storage essentials. Use your notebook to create lists while you organize. Make a maintenance list that contains all the side projects you find while organizing, such as tightening cabinet hinges or fixing cracked tiles. Simply writing down maintenance problems as you organize will make them less of a distraction as you work.

Create a shopping list of articles you discover need replacement, such as worn dish towels or broken utensils. Don't be tempted to purchase the items until you are completely through organizing your kitchen, though. It's easier to get a clear picture of what is actually needed, as opposed to wanted, when you have a complete shopping list. Items that you need are priority and should be acquired first. Items that you want can wait for a good sale.

The key to maximizing storage space is picking a storage essential that fit snugly. Visit various merchant websites or browse shops to pick out storage essentials. In your notebook's pocket section, store magazine photos of kitchens you like and keep product information and photos of organizers, so when it's time to shop you have all your research in one place.

Make a measurement list of all the storage compartments you currently have in your kitchen. For example, record the pantry's height, length, and width.

Create a storage-essentials list that consists of various organizers or storage systems you would *like* to purchase for your kitchen. Record each item's dimensions and cost and then plan your budget accordingly. Knowing the dimensions of both your storage spaces *and* organizers will help you plan your kitchen space with accuracy.

Step Two: Eliminate Paper Clutter

Before you begin your kitchen organizational project, complete all the kitchen chores, such as emptying the dishwasher or taking out the trash. The first thing to do before you start organizing the kitchen is to get rid of everything that does not obviously belong there. Paper clutter is the easiest thing to attack first. When you find newspapers, periodicals, bills, receipts, and the like littering the kitchen counters or drawers, it's time to devise a plan to stop this from happening in the future.

A good way to reduce this problem is to place mail and magazine organizers in entry ways, offices, hallways, or the kitchen. Use organizers—such as accordion expanding folders, file crates, hanging folders, desktop files, coupon organizers, check-file boxes, and photo boxes—to contain paper items. Such organizers can be stored in cabinets, drawers, and shelves at various locations throughout the home. A simple bin placed on a desk or console can collect papers that won't receive immediate attention, like unopened mail or unread catalogs and magazines. These strategies should help curtail some the paper clutter that commonly finds its way to kitchen counters and tables.

First, take all the paper clutter you currently have in the kitchen and sort it in a large open area like the dining room table. Group items into like piles, such as school papers, bills, receipts, and so on. While sorting the paper items, discard those you no longer need. If you have a paper shredder, use it. Safeguard fraud and identity theft by shredding all personal documents no longer needed. Keep warranties, bills, receipts, current schedules, calendars, tickets, bank statements, tax information, invitations, and the like.

Hang one or two pieces of your children's artwork on the refrigerator or frame the special pieces and toss the rest. (More is coming!) Keeping one or two old letters or greeting cards is reasonable, but a pile is not. Pitch any papers with information that can be generated via the internet. Eliminate the majority of directions for products or places and anything else that can be accessed on the internet. Keep only automobile, television, computer, or stereo manuals that would be cumbersome to replicate. These types of manuals are good to keep for when you sell the item. Lastly, always consider scanning and digitally saving first before keeping most forms of paperwork.

Step 3: Remove Unrelated Kitchen Items

Once you have eliminated the paper clutter, remove other items that have taken over the kitchen and really belong in other rooms. A good way to relocate items from the kitchen is to first sort them into similar groups and eliminate the useless items before you waste time transferring and containerizing them. Once done, select the most logical places for them in the home. For example, flashlights and candles make sense to store in a mudroom cabinet; store insect repellant next to the first aid ointments in the linen closet. Once you have determined where to best relocate those items, decide whether purchasing a container, organizer, or box is in order.

You may find that some of these items are left in the kitchen because they have no designated storage space elsewhere. If so, now is the time to devise a system to successfully containerize and relocate them. Through this process, it's common to find it's not possible to remove everything you want to out of the kitchen due to space limitations elsewhere. If this is the case, carefully select the most convenient ones to keep in the kitchen and find the proper organizers. When you transfer inventories to a disorganized space, you'll want to hold off on purchasing an organizer. For the time being, you can use an inexpensive cardboard box and record the contents on the outside.

Step 4: Declutter Kitchen Belongings

Now that you have cleared away unnecessary belongings from the room, you are ready to sort and reduce your kitchen items. Eliminating kitchen items is not easy, so the best way to influence quick decision making is always sort first and downsize second. When you sort everything first, it's easy to then get rid of stuff because you can see exactly how much you have of each inventory, making it easier to part with unnecessary excess. Alternatively, when you find that certain inventories are low, replacements or additions may be necessary. You can record the need for these items on a shopping list, which can be addressed once organizing is over.

Kitchenware

Kitchenware encompasses a broad range of articles found in a kitchen, but all are associated with preparing, serving, and storing of foods or beverages. These items can be broken down into categories according to function.

Food and Beverage Preparation

The preparation of foods and beverages can utilize different cookware, bakeware, preparation and cooking utensils, and small appliances. Cookware and bakeware are vessels used in the heating or freezing process.

Tableware

Tableware includes all the kitchenware utensils used to serve and eat food or beverages during mealtime. Common kitchenware items found at the table are dishes, forks, spoons, drinking glasses, serving platters and knives.

The following several chapters address each type of kitchenware. You can organize kitchenware items in any order, but here we will start with the cookware. Each step covers downsizing strategies and storage solutions. At these stages in your kitchen organizational project, make sure to completely reduce each inventory. Then put your kitchen items back in the most logical spots for their unique uses, even if that involves shifting other inventories around. Only *after* all the kitchen articles are completely reduced should you make final storage arrangements. Before you start the reducing process, have boxes ready for donation, selling, trash, and relocation.

Kitchens

Organizing a kitchen includes sorting, reducing, and arranging three primary areas:

1) kitchen utensils, appliances, dishes, cookware, and so on

2) all foods, such as dry goods and perishables

3) cleaning tools, appliances, and entire sink area

CHAPTER 25

Cookware

Cookware contains foods and beverages for use on a stove or range cooktop when cooking. Examples of cookware are stockpots and frying pans.

Organize the Cookware

Gather all your cookware from current storage locations, including any stored outside the kitchen area, and place it on a large workspace. Match all the lids with to their corresponding pots or pans. Begin by sorting the different types, such as the following categories:

1. Everyday/Frequently Used

Skillets, sauté pans, saucepans, frying pans/splatter screens, multipot sets (stockpot, pasta insert, streamer basket), and versatile bakeware sets (meaning your stoneware or glass bakeware sets that can also function like pots and pans).

2. Specialty/Infrequently Used

Tagines, braisers, sauciers, roasters, stockpots, ramekins, rondeaus, polenta pots, paella pans, buffet pans, chef's pans, crepe pans, soufflé dishes, Dutch ovens, fondue pots, risotto pans, lobster pot, egg poachers, pancake pans, fish poachers, lasagna pans, quiche dishes, meat loaf pan, double boilers, reduction pots, garlic roasters, smoker cookers, potato steamers, casserole dishes, tarte tatin pans, bamboo steamers, onion soup bowls, mini cocotte pots, stir fry pans/woks, pizza pans and stones, U-shaped roasting racks, and stovetop popcorn poppers.

3. Grills, Griddles, and Broiler Pans

Mesh pans, panini sets, broiler pans, presses, grill pans, and griddles.

Downsize Your Cookware

Once you have finished sorting your cookware, you can begin to downsize your collections. It's necessary to tabulate how often a piece of cookware is actually used, as compared with how many times you could possibly use it.

Reducing Everyday Cookware

Start with your everyday pots and pans. First, get rid of the ones that are badly worn, hard to use, or have damage not worth repair, such as broken handles. Then consider how many pots and pans you use at a given time to judge how low you can carry your cookware inventories. A few well-made, expensive pots and pans designed for multiple purposes are better than many lower-quality pots and pans you purchased at a savings because you bought the whole set.

Reducing Specialty Cookware

In almost every case, only one of each type of specialty pot or pan is necessary. The real challenge is determining which pieces you truly need and will use. In many instances an everyday, multipurpose pot or pan can be used in place of certain specialty cookware. Some specialty pieces overlap in function, which could be a reason why some of your specialty cookware is not used. Determine whether some of your specialty cookware pieces are being neglected because they're clumsy or hard to clean.

Reducing Stovetop Grills, Griddles, and Broiler Pans

Sort these items by first grouping them by type (grill, griddle, or broiler pan). Then separate them according to size. Group the double-burner grills and griddles together with the broiler pans. Keep the round and rectangular pieces designed for single burners separate.

Decide which pieces serve the most use in your kitchen. Households with many members would benefit from griddles or grills that span across two burners. Reversible grill and griddle combinations are most desirable and should be kept over pieces that serve only one purpose. At most, keep two

of each type of stovetop grill and griddle or the maximum amount the stove can handle at one time. Broiler pans must have different features in order to justify storing more than one.

Cookware Storage Solutions

Ideally, pots and pans should be stored in the low base cabinets near the stove due to their weight and size and for convenience. Base cabinets (those below counters) are generally deep, which make them ideal storage places for bulky cookware. Corner base cabinets, which are harder to access, benefit from a rotating lazy Susan organizer for heavy cookware that would not budge from spinning movement.

Full-extension pullout shelves and drawers are natural organizers for pots and pans in many base kitchen cabinets, closets, or pantries. These organizers come in different forms, from the common shallow-drawer versions to those with wire inserts to secure pot and pan handles, similar to how a dishwasher rack is designed. There are also rollout storage racks that can be installed in cabinets or pantries that secure pots and pans by their handles.

Pots and Pans Storage

There are different ways to arrange cookware in drawers and shelves in base cabinets. Nesting like pots and pans is the best way to conserve storage space. Use a lid organizer nearby, like a shelf lid rack or cabinet door-mounted lid organizer. Store pots that cannot nest with their lids intact. Keep frequently used pots and pans on the upper shelves or in drawers and lesser-used cookware, like stock pots, in lower shelves or drawers.

Kitchen storage arrangements for pots and pans will be influenced by the level of culinary skills household members possess. Some cooks maintain kitchens that are suited to frequent cooking for guests, in which multiple courses and generous portions are prepared. Therefore, specialized cookware would require accessible storage locations not required in the average home. In order to maintain convenient locations for large amounts of cookware, look to the wall, floor, and ceiling for storage solutions. Chances are such kitchen operators have a professional set of cookware that can be stored on pot racks or cookware stands to free cabinet space and provide convenient access.

Cookware stands are generally triangular in shape and tuck well in an open corner. Pot racks can hang decoratively over a kitchen island, or some can attach to an open wall. Kitchens with large collections of cookware can also benefit from wall-mounted pegboards to store small sauté or ladle pans. Floor roller baskets can store additional cookware out of sight in a pantry or closet.

When storing your cookware outside the base cabinets, make certain that you are keeping like pots and pans together. Seldom-used cookware, such as fondue pots, Moroccan tagines, and the like, can be omitted from base-cabinet storage when space is limited and stored with other entertainment items like punch bowl sets and chafing dishes.

Grills/Griddles and Broiler Pans Storage

Stovetop grills/griddles and broiler pans are also good to store in base-cabinet drawers, pullouts, or shelves due to their bulk and length. As one of the healthiest ways to prepare foods, convenient placement of this type of cookware can encourage use. If your kitchen is equipped with a double oven, use the lower or less-occupied oven to store stovetop grills/griddles and boiler pans. The drawer beneath the oven is made for the broiler pans, but griddles can also occupy this space. Sideways cabinet organizers that hold large cooking sheets and the like in individual compartments are also perfect for storing griddles, grills, and broiler pans.

CHAPTER 26

Bakeware

Bakeware (ovenware) includes the heat-resistant dishes, as of glass or pottery, in which food may be baked. Bakeware is more complicated to store than most cookware pieces because bakeware pieces vary greatly in shape and size. For storage purposes, it's usually easiest to sort and group bakeware by size, rather than type. Begin organizing your bakeware by first rounding up your entire collection and sorting everything by size on a large workspace. The following list should help you keep your groups in the best order:

- Pizza crispers, stones, and peels
- Cupcake, loaf, muffin, popover, biscuit, and donut pans
- Crème brûlée ramekins or any small set of baking dishes
- Baking and cookie sheets, jelly roll pans, cooling racks, baking mats, and pastry mats
- Angel food, cake, Bundt, tarte, torte, pie, and flan pans or dishes

Some bakeware pieces are versatile enough to bake meals, such as casseroles. Should you have a set of these pans, which typically nest, place them with the cookware if they store more efficiently at that location.

Make a separate pile for all your holiday bakeware. Remove these items from the kitchen and store them with other items holiday items in order to free up valuable kitchen storage.

Reducing Bakeware

Go through the different types of bakeware, downsizing each group separately. For example, examine all the baking sheets together so you can clearly see which ones are the best. It's easier to downsize inventories when you know exactly which ones you can afford to give up. Generally, no more than two of each type of bakeware piece is necessary unless you are certain you'll use more than two at any given time.

Closely analyze all your specialty bakeware since these pieces tend to receive infrequent use simply because they're used for desserts not typically eaten on a regular basis. To justify keeping such bakeware, it's important to be able to note how often you expect to use them and remember the last time they were used. If they receive little use, consider getting rid of them. Most specialty bakeware items, such as crème brûlée cups and scone or donut pans, are unique in shape and don't store uniformly with others. For these reasons, make certain you use what you decide to keep before making the extra effort to accommodate their storage space.

Bakeware Storage Solutions

Bakeware items come in many sizes and shapes, which make them challenging to store together. It's important to find storage methods for them where they're in the same location and easy to retrieve. The following storage strategies can help you decide the best ways to effectively contain your bakeware in the kitchen.

Silicone Bakeware

Silicone bakeware is storage friendly since these pieces can be stacked, crunched, squeezed, and rolled into tight spaces. The downside to silicone is that it can rip from sharp objects. Therefore, take advantage of silicone's flexibility and protect this bakeware in tightly packed containers. Label and store these containers alongside traditional bakeware pieces.

Baking Sheets and Pans, Cooling Racks, and Pastry Mats

Most baking sheets and pans (pizza pans, cake pans, etc.), cooling racks, and pastry mats are thin and long. Therefore, it's logical to keep these items together. When you have many different types of these items, it's best to use organizers to separate them.

There are a few ways to arrange baking sheets/pans, cooling racks, and pastry mats in base cabinets. First, you can use a freestanding wire-based rack organizer which comes both adjustable and fixed. These organizers mimic a desktop file sorter, where individual items are separated in between wire panels that attach to a weighted base. Similarly, there are individual wooden dowels or whole panels that are designed to permanently mount into the walls of the cabinets. These organizers offer stable organization for all your large shallow pans. A clever drawer organizer that can hold a number of stacked baking sheets and the like is one that is installed in the toe-kick region of the base cabinet. These are thin pullout drawers which can be added to existing cabinets.

In a pantry, versatile shelving can hold freestanding divider racks to separate items such as baking sheets, pans, cooling racks, platters, and the like. Divider racks come in short lengths to accommodate shallow upper cabinets or smaller bakeware pieces, like Jell-O molds, cake pans, bread pans, and the like. Some closet-pantry systems have accessory components, like divider racks, that attach to the shelving.

In kitchens that are short on storage space, the oven can house many bakeware items. They'll fit perfectly and be out of sight.

Flatware Organizer

Crock tool organizer drawer

Toe kick drawer

Mounted bakeware racks

Kitchen Organization

FIGURE 29.01
Base Cabinet Organization

CHAPTER 27

Food-Preparation and Cooking Utensils

Food-preparation utensils come in many different forms and serve various functions. Any kitchen utensil that helps prepare food for the actual cooking or baking process is considered a preparation utensil. Examples of food-preparation utensils are a paring knife, measuring cup, and grater. Cooking utensils are typically heat-resistant, long-handled instruments that may be used during the entire food-preparation process. Such utensils come in many different materials, such as silicone, metal, ceramic, plastic, and wood. Examples of cooking utensils are spatulas, slotted spoons, and tongs.

To begin the task of organizing your food-preparation and cooking utensils, first, gather all of them from their current storage locations and place them onto a large open surface, such as an empty countertop. Next, divide your kitchen utensils into like groups, as seen on the following pages. Then determine where each type should be stored for convenience and efficiency. Before storing your utensils properly, first remove those you don't need or are damaged.

Food-Preparation- and Cooking-Utensils Categories

Everyday Utensils for Daily Use:
- Basic set of knives: paring, serrated, cleaver, chef's, slicer, and fillet knives
- Can opener
- Corkscrew
- Ice cream scooper
- Ladle
- Measuring cups and spoons
- Mixing bowls
- Pasta fork
- Peeler
- Slotted and stirring spoons
- Spatula
- Tongs
- Whisk

Specialty Food-Preparation Utensils

Baking and Pastry Utensils:
- Bench, pastry, and bowl scrapers
- Cake divider
- Cake lifter

- Cake testers
- Crumb-cake pin
- Decorating comb and icing smoother
- Dough and pastry wheels
- Dough docker
- Dough doubler
- Flour dusters and wands
- Flour sifter
- Lame bread-slashing tool
- Mixing bowls
- Pastry bags
- Pastry blender
- Pastry brushes
- Pastry shaker and dredger
- Pie chain
- Pie dam
- Rolling pin
- Sugar dusters

Canning Utensils:
- Canning funnel
- Canning knife
- Canning labels
- Jar lifter
- Jar wrench
- Lid lifter
- Magnetic lid lifter
- Peach and cherry pitters
- Pear corer
- Tongs

Chocolate Utensils:
- Candy thermometer
- Chocolate chipper fork
- Chocolate shaver
- Dipping tools
- Wooden treat sticks

Cookie Utensils:
- Cookie cutters
- Cookie press

- Cookie scoop
- Cookie shovel
- Cookie spatula

Cooking Ladles and Spoons:
- Basting spoons
- Fruit and vegetable spoons
- Mixing spoons
- Slotted, wooden, and silicone spoons
- Soup, gravy, and sauce ladles
- Spoodles
- Spoonula

Egg Utensils:
- Egg beater
- Egg fry rings
- Egg piercer
- Egg poach pods
- Egg separator
- Egg slicer
- Egg timer
- Egg topper

Fish and Seafood Utensils:
- Clam knife
- Fish pliers
- Fish turners
- Fish-bone tweezers
- Lobster mallet and crackers
- Seafood scissors
- Shrimp deveiner

Fruit and Vegetable Utensils:
- Apple cutter
- Avocado slicer and pitter
- Cherry/olive pitters
- Citrus squeezers and zesters
- Corn zipper
- Grapefruit knife and spoon

- Handheld juicer
- Lemon reamer
- Mango splitter
- Strawberry huller
- Tater King scooper
- Tomato corer
- Zucchini corer

Garlic Utensils:
- Garlic chopper
- Garlic crusher
- Garlic keeper
- Garlic press
- Garlic slicer
- Onion/garlic cooker

Garnishing Utensils:
- Apple and pineapple slicer/corer
- Butter curler
- Canapé maker
- Carrot curler
- Carving sets
- Crinkle cutter
- Fruit kabobs
- Julienne peelers
- Skewers
- Twin curl cutter
- Vegetable curler
- Vegetable garnishing cutter
- Zesters and strippers
- Zigzag decorating knives

Herbs and Spices Utensils:
- Mincers
- Mortar and pestle

Knife Sharpeners:
- Electric knife sharpeners
- Manual knife sharpeners
- Sharpening steels

Knives for Prepping:
- Asian and Japanese knives
- Boning and fillet, carving, and slicing knives
- Bread, bench, and serrated knives
- Cake knives
- Channel knives
- Cheese knives
- Chef knives
- Citrus knives
- Cleavers
- Fruit and vegetable knives
- Grapefruit knives
- Paring and peeling knives
- Salmon slicer
- Sandwich spreader
- Tourne knives
- Utility knives
- Zigzag decorating knives

Measuring and Timing Utensils:
- Kitchen timers
- Measuring cups and spoons
- Scales
- Thermometers

Meat Utensils:
- Branding irons

- Choppers
- Grinders
- Injectors
- Meat hooks
- Pounders and hammers
- Presses
- Steak weights and markers
- Tenderizers
- Thermometers

Pancake Utensils:
- Batter dispenser
- Pancake rings

Pasta-Preparation Utensils and Accessories:
- Dough rollers
- Gnocchi boards or paddles
- Pasta bikes
- Pasta cutters
- Pasta drying racks
- Pasta forks
- Pasta guitar
- Pasta rolling pins
- Ravioli forms
- Ravioli stamps
- Rectangular frizz
- Spaghetti rakes
- Spaghetti tongs

Poultry Utensils:
- Baster and basting brush
- Fat separator strainer
- Injectors
- Lifters
- Trussing and roulade needles
- Turkey lacers

Scoopers:
- Ice cream scoopers
- Melon ballers

Miscellaneous Preparation and Cooking Utensils:
- Bottle, can, and jar openers
- Cutting boards
- Food mills and grinders
- French fry cutter, potato masher, and potato ricer
- Kitchen shears, cheese scissors, bone scissors, and herb snips
- Mandolines, graters, choppers, peelers, and slicers
- Pizza scissors, wheels, and choppers
- Strainers, drainers, skimmers, chinois, sieves, handheld colanders

Decluttering Food-Preparation and Cooking Utensils

Understanding how to locate damage done to your cooking utensils will help you determine when it's time to discard them. As you examine your cookware, look for corrosion, which is found on metal cooking utensils. Closely examine their seams where food-contaminating bacteria may lodge.

Check all wooden tools for deterioration. Make sure that wooden utensils are sanded smooth with nothing that could splinter off into your food. Splits in wood are bad because food can get trapped in the cracks. Mostly, only stains or mild roughness on wooden tools can be rubbed away with fine sandpaper. Although wood is naturally more antibacterial than any man-made object, wooden utensils still need to be inspected for potential germ and bacteria invitations. Check for soft or dark and mushy parts. These characteristics are often associated with rotten wood. Remember that the older the cooking utensil, the higher the probability that corrosion or bacteria has overtaken it. If you don't have the time or desire to hand wash, sand, and oil your wooden cooking utensils to preserve them, consider replacing the frequently used ones with more maintenance-free alternatives. Heat-resistant silicone is a wonderful material for a cooking utensil since it does not corrode, retain odors, or easily stain, and it doesn't scratch nonstick surfaces.

Check the rubber coating on cooking utensils to make sure that they're not too worn. Discard badly stained rubber or plastic components on cooking utensils since deep stains are almost impossible to remove from these materials. Throw out disfigured/melted cooking utensils because they'll never work like they should.

It's important that you enjoy the way a cooking utensil feels in your hand when you use it, or it won't be used. Cooking utensils that don't grip well or feel comfortable in your hand should be removed since you'll most likely never use them. Therefore, when you need to replace them, test them first in order to make sure that you like the way they handle.

Number of Cooking Utensils to Keep on Hand

One of the trickiest things to learn about decluttering cooking utensils is determining how many of each type to keep. As you downsize your cooking utensils, realize that keeping more than one of a particular cooking tool may be necessary. Generally, you need more than one of your frequently used cooking utensils, such as spatulas, spoons, ladles, tongs, whisks, mixing bowls, and the like. Spare cooking utensils are required when you cook often or with several pots and pans at one time. Also, it's convenient to have spares in case cooking utensils cannot be cleaned in a timely manner.

The best way to determine the number of each cooking utensils to have on hand is to first determine which pots or pans you use on a frequent basis. Then decide which cooking utensils are typically used for them, and these will be the ones in need of spares.

The Right Cooking Utensils Will Save Your Cookware

The material of your cooking utensils should also be compatible with the type of cookware you possess. For example, if your fry pans are nonstick, then you'll need nonstick turners in order to safely use your pan. If all your pots and pans are nonstick, discard any spatulas or turners that can potentially ruin the surface of your cookware.

Storing Food-Preparation and Cooking Utensils

Generally, cooking instruments are best stored in shallow base-cabinet drawers located just beneath the countertop. The frequently used stovetop cooking utensils should be located in the drawers closest to the stove or in a nearby crock on the countertop. They may also hang from wall-mounted organizers by the stove. Lesser-used cooking utensils can be arranged in shallow drawers farther from the stove, such as lower base-cabinet drawers.

Drawer Organizers

Cooking utensils that are stored in drawers need division, or they become impossible to find in a heap of metal or plastic. Storage compartments also prevent utensils from rolling all over the place when a drawer is opened. The best storage solutions are expandable trays or drawer dividers, such as snap-apart strips that create custom-size compartments for utensils of any size. Two-tiered, stacked tray organizers can hold cooking utensils in deep drawers. Keep the frequently used items in the top compartment of the tray and everything else on the bottom. There is also a silicone non-slip drawer mat kit that contains repositionable pieces which lock into a mat for securing cooking utensils. This organizer is designed to customize the layout of cooking utensils. A good one to purchase is by KMN Home called DrawerDecor.

When you have utensils that are used for a staple food, such as eggs, they can receive key storage placement. Egg utensils, such as piercers, slicers, rings, poachers, separators, and toppers can store in a single-drawer container or an open bin situated on a cabinet shelf.

Common utensils, such as pasta forks, tongs, and rakes are perfect for tossing, lifting, and serving pasta and other foods. These can be stored in a crock or with other everyday utensils. Due to the universal nature of these utensils, it's acceptable to have more than one of each kind. Handheld preparation utensils used to make pasta should be stored together in a labeled container or single-drawer organizer. Keep them next to the pasta makers or machines in places like a walk-in pantry, closet, lower base-cabinet shelf, or overhead compartment.

There are only a few pizza utensils: a pizza wheel, scissors, and chopper. Nearly every home has at least one of these. Since the utensils are sharp, they need to be stored in a single compartment in a drawer. You may also group them with related pasta or dough utensils.

Crock Organizers

The next best place to store everyday cooking utensils is in a counter crock, an easy-to-access organizer. Tools like spatulas, whisks, slotted spoons, tongs, and turners are good picks for a crock since they can be used for a number of meal preparations.

Some wall-mounted hanging systems have crock organizers that suspend from a hook. Deep cabinet drawers can be outfitted with tall containers or built-in crocks as an alternative location to a counter.

Storing Preparation and Cooking Knives

Don't store pointy objects like forks and knives loose in a drawer. Your best storage option is to store cooking forks with cooking knives, because these utensils both require special storage arrangements and they're often used with one another. Long-handled cooking forks are perfect for reaching into ovens to turn roasts and turkeys during the baking or broiling process. They're also useful to hold meats or other foods in place while cutting or carving. It's easy to get by with just one long-handled fork unless you prefer using two in place of a specialized heavy-duty lifter.

Many knife trays, especially those with flexible slots, can secure the body of a fork. You can also station forks in individual compartments of a cutlery tray, where other pointy utensils are gathered, such as turkey lifters, skewers, or meat needles. Position sharp instruments to face the rear of the drawer for safety. Long forks that can be hung may also rest on a wall rack designed for hanging utensils.

About Knives

The number and type of cooking knives necessary in a home are different for everyone. However, most meals are prepared with three main cooking knives: the chef, paring, and bread knife. When downsizing your knives, think about each knife's performance and how it feels in the cook's hand in order to determine which ones to keep. Knives should slice cleanly, evenly, and with minimal effort. A knife that has been sharpened but still is tough to cut food with is dangerous.

Much of what a cook likes about a knife is personal preference. Some people like lighter, more flexible, and thinner knives. Certain materials make a difference for the cook, such as whether the knife is ceramic or stainless steel. In most kitchens, a handful of high-performance knives is enough.

Cooking knives require special storage arrangements since they can be dangerous and their blades require protection from pitting and dulling. If you only have a few knives, it makes most sense to store them carefully with other cooking tools for space efficiency. You can accomplish this in two ways. First you can use rigid plastic knife sleeves that fully enclose the blade, making it possible to store cooking knives safely with other utensils. You can make a cardboard knife sleeve yourself by simply laying the knife out on cardboard and then tracing the blade. Cut out two of the same shape and tape them together to form a sleeve.

Invest in an expandable, in-drawer knife rack for larger collections of knives. A knife organizer should have slots that fit your knives and hold a sharpening steel rod. Countertop knife blocks, transportable traveling cutlery cases, or undermounted cabinet knife organizers can deal with large collections of knives and free up drawer space.

Sharpening and Honing Knives

Honing steels remove nicks, jags, and small burrs to maintain the knife edge in between sharpenings. Beyond honing steels, sharpening instruments like whetstones or professional home sharpeners are required several times a year, depending upon the frequency in which the knives are used. If you have these items, store them in an overhead compartment, closet pantry, or where other infrequently needed gadgets are kept. In your calendar, record a semiannual or yearly sharpening for your knives, whether you do them yourself or use a professional service. Establish a time that is easy to remember, like before the Thanksgiving holiday.

Other Food-Preparation Utensils

Prepping instruments used to grate, chop, peel, grind, mash, and slice (besides knives) are important, but usually don't qualify as everyday utensils. Often these utensils are used to prepare timely meals from scratch. However, when frequently used in your home, key storage placement may be necessary. Prepping utensils are responsible for hogging the most space due to their typical bulkiness. Therefore, make sure to keep only the

well-made ones and discard lesser duplicates. Drawer organizers that form various compartments like cutlery trays are necessary to keep utensils divided and separated so they're safe to grab and easy to find.

Larger prepping gadgets, such as food mills, mandolines, or choppers, can be overlooked due to the inconvenience of using and cleaning them. If this is the case in your home, and there are ample substitutes to use in place of them, consider donating or selling them. Prepping gadgets can be stored in deep base-cabinet pullout drawers, on pantry shelves, or in kitchen closets; avoid upper cabinet shelves since they can drop and break from heights. Any utensils designed to prepare herbs and spices should reside in a labeled

FIGURE 27.01
Kitchen Wall Organization

container and be stored alongside the spice rack, spice jars, or herb packets.

Nested Mixing Bowls

Mixing bowls are ideal preparation utensils for many foods. Mixing bowls nested together conserve space and conveniently keep them together in one spot, which is perfect organization. Mixing bowls are frequently used, so store them in an easy-to-access location. Any place close to the counter where they're used is ideal, whether in an upper cabinet, base-cabinet drawer, or pull-out basket.

Measuring and Timing Instruments

Measuring and timing instruments are helpful preparation utensils for many cooking and baking foods. Measurement of ingredients is centered on most recipes and boxed foods, so all homes should invest in a complete set of graduating measuring cups and spoons that can nest in order to conserve space. Also, save storage space by paring down to measuring tools that gauge several units, so you'll need only one all-purpose instrument versus many utensils that measure individual units.

Consider eliminating bulky kitchen scales, which are mostly only useful to a budding chef. Over time, many cooks develop a trained eye for portion size and refer less and less to measuring devices since they add an extra step to the cooking task and create another utensil to clean. In addition, much of what we buy has weight information on the packaging, further eliminating the need for a scale. Measuring instruments, aside from large scales, usually can fit into a basic kitchen drawer alongside other basic cooking utensils. Measuring devices can also be stored in a labeled container next to the flour, sugar, and spices.

Magnetic timers that hang on a refrigerator door or wall-mounted timers are great space savers. If you have a flat timer, try to get it onto a wall or appliance. If your timer is off the workspace, it will not get messy from food splatter or lost among bowls, pots, and pans. Thermometer/timer combinations can get also be stored with measuring cups, spoons, windup timers, and the like.

Strainers, Drainers, Skimmers, Chinoises, Sieves, and Colanders

Food-preparation utensils that perform different drainage functions are necessary for many food recipes. Keep food-draining instruments together and nested, if possible, next to the pots and pans in base-cabinet compartments, such as pullout shelves or deep drawers. Handheld skimmers and the like can be stored in drawers next to cooking utensils.

Chocolate Utensils

There are both specialty preparation and cooking tools for chocolate. Chocolate utensils qualify for kitchen storage when chocolate candies and desserts are regularly prepared or extra space is available. All chocolate utensils can go in a labeled container placed near your bakeware or on an upper cabinet shelf so they don't congest valuable drawer space. Pantries or kitchen closets are other possible storage options. If you find that you never seem to make time for creating chocolate treats or suspect a declining interest, let go of these utensils.

Fruit, Vegetable, and Garnishing Utensils

There are many specialty fruit and vegetable preparation utensils because there are so many different types of fruits and vegetables. Some utensils serve only one purpose, like a melon baller or apple corer, whereas others are more universal, such as peelers, zesters, and strippers. Make sure that you are using the specialized utensils and not substituting them for a multipurpose one that can accomplish the same goal. Generally, well-made utensils that perform many tasks will reduce drawer clutter, making things easy to locate. Additionally, a few multiple-function tools are easy to group in a convenient spot with the other everyday utensils.

Some fruit and vegetable utensils are good to store with other articles that go together with their purpose, instead of with other fruit or vegetable utensils. For example, a garlic press, chopper, and cooker can be stored together in one container on a shelf near the spices or dry goods. Specialized garnishing or carving tools are commonly sold with a tool case, which is the best and safest way to organize and store them in a drawer or on a shelf.

Cooking Ladles, Spoons, and Scoopers

Cooking spoons and ladles are frequently used in a busy kitchen and come in a variety of handle lengths and bowl sizes. It's always good to have one long-handled ladle and spoon for reaching into ovens and deep pots. Examine your collection of ladles and spoons and take notice of their bowl sizes as well. If you serve hearty stews and soups, you'll want to have a ladle that can hold at least eight ounces. Some ladles have graduated measurements up to a cup marked on the ladle. This is the optimal cooking ladle since it serves more than one function. You only need two cooking ladles. Keep at least one large ladle, approximately eight ounces, and one medium, approximately four to six ounces, with long handles for reaching into deep pots. Medium-sized ladles are important because they transfer to the table for serving.

Crocks are the perfect places to store everyday cooking ladles and spoons. Many ladles and cooking spoons are designed with hanging loops or hooks to store on rail, grid, or rack organizers. Ladles and spoons can also store with the frequently used cooking tools in a divided tray or drawer organizer located near the stove.

Gather all your scooping kitchen utensils like fruit melon ballers and ice cream scoopers. When applicable, check swing-lever functions and look for damage or wear. The best scooping utensils are nonstick, unbendable, and stainless steel with nonslip handles. Most kitchens can get by with just one of each type of scooping utensil. Fruit scoopers can be stored with garnishing utensils in a drawer near a food-preparation work area. Infrequently used garnishing utensils can also be containerized, labeled, and shelved.

Fish, Poultry, and Meat Utensils

Specialized utensils required for meat, poultry, and fish can be grouped together since they share a common bond in that they all prepare the protein element of a meal. Highly specialized preparation and cooking utensils are often limited to a single purpose. Therefore, it's important to determine if these utensils are actually being used at the appropriate times. Often, an everyday multipurpose cooking or preparation item can handle the job of certain specialized utensils. Declutter collections of highly specialized fish, meat, and poultry utensils with these principals in mind.

Duplicates of specialized utensils are almost always unnecessary, so when you have them, keep the higher-quality ones and donate the extras. Group your specialty utensils according to type and divide them in storage accordingly. Keep these cooking and preparation utensils stored separately from your everyday turners, forks, and knives, which are frequently needed and deserve priority storage placement.

Since they're not frequently needed cooking tools, store them in drawers beneath or besides those with the everyday cooking utensils. Deep kitchen drawers offer good storage with collections of specialty utensils that include bulky meat and poultry presses. Stackable trays with multiple compartments fill out deep drawers well and nicely divide utensils in specific groups. Stackable lidded containers can also divide these inventories and store in deep drawers. Label the tops of these containers so their contents are easy to see.

Jar, Bottle, and Can Openers

Preparation utensils, such as jar, bottle, and can opening devices, are commonly used in most kitchens. For this reason, store these items with your everyday cooking or preparation utensils so they're convenient to access and find. Only one of each type of opening utensil is necessary in the average home.

Examine all your opening utensils to ensure they operate well. Also, check for corrosion, which is common on these types of utensils since they're not often wiped down or cleaned after use. Test levers to make sure they turn easily. Can openers with completely sealed cutting mechanisms are best since they're less dangerous and food won't get caught in them.

Canning Utensils

Store canning items outside the kitchen area with holiday or seasonal items when they're used a couple times a year. Place all your small canning utensils inside the canners along with mixes, salts, and pectin. Store canning jars and lids in a sturdy box alongside the canning supplies.

CHAPTER 28

Food-Storage Containers

When you think about the fact that food-storage containers are used to keep leftovers, which is an economical choice, it's reasonable to invest in a good set. Food-storage containers have been upgraded tremendously, especially in product design, which helps with storage arrangements. To efficiently organize them, first gather your entire collection of containers and lay them onto a large workspace.

Decluttering Food-Storage Containers

Separate the containers by brand or material, such as Tupperware, Rubbermaid, glass, or plastic; then sort the lids in the same manner and match them to their corresponding containers. Make this the last ditch effort to find missing lids or bottoms, and toss the parts without a mate.

Discard warped, cracked, chipped, stained, and odor-absorbed plastic food containers. Determine whether your plastic and vinyl products contain harmful PVC toxins that have been added to these materials in the past. The additive called BPA is unhealthy, and older water bottles, storage containers, and baby bottles may be at risk. If you don't know the origin of your plastic storage containers and you have had them for a number of years, get rid of them.

Go through all the types of storage containers and decide which ones you use and like best. Make sure you have enough of the sizes you use most often. Perhaps certain sizes are never used, such as the very small or big containers; consider donating them or selling them at the next yard sale.

When buying new ones, look for the storage containers that allow the lids to adhere to the bottom of container so they don't get lost. Storage containers that come in graduated sizes for nesting save space. Popular storage container manufacturers have even come up with a line in which the pieces collapse and flatten for space-saving storage. Many food-storage containers are now made with a super clarified base to help see the contents.

Storing Food-Storage Containers

The greatest challenge in storing food containers is finding the best arrangements to contain both the lids and bases so they're easier to find and pair. It's best to store lids and bottoms separately, as they take up too much space and trap odors when stored whole.

To organize the lids, use a separate organizer for each different shape like square, round, and rectangular. Rack organizers can file lids by size, with the larger lids placed in back, graduating to the smaller in front so they're easier to see. A good substitute for a rack organizer is a sturdy napkin holder or desktop letter file.

Nest all the base containers with like shapes. It may be a good idea to get rid of a container when it's the only one of certain shape or it will be sitting alone on the shelf, taking up space. In homes tight on cabinet space, paring down to only one shape of container that nests with others can dramatically conserve storage space.

Glass and ceramic food-storage containers can follow the same storage protocol as plastic pieces, such as nesting and storing lids by shape. Store glass and ceramic ones at eye level or in a base cabinet where they're less likely to fall and break. Also since these pieces are heavier, lower storage placement is better.

Another way to maintain order among food-container lids and their counterpart bases is to number them so they correspond. This method works well if you choose not to invest in a lid-storage device. Keep the lids corralled in either a common drawer or designated container. Plastic bags can also separate the lids by numbers or shapes.

Store specialty food-storage containers, like large salad bowls or large party-size pieces, with entertainment items or roasting pans to save your most convenient kitchen storage locations for the items you use daily. Other specialty food containers, such as jelly jars used for canning jelly, jams, or sauces, are best stored outside your kitchen cabinets. Box and label all the canning containers and store them where canning supplies are kept in places such as a kitchen closet or storage area. If you use these food containers during a particular season, such as fall or the holidays, store these containers next to your Thanksgiving or Halloween decorations.

Specialized food-storage containers, like plastic refrigerator containers for onions, tomatoes, cheese, butter, lettuce, and lemons, should stay in the veggie compartments of the refrigerator, even when empty, to conserve cabinet space. Similarly, dry-goods containers for crackers or sugar can stay in the food pantry.

If you reuse food-packaging containers—such as yogurt, sour cream, and butter tubs—as food containers, keep only a few of the popular sizes. This way you can nest the like containers efficiently. Otherwise, it's likely that such containers will explode in number, and many different types and sizes will not store neatly. The disposable plastic containers largely manufactured by the leading makers of plastic storage bags can also be stored alongside other food-storage items, such as clear plastic wrap, aluminum foil, and plastic baggies.

Storing Beverage Containers

There are several types of pitchers: the lidded versions are good for keeping batters, juice, milk, and water fresh in the refrigerator and can also be transferred to the table. Classic pitchers without lids are ideal for serving cold beverages, such as lemonade, water, ice tea, and beer. Lidded thermos pitchers serve hot beverages and are often sold as a dispensing pot for coffee makers.

Gather all the pitchers throughout the kitchen and check them for chips, warping, stains, wear, or missing lids. Make certain they dispense well and don't leak. The ones dedicated for entertaining that have not been used at the last two parties should be donated or sold. Any everyday pitchers that have not been used in the past year should also go. Pare down inventories to keep a reasonable amount, such as two lidded thermos pots for serving decaf and regular coffee at parties. Keep only a few lidded everyday pitchers for refrigerated batters, juice, milk, and water. Keep display pitchers exclusively used for cocktails at a bar station or with the alcohol.

Jugs that dispense liquids through a spigot are great for entertaining or even for personal use. Only keep those you actually use, though since they're space hogs. Look them over to make sure they're in good working order; be sure to check that the spigots don't leak. Beverage dispensers used solely for entertainment should be housed outside the kitchen where other entertainment items are stored. Outdoor versions commonly used for team sports should be stored with sports accessories in places like the garage or shed.

Donate or sell any single-serve thermoses that have not been used in the past year. Consider moving thermoses that are packed away with your camping gear to where you keep the others, in order to utilize them more often. Keep enough small, single-serve thermoses to accommodate your personal needs, such as in children's lunch boxes, the car, the office, cold-weather spectator sports, or wherever they play a part in your life. Thermoses can all be contained in a single basket and stored on a base-cabinet shelf near related items, such as lunch-packing items.

CHAPTER 29

Countertop Kitchen Appliances

There comes a time when we need to evaluate the actual value of our various countertop kitchen appliances. These items tend to stick around because they're typically perceived as valuable. However, smaller kitchen appliances over a few years old hold very little resale value because newer technology usually equals technological advancement.

Decluttering Countertop Kitchen Appliances

When decluttering small kitchen appliances, it's common to find more than one of the same kind. This typically occurs when a replacement is purchased before the old one breaks, so it's kept as a spare. It's important to let go of the old one since there is a good reason you replaced it in the first place unless there is a need to use them simultaneously. Make sure to keep only what works well by checking over the blades, light bulbs, cords, and so on. When organizing small kitchen appliances, it's important to group them first by type to make it easier to notice which ones could overlap in function or discover duplicates.

There are important factors to consider when you access your countertop kitchen appliances. The following checklist will help you evaluate the usefulness and ideal placement for them:

- The appliance must receive regular use.
- A manual handheld device or tool should not be continuously replacing the job of a smaller appliance.
- The appliance must perform satisfactorily.
- The appliance should not be a nuisance to clean, such as having too many parts that require hand washing.
- Single-purpose gadgets, such as cotton candy machines, should have a high demand.
- Larger appliances that produce bulk quantities must be necessary, as they're heavy to move and are space hogs. Many of these appliances, such as food processors, juicers, coffee makers, mixers, and so on, come in compact or single-serve sizes, making them lightweight and easier to store off the counter.
- Appliances should not overlap in function since this is similar to keeping duplicates.

The following list of countertop appliances is broken down by type.

Brewing Devices

- Coffee maker, roaster, and grinder
- Espresso machine
- Tea makers

Cooking

- Convection, broiler, or rotisserie ovens
- Deep fryer, air fryer
- Electric grills and griddles
- Electric woks and skillets
- Fruit and jerky dehydrator
- Microwave
- Rice cooker, pressure cooker, slow cooker, Crock-Pot
- Roasters
- Sliced bread pop-up toaster, toaster oven

Food Preparation

- Blender
- Food processor and slicers
- Juicer
- Meat, spice, and nut grinders
- Mixers: stand and hand mixers

Specialty

- Ice cream, snow cone, and chocolate machines
- Single-purpose appliances: panini, crepe, waffle, bread, egg, cotton candy, donut makers, and popcorn poppers

Storage Solutions for Countertop Kitchen Appliances

When storing countertop kitchen appliances, there are many storage options. Many small- to medium-size countertop kitchen appliances can be stored together, where they're easy to find and access. A good place for a collection of countertop kitchen appliances is pantry shelves. Shelving must be sturdy for this purpose. In a pantry with multiple shelves, store the smallest ones at eye level, graduating in size to the bottom shelves, where the bulky appliances need to go. Don't place appliances behind one another unless on a pull-out shelf, which is the best type, especially for maneuvering heavier appliances.

Upper eye-level kitchen cabinets, rather than overhead ones that are dangerous, are another good place for small appliance storage. Reserve pullout base-cabinet shelves for the big appliances, such as Crock-Pots, pressure cookers, and deep fryers, but not near the stove or oven, because the cookware belongs there.

Locate kitchen appliances on the countertop sparingly. Even just a few can create a cluttered look on limited counter space. Invest the most money and time selecting countertop kitchen appliances that showcase nicely. Any counter-top kitchen appliance must receive almost daily use in order to claim such space. Kitchen cab-inets with pull-out shelves can disguise small appliances. Adding an interior electrical outlet allows the appliance to operate in this space. Refrain from investing in roll-top-door appliance garages because they're dated and are distracting to the eye.

There are several good cabinet upgrades that hide counter appliances. The most popular is an appliance lift, which is heavy-duty shelf with a lever that brings even the bulkiest appliance to counter height. There is also a hidden pulldown toaster shelf that flips out from a base-cabinet door front.

Countertop appliances can also rest on a wheeled tiered cart and moved from a pantry or closet when needed, which is easier than carrying them.

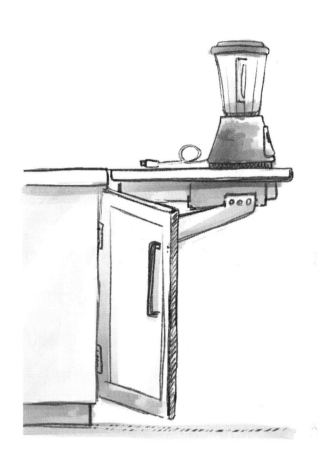

(fRoNt view)   (side viEw)

FIGURE 29.02
Storage solutions for countertop kitchen appliances

Base Cabinet Storage idEAS
Appliance Lift

CHAPTER 30

Serving Utensils

Serving utensils transfer foods from a large platter, tray, or bowl onto a single serving dish, like a plate or bowl for eating. These utensils come in a variety of forms designed to cut, spread, scoop, and so on. There is an extensive collection of serving utensils and a specialty utensil for nearly every kind of food. However, servers, such as tongs; large, long-handled spoons; and forks, are universal and can serve most foods. Examples of serving utensils are butter knives and salad servers.

When organizing your serving utensils, gather them from the kitchen, dining room, and any storage area that houses your entertainment items, as it's common for these items to reside throughout the home when they're used in various locations. After collecting them, form two separate piles when you have both formal and casual serving pieces. Divide servers by type, such as spoon or fork servers. The following information discusses ways to approach downsizing and organizing each type of server.

Serving Spoons

Separate serving spoons according to handle length and bowl size. Consider adding cooking spoons and ladles that have one-piece construction, as they're attractive enough to transfer to the table. Such division allows you to clearly see the differences among your serving spoons, which will help downsize inventories accurately.

Visualize yourself pulling spoon servers out to use for guests and focus on the pieces that you tend not to use; permanently remove them from your collection. Cut down an overstock of a certain spoon with a distinct handle length and bowl size by eliminating the hard-to-clean silver-plated spoons and those that don't match other servers or your flatware pattern. Eliminate the spoon servers that don't perform well, such as ladles that continue to dispense after pouring syrup, gravy, and soups. It may be worth your while to test some in order to determine which ones are best; you may have a well-designed, drip-free ladle and not even know it.

The handle lengths on your serving spoons coincide with the type of serving platters and bowls. It's important to skim through your platters and serving bowls to know exactly which serving spoons are necessary to keep on hand. Generally, it's best keep two serving spoons each in size large, medium, and small. In addition, two pierced spoons for fruits and vegetables are also necessary.

Serving Forks and Tongs

Sort your serving forks into three piles according to size: small, medium, and large. Remove all that are badly worn and never used. Notice whether there are any esoteric serving forks for which you cannot identify their intended use. Research those serving forks in order to find their purpose so you can receive more use from them or choose to eliminate them.

Small (Short-Handled) Forks

Smaller table serving forks suitable for side items, such as limes, lemons, olives, pickles, and the like, are helpful but not necessary. A miniature tong can also do the job. When you prefer using small serving forks for these items, make sure they're sharp enough to penetrate these foods. You only need to stock a few small serving forks.

Appetizer forks are another story. You can use one or two six- to eight-piece sets of appetizer forks, depending upon the number of guests you entertain at any given time. Appetizer, cocktail, dessert, hors d'oeuvre, or seafood forks are generally interchangeable.

Medium Forks

Many medium-size serving forks were named for the food they were intended to serve long ago, when times were more formal; however, they can usually be used to serve other types of foods. For example, a cold meat fork can serve lamb chops, waffles, or French toast. Medium-sized serving forks that serve multiple functions are good to stock in numbers.

Large (Long-Handled) Forks

There are a few important long-handled servers that you should keep one of each, if you possess them. The popular two-pronged holding fork contained in carving sets is absolutely necessary to assist in the cutting of hams, roasts, and turkeys.

A large, curved fork for transferring heavier foods is also good to have.

Long-handled banquet forks or cold meat forks are typically four-pronged and are useful when you entertain buffet style with chafing pans. Keep a number that would accommodate your largest buffet-style event. Banquet forks used exclusively with chafers can be stored inside the chafers.

Tongs

There are basically two types of serving tongs: standard and small. The larger tongs are used to serve salads, meats, vegetables, and potatoes. The smaller tongs can serve appetizers, ice, pastries, and the like. In many cases, tongs can easily be substituted with serving forks and flat servers. Therefore, you don't need to have more than two large and small tongs on hand unless you have a serving preference for them.

Select a single-drawer compartment to keep all the tongs together. Lay the tongs on their back to form a V. Then place all the serving tongs in a graduated pattern so that the smaller tongs fit inside.

Serving Knives

There are not many serving knives in existence because most of the cutting is done in the kitchen prior to serving foods on platters and in dishes. When you declutter, realize the number needed to keep for each type of serving knife. Stock one to two sets of carving knives, often sold in carving sets. Butter knives are good to stock in pairs, especially when two butter trays need to furnish a long table. Keep no more than two all-purpose serving knives, especially when you have other specialty knife varieties. Cocktail knives and spreaders are necessary for serving condiments, spreads, and a number of appetizers. Therefore, house a quantity that can accommodate your largest cocktail party, which is commonly two sets.

Flat Servers

Begin organizing your flat servers by first sorting them by type. To downsize your inventories successfully, recognize the different uses each piece offers. For example, a pie server can serve molded salads, pizza slices, fish, or frozen desserts.

In most homes, a few well-constructed, multipurpose flat servers are needed. Stock both multipurpose serrated and nonserrated flat servers. Uncommon flat servers, such as for sardines or asparagus, commonly receive limited use, and the space they hog may not be justified when you can easily use a universal server in place. Pack away any family heirloom servers or antiques for future generations, or sell those you don't use.

Cheese Servers

The varieties and amounts of cheese you serve at a time will dictate the quantities and types of cheese tools you'll need. To begin organizing your cheese tools, separate the serving tools that accompany the cheese boards from those only used in the kitchen. Common cheese tools used exclusively in the kitchen are particular cheese grates, shavers, scrapers, curlers, scissors, grippers, and some knives.

Learning how to properly serve cheese will help you eliminate unnecessary tools. Since it's courteous to cater to the many palates of guests, offering an array of soft, hard, mild, sharp, and strong cheeses will require that you maintain a diverse assortment of tools that can cut different textures of cheese.

Cheese knives follow simple rules. Generally, skeleton knives with holes in the blade prevent soft cheeses from sticking to the blade. Narrow, rectangular blades are good for semisoft cheeses. Spreader knives are perfect for spreadable cheeses. Two-tine knives cut soft to medium-hard cheeses. Wide, rectangular cheese knives cut soft, crumbly cheeses like blue cheese. Tear-shaped, pointed knives are for hard cheese like Parmesan. Two-handled knifes also cut hard cheeses in a seesaw fashion. Storing no more than two of each type of cheese knife can accommodate most occasions.

A chef's knife carrying case can also store cheese tools in a kitchen drawer next to other servers or on a cabinet shelf near the cheeseboards. Stackable containers can hold individual cheeseboards plus accompanying cheese tools. Use blade protectors for the cheese knives when they're stored loosely in a container. These containers can reside on a shelf or in a drawer.

Dessert Servers

Gather all your dessert servers and sort them according to type, such as pie, cake, jelly, and ice cream. Keep sets together, such as wedding cake knives that pair with a flat server. Formal sets used on rare occasions can move out of the kitchen drawers and into a buffet, hutch, or china cabinet.

In order to best determine how many dessert servers you need to keep on hand, consider the largest gathering of guests that you would ever entertain. Think about the types of desserts you present to your guests in order to determine which dessert servers to keep and how many.

Drawer Liners for Serving Pieces

Drawer liners are a good investment because they protect the guts of your cabinets from spills and markings. Many materials, especially wood, are porous; many liquids, such as oils, can permeate your drawers and cause stains and lasting odor. Drawer liners also cushion and stabilize your serving pieces to prevent them from sliding all over the place from drawer movement and creating disorder or scratches. Many drawer liners are absorbent or drain, taking in moisture that otherwise can create water spots and tarnish serving pieces; these liners should be avoided

There are several choices of drawer liners for storage of serving pieces. The drawer liner material and personal preference are the main determinants for selecting a drawer liner. The following is a list of the different types of drawer liners that are often promoted for serving pieces, along with storage facts.

- **CORK** drawer liners come with an adhesive backing so they stay in place well. Cork resists mold and mildew and provides a soft cushion for serving pieces.
- **NONADHESIVE LATTICE** or **GRID-PATTERNED** drawer liners have a breathable, open-weave design that provides drainage, so moisture/water does not lie stagnant on top of it. These nonskid liners are commonly rubber, washable, and antimicrobial, and keep contents from sliding around inside from drawer movement. However, they're not recommended for lacquered or urethane-coated cabinet surfaces or silverware because rubber contains sulfur, which can damage them.
- **PLASTIC** is a common material used for many types of drawer liners. They protect the drawer and are washable. However, the plastic must be ribbed or textured so it's not slippery and will stabilize serving pieces.
- **SILVER CLOTH** is a cotton flannel material chemically treated with anti-tarnishing properties that is best used to line drawers for silver or silver-plated flatware and serving pieces. It's designed to prevent tarnish and minimize polishing and also protects against dust and scratches. There are different grades of silver cloth, such as tarnish preventative that lasts decades or tarnish-resistant that requires replacement every few years. Silver cloth is commonly sold by the yard at fabric stores and various online websites. It's easy to measure and cut with a scissors.

Caring for Silver and Silver-Plated Serving Pieces in Storage

Silver and silver-plated serving pieces should not contact stainless steel. When these metals touch, stain damage will occur on the silver. As previously mentioned, silver-plated and silver serving pieces also should not contact rubber, which contains sulfur that is responsible for silver corrosion. Therefore, don't use rubber-padded storage devices for your fine silver. Regular cleaning with soapy water helps reduce tarnish on silver and silver-plated servers caused by sulfur in the air. Make certain to properly clean and fully dry silver servers before returning them to storage, especially when they come into contact with sulfur-containing foods, such as eggs, onions, and spinach, which can cause tarnish.

Also keep silver-based servers away from other elements that produce tarnish, such as wool, humidity, felt, latex gloves, carpet padding, and body oils. Silver is a soft metal and can scratch easily, so separate silver servers by placing them in individual compartments in order to prevent them from clanking against one another.

CHAPTER 31

Flatware

The two main types of flatware, or eating utensils, in the average home are everyday and formal. Most everyday flatware is made of a metal, such as stainless steel, which is easy to care for and store. Formal dining utensils, which are silver or silver-plated, require specialized care and have demanding storage requirements.

Everyday Flatware

Begin organizing your everyday flatware by sorting individual pieces into like groups, such as teaspoons and forks. Count the number in each group to see if you are missing any and decide whether replacements are in order. The manufacturer's name should be stamped on the flatware, in case you have forgotten where your set originated. When you track down the pattern name or number and the manufacturer, document the information. Another good reason to have the flatware manufacturer information is for warranty purposes since many flatware manufacturers offer lifetime warranties. Also, manufacturers know where to obtain discontinued flatware.

The number of place settings and the number of pieces that make up a flatware set is different in each household. The number of times meals are eaten in the home plus the types of foods consumed will be determining factors. Generally, two to three place settings per household member is standard. Deduct or relocate pieces that are not receiving use, such as uncommon flatware eating utensils like bouillon spoons or dessert forks. Alternatively, consider the need to add certain eating utensils to your flatware set, such as soup spoons. Now is the time to add or delete pieces to the flatware set before final storage arrangements are made for them.

Store flatware in the shallow drawers just below the counter near the dinnerware, glassware, or dishwasher. Expandable cutlery trays that enlarge both horizontally and vertically are ideal for wide drawers. Custom drawer divider kits and spring-loaded divider devices can also achieve this goal. In deep drawers, stackable flatware trays can also hold additional flatware pieces; place the frequently used pieces in the top tray and the less-required utensils on the bottom.

Custom cabinet accessories like built-in, foldout caddies can hold flatware upright, which conserves lateral space. Handled silverware caddy organizers are useful storage devices when your kitchen is short on drawer space. A flatware caddy is transportable, which makes it easy to move from cabinet to table. Office wall-mounted cup holders designed to store pencils can also be used to store flatware. Countertop flatware storage devices include decorative serving caddy organizers and stainless steel cylinder holders commonly obtained through restaurant suppliers.

Formal Silver and Silver-Plated Flatware

Silver-plated flatware is coated in a very thin layer of sterling silver, so it has all the same features as actual silver. Therefore, it only makes sense to care for silver and silver-plated flatware in the same way.

The following is a list of storage tips for silver and silver-plated flatware:

- Avoid wrapping silver flatware in plastic, aluminum foil, newspaper, or rubber bands, which causes damage.

- Exposure to air and light (even artificial light) promotes tarnishing. Something as simple as a frequently opened drawer near a light will accelerate tarnishing.
- Common kitchen-drawer storage often leads to silver damage or premature tarnishing. For example, wood drawers, rubber drawer liners, stainless steel flatware, stove/oven heat, and humidity all negatively affect silver.
- Silver scratches easily, so never store it loosely anywhere.
- Overpolishing, especially on thinly coated silver-plated flatware, removes silver.

Following proper storage arrangements will prolong the life of your formal flatware and prevent tarnish. The best way to store silver flatware is in a flatware chest, which is a fully sealed container lined with treated, tarnish-prevention silver cloth. The chests feature individual slots for storing each flatware piece separately so they don't pile together and scratch. Flatware chests need to be stored in a dry, dark area that has a consistent temperature, such as a closet or base cabinet. When possible, store your silver where it can receive frequent use since regular washings prevent tarnish, and your silver should get put to good use.

CHAPTER 32

Dishware

Dishware includes the dishes used for serving and eating food. There are two types of dishware: a casual, everyday set and a dressy, formal set. Casual dinnerware is made of durable material, such as stoneware or earthenware that is able to withstand the microwave and dishwasher. Casual dinnerware is mostly used in the kitchen.

Bone china, fine china, and porcelain china dishware are classified as formal. These pieces tend to be delicate, lightweight, and require careful handwashing. Formal sets are traditionally used in the dining room for special occasions.

Everyday Dishware

Start organizing your dishes by first gathering all your everyday bowls, saucers, chargers, and plates, *not* the fine china. Use a large work area, such as a kitchen table, and group the dishes by type. As you sort your dishes, discard those with chips or cracks. Establish a miscellaneous pile for mismatched plates, such as those from a previous set. Dinnerware is commonly sold in sets that include plates, bowls, and cups and saucers.

When you have a couple sets of kitchen dishes, it's important to ask yourself why. Two like sets of dishes are acceptable when you use them for entertaining or have a large family. However, should the second set of dishes be an old set that you replaced with a current one, it may be time to donate or sell them if they receive no use. Organize your dinnerware as follows.

Plates

The plates in dinnerware sets generally come in two different sizes: a larger dinner plate and a smaller luncheon plate. Therefore, many homes have these two types of plates in their cabinets. There are other plate sizes that are less common in the average household. For example, a charger plate, which is placed underneath a dinner plate for a decorative touch to tablescapes, and smaller plates typically named by their individual functions, such as fruit, bread, salad, dessert, tea, and cheese plates. Many of these specialized plates are recognizable by ornamentation in a food pattern.

Dinner Plates

Start by counting how many dinner plates you own. You need three to five plates more than the number of people living in the house, in case you have a guest or two. Also, you need extra plates so there are some available on the shelf when the dishwasher is full. If you have too many dinner plates, especially a number not suited for the storage space, pare down or move a portion of them elsewhere. Two sets of identical dishes may be unnecessary for daily use, but keeping them around for parties and replacements is worthwhile. Store any overstock dishware in overhead kitchen cabinets, closets, or pantries. If you find that you are low on dinner plates, locate replacements by contacting the manufacturer. It's best to maintain a correct inventory of dinner plates, especially if you have matching salad plates, bowls, cups, saucers, and serving pieces.

Luncheon and Salad Plates

Typically, the luncheon and salad plate are produced in the same size, which is usually nine inches in diameter, two inches smaller than a dinner plate. For this reason, you need only one or the other unless you desire a different shape for each. You can stock more luncheon plates than dinner plates, two per household member, because their smaller size makes them ideal for snacks, desserts, and appetizers. When your household members prefer smaller dinner portions, luncheon or salad plates are good substitutes. In those cases, you may want to keep your luncheon or salad plates on an eye-level, easy-to-access shelf and move the dinner plates to a less convenient upper shelf.

Keep luncheon plates next to the dinner plates. Avoid stacking smaller luncheon plates on top of the dinner plates for access purposes. Either position luncheon and dinner plates beside each other, or use a lateral-tiered plate organizer to separate the different sizes. Plates can also file upright in a built-in cabinet, dowel-rod plate organizer.

Upper cabinets or deep pullout drawers near the dishwasher or sink are also convenient places to store plates. In drawer storage, secure plates by using a pegboard at the base of drawer and inserting dowel rods to hold them in place. Also, rack-style organizers or even a dish drying rack can be added to a deep drawer or pullout shelf for storing plates in a convenient upright position.

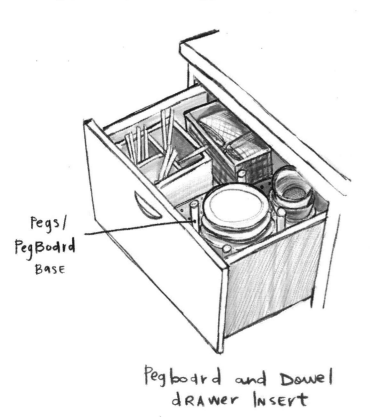

Pegs / PegBoard Base

Pegboard and Dowel dRAWeR InseRt

FIGURE 32.02
Pegboard & Dowel Drawer Storage

Small Plates

The number of small plates to have on hand should correspond with the number of dinner plates you stock. Most bread, appetizer, and dessert plates are smaller: five to seven inches in diameter. Since all these plates are relatively close in size, they're interchangeable. Therefore, one to two sets are necessary, depending on your need to serve salads, snacks, desserts, breads, and hors d'oeuvre. When paring down multiple sets of small plates, keep the larger sets that best match your other dinnerware and donate the rest.

Small plates are great for snacks and promote healthy, small portion sizes, so they should receive key storage placement in a convenient kitchen cabinet. However, small decorative plates and unusual specialty plates, such as fruit, cheese, or fish, can store outside the kitchen in places like a dining room buffet, china cabinet, hall closet, or a designated storage location where entertainment items are kept.

Chargers

A charger is a large decorative base upon which dinnerware is placed for formal occasions. These plates make great substitutes for platters, so if you want to donate a set, keep a couple for this purpose. Since chargers receive infrequent use, store them in overhead compartments, closets, or pantries. Buffet cabinets or storage armoires located in the dining room are also good storage spots. Those limited to certain occasions, such as festive-patterned Christmas chargers, can be stored with the decorations.

Specialty Plates

To justify keeping specialty plates like sushi or fondue plates, pull them out when such foods are served instead of using the regular dishware.

Commonly, specialty plates are accompanied by specialty utensils and accessories. For example, sushi preparation and serving involve specialty mats, sauce dishes, and chopsticks. It's best to store all those types of items together in a single compartmentalized handled container, saving regular drawer and cabinet storage for common dishware used daily. Label these containers and store them in base or overhead compartment in a kitchen pantry, closet, or cabinet.

Bowls

Gather all the bowls you have in your home—except for the fine china, holiday, or outdoor acrylic set—and sort them according to type: cereal, soup, fruit, and the like. Any obvious sets that are never used or depleted should go straight to the donation or resale box. Sets to eliminate are those that don't match the rest of the dishware, are not microwaveable, or are hard to nest in storage. Generally, it's best to keep multipurpose bowls in small, medium, and large.

Small Bowls

Often produced in smaller sizes, fruit bowls are perfect for single servings of any food that promotes healthy portions. Keep an extra five to eight additional small bowls over the number of household members since they're used for so many different purposes. Keep small bowls where they're easily accessed since promoting their use is beneficial. However tempting, don't nest small, medium, and large bowls together. Bowls can stack separately according to size with or without an organizer on a given shelf. Tiered dinnerware organizers can separate different size bowls while optimizing available vertical storage room in cabinets. Pullout drawers lined with pegboard can also separate various sizes of bowls.

Keep the frequently used bowls in front and the less-needed bowls in the back row of a drawer.

If you decide to promote more use from your specialty bowls, establish storage modifications as a solution. For example, decorative specialty bowls, such as painted dessert bowls, can be displayed in a hutch, while functional specialty bowls, such as bouillon bowls, can receive convenient drawer storage.

Medium Bowls

Soup and cereal bowls are classified as medium-size bowls. The number of these bowls should correspond to the number of household members plus an extra handful for guests or spares. Soup and cereal bowls tend to be the most used. For this reason, store them with other frequently used dinnerware items, like dinner and luncheon plates. They don't need to be grouped with other bowls that are infrequently used. Use a freestanding dishware organizer on a shelf that holds a combination of plates, bowls, and cups and saucers to store the items used daily. Base-cabinet

pullout shelves or racks can also group the everyday plates and bowls.

Thicker chili and French onion soup bowls are usually bulky and take up a good amount of space. In some cases, such bowls are only used during the fall and winter months. For these reasons, consider rotating storage locations for seasonally used bowls and offer key storage placement only when they receive a good amount of use.

Handled chili or French onion soup bowls are best stacked together so alternate handles face in opposite directions for balance. Lids pertaining to such bowls can keep in a single container.

Large Bowls and Bowl Saucers

Larger single-serve bowls, like a pasta bowl, have advantages over flat plates. Pasta bowls are ten inches in diameter and are shallow; they hold messy food, such as saucy noodle dishes and salads, better than flat plates. These bowls are also great for mixing and tossing foods— another great advantage over flat plates. For these reasons, pasta bowls can easily replace dinner plates for certain

FIGURE 32.01
Pull-out Dishware Rack

Base Cabinet Stordge Ideas
dishware Rack

meals, so it's worthwhile to acknowledge their versatility. If you use them in place of dinner plates for some meals, it's important to stock a number of bowls that can accommodate the family plus extras in case of breakage or guests. Encourage more use from these practical bowls by offering key storage locations, such eye-level shelving, deep drawers, or convenient pullout shelves alongside other daily used plates and bowls.

Bowl saucers are useful for catching spills and holding crackers, breads, and soup spoons. However, they're easy to substitute with other plates. Therefore, should you have a depleted set or find they're not receiving enough use, consider eliminating them altogether and opt for more storage space. Regularly used bowl saucers can be stored on a tiered-shelf organizer with the bowls above the plates. On a shelf or in a drawer, nest bowls and accompanying saucers side by side or keep the plates behind the bowls.

Specialty Bowls

Many specialty bowls, such as banana split, ice cream, or bouillon bowls, are novel but inconvenient since they tend to be glass and fragile or need to be washed by hand. Many times, specialty bowls are simply overlooked because they're commonly buried away in a poor storage spot and, as a result, are never used. Move them to a visible storage location only when there is a potential to use them, or they need to go.

Fine China

Fine china is often acquired in sets that include the same types of pieces found in everyday sets. It's important to recognize the significance of your fine china. How often and where your china is used should determine its storage location. China

that is used at least one a month can be stored in places like kitchen base cabinets, buffets, china cabinets, armoires, pantries, hutches, and so on. Infrequently used fine china, used just a few times a year, can be stored in overhead kitchen-cabinet compartments or in dining room furniture pieces. In some homes, fine china plates are openly stored for display in furniture pieces, such as a Welsh dresser or a glass-front hutch.

All fine china needs careful storage arrangements to prevent scratches, cracks, and chips. Stacked plates need packing paper, foam sleeves, paper towels, or napkins inserted in between them. Store cups and footed or handled bowls in individual compartments with divider inserts to prevent breakage. It's best to invest in a specialized storage set for fine china, easily found at stores that carry housewares. Most fine china storage sets are padded, quilted, nylon, or vinyl that are top-loading, zippered storage containers. Many have a see-through window or label holder on the outside to identify contents. These organizers are easy to access and perfect for storing any fine china.

Long-term storage arrangements can entail the use of a plastic container, where each piece of china is fully wrapped and stored sideways for less weight pressure than stacking. Use small to medium-size containers for fine china storage since it's heavy. It has become more popular over the years to entertain more casually with disposable dishware that closely replicates actual tableware. This is even more evident when serving large parties. Rethink keeping any fine china that is not consistently being used. Antique or heirloom china sets that are worth passing on can be packed away in long-term storage arrangements. Other options include donation or selling through consignment.

CHAPTER 33

Drinkware

Drinkware includes any vessel used to hold a liquid for consumption. There are many different ways that drinkware is categorized, which makes it impossible to have one universal classification system. It can be classified by material, purpose, or the type of liquid it holds, and such categories may overlap. For example, the stemware category of drinkware is glasses that have a long stem between the bowl and the base, like many wineglasses.

Stemware can also be found under the drinkware classifications of glassware and crystal. For this reason, it's best to approach organizing your drinkware by first separating the everyday drinkware—such as cups, mugs, drinking glasses, juice glasses, and so on—from the formal drinkware and barware that include wine and crystal glasses. This way, categories are easier to simplify by material, which plays a major factor in how they should be stored.

Before you start organizing all your drinkware, have protective packing materials, such as partitioned boxes, for fragile glasses or cups that need to be packed away or sold. It's best to organize one category of drinkware at a time since each type is so different.

Everyday Drinkware

The primary types of vessels used in the home on a daily basis are cups, mugs, drinking glasses, tumblers, and juice glasses; these are considered your everyday drinkware. However, other drinkware can also be used daily. Alcohol consumed daily can mean bar glasses may also need to be stored in the kitchen with other everyday glasses. In some homes, specialized stemmed water glasses, called goblets, are used daily in addition to regular drinking glasses at mealtime, requiring a storage location near the everyday drinkware.

Tumblers are flat-bottomed, heavy-based beverageware designed to withstand daily use. Tumblers commonly come in glass, aluminum, and plastic. They hold an array of beverages like milk, water, shakes, soda, juice, and many mixed drinks poured over ice.

Glassware

Glassware is drinkware made of glass. Many glassware tumbler sets are commonly purchased to accommodate everyday drinking needs for kitchen use. Since they're glass, they can be transferred from a casual to formal table and look fine. Typically, a glassware set includes both tall (sixteen-ounce to eighteen-ounce) glasses and short (nine-ounce to twelve-ounce) tumblers. The tall glasses are also referred to as highball glasses, and the shorter ones as rock or old-fashioned glasses. These glasses can serve both alcoholic and nonalcoholic beverages.

Juice glasses are the smallest tumblers, usually nine ounces and under; they're found in the average kitchen to serve a side of juice with breakfast. Iced tea tumblers are the tallest and tend to find their way in kitchen cabinets. These glasses also come in acrylic to accommodate outdoor use.

It's important to sort your glassware sets and count their numbers. Unfortunately, maintaining a complete set over time is almost impossible due to breakage. Check glasses for chips and cracks and discard sets that have dwindled to just a few since they cannot furnish a properly dressed table.

Glassware sets should contain a number that satisfies the household. Beverage glasses should outnumber plates since beverages are typically consumed more often than foods. Generally, two large and small glasses per household member is a safe number, which covers guests and replacements. When you really love your glassware, it's a good idea to buy one extra set of glasses to stash away in the storage room. This way, you can easily replace any that break.

Don't overstock glassware in your daily used cabinets, because there are limited storage options for them since they cannot stack. Glasses are not safe to place on overhead shelves; rather, they should situate at waist or eye level. They can also go in base-cabinet drawers or shelves. You can design a drawer with a grid divider, so each glass fits securely into an individual compartment and does not tip over. These dividers are similar to how ornament organizers protect and separate individual pieces.

On a shelf, line up the glasses in separate rows according to glass type or size. Having a random arrangement of various size glasses in a row makes it clumsy to reach for a certain size. Curios, breakfronts, hutches, armoires, and any tall cabinet in the kitchen area are good places to store glassware. Any cabinet with glass doors is meant to showcase glassware, so the good sets can go there.

There is no right or wrong way that drinking glasses should be stored. Every household has unique variables that influence the decision about storing drinking glasses upright or upside down. Your environment can be a strong factor in determining how glasses are best stored. For example, certain warm-weather climates have noteworthy bug problems, which persuade people to store their drinking glasses upside down. The common complaint people have with storing drinking glasses face down is that they don't look as nice in this position when on display.

Some people have health concerns about storing drinkware upside down. Drinking glasses stored upside down on cloth can trap air and water, which can encourage mold. There are also fears about the shelf contaminating the glass rims. People who are allergic to dust or annoyed by dust inside their drinking glasses may want to store their glasses upside down. To ward off contamination dangers and possible foul odors, elevate drinkware by using a mesh shelf liner and frequently disinfect it. Regular shelf cleanings and fully drying drinkware on a rack prior to storage is another safeguard.

Mugs, Cups, and Saucers

Both cups and mugs are used to hold mostly hot beverages. Cups traditionally hold hot tea, whereas mugs are associated with drinks like coffee, beer, and hot cocoa. Mugs are heavier, thicker, and sometimes made without handles. Mugs don't have accompanying saucers. They're often sold separately as a one-of-kind item added to a collection. Many people elect to showcase such collections outside the cabinets, which frees up storage space. Common places for this are on wall organizers, such as shelves, racks, or on furniture shelving. They're also featured on countertop organizers like cup trees or hung from hooks placed on the underside of upper cabinets.

Cups usually have an accompanying saucer. Traditional cups always have handles. There are many cabinet organizers designed to store cups and mugs. Popular cabinet organizers are pullout racks that install to the underside of a shelf. These organizers suspend cups and mugs by the handles so they don't take up shelf space. Accompanying saucers can be stored on the shelf below the hung cups. There are also freestanding cabinet racks that store mugs and cups by the handles from hooks, with a compartment for saucers.

It's important to recognize how your cups are being used in the home. It's not necessary for a coffee cup to be used exclusively for that beverage. Many times, cups are chosen for a size preference or because they include a matching saucer. Mugs are not part of this category.

Make sure to get rid any cups that are chipped or never used, like the common promotional cups that have collected over the years. Since cups are usually ceramic or glass, there is a good chance many have been broken along the way. Therefore, count sets to make sure they have not dwindled away to almost nothing, in case you need to replenish or invest in a new set altogether. Keep the number of cups on hand you actually need, not the amount that satisfies the number of people in the home since everyone may not use them. Figure that the number of cups to stock should equal the amount used in a two- to three-day period,

allowing enough time to wash them in between. Recognize that replacement cups are needed when you often find yourself grabbing cups from the dishwasher to clean for use.

The number of cups saucers you stock should correspond to the number of matching cups. If you frequently use cup saucers stack them next to the cups. Don't store saucers for the cups next to the regularly used cups if they're not used. Many people find it less work and less formal to use their cups without saucers, in spite of cup rings. In these cases, place them on a high shelf or with entertainment items, reserving them for guest use.

Plastic Drinkware

Polycarbonate and acrylic drinking glasses are shatter-resistant substitutes for glass. Such drinkware is safe for children and practical for outdoor use, and makes for worry-free entertaining. Place them into groups, such as those used daily, outdoor, entertainment, and so on, to inventory this category of drinkware. Decide which sets deserve cabinet space and which to store elsewhere. For example, store only the daily use drinking glasses in the upper kitchen cabinets. Move acrylic bar glasses to a bar station or an upper shelf where entertainment items are kept. Make certain to remove any that never receive use, such as outgrown children's sets.

Stacking plastic drinkware is the most efficient way to store them. Plastic tumblers used daily can reside next to the drinking glasses. Since plastic is unbreakable, they can also be stored in a basket or container on a base-cabinet shelf or drawer where small children can access them.

Plastic amusement park and festival cups don't store well unless you have a collection of them that nest together since alone they tip over from even the slightest touch. Generally, such cups are clutter in homes that have complete sets of drinkware unless there is a good reason to hold onto them. Plastic souvenir cups with lids that are used to safely transport hot or cold beverages don't need to occupy valuable shelf space; containerize them in a basket on a closet shelf or in a base cabinet. Store any sentimental souvenir cups with memorabilia items, and children can keep their favorites with their toys.

Formal Drinkware and Barware

Most formal and barware drinkware is made of glass or crystal. Crystal is glass with a lead content, which means it costs considerably more than regular glassware and is higher end. However, there is lead-free crystal to appease those opposed to lead. The lead component does have many attributes, though. Lead makes the glassware easier to sculpt for more ornate designs. Lead creates more clarity and is more refractive, which makes the glassware sparkle. Crystal should always be hand-washed.

Stemware

Stemware is drinkware commonly made of glass or crystal on footed stems with a bowl top. Stemware can be formal or casual. Crystal stemware usually comes in formal drinking glasses called goblets, champagne, and wineglasses to furnish dressy dining tables. The following are the most popular stemware glasses:

- Goblets
- Wine glasses
- Margarita
- Martini
- Brandy
- Sherry snifter
- Champagne
- Hurricane

Most stemware glasses hold alcoholic beverages, making a bar the natural place to house them. Many bars feature glass shelves for glassware storage or cabinets with clear door fronts. A bar can also be hidden in an armoire, cabinet, kitchen pantry, or closet. Closed storage locations, such as these behind doors, are best to keep fragile stemware safe and dust-free since they're not exposed to open air.

Stemware stored on a shelf cannot store upside down or rim down because the weight of the glass can crack the bowl, especially when they're thin. Always store stemware in single-file rows with the same glass, size, or type so there is no reason to reach into the back and risk knocking them over.

Many organizers are designed to safely store wineglasses, probably because the beverage is so popular. However, other stemware that share similar bowl dimensions can be stored in the average wineglass organizer. Most wineglass organizers are racks that suspend the glasses upside down, where the stem inserts into a fitted channel slot so it can hang. There are wall-mounted, under-the-cabinet, shelf, and countertop rack wineglass organizers that can be in almost any room of the home.

In homes short on storage space, stemware can be moved to specialized storage containers designed to safely house them. These organizers are made to store anywhere from six to twelve glasses in sectioned compartments, separating each glass so it does not break. These organizers are usually padded or quilted and have a zipper enclosure so the glasses stay dust-free. Use such organizers to store away the bulk of a large stemware collection for next party, keeping a few glasses in cabinet storage for daily use. Also, these organizers are good for packing antique and heirloom stemware for long-term storage.

CHAPTER 34

The Pantry: An Overview

A kitchen pantry is a specialized storage area designed to hold a large number of items. In the past, pantries were small rooms or walk-in closets off the kitchen that were lined with shelving for storage. Today, pantries have been brought into the kitchen for convenience. A kitchen pantry can be integrated in kitchen cabinets configured with tall double doors that extend twenty-four inches to thirty-six inches across. They're usually lined with a series of vertical shelving or pullout storage shelves.

Some kitchens have tall, freestanding, double-door storage cabinets for pantry use. A used wardrobe closet or armoire can easily be repurposed as a freestanding kitchen pantry. An attached reach-in kitchen closet could also be converted into a kitchen pantry by installing shelves or even a closet system for holding kitchen-related items.

A kitchen pantry was traditionally used as a stocking center for dry goods, such as canned goods, pasta, rice, spices, oils, and so on. But people now store other items in pantries, such as small appliances, serving pieces, entertainment items, alcohol, bottled drinks, canned drinks, canning supplies, pet supplies, and the like.

Organizing an Established Pantry

Your existing pantry will need to be decluttered then put back together so the items are arranged correctly for convenience and efficiency. Before you begin a pantry organizational project, gather trash liners, sorting boxes, and recycling bins. Label boxes for donation, relocation, garage sale, and food pantry. Clear a large area in your kitchen for sorting near where you can easily discard expired foods and recycle food packaging.

Depending upon how much is now in your pantry, you can empty it out completely or pull out one group of items at a time to sort and declutter. For example, if it's simply overwhelming to clear everything out at once, just start with one group, such as small appliances, to downsize.

Once your pantry areas are completely empty, clean them and record all the dimensions. Use these measurements to help you lay out the pantry space with your items and storage organizers.

Now is the time to determine what is not working for your current space and decide how to fix it.

Pantry measurements are especially important if you need to fit (or refit) your current space with new storage essentials. Determine a budget and then rank which pantry items need the most structure. Research various pantry organizers designed to accommodate your space. Once you select your favorite organizers, record their dimensions and costs. Then, decide which pantry items should go in those organizers and determine how many of each size/shape you'll need. You can make a sketch of your pantry and plot the placement of your organizers and pantry items. Design your pantry for logical uses and omit dead space by using all the height, width, and depth of the space.

Use your limited organizational time wisely; apply it to straightening rows, rotating inventories, condensing packages, cleaning shelves, and checking expiration dates, rather than keeping detailed lists. Alphabetizing canned goods and labeling pantry shelves is tedious organization and commonly fails. Likewise, labeling pantry shelves is difficult to follow since food packaging, quantities purchased, and food choices do change. Don't waste time trying to arrange things to fit into predetermined places. It's easiest to find canned goods when they're just arranged by food group: fruits, vegetables, beans, and the like.

Regulating Food Pantry Items

The types and quantities of foods we buy play a major role in how food turns over and occupies storage space. Understanding how food-purchasing decisions affect pantry organization is one of the best ways to keep your pantry in order.

Power Shopping

It's a great convenience for people to shop less often and save money by purchasing their food in large quantities at warehouse clubs. A surplus of a particular food may need to be divided between two storage locations: one in the kitchen and one elsewhere, which leads to rotating and managing food inventories.

Power buying has its merits, but be careful about choosing which items to purchase in mass quantities. Generally, foods with a long shelf life and those that prepare a number of meals, such as pasta, rice, or tomato sauce, are a safe bet, but many others are not.

Analyze the results of your bulk shopping and gain awareness of the consequences of your buying behavior by asking yourself the following questions:

- Which items are expiring before they're used?
- Is your family bored and tired of a food by the time you are halfway through consumption?
- If you purchase bulk products that come in variety packs, are the various assortments equally enjoyed, or are some discarded?
- Are the bottles or cans too big and difficult to situate in storage or the refrigerator?
- Are you purchasing items you would normally not buy if they weren't offered in bulk?
- Have you actually figured out if your bulk purchases are saving you money over discount stores that carry the items in smaller quantities?

Pantry Waste

First, determine why some of your pantry foods are discarded or expired before use. Pantries may become mismanaged for several reasons. In a disorganized pantry, the same foods tend to be bought over and over again because it's difficult to find out what is already in stock.

Our spending habits can play a big role in the problem. Many times, random foods are bought simply because we have a coupon or they're on sale, with no thought given as to whether they're needed or wanted. Keep a small whiteboard in the pantry and encourage family members to write items they want you to buy or to record when items run out. Then transfer the list onto a grocery shopping list. This way, you'll really be buying what the household needs.

Shopping without a well-planned shopping list is the number one reason people purchase too much food, which creates food clutter in the pantry. This happens because without a clear idea of what foods are really needed, too much time is spent in each and every grocery store aisle trying to remember what you need and tempting you to buy other things. Plus, you may return home only to discover you forgot something, which brings you back to the store for some more unnecessary buying.

A sure indicator that the wrong foods are coming into the home is when you feel worried things are not being eaten or household members are complaining that there is nothing to eat when the pantry is full.

Store Less to Save More

One of the best ways to keep your pantry organized is to stock a minimal number of food items, thereby creating less congestion and clutter so it's easier to clean, arrange, and find things. Smaller quantities of food items also decrease the probability that food will expire before use. Having smaller quantities of foods may also force household members to be less picky, making it surprising what they'll eat given fewer options. Good shopping strategies include:

1. Stock items that are key ingredients for many dishes and have a long shelf life in the largest quantities: canned vegetables and fruits, noodles, beans, rice, oats, dried fruits, sugar, oils, preserves, syrups, flour, salt, and so on. Purchase all other pantry foods in small quantities.

2. Buy only what is on the shopping list. Before you shop, straighten, arrange, and reconcile your pantry inventories. Keep the shopping list in a convenient kitchen location and update it on a daily basis.

CHAPTER 35

Efficient Pantry Arrangements

Almost every kitchen pantry could use some changes, and even the smallest modifications, like adding baskets or shelf dividers, can create additional order. Putting items back in the pantry in a successful layout requires that you carefully plan how to replace everything instead of simply putting items back where they were before. It's important to play around with moving existing organizers to different places that might be better or think about relocating items that were hard to find or access.

Usually, when you can visualize an organizer to solve a storage situation, it's probably out there, so spend the time hunting around at stores and websites that sell home organizational items. Every pantry is different. A walk-in pantry may have some floor or wall space to utilize for storage. A kitchen-cabinet pantry can be fitted with pullout shelves. It's important to capitalize on all the potential your pantry has to offer.

Planning the Pantry Space

To help plan your pantry space, use the following information as a reference. The different sections of the pantry each have special storage specifications.

Wall Space

Empty pantry walls can hold wall-mounted organizers, such as bulletin boards, hanging hooks, shelves, spice racks, and baskets. What you can store in these organizers is endless: packages of foods, cleaning tools, cups, canisters, tools, aprons, reusable grocery totes, and so on.

Floor Space

Use the floors of walk-in pantries for heavy goods or large, bulky items. Wheeled crates or dollies are convenient for maneuvering these goods around to other places outside the pantry. Good items for these organizers are pet food, soda, paper towels, linens, trash liners, bulk foods, outdoor accessories, holiday dinnerware, punch bowls, small appliances, and cookware.

Other key items to keep on pantry or closet floors are trash cans, water coolers, vacuum cleaners, step stools, compost bins, dry pet food bins, recycling bins, and cases of spirits, sodas, and water.

Lower Shelves

Shelves closest to the ground should hold heavy, bulky items, such as small appliances, bulk-size bags, jars, or cans of foods and beverages. Drinks that come in cardboard or plastic packaging with handles should stay intact while in pantry storage because it makes transportation to the refrigerator easier. Also, housewares, such as glass floral vases, soup tureens, fondue sets, punch bowls, and so on are good picks for these shelves.

Most organizers designed for a base cabinet can be incorporated into low pantry shelves. You can also create a vertical compartmentalized storage station in the pantry to store infrequently used trays, cookie sheets, platters, cupcake pans, stovetop griddles, and the like. Consider replacing lower shelves with pullout bins, baskets, or specialized racks when you have the budget to do so since seeing and accessing items on lower shelving is a common problem.

Use shallow pullout baskets for smaller items like serving utensils, flashlights, candles, batteries, and so on. Medium pullout baskets can hold things like loose produce and single-serve snacks. Use the larger pullout baskets sparingly since few items store well in them. You can also use specialized pullout or stationary beverage racks that hold bottles of wine and soda liters on their backs so they don't stand and take up lateral space.

Plastic dishpan tubs are an inexpensive alternative to storage baskets and containers; they're roomy enough to store a good amount and work well on middle and lower pantry shelves. These organizers are good for separating many groups of common kitchen items, such as vitamins, birthday supplies, storage bags, baking ingredients, plastic silverware, trash liners, and so on. These tubs have handles, so they're easy to transport to the kitchen counter where they're needed.

Middle Shelves

The middle shelves, which are at eye level, offer the best view and access for things you frequently need. Small to medium-size items are also best to store at eye level because they're harder to see on the upper or lower shelves. Also place fragile items, such as glass or ceramic serving pieces, at eye level, as upper shelving is a more dangerous place for them. Middle shelves don't necessarily need to have pullout shelving because items are easy to access at this level.

Organizers for Middle Shelves

- **GRADUATED STEPPER SHELVES**: Staircase-style shelf organizers are perfect for smaller upright items like spices and canned and bottled goods.
- **HELPER SHELVES**: These freestanding shelving units rest on top of an existing shelf, thus creating another platform for using vertical space. They're good organizers for fixed shelving.
- **UNDER-SHELF BASKETS**: These baskets slide under a fixed shelf to offer storage compartments and capture dead space.
- **TURNTABLES OR LAZY SUSANS**: Circular, revolving disc organizers such as these come in one or two tiers. They're great for hard-to-reach corners.
- **STACKABLE CONTAINERS**: These organizers are good for holding loose articles, such as batteries, plastic eating utensils, flashlights, or any small collection of items.
- **OPEN BASKETS OR CONTAINERS**: These organizers are perfect for holding grab-and-go, single-serve snacks. Also, hard-to-file or stack bags of chips and the like can be corralled in open containers. To keep order, each container can hold a separate type of snack. Open baskets are a great tool for arranging children's snacks so they're easy to see and reach and the kids don't have to rifle through the pantry and leave a mess behind.

- **CLEAR, AIRTIGHT FOOD-STORAGE CANISTERS:** Modular, stackable containers are perfect for transferring certain dry goods commonly sold in flimsy packaging, such as beans, rice, pasta, flour, and sugar.

Upper Shelves

For safety reasons, the upper pantry shelves should not store heavy containers or fragile items. Label all your containerized items with large clear letters so their contents are easy to read from a distance. It's best to store infrequently needed seasonal, entertainment, and holiday items overhead. Hard to stack or store snack trays, serving platters, baking pans, table placemats, cutting boards, cupcake pans, and cooling racks can be vertically arranged in bakeware racks, placing such items sideways so they're easy to see and grab. Surplus paper products, such as paper towels, napkins, and toilet paper are also perfect for upper-shelf storage. Any lightweight boxes of bulk snacks, pasta, and so on purchased from warehouse clubs are fine here.

Inside the Pantry Door

There are many organizers created to house items on the insides of cabinet or pantry doors. They can be mounted or hung over the top of the door. You can also use a fabric shoe organizer, which offers many pockets to store small items like spice packs, flashlights, bag clips, aluminum foil, clear wrap, parchment paper, sandwich bags, paper lunch bags, twist ties, grocery lists, writing tools, napkins, straws, and the like.

These lightweight organizers are perfect for thin doors or shallow pantries. Thick, heavy doors can support mountable spice racks, baskets, or shelves and can hold almost anything that could rest on a pantry shelf. Mountable rail organizers

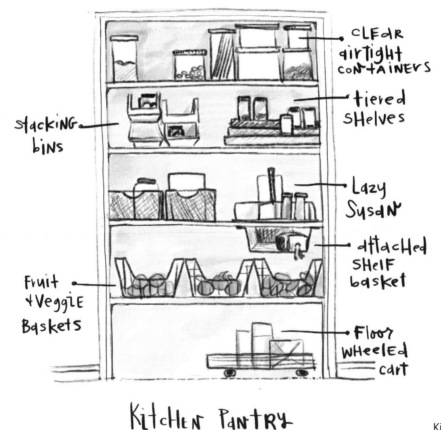

Kitchen Pantry

FIGURE 35.01
Kitchen Pantry Organization

that attach baskets and shelves are adjustable so the baskets and shelves can be rearranged when storage needs change.

Pantry and Cabinet Storage for Food

While you declutter and organize dry goods, consider the pantry's location in relation to the kitchen. Items used on a daily basis should be stored in a pantry only if it's located in the hub of the kitchen. It may be necessary to move certain items out of the pantry and into other places where they would be better suited, such as kitchen cabinets or closets. It's also important to learn how to properly package foods and know when it's time to dispose of them. Understanding the manufacturer's terminology for how long a food stays fresh or safe to consume helps you make the right downsizing decisions for different foods.

A food product's best-when-used-by date is different than its expiration date, which is the last date a product should be consumed. The manufacturer establishes a best-when-used-by date to ensure optimal food flavor and quality, not for home-storage purposes. Even among similar products, such as instant hot chocolate, various manufacturers have different expiration dates because ingredients vary. Therefore, it's a good practice to contact the manufacturer or reference their website to find out how long a given product can safely be stored in your cupboards after the best-when-used-by date. Then with a permanent marker, record this information on the package next to the best-when-used-by date.

Alphanumeric hodgepodge on a container is a code that manufacturers use for tracking or packing data. Since there is no standardized coding system for foods, it's up to you to contact the manufacturer to find out the how long the product is good, given its code. Record the actual calendar date on which the product expires with a permanent market right over the cryptic code.

Boxed and Canned Foods

Most boxed foods and canned goods can stand or stack on shelving without organizers. In fact, certain organizers designed for them—such as the gravity-feed can rack organizer that consists of slanted tiered wire shelves so cans resting on their sides roll forward to dispense one at a time—can actually waste space. These organizers are bulky and, when not stocked to capacity, waste space. Also, cans in the back of the organizer are hard to access. Therefore, stack cans since they're designed to do so. Store boxed foods separate from canned. Always keep similar foods grouped together on the shelving, so you find things easily and know how much you have of each type. Face can labels forward and boxed items so that their contents are easy to identify.

Bottles and Jars

Similarly, face bottles and jars forward to see their contents. Generally, bottles and jars cannot stack, so they need to stand in neat rows. Keep like items grouped together in general classifications, such as beverages, condiments, or marinades.

Which cans, bottles, jars, or boxed foods you place in the pantry or kitchen cabinets will depend upon your personal preferences. Some people like to use their pantries as a storage center for excess and keep smaller amounts of each food type in their kitchen cabinets. Others like to divide types of foods according to usage: keeping the cans of soups or boxes of cereal used daily in the kitchen cabinets, but less-used ingredients, such as unopened jars of minced garlic or olives, in the food pantry. It's important to note that shelves supporting multiple cans, bottles, or jars need to be strong since many shelving materials are prone to buckle from excessive weight.

Baked Goods

Donuts, cakes, pies, breads, and the like are great for pantry storage, especially if you don't want your countertops congested with these items. It's important to recognize the shelf life of these goods, especially those without best-when-used-by dates, like homemade treats or items purchased from a bakery. Most baked goods keep well only for a few days.

Baking Items

A good number of baking items, such as sugar, flour, chocolate, honey, spices, herbs, oils, and marshmallows, can be stored in more than one location since they may serve multiple purposes. The most important thing to consider is their proper storage, which is commonly misunderstood by many. The following information addresses the best ways to preserve baking items and good storage options.

Sugar and Sugar Substitutes

Sugar substitutes and granulated or unrefined sugars that are used daily in your beverages should be stored with the coffee and tea products by the brewing machines and cups. Such sugars can be contained in a pourer or serving dispenser. Keep sugar packets and sticks in a caddy designed for them. Sugar cubes or tablets can be stored in a lidded serving bowl for easy access.

Store bulk supplies of granulated white sugar, unrefined raw sugar, and sugar substitutes with your baking items or with spices in a pantry, if there is one. Bulk packaging for sugar is sold in plastic zip-seal pouches, paper bags, boxes, or plastic containers. The paper bags are too fragile and leak the sugar through the seal, so when you purchase your sugar in bags, transfer it into a lidded container. You can reuse a plastic coffee container or glass jar with a tight fitted lid and store it in a cool, dry place.

Sugar has an indefinite shelf life when stored properly, which is why best-when-purchased-by dates are not posted on packaging. However, brown sugar's flavor is at its best for only six months after opening. Therefore, freeze surplus in airtight packages to extend its flavor life. Sugar substitutes, granulated white sugar, and unrefined raw sugars will get lumpy and hard from moisture, so keep their containers dry and away from humidity. Brown sugar requires more storage maintenance because it's prone to hardening once it comes into contact with air. To prevent this, place an apple slice, lemon wedge, or piece of bread with the brown sugar. Shaped terra clay, commonly sold in disk form, is made for this purpose and can be found at most specialty kitchen stores. Brown sugar should be stored in an airtight container with a scoop.

Honey

Honey has an indefinite shelf life due to its high sugar content. Therefore, keep honey away from the same elements that deteriorate sugar. You want to store honey appropriately so that it keeps its texture and flavor. Don't refrigerate honey, because extreme temperatures cause honey to become cloudy, which is referred to as crystallization. This does not ruin the honey, but you'll have to liquefy it again to get its texture back.

Kitchen cabinet and pantry storage is ideal, provided it's away from a heat or moisture source. If needed, you can keep just one small jar of honey near the coffee and tea items. Store the excess with baking items or in a storage pantry. Make sure that the cover or lid to the honey is sealed tightly before returning it to storage so it does not absorb moisture or odors from the air. When you have more than one bottle of opened honey, condense the two, provided they're the same brand. Don't mix together processed and raw unpasteurized honey since their ingredients vary too greatly.

Spices and Herbs

Spices and herbs don't go bad in the sense that they go rancid, but they'll lose their potency over time and not flavor foods as intended. Spices and herbs are adversely affected by heat, moisture, light, and air, which all speed up flavor loss. These elements are responsible for shortening the shelf life of spices and herbs by staling, fading, caking, and deteriorating their contents. This means that you need to guard your spices from the stove, sink, dishwasher, windows, radiators, and heat vents. Also, handling your spices and herbs properly helps preserve them. Therefore, don't pour them over a steamy beverage; rather, premeasure them beforehand with a clean, dry utensil.

Generally, whole spices can be inspected for quality by simply smelling them for a solid aroma. The stronger the scent, the fresher the spice or herb. Whole spices and herbs should last up to five years in proper storage arrangements. Ground spices and herbs last up to three years when stored well. Test your ground spices and herbs by immediately sniffing them after they have been gently stirred or shaken. A lack of aroma indicates flavor loss or lack of freshness.

Don't overstock spices and herbs, because they're typically used in such small amounts and you want it to still be fresh by the time you reach the end of the container. For this reason, it's best to wait to restock your spices and herbs until they're nearly gone and limit the supply to one bottle each.

One centrally located, well-organized spice rack is enough, provided it has easy access for beverages, baking, and cooking preparation. A cool, dry place away from moisture and heat is necessary, and you can use a drawer or cabinet. There are drawer organizers for spices and herbs that can keep them from rolling around. In an upper cabinet, use a tiered shelf for your spices or a lazy Susan so they're easy to see and access. Store them in a food pantry only when it's located in the kitchen near the cooking areas. A mountable spice rack placed on the inside door is a good pantry organizer.

Chocolate

Store chocolate in a slightly cool, dry, dark place. Sunlight will melt chocolate and can cause white chocolate to go rancid. Keep your chocolate away from all the heat sources in your kitchen, such as heat vents, steamy appliances, stoves, windows, and the oven.

Milk and white chocolate are good for about one year, and darker chocolates can last up to two years under proper storage conditions.

All chocolate has a best-used-before date and is safe to consume when this date has lapsed. However, for best taste, keep regular chocolates no more than four months past this date., They taste best for six months when stored in the refrigerator and for eight months in the freezer.

Fine chocolates taste their best only for a couple weeks past the best-used-before date. In refrigeration, fine chocolates stay fresh up to four weeks and in the freezer only four months.

Oils

Most oils used in cooking and baking need to reside in a cool, dark place, such as a cupboard or pantry. Light, heat, and oxygen will cause oxidation and eventually turn oils rancid. Heavily processed refined oils are shelf stable for dry storage, whereas the purer, unrefined oils need refrigeration. Shelf-stable oils include canola, soybean, palm, vegetable, peanut, coconut, and processed olive oil.

Marshmallows

Marshmallows are a popular item to place in hot beverages. They're also used often in baking. Therefore, you can store them with your baking goods, beverage items, or both. Marshmallows usually have just under a year of shelf life from the manufacturer's date, whether opened or unopened. Any marshmallows past their expiration date should be discarded, especially if they have lost considerable texture.

Marshmallows need airtight storage accommodations, as they're prone to harden and stick together from the slightest exposure to air or humidity. Keep marshmallows in an airtight plastic container and store in a cool, dry place.

Coffee and Tea Storage

Coffee can lose its freshness and flavor over time. Storage arrangements play a big part in preserving coffee. It's important to note that once coffee loses freshness, you can compost it or directly sprinkle onto soil as fertilizer. There are different forms of coffee, starting with the coffee bean itself. Then there is commercially ground, freshly ground, coffee pods, and instant coffee, all of which require distinct storage arrangements.

Coffee Beans and Ground Coffee

Coffee beans and freshly ground coffee, which is coffee just grinded from the bean, have similar storage requirements. Strong odors can be absorbed into coffee, changing its flavor. Air, light, and heat also adversely affect the flavor and degrade the quality of coffee. For these reasons, it's best to store ground coffee and beans in airtight, opaque containers in a dry, dark cabinet or pantry near the brewing devices. Use ceramic containers since plastic or metal taste can leach into the coffee flavor. In proper storage, roasted beans last a couple weeks, whole green beans one year, and freshly ground coffee only a few days.

Commercial ground coffee, which is the kind lining the shelves at the grocery store in metal or plastic containers, has a best-when-used-by date. However, after opening, it's good for six weeks or so in refrigerated storage, which is recommended.

Coffee Pods

Coffee pods, the tiny cups designed to brew a single serving of coffee, are commonly sold in lots of ten or twelve contained in cardboard boxes marked with a best-when-used-by date. Usually coffee pods can maintain flavor up to several weeks past their dates, but it's best to go by taste. Coffee pods are airtight, so they can store outside a pantry or cabinet. There are several coffee-pod organizers designed to store individual coffee pods labeled with their contents. These organizers can reside in a cabinet or next to the brewing machines.

Instant Coffee

Instant coffee has an extensive shelf life, sometimes two years. However, once opened, instant coffee stays fresh only for a month. It's recommended that instant coffee be stored in a dry, dark place, such as a cabinet or pantry.

Coffee Condiments

Coffee condiments, such as syrups and creamers, are generally best stored alongside coffee for convenience in cabinet or pantry storage when they're shelf stable. Coffee syrups will degrade in color, flavor, and aroma from moisture or heat.

Therefore, never store them on the counter by sunlight or next to steamy espresso machines.

Keep nondairy liquid coffee creamer concentrate, which does not require refrigeration, in a cool, dry place. This type of coffee creamer comes in individual tubs or in a multiple-serving plastic bottle. The tubs generally come in cardboard boxes with an opening for dispensing. The bottles can include a pump that exposes the product to air, thus reducing the shelf life to a month. Such bottles commonly have a section to mark the date when opened. Refrigeration clogs these pumps, and the cold does not extend the life of this type of creamer. Powered creamers stay fresh up until their marked expiration date, whether opened or not.

Tea

Tea is purchased either in loose-leaf form or in permeable bags for steeping. Tea leaves are both porous and fragile. Elements such as air, heat, moisture, light, and pungent odors can eventually deteriorate tea taste. Therefore, avoid refrigerating your loose tea and tea bags, because it creates condensation and hence moisture. Also avoid storing near strong spices, which can permeate the leaves, and never keep tea near a heat source, like a stove, or in sunlight. Airtight, opaque containers, such as popular tin canisters sold at tea shops are the best storage organizers for loose tea. Cabinet or pantry storage is recommended.

Although tea varieties vary, most loose tea has a one-year shelf life when stored properly. Most tea bags have the best-when-used-by date stamped on the carton, pouch, or canister. Whether they're made of nylon or paper, tea bags are porous and will degrade from exposure to air, light, heat, moisture, and odors; they should be stored in airtight opaque canisters. Label the type of tea plus the expiration date on the canister, and store these canisters in dry, dark pantries or cabinets.

Powdered Drink Mixes

Most powdered drink mixes have a two-year shelf life. Make certain that you store these items in their recommended places after opening, because some may require refrigeration whereas others can be damaged by such storage conditions. Drink mixes that don't require refrigeration should be stored at room temperature in a cool, dry place, such as in a cabinet or pantry.

Check how long your powdered mixes stay fresh upon opening; some are even good past their best-when-used-by dates, while others have only a few months. It's best to record with a permanent maker how long a drink mix stays fresh upon opening on the container. Make certain your powered drink mixes are being consumed, especially those made to for daily use, such as meal replacements. Be careful to check expiration dates on seasonal drink mixes like lemonade for summer or hot chocolate for winter. It's common for seasonal drinks to expire before they're used up since they do not receive regular consumption.

CHAPTER 36

The Refrigerator

The first step to refrigerator organization is getting acquainted with your refrigerator's operational manual. Understanding how the refrigerator operates and knowing which compartments are designed for what foods will help you arrange everything effectively. You should also know the temperature differences in your refrigerator since many foods need certain conditions to stay safe for consumption. You may want to invest in refrigerator thermometers and place them in different areas, such as the top, middle, and bottom doors and drawers. You should also know how to regulate the humidity controls on the crisper drawers, because some types of produce require certain humidity levels.

Decluttering the Refrigerator

Begin organizing the refrigerated foods by getting rid of unwanted and expired foods. Set a large garbage can or compost bin next to the refrigerator. Clear off counter space next to the sink to place foods that need to be discarded in the disposal and those that need their packaging cleaned for recycling.

When you are uncertain about a food's expiration date or age, discard it. Never go by how the food the smells or tastes. Expired foods can contain harmful bacteria. Obtain a chart online that lists the shelf life of different foods once they have been cooked or their packaging has been opened. Properly repackage any foods that are not sealed well. When you have more than one opened package, bottle, or jar of the same item, to be safe condense them into the one that has the closest expiration date.

Cleaning the Refrigerator

It's convenient to perform a deep cleaning of the refrigerator while you organize. If you think the job will take a long time, fill a couple coolers and the sink with ice to safely store your refrigerated goods while you work.

Start by emptying the entire contents of the refrigerator. As you take items out of the refrigerator, place like items together. For example, keep all the produce in one group and the meats in another pile.

Clean the entire refrigerator by removing the shelves and compartments. Follow manufacturer cleaning instructions or fill your bathtub with hot soapy water and soak these parts. Don't forget to clean the walls and ceiling of the refrigerator unit. Completely dry the refrigerator parts before returning them. Prior to reinstalling the shelving, you'll want to plan what goes where, so you'll know the correct distances to mark between shelves.

Additionally, clean items before you return to them the refrigerator, but don't use a cleaning product with chemicals. Dilute vinegar with water or use a mild soap and wipe off gunk on the outside of bottles, jars, cartons, etc. You may also choose to clean them with only water from your sink's faucet and a paper towel. Be careful when cleaning the rims or spouts of containers, because you don't want anything to leak into the food that might be contaminating.

Proper Produce Storage

The good thing about produce is that it's obvious when it expires. Most produce, once ripe or at its peak, will keep only for several days. Knowing the shelf life of different produce is invaluable when you shop since you can determine how much you'll use in a given period of time.

Generally, replicate in your home how produce is packaged and displayed in a store. Farmers, packers, and grocers don't want their merchandise to go bad or they can't sell it, so they reference trained professionals to learn how to achieve maximum shelf life for their produce. In some cases, produce sold out in the open is still ripening, and once that process ends, refrigeration can take over for preservation. However, certain fruits and vegetables are damaged by cold storage. Some lose flavor and texture from refrigeration. In particular, tomatoes lose nutrients, flavor, and texture in the refrigerator. Eggplant actually spoils faster in cold storage.

Other fruits and vegetables that are not recommended for refrigeration prior to cutting are citrus fruits, cucumbers, potatoes, bananas, squash, papayas, mangoes, garlic, basil, ginger, pumpkin, apples, peppers, melons, pineapples, and pomegranates. It's important to understand proper fruit and vegetable storage procedures; also, consider how your household members like to eat their produce, in spite of nutritional benefits. Sometimes chilled is the only way they enjoy it.

Specialized Produce Storage Organizers

Experts offer varying opinions about how and where particular fruits and vegetables should be stored. For this reason, the best thing to do is to first follow good advice and then try alternative suggestions until you achieve optimal longevity for your produce.

Green Bags

These special produce bags are designed to keep produce fresher ten times longer, but they have received mixed reviews, which creates skepticism. The basis of this product is that the bags absorb the ethylene gas released by fruits and vegetables while ripening. Although expensive, the bags are reusable up to a certain point. Green bags are not microwaveable or freezer friendly. They may be worth a try, but realize that you could preserve your produce very well on your own with just some basic storage knowledge.

Veggie and Fruit Keepers

Veggie and fruit keeper organizers are ideal for cut produce. These storage products are designed to trap odors and even extend the life of produce. Some are designed in the exact form, size, and color of a given fruit or vegetable, making them easy to identify and find. You can find produce storage organizers with built-in colanders that both wash and store. Some have adjustable vents to regulate air circulation and water reservoirs to create needed moisture for certain produce. Such storage organizers usually have printed venting and moisture instructions.

Crisper Drawers

Crisper drawers, also called humidity drawers, are designed to provide the humidity important for preserving many types of produce. Refrigerators typically have two separate crisper drawers for organization: one for fruits and the other for vegetables. Generally, fruits require low humidity levels and vegetables high, but this is not always the case. For example, fruits that wilt easily, such as strawberries, watermelon, and okra, require a high level of humidity. Crisper drawers have a sliding humidity control setting that ranges from high to low. A high setting cuts off airflow so humidity is locked inside the drawer, keeping in moisture. A low setting opens up a vent so moisture escapes, decreasing humidity

Separating fruits and vegetables in storage is important because many fruits emit high levels of a ripening agent called ethylene gas, which speeds up decay for many vegetables that are sensitive to it. Exceptions to the rule are watermelon and unripe bananas, which are ethylene-sensitive fruits and not high producers of the gas.

Within the crisper drawer, divide produce by type with plastic bags. Use perforated bags or simply slice openings in regular plastic bags to release the carbon dioxide that becomes trapped in sealed packaging, as it causes food to rot. These bags will stop the produce from dehydrating, especially beneficial for those with no outer skin. Nonperforated bags generate too much humidity, which leads to condensation and mold or bacteria growth.

One of the biggest problems with crisper drawers is that produce is often forgotten in these places: out of sight, out of mind. If this is a common problem in your home, cut up your fruits and vegetables and store them in sectioned vegetable trays or transparent containers. Keep them handy and visible on the refrigerator shelves. Use spare crisper drawers to stash items like excess soda or juice boxes, and turn down the humidity. Remove the drawers if you just want an open-storage look, so items are easy to view.

When Produce Enters the Kitchen

The first thing to do when you arrive home from the grocery store is sort your fruits and vegetables. Anything that is still ripening can be stored in an open, well-ventilated bowl or basket in a cool place away from sunlight and heat. Once ripened, most produce can be transferred to the refrigerator to maintain the ripeness level. Don't wash most produce prior to refrigeration, because moisture can cause it to go bad more quickly.

Home refrigerators are generally cold and dry. Temperatures stay a little below 40°F, with humidity levels at 50–60 percent. It's also important to note that some produce types with many varieties don't all have similar shelf lives. For example, apples come in many varieties, but don't all have the same shelf life.

The following storage tips are for common produce items.

Fresh Fruit

- APPLES: Keep in the fridge from the start in a perforated plastic bag, not in the crisper since they need air circulation and less humidity.
- BANANAS: Ripen at room temperature. Suspend on banana tree to lessen bruising. Store ripened bananas in refrigerator, where they'll turn brown but still be good on the inside.
- BLUEBERRIES: Refrigerate from the start since they don't ripen after harvest. Keep in a firm container covered in plastic; the crisper is too humid.
- CHERRIES: Refrigerate immediately since they don't ripen after harvest. Store in shallow, loosely covered bowl to disperse their weight and prevent bruising. Plastic bags also work. Keep in colder part of refrigerator: bottom shelf or near fridge walls.
- CITRUS: Stays most juicy at room temperature; don't bag. Refrigeration can prolong shelf life, but they lose water during refrigeration. For long-term storage, individually cover in waxy paper. Store inside a cardboard box and keep in a cool, dark place.
- CRANBERRIES: Refrigerate from the start since they don't ripen after harvest. Store in tightly sealed plastic bag, airtight container, or heavy-duty freezer bag.
- GRAPES: Refrigerate at once, because they don't ripen after harvest. Keep on the vine and store in perforated plastic bag. They require less humidity so upper shelf is fine, but not the crisper.
- MELONS (WATERMELON, HONEYDEW, CANTALOUPE, AND CRENSHAW): Store at room temperature in a cool, dark place until ripe. Store whole ripe melon in the refrigerator crisper, where humidity levels are high. Cover and store cut melon on a refrigerator shelf.

- PEACHES, PEARS, PLUMS, NECTARINES, MANGOES, APRICOTS, AND KIWIFRUIT: Ripen at room temperature away from sunlight and then refrigerate. Store in perforated plastic bags.
- RASPBERRIES, HUCKLEBERRIES, BOYSENBERRIES, BLACKBERRIES, AND CURRANTS: Refrigerate at once, because they don't ripen after harvest. Place in single layer in a shallow container since they're too fragile for deep containers. Cover with plastic wrap or a tea towel.
- STRAWBERRIES: Refrigerate at once, because they don't ripen after harvest. Store uncovered in perforated container. Crisper is too humid.

Fresh Vegetables

- ASPARAGUS: Trim ends and stand them upright in a jar with water at the bottom. Refrigerate and cover in plastic.
- AVOCADOS: Keep at room temperature. Store cut halves with pit intact tightly wrapped in plastic in the refrigerator.
- BASIL, CILANTRO, AND PARSLEY: Snip off bottoms and stand upright in a jar/cup of water. Don't rinse leaves. Store basil at room temperature, parsley either in fridge or at room temperature, and cilantro covered in loose plastic in fridge.
- BROCCOLI, CABBAGE, CAULIFLOWER, BRUSSELS SPROUTS, AND RUTABAGA: Refrigerate in the crisper drawer inside perforated plastic bags.
- CARROTS, BEETS, PARSNIPS, AND TURNIPS: Remove leafy tops and store in crisper drawer. Use perforated plastic bags.
- CUCUMBERS, EGGPLANT, PEPPERS, PASSION FRUIT, AND SUMMER SQUASH (ZUCCHINI): Store in a place with cool temperature outside refrigerator. Cut produce gets wrapped and stored in refrigerator.
- CORN: Remove husk if not consumed immediately. Vacuum seal and store in the freezer.

- **GARLIC:** No refrigeration. Store in a dark, cool spot where air can circulate without moisture.
- **GREEN BEANS AND PEAS:** Refrigerate in crisper. Store in perforated plastic bag and don't trim or cut until used.
- **LETTUCE (ROMAINE, ICEBERG, ENDIVE, SWISS CHARD, SPINACH, RADICCHIO, WATERCRESS, RAPINI, RHUBARB, ETC.):** One of the very few produce goods that can be washed prior to storage. Refrigerate in crisper. Wrap in plastic, along with white paper towel, to absorb excess moisture.
- **WINTER SQUASH AND PUMPKIN:** Store in a dark, cool, dry place outside the refrigerator.
- **CELERY:** One of the few produce goods that can be washed prior to refrigeration storage. Remove leaves or ribs that are bad. Wrap in aluminum foil or plastic and store in crisper or submerge cut pieces upright in water within a sealed container in refrigerator.
- **CELERY ROOT:** Remove stalks. Refrigerate in perforated plastic bag.
- **CHESTNUTS:** Store unpeeled at room temperature in a dry, well-ventilated place. Extend shelf life by placing them in perforated bag in refrigerator crisper. When peeled, wrap in aluminum foil or airtight plastic wrap and freeze.
- **FRESH FIGS:** Wrap in plastic and refrigerate in coldest section (bottom shelf or near fridge walls).
- **FRESH DATES:** For short term, store in airtight container at room temperature. Refrigerate for long-term storage.
- **JICAMA:** Store whole and uncovered at room temperature. Cover and refrigerate cut pieces.
- **LEEKS:** Wrap in damp paper towel and seal in perforated bag. Refrigerate in the crisper.
- **MUSHROOMS:** No refrigeration. Keep in a cool, dark place. Store in a paper bag or cardboard container in which they're commonly sold. Cover loosely with paper towel.

- **ONIONS:** No refrigeration. Store in cool, dark, well-ventilated place separate from potatoes. Hanging baskets offer good ventilation. Cut pieces can be stored in a sealed container in the refrigerator.
- **POTATOES:** Keep in a dark, dry, cool area or brown bag. Refrigeration converts their starch to sugar, thus altering taste.
- **SPROUTS:** Refrigerate in crisper in perforated bags. Leave delicate sprouts, like alfalfa sprouts, in original ventilated plastic container and refrigerate.
- **TOMATOES:** Ripen at room temperature in an aerated basket away from sunlight. Refrigeration causes flavor and aroma loss. Refrigerate only cut tomatoes.
- **TOMATILLOS:** Keep in paper bag with husks intact and store in crisper or in a bowl with a paper towel over them in the refrigerator.

Proper Meat, Poultry, Fish, and Seafood Storage

The main concern when storing uncooked meat, poultry, and fish is the potential harmful microbes that can be present in either the food or its juices. Don't let raw meat, poultry, fish, and seafood contact any other foods, especially items that cannot be cooked to kill bacteria, such as produce or ready-to-eat foods. This type of cross contamination can easily be avoided by using a few simple storage strategies.

Leave meat, poultry, fish, and seafood in their original packaging; simply double wrap the product in a leakproof bag or container or place it on a plate. It's neither necessary nor advisable to repackage these items. The less you handle raw meats or have them in contact with other parts of the kitchen, the better. Wrapping meat well also prevents dehydration from the dry and cool refrigeration. Plus, well-wrapped meats and fish don't absorb other food odors that get trapped inside the refrigerator.

Store raw meat, poultry, and seafood on the lowest refrigerator shelf where temperatures are the coldest. At this location, there is no chance that potentially contaminated juices can trickle down onto other foods and expose them to harmful bacteria. Know how long raw meats can store safely in your refrigerator. Go by the packing date and if it's not clear, consult the meat or seafood department of the store where it was purchased or call the USDA's meat and poultry hotline number at 800-535-4555.

Proper Dairy Storage

Natural, processed, and imitation cheese (sliced, block, string, shredded, and cubed) should be stored together on a shelf in a basket, refrigerator cheese drawer, or crisper drawer set on high humidity. There are clear plastic storage containers designed to store slices of cheese and others that fit big blocks of processed cheese products. These storage devices are perfect for refrigerator drawers since they keep the cheese squish-free. Jarred or containerized cheese sauces and spreads can be housed on a refrigerator shelf with other ready-to-eat foods or with the condiments on the door shelves.

Natural Cheeses
Most varieties of natural cheese should be wrapped in cheese paper, parchment paper, or wax paper after being opened. Double wrap strong pungent cheeses, such as blue cheese and gorgonzola, to avoid their aromas permeating other

foods. Change paper after each use and write the cheese type on the outside. Then, enclose it in loosely wrapped plastic or a vented plastic storage bag; natural cheese needs to breathe because it contains enzymes and bacteria.

Another option is to use a vented plastic container that offers air space for cheese to breathe. Tupperware makes a specialized one for blocks or wedges of natural cheeses. These containers can store in a compartment or on a refrigerator shelf. Natural cheese should be kept at 35°–45°F. In a crisper drawer, set the humidity at a high level.

Naturally dried cheeses, like Parmesan or Romano, should stay in closely sealed containers to prevent moisture loss and will remain fresh for a month after opening. Soft to semisoft cheeses, such as feta, ricotta, and mozzarella, last several days once opened. They should remain in their store-bought plastic containers and kept well covered. Cream cheese in foil should be wrapped in a plastic bag after opening or transferred to a plastic container, where it's good for about ten days; the same goes for cream cheese purchased in a tub. Cottage cheese is good for several days after opening.

Processed Cheese
Due to preservatives, processed cheeses, such as Velveeta pasteurized process cheese or Kraft American slices, have a longer shelf life than natural cheese, and they're often packaged ready for refrigerated storage. The sandwich-size processed cheese slices usually come individually wrapped in plastic sheets, and the outer packaging marks their best-when-used-by date. When the outer packaging is flimsy and no longer holds the cheese slices together, transfer them to a plastic baggie or lidded container and place a sticker with the best-when-used-by date on the front.

Processed shredded cheese should stay in its store-bought package, which is typically a resealable pouch. Cheese spreads, sauces, dips, or any processed cheese food that was sold outside the refrigerated section should stay in the cupboard before being opened; after opening, refrigerate only the ones that indicate it's necessary.

Imitation cheese will have a name like "sandwich singles" or "sandwich mate" and will not be called a cheese. Since there is little dairy in these products, their shelf life is quite long. These products usually come in ready-to-store packaging, such as individually wrapped sandwich slices or resealable pouches that contain a shredded version of imitation cheese. Imitation cheese needs to stay in protective wrapping or it will dry out.

Eggs

Keep eggs in their original container that marks their sell-by date. The carton protects the eggs from absorbing other food odors in the refrigerator. Also, the carton is designed to store eggs with the large end up so the yolk stays centered. Don't store eggs in door shelves where temperatures fluctuate. Eggs need cold spots in the refrigerator, like middle or lower shelves.

It's important to note that an egg carton stamped with a sell-by date is different than a use-by date. Sell-by dates usually give you a few weeks after the date to consume properly stored eggs.

Hard-boiled eggs will last one week in the refrigerator. Place them in a covered container and label when they were cooked.

- Raw egg yolks keep for one week and egg whites two to four days. Keep them in a date-stamped, lidded container.

- Egg substitutes commonly sold in cardboard cartons will keep for three days after opening. Note the date when the carton was opened with a permanent maker or freezer sticker.
- Open packages of dried eggs should be tightly sealed in refrigeration. Keep unopened packages in a cool, dry place like a pantry or cabinet.

Butter

Many butter manufacturers recommend that butter should receive cold storage in accordance with the USDA and Federal Department of Agriculture (FDA) guidelines. However, opinions vary, and some claim butter can be stored at room temperature for up to two weeks, provided the room temperature is below 70°F. Keep unrefrigerated butter in an airtight, lidded butter tray, because oxygen will cause it to become rancid. You can find "French butter dishes" or "Acadian butter dishes" that are intended to store butter outside the refrigerator. These butter dishes use water to form a seal between the butter and the air. To be safe when storing your butter outside cold storage, keep it out of sunlight.

Keep refrigerated butter in its original wrapper to prevent odor absorption. Wrapped sticks should remain in the original package that marks the best-when-used-by date; transfer to the freezer when close to this date, where it will stay fresh for up to six months (record this date on package before freezing). Contain unwrapped butter in a lidded butter keeper, where it will stay fresh for a few weeks.

Butter Substitutes, Margarine, and Spreads

There are a number of butter-like spreads on the market that have ingredients such as various oils that may require refrigeration storage in order to keep the spreads' shape, flavor, and texture intact. For this reason, it's best to consult the manufacturer of the product for storage information once the product is opened. Most opened butter spreads keep for about one month in refrigeration.

Milk and Milk Products

Store milk on an upper shelf, along with cartons and bottles of other beverages. Don't store milk inside the door shelves, because the temperature fluctuations from opening the refrigerator makes this location too warm for dairy products. Open milk keeps for about a week; the higher the fat content, the longer it will keep. Exposure to light and heat decreases milk's shelf life.

Half and Half and Cream

Once cream is opened, it's usually good for one to two weeks, regardless of the date stamped on the label; once spoiled, it will curdle. Store these products on the same refrigerator shelf where you keep sour cream, yogurt, cottage cheese, and other dairy products.

Sour Cream

Store-bought plastic tubs of sour cream stay fresh anywhere from one to two weeks after opening, until a pinkish tint or foul smell forms. Most containers of sour cream can be stacked with other dairy items, such as custard and yogurt, on a cold shelf; don't store in the door, where the temperature fluctuates.

Yogurt, Pudding, and Custard

Yogurt needs to be kept in a sealed container and always refrigerated. Yogurt sealed in foil can be transferred to a lidded plastic storage container after opening, if plastic lids are not provided. How long a yogurt stays fresh after opening varies greatly by brand; the range is anywhere from two to ten days. Record the date yogurt expires with a permanent marker for all opened yogurt.

Pudding and custard are a combination of a milk or cream and egg yolk, so store them with similar items, such as sour cream, on a colder shelf. Puddings prepared from package mix should be placed in a covered container in the refrigerator for no more than a few days. Individual packs of pudding cups—commonly sold in a cardboard container—can be stored in the fridge (for temperature preference) or in the pantry to conserve space. These products are stamped with their best-when-used-by dates.

Custards can be stored in the same manner as pudding. Custard begins to separate within a few days, which is when it needs to be discarded. Don't store custard in a can; instead, transfer it to rubber, glass, or plastic containers in cold storage.

Whipped Cream and Toppings

Homemade whipped cream stays fresh only for one or two days in the refrigerator. Therefore, make only what you'll use. Store it covered in a lined colander so the cream stays formed and the liquid drains into a pan.

Canned whipped creams and toppings should last up to their best-when-used-by date, whether opened or not. Whipped topping is an imitation whipped cream with very little dairy, but it still needs very cold temperatures to hold its volume. Tubs of whipped topping should be stored in the freezer and transferred to the refrigerator for use, where it will keep for about two weeks.

Proper Beverage Storage

Store beverages contained in tall bottles, cartons, pitchers, and jugs on the upper shelves of the refrigerator, as opposed to the coldest lower shelves, which are more suitable for foods such as meat products. Use the height of these items to mark the distance from the top shelf to the ceiling of the refrigerator. Nondairy beverages like soda and water can also be stored in refrigerator door compartments.

Arrange single-serve bottles, pouches, or cartons in like beverage groups with their labels facing forward. To keep the refrigerator from being congested, keep only a dozen or fewer of each type of single-serve beverage; store the rest in a pantry. Use refrigerator organizers like under-shelf baskets, racks, or bins designed to hold beverage bottles, cartons, or pouches sideways when you need to conserve lateral space.

Consider a second refrigerator to stock single-serve beverages to free space in a main fridge. A garage location is convenient since you can simply unload heavy cases of beverages right from the vehicle instead of lugging them into your home. A garage location for a second refrigerator

Refrigerator Organizers

FIGURE 36.01
Refrigerator Interior

will also help you to remember to take your beverage along to games, the gym, and the office.

Storing Miscellaneous Refrigerator Products

Outside of the five main food groups—dairy, fruit, grains, meats/poultry/fish, and vegetables—a refrigerator can store many other odds and ends. The largest categories of miscellaneous foods that seek refrigeration storage are condiments, dough products, and leftovers. Many condiments need cold storage immediately and some after opening, so it's always best to read the labels.

Dough-related products, such as bread rolls, ready-to-bake cookies, and cakes, require refrigeration mainly because they contain eggs. Lastly, leftovers are trickier to store in the refrigerator because they don't come with food wrapping and are not stamped with expiration dates.

FIGURE 36.02
Under-the-Counter Refrigerator Drawers

The following information explains the best refrigerated-storage strategies for these items.

Refrigerated Dough Products

Ready-to-bake pressurized tubes of biscuits, rolls, and pizza dough are fresh until their best-when-used-by date and cannot be stored once opened. Most of these products are not recommended for freezer storage before baking. The store-bought tubes can stack, lie, or stand, offering many storage options.

To remain fresh until their best-when-used-by dates, prescored sheets of cookie dough ready for baking must be securely wrapped in plastic after opening. Most of these products accept freezer storage prior to baking, which will extend the shelf life by several months.

Ready-to-bake pie crusts remain fresh only up until their best-when-used-by dates. Once their vacuum pack seals are removed, they should be consumed immediately. These should be stored with all ready-to-bake dough products on a refrigerator shelf or bin.

Cakes and Pies

Homemade or store-bought cakes and pies are at their peak for just a day or two, so make or buy only what you can consume. Optimal taste and freshness is degraded by refrigeration and freezer storage. Generally, depending on ingredients, they can be stored in the refrigerator for three days and in the freezer for three months unbaked or four months baked. The more fat that a pie or cake has, the better it will freeze. Only cakes and pies that contain perishable frostings and fillings—like cheese, custard, whipped cream, fresh fruit, and uncooked eggs—require refrigeration. Cheesecake and meringue need to be stored in a well-sealed cake keeper or under an inverted bowl so they don't dry out.

Dome-like pie and cake containers from the store are fine for refrigeration storage. Bakery cardboard boxes should be sealed in plastic wrap and taped on all sides or transferred to cake or pie containers. Place frosted cakes in the freezer for a few hours so they harden, before wrapping them in several layers of foil or plastic wrap. Then transfer to an airtight food, cake, or pie container to prevent them from being crushed in the freezer.

Condiments

Whether out of habit or lack of knowledge, it's common for people to store all their condiments in the fridge, even when some don't need it, so read the labels. To conserve refrigerator space, store all condiments in a dry location until they're opened unless they were purchased from a refrigerated section of the store. Once you open a condiment, don't go by the marked expiration since the shelf life of most food products dramatically declines upon opening the freshness seal. Unfortunately, this type of information is usually not given on the food container, so reference food-storage charts or the manufacturer of the product. Most opened condiments are hardy enough to store safely in the fridge door, which is the warmest place in the refrigerator.

Turntable lazy Susan organizers and slim-handled bins situated on an eye-level refrigerator shelf can successfully store groups of condiments. Slim-handled bins are easy to maneuver and hold condiments securely. Lazy Susans should have bottom suctions to keep them stationary on a slippery glass refrigerator shelf. Also, keep taller condiments in the middle of the turntable and the smaller ones surrounding the edge, for best view and access.

Safely Storing Leftovers

When storing your leftovers, follow food-safety guidelines to guard against foodborne illnesses. The problem is that bacteria does not alter the taste, smell, or appearance of food. Generally, anything containing mayonnaise or egg-based products usually cannot make it past a day in the refrigerator. Refer to reliable sources like the US Food and Drug Administration and the Center for Food Safety and Applied Nutrition (1-888-SAFEFOOD) to obtain comprehensive cold-storage charts that detail the shelf lives of various leftovers.

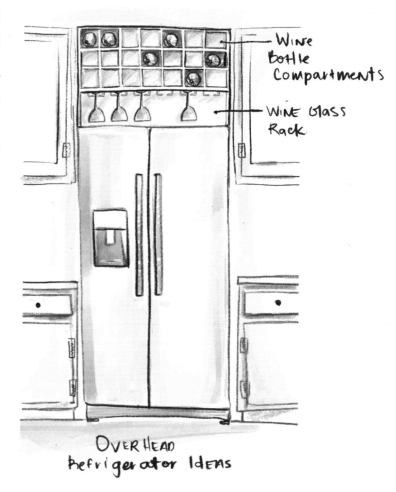

FIGURE 36.03
Over-The-Refrigerator Storage Ideas Wine & Glass Storage

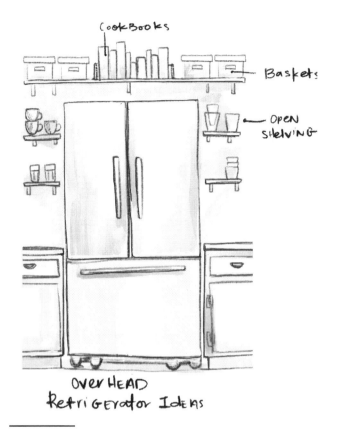

FIGURE 36.04
Overhead Shelving for Miscellaneous Kitchen Items & Décor

When handling leftovers, always wash your hands, use clean utensils, and make sure that work surfaces, like cutting boards and counters, are clean. Store leftovers in the refrigerator or freezer within two hours of preparation. Hot weather cuts this time in half since bacteria will multiply rapidly in these conditions. Transfer leftovers into single-serve, stackable, shallow, microwaveable, and freezer-friendly containers. Such containers are convenient to transfer to the lunchbox, freezer, and microwave and promote the consumption of leftovers. Use freezer-safe labels to jot down the date and contents. To avoid contamination, don't store leftovers in the cookware used to prepare the food or use any dishware that is difficult to seal properly with foil or plastic wraps, which can drip.

Serving your foods separately, thereby leaving the mixing to the family members, can increase the likelihood that leftovers don't go to waste. When you keep your noodles, sauces, meats, vegetables, and the like separate, you can easily invent new dishes later with some of the sides and freeze what you don't need.

Miscellaneous Refrigerator Tips

- **ALL-PURPOSE FLOUR** will stay fresh after opening for up to two years when concealed in an airtight container in the refrigerator, but not after the best-when-used-by date. You can house it in a refrigerator door shelf, along with condiments. Label the expiration date on the outside of the container. Flours made from other grains have a much shorter shelf life because they contain oil. For instance, wheat and barley flours are good for only six months in refrigeration.
- **CORNMEAL** should be refrigerated after opening, where it can stay fresh up to one year, but not after the best-when-used-by date. Keep cornmeal in an airtight container and store it in the door next to your condiments. Label the expiration date on the outside of the container.
- **NUTS** are best kept refrigerated to prevent oxidation of their oils. Store them in an airtight, translucent container so they're easily identified. The refrigerator door or upper-shelf storage is fine.
- **READY-MADE FROSTING** in a can should be refrigerated after opening, where it can stay fresh for about two weeks. Keep it on an eye-level refrigerator shelf where other small containers reside, like yogurt, pudding, and sour cream. You can also store frosting in the door of the refrigerator where your condiments are kept. Label the

expiration date with a permanent marker or cold-storage sticker.

- **UNREFINED, DELICATE PURE COOKING OILS** are prone to going rancid. Some oils will spoil if not kept in a cold place. Keep such oils in an airtight container with caps or enclosures well sealed at all times. The main oils that are recommended for refrigeration after opening are avocado, corn, mustard, safflower, sunflower, truffle, sesame, grapeseed, hazelnut, walnut, and premium extra virgin olive oil.

- **BREADS** that have been approved for refrigeration by the producer are the only kinds recommended for this type of storage. Most bread placed in the refrigerator will become stale quickly due to loss of moisture.

- **TORTILLAS** found in the refrigerated section need refrigeration in the home, or they may grow mold before the best-when-used-by date. Keep refrigerated tortillas well sealed in a plastic or a lidded tortilla container. Tortillas purchased from the dry grocery shelf usually don't need refrigeration after opening. Freezer storage varies by brand, but refrigerated tortillas can be transferred to freezer storage to extend their shelf life.

- **DRIED FRUIT** that has been opened should be stored in the refrigerator, where it can stay fresh up to six months, but not after the best-when-used-by date. When refrigerated, dried fruit must be sealed in an airtight container or plastic bag to prevent moisture loss. Humidity levels should not be excessive, so avoid crisper drawers set to a high-humidity level. Dried fruit can freeze indefinitely when packed correctly.

- **JARRED BABY FOOD** requires refrigeration after opening and it's good for only one to two days, maximum. Record the expiration day on the lid or label and store it next to other baby food

and beverage products, like formula. Keep all refrigerated baby products together in a small bin on a refrigerator shelf.

Refrigerator Maintenance

The key to keeping your refrigerator in the best state possible is to develop an ongoing habit of decluttering and cleaning the contents. Even basic cleaning tasks such as regularly wiping bottles and jars before returning them back to the refrigerator after use will add to tidiness. Other efforts would be to rewrap flimsy packaging and condense half-consumed foods into smaller containers or bags. Right before garbage pickup or prior to grocery shopping, check expiration dates, toss

FIGURE 36.05
Infrequently Used Pots & Pans

leftovers, and discard refrigerated goods that no one is eating.

Another key element to keeping your refrigerator well maintained is good inventory management. Keep your refrigerator minimally stocked with the all the basics like eggs, cheese, butter, milk, juice, and so on. Then buy produce and meat in quantities typically eaten in the time frame of their expiration dates. Don't overbuy anything you cannot transfer to the freezer.

Before going to the supermarket, first shop in your refrigerator. Figure out ways to use the foods in upcoming meals, especially those approaching the end of their shelf life. Write these items and their amounts on a separate piece of paper and attach it to your grocery list. While at the store, you can pick up other foods that can combine with them in order to create a full meal. Also, always double-check your grocery list against the actual inventories before leaving the house for the grocery store.

Refrigerator Exterior

The refrigerator doors are often used to display photos, calendars, shopping lists, schedules, coupons, and the like. If your refrigerator is filled with such items, take everything off and see how it looks. A cleared refrigerator offers such a clean appearance that you may not want to put things back on it.

Artwork and photos always look best framed, even on the refrigerator. Therefore, invest in cardboard picture frames, which typically come in sizes such as four-by-six inches, eight-by-twelve inches, or nine-by-twelve inches. Consider using removable adhesive products, such as "tacky tape" or magnetic strips, behind the artwork or photo frame, rather than unattractive tape. Limit artwork to one piece per artist and a few meaningful photos.

The space over the refrigerator is typically awkward and difficult to access. Therefore, place infrequently needed items there, such as stockpots and small kitchen gadgets, to free up easier-to-access spots like base cabinets.

If there are no cabinets over your refrigerator, incorporate baskets or cubbies to conceal items. Some organizers, such as wine racks, can be installed over the refrigerator, suspending from the ceiling, and they look good. Typically, the top of refrigerator is hot, so avoid placing foods at this location.

CHAPTER 37

The Freezer

Commonly, the freezer is a congested space due to its typical small size. Also since freezing dramatically extends the shelf life of many foods, they remain in the freezer longer, pile up, and tend to be forgotten. Organizing the freezer calls for a deep cleaning since the space is not cleaned on a regular basis, unlike a refrigerator.

There are two types of freezers: manual and automatic defrost units. The more mainstream automatic defrost freezer is attached to the refrigerator, usually as a side-door compartment or pullout base drawer. Automatic defrost units are popular since they're maintenance-free and easy to clean, although it's important to establish proper air circulation in these units by not overloading them. Doing so and properly sealing foods should improve conditions and minimize the likelihood of freezer burn.

A manual defrost unit also comes attached to the refrigerator, commonly as a top compartment with a swing door and the refrigerator section below it. The manual defrost freezers are distinct in that ice will build up on the unit walls. These are reminiscent of freezers from the past, but their basic concept still exists since they have benefits:

- Manual defrost units are less expensive to purchase and operate because they consume around 40 percent less power.
- These freezers have fewer moving parts than automatic defrost units, so they're less likely to break down.
- Foods keep longer in these freezers because they don't cycle on and off like the automatic units, which promotes freezer burn on foods, especially those not properly sealed.

The downside to manual units is that they need a yearly labor-intensive defrosting procedure to break down ice buildup and perform a deep cleaning.

Both types of freezer will require a thorough organizing and cleaning from time to time. The main difference will be that the manual defrost unit will require a detailed process that requires a series of steps to melt excess ice, whereas the automatic defrost freezer will only need to be turned off so it can become washable. Manual defrost units can take anywhere from eight to twenty-four hours to thoroughly defrost, depending on the freezer type, brand, and the amount of ice buildup.

Speeding Up the Defrosting Process

If you don't want to wait the hours it may take to manually defrost a freezer, you can speed up the process by using other means. Before manually defrosting the freezer, lay newspapers and shop towels around the floor to absorb any water. Carefully run a handheld hairdryer several inches away from the freezer walls and storage components. Keep the heat away from any mechanical parts, such as coils and the icemaker. When the home is being heated by a furnace, use a fan to draw warm air into the freezer. A pot of hot water placed on a trivet inside the freezer with the door closed will produce steam to will melt ice buildup, as well. Keep the pot inside anywhere from thirty to sixty minutes.

If formed, a fine layer of ice can be removed with a rag and rubbing alcohol. There also frost remover agents for freezers sold in the marketplace. Use only plastic tools to loosen ice and remove ice chunks from the freezer quickly. To avoid deep scratches, never apply metal tools or too much force to chip ice away.

Once the freezer is defrosted, remove all the storage components and clean everything with a safe, nontoxic, noncorrosive but powerful cleaning agent. You can purchase safe and gentle specialized cooler/freezer cleaners or make your own using equal parts of mild dish soap, vinegar, and water. A baking soda and water mix can deodorize. Freezer components, such as shelving and drawers, can soak in a tub or sink. Completely dry all the storage organizers before returning them to the freezer.

Organizing Freezer Contents

Discard all the expired foods and those you know won't be eaten. When you are unsure about the age of an item, it must go. Check that everything is packed airtight. Look for freezer burn on items, and decide if you can cut off the damage; if so, then repackage it well. Freezer burn will most likely change the texture and flavor of the food, but it's still safe to consume. Transfer anything approaching its expiration date to the refrigerator, where the defrosting process can begin and the item can be eaten.

It's sometimes impossible to repackage foods the way you should—or you may not want to, if they're frozen. So these items will have to stay in their current form, but you can package all incoming foods to help organize and promote food use.

Packaging Strategies

Package cooked foods for the freezer when they're cool, in order to prevent freezer burn. Also, tightly pack foods into airtight containers to seal out oxygen and compact space. A vacuum-sealing system can successfully bind foods airtight without requiring additional packaging or a container that can take up additional space. Vacuum-sealing systems are worth the investment when you often buy in bulk or cook in advance. It's easy to make vacuum seal packs for many foods—even sauces—and freeze them to a shape that offers a space advantage, such as flat, making them easier to stack or file.

Most store-bought meat, poultry, and seafood products are sold in a plastic wrap designed for freezer storage. However, this type of packaging usually has a limited freezer storage time. Therefore, it's always best to receive freezer storage information from the store's department where it was purchased. Small containers thaw faster and offer more storage arrangements than large ones. Use single-serve size containers for individual portions and plan to defrost multiple servings for a group.

Use microwave or oven-friendly freezer storage containers and color-code them for easy viewing. For example, put soups in red- and sauces in green-lidded containers. Square or rectangular containers take up less space than circular ones. Record the type of food and the expiration date on all freezer containers. Sometimes, thawing, cooking, and weight information can also be added to the label.

Arranging Freezer Food

When placing things in the freezer, store like items together so things are easy to find. Categories like desserts, meat, poultry, fish, vegetables, fruits, leftovers, soups, sauces, and breakfast foods are good groupings.

Most kitchen freezers are either in a side-by-side, top, or bottom pullout configuration relationship to the refrigerator. Each type of freezer has unique storage arrangements and therefore may require different organizers to separate foods. The following storage ideas are recommended for each type of freezer.

Side-by-Side Models

These refrigerator/freezers usually have a series of shelves with some pullout baskets or drawers. An icemaker typically dispenses ice cubes into a designated plastic pullout drawer. The shelving system makes separating different inventories easy since a given food category can occupy each shelf. Shelf baskets or bins can further subdivide foods on each shelf. Color-code baskets for easy identification, such as red for meat or green for vegetables.

Under-shelf bins can take care of any dead space that resides between two shelves. Items like tubes of cookie dough or concentrated juice cans are good for these organizers.

Top Freezers

Top freezers usually are in the form of a rectangular box with a shelf or two and a compartment for holding ice cube trays. Stackable bins or tray organizers are great for dividing inventories and effectively using lateral space. These organizers also make accessing items easier. Bins with easy-to-grasp handles are helpful when items need to be transported in and out of the freezer.

Bottom Freezers

These freezers are the large pullout drawers located below the refrigerator unit. Typically, these freezers feature slide-out wire baskets or bins that fully extend. Some freezers may also feature built-in organizers, such as indoor pockets, both upper and lower slide-out bins, or wire baskets to offer many useful compartments.

It's best to file items rather than stack them in a base freezer, so you can actually see everything; if you stack items, only the top one is visible. For example, stand boxed frozen items upright so the sides of the packages are seen when filed.

CHAPTER 38

Organizing the Sink Areas

The kitchen is a busy, messy place that requires constant cleaning. It's important to have cleaning products and agents well organized in convenient places with easy access. Primarily, the areas near and below a sink constitute the hub of cleaning activities because they're near a water source. This space is also the best storage and organization center for cleaning products. When organizing your sink areas, plan to begin with what is currently in the base cabinet under the sink.

Decluttering the Sink Areas

Heat and moisture generated from the hot water pipe and the dishwasher hose can make the under-the-sink space dank and smelly, so test the disposal and check for plumbing leaks before organizing. Empty the entire under-the-sink area and then wash the cabinet floor, walls, and pipes. Measure the storage area and record the dimensions. Record the location and the amount of space occupied by the plumbing. Paint the area, if possible, and cover warped cabinet flooring with inexpensive vinyl or a sheet of laminate.

You can add adhesive air fresheners and mount a battery-operated light to help locate items.

Gather all the soaps and lotions used at the sink that are now stored under-the-sink. Discard old bottles and the stuff you don't like to use. Condense half-used bottles and jars into as few as possible. Keep one bottle of dish soap by the sink, and store the spares with the cleaning products under the sink.

Surplus cleaning sponges and tools can be stored under the sink in a handled caddy. Keep these items in their original packaging or safely conceal them to protect from possible chemical exposure or bacteria.

Gather all your rubber gloves and cleaning tools used at the sink, such as such as sponges and cleaning brushes. Discard all the old, broken, and worn items. Pitch anything that carries a bad odor, because that usually means bacterial growth. Keep one tool for dishes, glassware, and flatware and one for difficult scouring jobs. When necessary, one bottle brush can reside in the sink area, as well as a specialized fruit and vegetable brush. Sanitize and move all rest to a container.

Under-the-Sink Storage

There are many good organizers designed for under-the-sink storage. One popular organizer designed for this space is a two-tiered wire shelving unit, commonly referred to as an **EXPANDABLE UNDER-SINK ORGANIZER**, which easily adjusts to fit around sink pipes and garbage disposals. It's made to stretch the width of the cabinet and has adjustable shelves. This organizer typically incorporates pullout baskets so items are easy to access in this hard-to-reach storage space.

An assortment of two-tiered base-cabinet organizers is available, offering pullout compartments that are ideal for under-the-sink articles. A handled caddy organizer is another good one for this space. Handled caddies can carry cleaning products, dishwasher accessories, air deodorizers, sink accessories, and other household odd and ends to and from the places they're needed in the home. The following items are logical belongings to keep in this space, along with good ways to organize them.

Cleaning Tools

Hanging any cleaning tool or accessory to fully dry in between uses is a good idea. The interior side of the under-the-sink cabinet door is a place to mount hanging hooks for such articles. It's possible to hang items that don't have holes or loops by creating tearproof ones using a grommet-setting kit.

Dishwasher Accessories

Since dishwashers are placed next to a sink, their accessories and detergents naturally gravitate under the sink. Store dishwasher detergents alongside dish soap, sink cleaners, brushes, scrubbers, and sponges to keep all cleaning items together.

All these items can be stored in a container for easy access, like a handled tote.

In order to free up the tight space associated with an under-the-sink location, keep just one box, bottle, or tablet pouch container of detergent plus a single bottle of dishwasher rinse aid in this area. Place excess products with the cleaning supplies. Store dishwasher bags, ball cap washers, spare flatware baskets, or any device that is taken in and out of the dishwasher in one spot.

A storage location under the sink might be too cramped to store these bulkier items. Since they tend to be used infrequently, store them in a single, labeled container and move it to an upper shelf, kitchen closet, or pantry.

Trash Liners

A wall-mounted rack organizer attached to the inside wall of the sink cabinet is a good place to keep trash liners. Use a handled container if you chose to store trash liners on the floor of the sink cabinet so they're easy to access.

Portable Dust Pan Set and Plunger

A portable dust pan and brush set is a good item to store below the sink. The volume of spills that take place in a kitchen warrants easy access to a cleaning tool when full-size versions are stored outside the kitchen. Many companies that sell car care or camping products also sell these sets. Typically, portable brush and dust pan sets nestle together and have holes for hooks in their handles; hanging them anywhere below the sink is best.

A short-handled plunger is an important tool to have under the sink. Mount a single-utility holder designed to store a broom on the interior wall of the sink's base cabinet to hold the plunger and free up the cabinet's floor space.

Towels and Rags

Keep towels near the sink out of sight by placing them on a mounted towel bar attached to the inside door of the under-sink cabinet. At this location, they're easy to access and can line dry.

Another idea is to mount a paper-towel organizer that holds a single roll onto the inside door of the under sink cabinet. This organizer can hold disposable shop towels, which are thicker and more absorbent than regular paper towels. Disposable shop towels are designed to soak up garage oil, making them good for common kitchen oil spills and messes.

In and Near the Sink Storage

Given that water, grime, and goopy soaps will constantly find their way around the sink region, keep a minimal amount of belongings in that space. Usually, a cluttered sink area is due to the lack of successful storage arrangements under the sink, which is why it's always best to maximize that space for as many countertop items as possible. However, some items are better stored either in or near the sink, either due to their function or your personal preference.

Hand and Dish Soap

It's convenient to place hand-pump bottles of dish and hand soap on the sink counter. Some dish soap is gentle enough for handwashing, which is good for this spot and eliminates the need for two different soap dispensers at this location.

Sink or countertop holes once used for spray hoses or instant hot-water devices can be repurposed to hold a stationary pump, where the spout rests at the top and connects to a soap bottle beneath the counter. When you like to keep hand lotion near the sink, consider storing a tube in a kitchen drawer rather than a dispenser next to the faucet to reduce counter clutter.

Dish Racks

Opt for an over-the-sink adjustable dish rack whenever possible to free counter space since dish racks are counter-space hogs. Often times, countertop dish racks conveniently become storage centers for those who do not want to put things back in the cupboards. When hand-washing demands are low, simply laying out dish towels on the counter for wet dishware and glassware can get the job done without the need for a dish rack.

Make a solid investment in a countertop dish rack when there is a demand for one. The best ones on the market are made by a company called Sabatier. Their dish racks have a slim design with removable parts so they store away easily. They are equipped with an expandable drain board for additional storage which has an attached bi-directional spout for draining water into the sink. These dish racks also come with unique organizers such as removable stemware and flatware holders.

Invest in a wine glass drying rack if you use wine glasses daily. Not only do wine glass drying racks display glasses well, but also they securely air dry them and eliminate drying streaks. You can situate this rack on your countertop near where you serve wine, not necessarily right next to the sink itself.

Cleaning Tools

Cleaning tools that reside in the sink region need to stay sterile and dry between uses, so their storage essential should both shield and offer drainage. A good organizer for this is a suction-mounted sink organizer with drain holes at the base. Another useful tool organizer is the compartmentalized saddle caddy that rests on the partition dividing a double sink.

Most cabinet sinks have room in the front of the basin to install a hidden tip-out tray, which folds out from a concealed false-cabinet drawer and has compartments to hold sponges and brushes. Handled bottle brushes can be stored in the flatware compartment located on a dish rack.

Sink Strainer Baskets and Disposal and Suction Stoppers

A spare removable strainer basket and disposal and suction stopper are handy to keep on hand since these smaller items have a tendency to disappear. Store these related items in the same spot, like in a drawer or cabinet next to the sink. Use an organizer caddy, labeled container, or cabinet door rack device to house them. Don't store these items too far from the sink, because you could run the risk of forgetting about them: out of sight, out of mind.

Dish Cloths and Towels

Separate your "cleaning" dish cloths from the dish towels used for drying or display. Dish clothes are usually smaller and square in shape, whereas dish towels are larger and rectangular. Count and inspect these items for tears and stains. Forward those in poor condition to your cleaning-rag supply, if you can spare them.

It makes the most sense to keep twice as many dish cloths as dish towels on hand because they tackle more jobs. The frequency in which you use your dish cloths and the number of days in between doing laundry will determine how many to have. Generally, four to six are enough if the laundry gets done once or twice a week. Dish towels, on the other hand, are largely used to dry items that are already clean or for display. Therefore, two to four dish towels are sufficient in the average home.

Dish cloths and towels can be stored in a drawer near the sink or dishwasher since they're mainly used there. You can also mount a stationary or slide-out towel bar on the cabinet door to hang dish linens. Hooks can also be mounted on a cabinet door when you install grommets to the cloth that forms secure holes for hanging. Base-cabinet pullout storage devices, like slide-out shelves and baskets, can house dish linens for easy access. Containerize linens stored below the sink to keep them dry and clean.

Paper-towel organizers can also be installed near the sink. The underside of an upper base cabinet near the sink marks the perfect spot for such an organizer. They can also be mounted on a wall near the sink. A good assortment of countertop paper-towel organizers are available for this purpose.

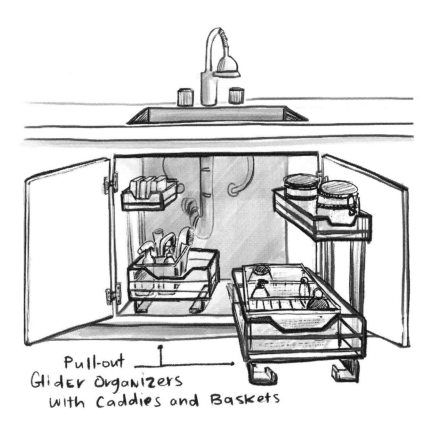

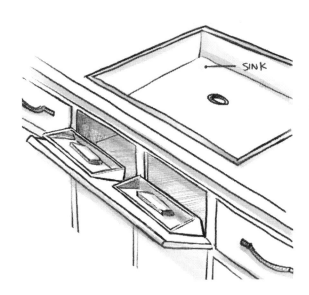

Pull-out
Glider Organizers
With Caddies and Baskets

FIGURE 38.01
Under-The-Sink Kitchen
Organization

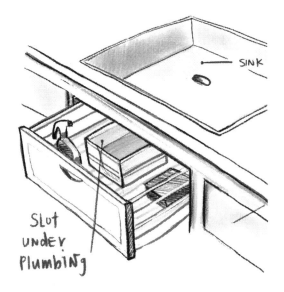

Slot
under
Plumbing

Pull Out Wire Sink
Organizers

Tip out Tray Sink
Organizers

PART FOUR

Bathrooms and Laundry Rooms

CHAPTER 39

Organizing Bathrooms

A bathroom is defined as a room with at least a toilet and a sink where basic personal hygiene takes place. Plumbing fixtures—meaning any device connecting a water source to a bathroom, such as a shower or tub—can also be included in this definition. In real estate terminology, which varies in actual sales listings throughout the country, there are three different types of bathroom configurations categorized by the number and types of water-bearing fixtures in the bathroom:

- A full bathroom will have all four plumbing fixtures: toilet, sink, shower, and bathtub.
- A three-quarters bath has a toilet, sink, and either a shower or tub.
- A half bath or powder bathroom has just a toilet and sink.

A bathroom's arrangement will dictate what types of organizers can get included in the space and will also influence the kinds of belongings to store. For example, a master bathroom, which adjoins the largest bedroom of the home, may have the need for a makeup station, whereas a small powder room near a kitchen would not.

There are different budgets involved when organizing any bathroom. High-end custom bathrooms will have an entirely different set of organizational features than budget-friendly alternatives. The following covers both upscale and economical ways to outfit a bathroom with storage organization.

Upscale Bathrooms

The main distinction that marks a bathroom as high-end is plenty of upgraded cabinetry. The best part about cabinetry is that it hides and organizes bathroom essentials well.

Cabinets

The following are some of the best ideas for upscale cabinetry:

- Countertop cabinets, which are cabinet compartments stationed on a countertop, mimic a hutch, making them a great place to store daily needed toiletries and medications. Drawers are also possible on such cabinets, which are suitable for many bathroom essentials such as makeup, hairbrushes, jewelry, hair accessories, hand towels, oral care supplies, and so on.

- A makeup vanity station can be created using cabinetry by eliminating the lower base cabinet, keeping just a drawer below the countertop. This leaves room for a stool.
- Several slim pullout shelves can be installed in a tiered manner in a single cabinet. They're perfect for the many small items commonly needed in a bathroom, such as makeup, hairbrushes, manicure supplies, hair accessories, skincare products, oral care items, and so on.
- Built-in components are possible to incorporate in drawers rather than purchasing separate organizers.
- Base cabinets are best organized with pull-out drawers, baskets, or shelves.

- A pullout hamper or garbage can is an ideal built-in organizer for a bathroom with a base cabinet.
- It's a good idea to install a power outlet inside a bathroom drawer for charging small personal oral, skincare or grooming appliances, such as water picks, electric toothbrushes, trimmers, shavers, hair-removal lasers, and so on. This keeps them from congesting the countertops and makes them easily accessible where they're commonly used.

Heated hairstyling appliances are probably one of the larger items that can congest bathroom countertops. It's possible to store, organize, and operate hot styling products right from the drawer. A pullout hair-appliance valet organizer designed to retrofit an existing cabinet drawer is a good option. They come in standard drawer sizes, so you'll likely to find one to fit yours.

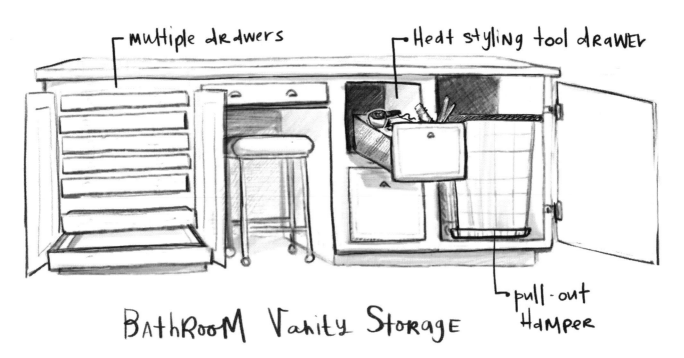

FIGURE 39.01
Bathroom Vanity Organization

Many of these organizers have a spot to install a power strip to plug in and use your hair appliances right from the drawer. These organizers also tend to have quick-release knobs that eliminate cord tangles. Ventilated, metal-capped tubes are used to hold the styling appliances for safe heating and cooling.

It's also possible to customize your own hair appliance storage drawer with some DIY carpentry skills. Ventilated, stainless steel tube and cap sets, which are the docking stations for these appliances, are sold separately at many home centers or hardware stores. Cuts in wood can be made to insert these pieces for safe storage of hot styling appliances and related accessories, such as brushes and combs.

Showers

Walk-in showers and steamers are a common feature in an upscale bathroom. These showers are large, with spacious wall and floor room. A popular upscale shower organizer is a recessed one called a *shower niche*: basic wall shelving used to hold bath essentials. Shower niches are inserted into the drywall in between wall studs, so a cutout in the shower wall needs to be made.

Make certain to find one that has pitched shelving so that water sheds out and does not collect in the organizer. Most tile stores and home centers sell shower niches prepared for tiling. Some are sold as a continuous porcelain piece, while others are already tiled inside a frame to avoid intricate tile cutting. These organizers are installed *before* the tiles, making them a must for new bathrooms or renovation projects. The main benefits to these shower organizers are that they don't use valuable shower space and they offer a custom, high-end look to your bathroom.

Mountable shower wall organizers, such as stainless steel baskets, should be anchored directly into the wall studs before tiling, as well, to eliminate the risk of cracking the tiles. These organizers require foresight when building or renovating a bathroom shower.

Another clever organizer to incorporate into a walk-in shower renovation is a built-in tiered shelf or a pullout cabinet behind a tiled shower wall. These shelves are suitable for holding towels, washcloths, and all bath products. Other practical organizers to tile or build into a shower are external bench seating, corner shaving steps, and corner shelving.

Bathtubs

Drop-in and Jacuzzi bathtubs are popular luxury bathroom options. These bathtubs sometimes have a platform around the tub's rim. Take advantage of that space to contain towels, bath salts, soaps, sponges, and on the like in decorative organizers like glass jars, wicker baskets, bowls, and trays. There is a caddy tray organizer designed to extend across the body of almost any type of bathtub. This organizer is supported by both ends of the tub's edge and has compartments to hold bath essentials, books, eyewear, candles, and whatever else is used while soaking in the tub.

Other luxury bathtubs include the freestanding and claw-foot types, which are both unconnected to walls and require more space. The claw-foot tub is elevated on four feet, while most freestanding tubs sit on the floor. Both these bathtubs will rely on wall shelves, wall cabinets, and freestanding or fixed cabinets to store toiletries and towels.

Budget-Friendly Bathrooms

Many showers and bathtubs are combined for space conservation in smaller bathrooms, and cabinets may be small or nonexistent. Some bathrooms may have only a small shower and no bathtub. Even in these more confined spaces, it's still possible to create effective storage solutions, which are important so that bath products are off the shower floor and tub ledge.

Cabinetry

It's common for many economically arranged bathrooms to have just a freestanding pedestal sink or cabinet-style vanity sink. Bathroom vanities come with a single or double sink over a base cabinet. Even in budget-friendly bathrooms, it's important to select a durable or well-finished cabinet, because water and humidity can warp and crack them. A bathroom with some cabinet space will have countertops that can be outfitted with budget-friendly tabletop organizers to expand storage significantly.

Bathrooms with just a pedestal sink and no cabinetry will still need storage places for necessary items, such as toiletries, toilet paper, hand towels, guest towels, room deodorizers, and the like. Good organizers for small spaces include wall-mounted cabinets, freestanding tower cabinets, or shelving units to gain this needed storage space.

Showers

There are economical ways to create storage solutions in any bathroom shower that don't require invasive remodeling like tile removal. Most home centers and tile shops sell baskets and shelving designed to mount on shower walls with either screws or suction cups. These organizers come in different materials, but the best ones are made of aluminum or stainless steel that is guaranteed rustproof. Don't select chrome, because it rusts. Look for organizers backed by either a five-year or lifetime rust-free guarantee.

Use suctioned organizers for lighter items, such as bar soap, disposable razors, or loofahs since they're prone to lose suction and fail. Silicone caulk can hold them in place, but refrain from placing too much weight on them. Organizers attached with screws usually require wall-stud installation to ensure a higher load capacity for holding heavier items, such as shampoos, liquid body soaps, and shaving cream. Drilling into the tile requires careful work to prevent cracked tiles. It's recommended to gently drill through masking tape applied to the tile with a masonry drill bit. However, even a professional can still crack the tile, so it's best to either have spare tiles or drill only through the grout lines. Since tiered shower organizers may not line up to multiple grout lines, it's best to use several single baskets or shelves.

Besides wall-mounted organizers, a corner pole organizer with attachable storage baskets is a good budget option. These organizers are freestanding tension mounted and stretch from floor to ceiling, thus requiring no installation. There is also the popular shower caddy organizer designed to be suspended from a shower head. Both of these organizers have tiered baskets sturdy enough to hold shampoos, body soaps, razors, and the like. You can also attach suction cups to these organizers for stabilization. These organizers keep everything in the most convenient location where the water does not directly hit the items stored.

Some showers areas are outfitted with a recessed window, often with block glass for privacy. It can be advantageous to use that space for storage by boarding up the glass with drywall and installing waterproof shelving in its place. Today, even the feel of natural light is easy to manufacture with artificial light.

Corner shelving is another storage solution for an existing small, tiled shower. Basic white porcelain corner shelves are easy to find at home improvement or tile shops and are simple to install securely with silicone caulk; they're often sold as kits.

The look of various bottles and jars displayed in open shower storage organizers is bothersome to some people. One way to solve this problem is to transfer products into uniform containers and label them with their contents. It's amazing at what a transformation this can make in a shower area. Wall-mounted shower soap dispensing

organizers used to hold shampoo, conditioners, and body soap also look tidy.

Storage can be gained from a shower door or curtain enclosure, as well. A regular standard single shower curtain rod can easily be changed to a double shower rod. The outer rod can hold the shower curtain/liner and the inner rod makes for an organizer. This inner rod is a perfect organizer to drape towels on and hang many bath essentials from S hooks, such as body sponges that need to fully dry. This rod can also suspend a pocketed hanging organizer designed for showers, which is made from water-friendly material like nylon and has mesh pockets for draining water. Pocketed organizers are great for holding small

BathRoom Organizers

FIGURE 39.02
Shower Organization

bath items, such as shower brushes, facial soaps, or disposable razors. There are also tiered basket organizers with hooks at the top that can suspend from the rod.

Shower doors offer another storage opportunity. Most shower doors have an overhead rail or door trim that can accommodate an over-the-door organizer consisting of tiered storage baskets, pockets, or pouches for holding small items. Look for those made of water-friendly materials.

Bathtubs

Alcove bathtubs enclosed within a three-sided tiled wall tend to include a shower; they have either a plastic shower curtain or door enclosure. These tub/shower combos are popular in budget-friendly bathrooms due to their compact size and dual capability. Since these bathtubs have tiled walls, they lend themselves to the same organizational options as showers. In addition, bath items such as toys and sponges can be stored inside nylon mesh bags attached to the tiled walls by suction cups to drip dry between uses.

Utilizing Bathroom Countertops

Since nearly all bathrooms have some sort of countertop, either atop cabinetry or on a freestanding storage unit, bathroom countertops are the easiest place for clutter to form. Items that are continuously gravitating to this spot may as well be containerized here, especially if their current storage places are insufficient. It's important that you are fine with open storage in this highly noticeable location, though. Organizers intended for drawer or cabinet use may not be decorative enough for a visible countertop location, which can discount the space.

Use countertop organizers sparingly to prevent a cluttered appearance. Select easy-to-clean organizers in high-traffic and messy places, such as bathrooms. Organizers that conceal by using drawers or closed compartments are also helpful in creating a more orderly presentation. The following covers the best bathroom organizers for bathroom countertops.

Styling Stations

There are many countertop styling stations for electrical hair appliances, so finding the perfect one for your needs is doable. Most countertop hairstyling appliance organizers are designed to store just a few appliances in ceramic or metal sleeves for safety, which presents a neat look. Some have additional storage places, such as compartments or drawers for holding hair-care essentials like brushes or hair spray. Many also have internal compartments for concealing a power strip so countertops stay free of dangling appliance cords.

Oral Care Organizers

Oral care supplies, such as toothbrushes, toothpastes, and dental floss that are used daily, are convenient to store at arm's length from the sink. There are specialized toothbrush stands that also hold the toothpaste and floss. Many are decorative, so look for one that matches your bathroom.

Accessory Trays

An accessory tray is a flat, shallow decorative container used to openly house many small items, such as candles, air fresheners, cotton balls, cotton swabs, cologne, shavers, soaps, makeup sponges, toothpaste, and just about any item needed at the sink. You can also use traditional perfume trays for this purpose. Accessory trays are good for corralling items and keeping them tidy in a designated spot. Similarly, a guest towel tray, which is a flat, shallow, decorative container scaled for paper or cloth hand towels, works well.

Apothecary jars, or decorative glass lidded containers, are perfect organizers and look esthetically appealing on a counter for storing bath salts, cotton balls, cotton swabs, soaps, hair accessories, makeup sponges, and the like. These organizers can stand on or near a decorative tray or plate.

Common serving organizers, such as tiered food or cake stands with multiple levels for holding pastries, fruits, cakes, finger sandwiches, and the like used for entertaining, are good to repurpose for bathroom counter storage. Food stands come in many decorative styles, so finding one to match your bathroom is easy. The best thing about these organizers is that they're decorative and have multiple storage levels (usually three), allowing for division of belongings, such as rolled hand towels, soap dispensers, candles, makeup, shavers, nail polish, hand creams, hair-care products, oral care products, and just about any smaller bathroom essential.

Cosmetics Organizers

Many cosmetics organizers are specifically made for countertop display. The best ones have two-tiered storage with several small compartments to fit specific articles, such as lipstick, nail polish, mascara, face powder compacts, and so on. Many are acrylic and wood with molded compartments shaped to fit certain items. Some are circular and fully rotate. The best ones are made from easy-to-clean materials like mesh, wire, or perforated plastic so dust and debris don't accumulate inside the compartments.

Utilizing Base Cabinets

Commonly, base cabinets or under-the-sink areas tend to be disorganized due to a number of contributing factors. The main problem associated with base-cabinet storage is the difficultly in arranging space that is both low to the ground and deep. Another aspect that plays a role is trying to arrange too many small articles, such as toiletries, makeup, soaps, and hair and nail grooming accessories, in a relatively large base cabinet.

The organizers used in this space will play a significant role in how well it functions. Therefore, take the time to plan for and invest in good organizers. The following are recommended storage options to use under the sink and in base cabinets for bathroom essentials:

1. The most important investment to make in bathroom base cabinets and in under-the-sink arrangements is to install slide-out shelves or baskets that fully extend to bring the stored articles out in the open where they're easy to see and access. Since base-cabinet space is usually around thirty to thirty-five inches tall, it's best to create two storage levels, splitting the space between a few organizers. Install a pull-out organizer at the base and add another above this one. Larger items, such small appliances like foot-soaking tubs, humidifiers, fans, and so on, may require only one pullout organizer.

2. There are many freestanding two-tier, sliding-basket organizers designed with this space in mind. They're tall and narrow enough to capture the lateral space and fit around plumbing obstructions.

3. Organizers like stacking, clear, drawer-style shoe box organizers or stackable drawer units have both the slide-out feature and the capability to offer multiple levels of storage.

4. Handled totes or caddy organizers are good to place on base-cabinet shelves because they're easy to grab. There are many bathroom essentials that would be convenient to transport in a caddy from a base cabinet to the location where they'll be used. This keeps items off the countertops and neatly tucked away when not in use.

   Some of the best items to store in a caddy or tote organizer for this purpose are heated hairstyling appliances. There are specialty totes that safely carry and store hot styling products. Some have attached hooks designed to attach and hang from a towel bars, thus keeping the appliances safe from contact with a water source. Other good items to keep in a portable caddy or handled tote are first aid essentials, medications, bath products, hair products, bath toys, makeup, cleaners, sanitary products, shaving essentials, body lotions, and deodorants.

5. The inside of a base-cabinet door is the perfect place to house many bathroom articles. It's best to stick with lightweight items for door storage because larger, bulky items clank loudly from door movement and can also loosen door hinges. A basic towel bar can be installed to hold washcloths. A wall-mounted paper-towel organizer is another good option for this space. Wall-mounted cup organizers can hold toothbrushes, toothpaste, nail files, brushes, shavers, makeup, air fresheners, hair spray, cologne, and just about any small toiletry item here, as well.

There are many types of adhesive-backed organizers that can adhere to hard, flat surfaces. Utility hooks with pressure-sensitive adhesive strips are capable of bearing up to five pounds. Such organizers are good for holding lightweight appliances, like curling irons or flat irons, by their bound cords. They can also hold any bathroom essential that has a hook hole at the end. There are clear cosmetic adhesive organizers designed for cabinet door storage that have specially shaped compartments to hold lipstick, nail polish, makeup brushes, and compacts. Consider placing a waterproof backing on the inside of the cabinet door and attach hooks for holding wet articles, such as toilet bowl brushes or bath essentials like exfoliating gloves or loofahs.

Utilizing Drawers

Drawers in a bathroom are found on cabinetry and sometimes on sink vanities. The drawers' locations will determine what to store in them since things should be stored close to where they're used. The drawer size also dictates what it can hold with little to no leftover space. Since many bathroom items are grouped in quantity, such as cosmetics, Q-tips, cotton balls, toilet paper, face wipes, and so on, these items will need their own compartments when stored in a drawer.

Some bathroom belongings should *not* be stored in drawers. For example, don't keep bottled products with liquids in a drawer, especially lying flat, no matter how tightly you think the cap is screwed on. It's easy for bottles of liquid product to fall over and leak from drawer movement.

Also, refrain from keeping articles that take time to dry in drawers, such as loofahs, sponges, facial brushes, finger nail brushes, facial exfoliating sponges, and the like.

Small, Shallow Drawers

Small drawers are also shallow, ranging around three inches to five inches in height, and are stationed right below the counter or in the center of a cabinet. When these drawers are wide, they need organizers to separate belongings. However, narrow drawers, fewer than five inches in width, may not require organizers if they can fit only one item or group of articles. Small drawers that are conveniently located are good for holding daily needed bathroom essentials, such as oral care items, washcloths, shavers, trimmers, hair brushes, hair accessories, acne treatment products, and so on.

Small drawers can benefit from expandable tray organizers that open to the exact width of the drawer. These organizers have several molded compartments in various sizes to divide multiple bathroom items. Another type of organizer that functions in the same way is drawer-organizer strips that snap together. These organizers consist of heavy-duty, grooved plastic strips that interlock to create custom-sized sections. Depending on the height of the strips, these organizers are good to use for both small- and medium-size drawers.

Medium and Deeper Drawers

Deeper drawers are a benefit in a bathroom since they're suitable for a number of items. Many bathroom items are purchased in bulk because they're used and disposed of quickly. Such products can be divided in deeper drawers with simple organizers, such as expandable spring-loaded dividers that stretch across the drawer and are held in place by tension. Also, deep modular containers or baskets, which come in different sizes, can puzzle together in a drawer where, collectively, they can occupy all the space. Each basket or container can hold a given type of item.

Even without organizers, many packaged products can be stacked in deeper drawers. The following items are perfect to store with or without organizers in deeper bathroom drawers:

- Bagged cotton balls
- Boxed cotton swabs
- Bagged razors
- Boxed incontinence products
- Boxed sanitary products
- Facial tissue boxes
- Heating pads
- Hot water bottles
- Packaged diaper/facial wipes
- Packaged diapers
- Paper napkins
- Paper towels
- Toilet paper
- Towels

Containers or kits, such as first aid supplies, sewing boxes, manicure/pedicure items, makeup cases, and shoeshine supplies are also good to contain in deep bathroom drawers. When an electrical outlet is installed in a drawer, many electronic grooming gadgets, such as razors or skincare devices, can be stored and charged there.

CHAPTER 40

Alternative Bathroom Storage Options

Most bathrooms, even small ones, have storage potential. It's important to utilize walls, floors, and closets for as much storage as possible. Usually, it's possible to find organizers to fit these spaces that suit your open or closed storage preferences. Also, storage organizers that match the decor of your bathroom and create a statement are abundant in the marketplace. The following covers different ways to use such spaces for storing many different bathroom essentials.

Utilizing Bathroom Wall Space

The wall space in a bathroom is more valuable than in most rooms because bathrooms tend to be small and cabinet storage space is often limited. Many wall organizers are designed for bathrooms for this very reason. The following are the best ones for bathrooms.

Towel Racks

Vertical wall-mounted towel racks can hold several folded towels and are common in hotel rooms. Hotel designers are proficient space-saving experts who know how to stylishly and efficiently select organizers. Therefore, it makes sense to use their expertise for storing towels. These organizers are easy to find online by searching for "hotel-style towel racks."

Swivel towel holders are vertical open-ended bar rods that swivel fully to the left or right. These organizers are wall mounted and can hold towels, hangers, and clothing accessories, offering multifunction storage options.

Ladder-style, heated towel racks with multiple rungs are great organizers for neatly storing a large number of towels. This is important for homes with many members who share a bathroom and need a place to store several towels. Heated towel racks can be found at your local bath supply store or online. Depending on DIY skill levels, professional installation maybe required.

Shelving

Shelving, towel racks with shelves, and cubbyhole organizers are inexpensive and effective organizers for bathroom walls, especially when over-the-toilet space is available. It's best to use these organizers rather than the highly marketed over-the-toilet tower organizer—a one-piece freestanding tiered shelving unit (some contain cabinets)—since they look inexpensive and have a flimsy, wobbly construction. Furniture-grade étagères, or leaning-ladder shelving units, are good substitutes for such organizers since they offer more stability and look substantial. Étagères have multiple shelves for storage that can also hold bathroom essentials in decorative containers.

Shelving and cubby compartments placed above the toilet or sink need to store bathroom essentials for accessibility but also be appealing to the eye. From an esthetic point of view, when storing items such as toiletries, oral care, and hair-care supplies on open shelving, it's important to place them in neutral containers that blend well in the room. This is the best way to create order, where

each container stores a particular type of item so they're easy to find and remove.

Decorative baskets and wood, metal, and plastic containers are good organizers to use in open-storage arrangements. Breakable ceramic and glass containers may be dangerous in a bathroom, especially when managing them with wet, slippery hands.

A single sturdy shelf can be placed on the wall above the bathroom door and just below the ceiling. This space is generally ignored, but it's an ingenious spot for additional storage. You'll need a ladder or stool to access this shelf, though. Since it's not easily accessed, use this place to

Over the toilet shelves

Recessed Cabinetry

Recessed Toilet Paper Holder with Storage

Bathroom Organization

FIGURE 40.01
Bathroom Organization

store infrequently needed items or excess, such as humidifiers, toilet paper, or liquid soap refills.

Medicine Cabinets

Medicine cabinets are a traditional fixture in a bathroom and have been around for a long time because they're such effective organizers. These organizers are wall-mounted, shallow cabinets that contain many shelves for storing small articles, such as medications, oral care products, and deodorants. The medicine cabinet doors are mirrored for grooming purposes and store related essentials within reach, typically over the sink. Medicine cabinets can be mounted on a surface or recessed into a roughed-in opening or a cutout in the wall. These are well-designed organizers because their shallow shelves mean the small items can't get lost behind any larger ones.

A medicine cabinet does not need to be conventional. There are shallow wall cabinets that are longer than traditional medicine cabinets but can still fit over a sink. Some are as long as five feet, so they can store additional items, such as toiletries, toilet paper, tissues, and so on.

Consider adding a second medicine cabinet to the one situated over the sink: a wall located at the side of a sink can hold another medicine cabinet for additional storage. A second medicine cabinet does not necessarily have to be mirrored. The cabinet door can match the other cabinetry in the room. You can also disguise the cabinet by attaching a piece of framed art to the cabinet door.

Recessed In-Wall Cabinets

Recessed in-the-wall cabinets and shelving are brilliant ideas for using dead wall space in bathrooms. Taking advantage of dead space behind the drywall to insert shelving or cabinets is the perfect solution to limited storage options in small

spaces. Work can be involved in locating the space beyond the drywall, however. You'll need to find room in between the wall studs or perhaps cut into the studs to make that room. Also, the area needs to be free of electrical lines, plumbing, and vents, which may require professional help.

Ready-made recess cabinets are available that typically come with adjustable shelving and many door options to match your decor. This narrow space is best for shallow storage, which is perfect for hundreds of bathroom essentials, such as toiletries, makeup, oral care products, medications, vitamins, first aid articles, and the like. You can create an in-the-wall shelf by the toilet to store a toilet paper holder, plus shelves for extra rolls and air fresheners.

Utilizing Bathroom Floor Space

Available floor space in a bathroom can be put to good use with a freestanding organizer. Some of the best organizers for bathrooms tight on space are linen tower cabinets—tall and narrow freestanding cabinets that wisely occupy a small section of the floor, often just fifteen square inches of space. However, they're tall, usually sixty inches high, so they take advantage of commonly untapped vertical space for storage. There are countless linen tower cabinets on the market. They come with cabinet doors, shelves, and drawers for your storage preference. Cabinets and drawers will hide visual clutter, whereas shelving on these units should have baskets or containers to contain loose items. These cabinets are also designed for hard-to-arrange corners, when in a triangular shape.

There are many narrow shelving units that can also take advantage of lateral space. Some are even outfitted with pullout drawers and roller wheels for easy access. Common decorative étagères and ladder-style shelving pieces are useful for this purpose, but usually require baskets or containers to conceal and organize bathroom essentials. These space-saving organizers work nicely next to a sink or toilet where many bathroom essentials, such as toilet paper and soaps, are used.

A freestanding towel rack with multiple bars for holding a number of towels in between showers or baths is a good solution for households with many members. There are also freestanding heated towel racks that can hold multiple towels. These organizers are important to place right next to the shower or tub for convenience. Many alternative bathroom storage organizers for airing towels have limited hanging storage space, such as a wall-mounted towel bar or towel stand with only one or two bars.

Rolling cart organizers are great for the bathroom because they can station in the room while in use and then easily retreat to an adjoining closet for storage. Many rolling cart organizers have tiered compartments to hold bath essentials, hair appliances, and accessories, skincare products, towels, and makeup. For serious hair-care, a professional-grade, wheeled trolley cart specifically designed to store hairstyling appliances and accessories may be in order. Such carts are found through hair-salon supply stores.

Freestanding toilet paper holders generally have a long pole that connects a weighted base to a dispensing toilet paper roll at the top. Some freestanding toilet paper holders have storage compartments for holding additional rolls in lieu of a connecting pole. In conjunction with a toilet paper holder, separate freestanding toilet paper canisters offer an additional place to house excess rolls. Such organizers are great alternatives to

traditional wall-mounted dispensers which tend to loosen and fail; plus many don't offer a convenient storage spot for extra toilet paper.

Toilet plungers and brushes can usually be inserted into freestanding floor organizers. Many are designed to fully hide the plunger or brush in a container, leaving only the handle visible. You can find both the plunger and brush designed for one organizer unit or separately. Usually, these organizers openly reside on the floor next to toilet, so it's best to select an organizer that can hold both items, or keep just the frequently used brush organizer next to the toilet and move the plunger under the sink.

Utilizing the Toilet Area

The toilet itself has storage possibilities. The top part of the toilet tank often has a surface space to hold a decorative basket or tray organizer for hand towels, guest napkins, hand sanitizer, perfume, makeup, tissue, toilet paper, candles, and so on. Add a plant or artifact to this organizer as a decorative element.

There are toilet paper holders and magazine racks made to hook onto the toilet tank rim where they hang from the sides of tank. Using organizers on the toilet itself is ingenious since you can keep necessary items within reach and not occupy floor space or crowd walls with organizers.

Utilizing the Bathroom Door

An entrance or closet bathroom door can be a good storage opportunity. The best bathroom items for doors are space-demanding towels, especially those that need to air dry in between uses. There are many over-the-door towel organizers that hook onto the top portion of the door with multiple tiered hanging rods for increased towel storage.

Regular wall-mounted towel bars can be used on the inside of the door, as well. Other common towel-rod door organizers are four-bar hanging valets that fasten to the door hinge. Valets are easy to install by simply popping out the door hinge pin and inserting the organizer. These organizers have four hanging parallel bars that swivel independently.

Utilizing an Available Bathroom Closet

A closet in a bathroom is clearly a great asset. How a bathroom closet is organized will depend on a few factors. Largely, the number of bathrooms in a home, as well as how many contain closets, influences contents and arrangements. Bathtubs or showers greatly contribute to storage requirements for bathroom closets. Also, a bathroom closet's storage demand is lessened in homes with nearby hallway linen closets that can hold excess bathroom linens and toiletries.

A closet is the best bathroom organizer because it's typically roomy, and most storage organizers can make the closet a highly versatile and functional space for storing all bathroom items, both large and small. However, closets can become the catchall place for everything, which is why they can become disorganized and congested. Also, closets tend to be deep, which can create problems when arranging smaller bathroom essentials, such as toiletries.

Bathroom Closet Storage Solutions

In deeper closets, pullout shelves and baskets can bring items from the back of the closet out into the open for easier viewing and retrieval. Use deeper pullout baskets for bulky articles, such as bath towels, humidifiers, small fans, foot soakers, massaging gadgets, paper products, beach towels, bath toys, and hair dryers. Place the largest pullout baskets at the bottom of the closet, graduating upward to the smaller baskets. Position smaller shelves or baskets at waist level. These shelves or baskets can accept common drawer organizers, such as smaller baskets and divider trays, for grouping like things together. Makeup, manicure/pedicure supplies, nail polish, wipes, hand towels, skincare products, or toiletry tubes are some of the articles that will store well in this space.

Pullout hampers and trash cans are other storage accessories that can be installed at the base of a closet. These organizers are sold in kits at home centers and online. A freestanding hamper or trash can is an alternative organizer for the closet floor. Mobile organizers, such as wheeled baskets, tiered drawer organizers, and carts, make great organizers for the closet floor where they're easy to access and move, should they be needed elsewhere. Another good floor organizer is a handled caddy organizer to fill with bathroom cleaning products and paper towels for quick or daily cleanups.

The middle and upper sections of a bathroom closet are best outfitted with adjustable shelving. Don't go too deep on the shelves, however, even if the closet is deep. It's always harder to arrange items, especially common bathroom essentials like small bottles and jars, in too big of a space where they can become lost. There are easy ways to arrange the many groups of small articles found in bathrooms so they store nicely on open closet shelving.

Common small- to medium-size handled or easy-grip baskets/containers are ideal for dividing everything. Use open baskets/containers and don't stack or use lidded containers for items needed, because stacked, lidded containers are hard to access and are especially a nuisance on a busy morning bathroom rush. It's best use a single open basket on a shelf and space the shelves close together. However, when dealing with fixed shelving, use cabinet organizers that can take more lateral space. A popular "helper shelf" creates an additional shelf platform to place containers or items on.

There are also organizers shaped like two-tiered round plates that spin 360 degrees for easy accessibility and additional lateral storage often referred to as a Lazy Susan. Store only weighted toiletries on them since they're more stable and will not tip over from movement. Under-shelf baskets are another organizer to use because they also capture free space in between fixed shelves. Handled storage containers are great for transporting items around. In small bathrooms, it may be wise to create separate caddy organizers to hold first aid supplies, bath essentials, makeup, skincare and hair products, and so

on, with the intention of using them at the sink but storing them on a closet shelf.

Overhead shelves in a bathroom closet are good places to store excess toiletries so you don't make the mistake of opening three bottles of the same type of product simultaneously. This strategy will also declutter shelf space. Simply use containers and label their contents for items like shampoo/conditioner, shaving cream/razors, deodorant/body spray, and so on. Refill-size products used in soap dispensers and the like are also good to store overhead. Other items for overhead compartments include: paper goods, seasonal beach or picnic towels/blankets, excess bath towels, and infrequently used gadgets, such as massagers or humidifiers.

The inside portion of a bathroom closet door that is a slab style—which opens in either a right or left swing—has storage potential. Towel bars can mount on them to hang wet or new towels. Rails that attach baskets can hold a number of bathroom essentials, such as small appliances, paper goods, and toiletries. Many first aid kits come mountable, which are also great for door installation. A simple hook can be used to store a number of bathroom articles, such as a robe or towel. A clever idea is to hang a basic nylon mesh bag from a door hook to hold items such as laundry, bath toys, or clothes.

CHAPTER 41

Organizing Bathroom Items

A number of articles would be convenient to store in a bathroom, but sometimes not everything can fit in the space. It's important to be selective about choosing which products are absolutely essential in a given bathroom and determining whether it's feasible to keep surplus in another room or closet. The following are the most popular items to store in the bathroom. Strategies on how to downsize and manage them are included.

Bathroom Towels

A towel is any absorbent fabric or paper used to dry a person or object. Most bathroom towels are made of cotton terry cloth due to its high absorbency and durability. Some hand towels are made of disposable paper. Different types of towels are stored in most bathrooms.

- A washcloth is a small cloth used for face and body washing, usually measuring approximately nine inches square up to eleven inches square.

- Hand towels are generally decorative smaller towels typically displayed near a sink for hand drying.
- Bath towels come in various sizes, depending on preference, and are used for drying the body after taking a bath or shower.
- Specialty towels:
  - Guest towels are bathroom towels, but they're typically newer and set aside exclusively for company.
  - Beach towels are longer towels used at pools, beaches, and other outdoor activities.

Bathrooms shared with visitors, such as powder rooms and guest bathrooms, receive the better towels. In these rooms, it may be necessary to rotate between two sets of towels. One can be displayed on towel bars, exposed shelves, counter organizers, and so on, while the other is stored in a closet, cabinet, or sink drawer. If the bathroom doesn't have sufficient storage, guest and beach towels are typically stored in a linen or spare bedroom closet.

Bathrooms used by household members on a daily basis will need a quantity of towels based on the number of people using the room. Generally, each household member will need his or her own bath towel easily accessible near the tub/shower and a place to dry them between uses. Bathrooms shared by many household members may benefit from a system that identifies an individual's towel with an embroidered name initial or sewn name label. Another option is to color-code towels with a ribbon or patch. This approach is less confusing to use over trying to maintain a certain order with towel organizers. Unused bath towels should be tucked away in an organizer, such as a wall shelf, cabinet, drawer, or closet. Store towels rolled or uniformly folded in stacks with the fold facing forward, especially if they're openly stored.

Bathrooms shared by many members can use paper hand towels, which are more sanitary and easier than cloth ones. These towels are also handy for quick cleanups. Disinfectant wipes or perforated paper towels on a roll, plus a bathroom cleaner, can be kept under the sink for this purpose.

Downsizing Towels

Towels that are visibly displayed in a bathroom should look their best since they greatly impact the overall appearance of the room. Once or twice a year, sort these towels and reduce them. The best time to organize your towels is when linens typically go on sale, in case you need to replace them. In January, stores hold "white sales," meaning all linens are on sale. Sometimes, by February, linens will go on clearance. In August, retailers want to capture those who need college dorm linens, so sales are common at this time, as well.

It's necessary to group all bathroom towels by type, such as washcloth, hand towel, and bath, so you know how many you have of each kind. Then check them over for pulled threads, shrunken bands, stains, frayed hems, fading, or rips. Get rid of any towels that are in bad shape. Plan to recycle them into rags or donate them to an animal shelter.

Decide the number of towels absolutely necessary to have on hand so that a fresh washcloth and bath towel are available at all times for a household member or guest. Notice whether you are running out of towels before you can get to laundering them. On the flipside, towels that are not in the regular laundry rotation and have not left the shelf in some time indicate a surplus.

Medications and Vitamins/ Supplements

Most vitamins, supplements, and OTC and prescription medications must be stored at room temperature in a cool, dark, and dry place. Extreme temperatures, either cold or hot, can break down the active ingredients in a drug, making it ineffective. High humidity or moisture can also degrade medicines. For these reasons, a bathroom that is prone to warm, moist, and humid conditions is not a recommended storage place for medications. This is important to acknowledge, especially when life-saving or preserving medications are involved. In spite of these findings, some people simply prefer to store their medications in the bathroom due to the convenience of a medicine cabinet. In these cases, it's important to make certain your bathroom is well ventilated.

First, check your exhaust fan's suction by performing a simple test. Just hold a piece of toilet paper up to the exhaust fan when it's on; if the paper stays on the fan, the suction is working fine. Mold formation anywhere is a sign of poor ventilation. Combat poor ventilation by installing a few exhaust fans near the water sources, and make certain they vent outdoors. Always leave shower doors open or pull shower curtains back so moisture isn't trapped in the room. Keep the bathroom door open, especially while the exhaust fan runs, which should be for at least fifteen minutes at a time, allowing for air exchange from other parts of the home. Any bathroom windows should stay open, even a crack, for at least as long as the exhaust fan runs.

People taking up to five medications a day can benefit from date-stamped, compartmentalized pill containers to group their medications together. There are also specialized online pharmacies that will make individual packets for prescriptions and OTC medications by the dose.

As a general rule, don't transfer medications from an original container to another one unless they're consumed in a short period since dosages can change and important label information—such as the expiration date—is lost. Most prescription bottles are designed with push-and-turn, child-resistant caps. The bottles are opaque to protect the contents from light. However, they're not airtight, waterproof, or ultraviolet (UV) light protected. Therefore, still handle them with care. There are specialized herb storage and preservation jars designed to be airtight and block UV rays. Find those that can fit a prescription bottle inside for important medications if you think your current storage locations are compromised by too much moisture. Before transferring medications to another organizer, it's best to consult your physician and pharmacist.

In a well-ventilated bathroom, keep medications and vitamins away from any windows. Consider installing a shallow recessed wall or medicine cabinet as far away from the shower or sink as possible. These organizers are best for bottles of vitamins and medications because they won't get lost like they might on a deep shelf or in a container. Such organizers can be placed at eye-level locations on the wall for better visibility and accessibility.

Many kitchen organizers designed to hold spice bottles are also ideal for storing small bottles of medications and vitamins. Cabinet organizers, such as tiered step shelves, are good options. Some tiered step shelves for cabinet shelves run along the interior walls to form a U shape. These are great organizers because they leave the center of the cabinet open, allowing for easy viewing and access to items.

Stacking lidded containers, such as shoebox-style organizers or tiered pullout drawer organizers, are not the best choice for storing medications because most items, especially bottled medications, are impossible to stabilize. Stacked organizers are inconvenient for accessing items because each one needs to be taken out individually to see its contents. Tiered drawer organizers are mainly useful for small loose articles, such as many first aid products like gauze, ice packs, tapes, splints, ear plugs, and so on.

When children are present in the home, storage modifications must be in place. Medications must be stored in locking cabinets or high shelves. Most medications are placed in child-resistant packaging, which is different than childproof packaging. Therefore, it's still possible for a child to open them.

Downsizing Medications and Vitamins/Supplements

All medications and vitamins need regular attention; they should be sorted and reduced several times a year, especially before the cold, flu, and allergy season, or in spring and fall. Always begin organizing these items by removing everything from storage then sort into like groups, such as allergy, prescription, cold, and flu.

Discard all expired products and anything without a date. Use a permanent marker to go over the faint or small expiration dates. It may be a good idea to have a pad and paper to record which items you are low on or out of stock. Then attach it to your shopping list or keep it in a coupon organizer and purchase these items when they go on sale. Prescription refills can also be noted. Keep all medications in their original packaging, which makes for easy identification and clear expiration dates. For example, capsules or tablets contained in molded plastic sheets and sealed in a foil covering can become hard to identify outside their boxed packaging.

Unlike most edibles, opened medications, such as liquid cough syrup or topical creams, stay effective until their expiration dates, provided they're well sealed. While organizing, don't condense two liquid medications together; you want to keep medications as sterile as possible. On the same note, don't run sticky syrupy bottles of medicines under a faucet to clean them, especially near the rim where water can seep inside and potentially cause contamination. It's best to stick with damp, white paper towels free of cleaning solutions.

Arrange your medications as logically as possible and in general categories, for several reasons. First, there are so many different types of medications that sorting them would create numerous categories and unnecessary complications. Also, broad categories make finding common medications easier to locate when they're needed.

In general, keep oral medications together by type, such as sleep and allergy. Topical liquid remedies, such as hydrogen peroxide, rubbing alcohol, and itch relief lotions can be kept together. Most first aid supplies, such as finger splints, adhesive tape, and bandages, can be stored in drawer organizers or specialized containers. Mix in homeopathic medications with the regular kind.

The following is a list of general classifications to help you group these items in storage.

- Allergy and sinus: asthma, nasal sprays
- Children's medications: keep all types of children's medications in one location
- Cough, cold, and flu medications
- Digestive and nausea: antacids, diarrhea, laxatives, constipation, probiotics, gas, fiber, motion sickness
- Home testing kits: fertility, diabetic, pregnancy, drug
- Pain relief: aspirin, nonaspirin, migraine, joint/muscle pain, arthritis, oral pain, menstrual pain
- Skincare: rash, eczema, psoriasis, wart, scar, wound, foot care
- Sleep and snoring aids
- Vitamins and supplements

Lastly, laminate any pertinent medical dispensing instructions, daily dosage information, pharmacy locations/numbers, or prescription records and refill information and post it on a cabinet wall or door. Medical books and pamphlets can also be kept with medications for convenience.

First Aid Kits

First aid kits are really important, especially in homes with small children and elderly people prone to more accidents. These kits are best when portable, so they can be taken to the scene of an accident. There are many ready-made first aid kits in the market, but it's easy to create your own. A basic handled caddy organizer, fishing tackle box, sewing box, or tool box can be repurposed as a first aid container. Customize the contents to your specifications. Select the type of bandages, topical antibiotic, and size gauze pads you like to use. Opt for smaller-size tubes and jars of medications to fit a larger variety of items in the kit.

Cosmetics

For most women, a specialized vanity table equipped with storage drawers, a seating bench, and a mirror with proper lighting is a fantasy place to apply facial cosmetics, which are any products applied to the face: makeup, lotions, and makeup applicators (e.g., brushes, sponges). Many of us resort to basic bathroom accommodations to put ourselves together every morning, but there are ways to contain makeup in specialized organizers that can add a bit of glamour to a bathroom.

Fortunately, many makeup organizers are decorative and functional enough to dress up any space. Then there are those that can be concealed in a cabinet or drawer. Decide which type of organizer suits your space and tastes. The following are various organizers you can use to store your cosmetics and related accessories in a bathroom.

Countertop Cosmetic Organizers

These organizers can sit on any open space (counters or shelves) and in cabinets and closets. Most are designed with tiered levels of storage to compartmentalize several small groups of cosmetics, such as compacts, mascara, or lipstick. It's important to think about which organizer best suits your belongings, because you want the compartment sizes to fit the types and number of cosmetics you possess.

Popular translucent acrylic cosmetic organizers make stored articles easily identifiable. These organizers are attractive for the countertop. You can find such organizers with drawers and individual compartments designed specifically for particular items such as lipstick or nail polish.

Another efficient countertop organizer is the tiered 360-degree rotating cosmetic organizer. This organizer can fit in corner spaces and offers great access to cosmetics.

For those who don't like the look of open storage, there are organizers that conceal the entire contents inside a countertop cabinet similar in design to many jewelry boxes. These organizers have doors that open to many small drawer compartments.

In-Drawer Cosmetics Organizers

Most in-drawer cosmetic organizers are compartmentalized trays found in stores that sell bathroom or home office organizational items. Modular drawer containers and kits designed to compartmentalize drawers are several inches tall and fit in deeper drawers to hold larger cosmetic items.

Freestanding and Portable Cosmetics Organizers

Tiny or congested bathroom spaces benefit from wheeled or handled cosmetic organizers that are easy to transport. Wheeled, tiered cart organizers with pullout drawers can also hold cosmetics. These are convenient to roll into a closet for storage in between uses.

There are also portable, handled cosmetic totes and caddy organizers that can move to a counter when needed and then nicely tuck away in a deep drawer, cabinet shelf, cart, or closet when not in use. There are clever freestanding changing mirrors that open into a storage cabinet for small items and are great if your bathroom can spare just a little floor space.

Downsizing Cosmetics

Many people don't realize that makeup has a shelf life or are misinformed about actual product expiration dates. Most cosmetics have a period-after-opening (PAO) symbol on the label, which is marked by a photo of an opened container along with the number of months it can keep once opened. For example, "6M" means six months. Shelf life is also determined by how a product is stored and the type of packaging used.

Makeup can go bad and form bacteria, which could damage the skin. Help prevent bacteria formation by applying makeup with clean hands and makeup applicators. On a monthly basis, deep clean all makeup applicators, especially heavily soiled brushes used for liquid or cream-based makeup. Treat them with a specific brush cleaner or make your own with a degreasing liquid soap, a little olive oil (which actually removes oil), and a new sponge. Makeup brush cleansing wipes can be used in between deep cleanings. Depending on the quality of the sponge and how it's maintained (daily rinsing is recommended), most blending sponges should be discarded after three months.

Makeup is usually marked with a manufacturer's expiration date, but once opened, this date changes. The following are general expiration dates for various types of opened cosmetics. However, these dates vary by specific product ingredients and packaging.

Natural Products

Any product made without preservatives will have a short shelf life. It's best to contact the product's company for expiration information.

Cream Concealers, Liquid Foundations, Eyeliners, and Mascaras

All these products are water based; so they're prone to bacteria formation after opening. Eyeliner and mascara have the shortest lifespans: only four to six months. Therefore, consider buying inexpensive eye makeup and replacing it often, because bacteria can lead to eye infections. Foundations can last up to one year when properly stored. Don't place a used sponge on the rim of a liquid makeup bottle to dispense the product because a bacteria risk is present.

Face Powders, Blush/Bronzers, and Eye Shadows

Dry textures like powder are less likely to develop bacteria. Keep pressed powder, blush/bronzers, and eye shadow compacts clean by gently wiping off a fine top layer with a dry white paper towel once a month. If well sealed, these products can keep for up to two years.

Brow and Lip Pencils

Keep makeup pencils well sharpened, and wipe them down with makeup wipes regularly. Brow pencils last a few years and lip pencils approximately one year.

Lipsticks and Lip Gloss

Lip gloss is prone to discoloration and will thicken to the point where it goes on too clumpy, which is a sure sign to discard it. Lipstick and lip balm sticks can be cleaned with a makeup wipe. Lipstick can last up to two years and lip balm one year when properly resealed.

Cosmetics Organization Tips

Organize cosmetics by grouping them by like items, such as bronzers, eye shadows, and mascaras.

- Discard anything missing a lid or with a cracked case, because air exposure degrades makeup.
- Get rid of pressed powders that have cracked, because they'll inevitably break down and create a big mess.
- Toss any expired makeup or anything that has clumped, separated, dried out, discolored, or changed texture.
- Sharpen all pencils.
- With a clean, damp white paper towel or makeup wipe, clean all cosmetic containers thoroughly and carefully around the rim without making contact with the actual product.
- Invest in makeup expiration stickers, or use any small blank sticker and start recording the date a product is opened. Keep the stickers with all the unopened makeup outside of the cosmetics organizer.
- The amount of makeup to keep is such a personal decision; however, it's best to keep only what you regularly use. Makeup that has not been touched in a few months will most likely not be used. Due to short shelf lives, this makeup should be discarded.

Hand and Foot Care Supplies

A manicure and pedicure are cosmetic treatments. A manicure involves grooming hands and fingernails; a pedicure treats the feet and toenails. Both entail procedures that file, trim, cut, and polish the nails and may include exfoliating, moisturizing, and massaging the skin in these areas. A manicure is similar to a pedicure, so most of the lotions and tools involved are shared. For this reason, keep all your manicure and pedicure supplies together in one spot. Regardless of their number, an organizer is necessary to corral them. Otherwise, many hand and foot care items, which are mostly small in size, wind up throughout the house and are difficult to find when needed.

The bathroom tends to be a popular spot to house manicure and pedicure supplies, even though it may not necessarily be the place you like to perform home manicures and pedicures. In that case, a portable organizer is convenient. There is a popular cosmetic organizer used by many professionals in the beauty industry called a *train case*, which is a hard-shelled carrying case designed to

Cosmetic Tips

→ Invest in makeup expiration stickers, or use any small blank sticker and start recording the date a product is opened.

→ Natural products have a short shelf life. Contact the product's company for expiration information.

Product Life Spans

Eyeliner & mascara	4 to 6 months
Foundation	up to 1 year
Powder & eye shadow	up to 2 years
Brow & lip pencil	up to 1 year
Lipstick	up to 2 years
Lip balm	up to 1 year

store several small articles; some train cases have specialized compartments for holding items like nail polish. This organizer—or any handled tote, case, or caddy with several compartments—is a good option for dividing supplies, such as nail files, pumice stones, nail trimmers, and so on. Bathroom shelves, closets, or cabinets are great places to keep these organizers.

Store manicure and pedicure implements made of high-quality stainless steel in a protective case to safeguard their sharpening surfaces. Sets of manicure and pedicure tools usually come with such cases, but they're also sold empty.

Tiered wheeled carts with drawers can store everything needed for a manicure or pedicure, such as cotton balls, nail polish and remover, pedicure sandals, toe separators, files, stones, and so on. These organizers can sit in a bathroom closet and be rolled out when needed.

Downsizing Hand and Foot Care Supplies

Manicure and pedicure supplies are easy to reduce because it's obvious when they're worn down. Items like nail polish are also easy to recognize when they're past their prime since these products become thick and impossible to apply. Also, discoloration in old polish is common. It's a good idea to downsize large numbers of manicure and pedicure supplies to the following, keeping only those in the best condition:

- one complete set of metal-based implements, such as a cuticle trimmer or nail clipper;
- a handful of nail files;
- one pumice stone or foot file;
- one bag of cotton balls or pads;
- one bottle of nail polish remover; and

- a pair of pedicure sandals and a set of toe separators.

Toiletries

Toiletries are personal care items used for hygiene and grooming the body. Toiletries cover a wide range of body cleaning and grooming products and utensils, and most tend to be used in the bathroom. The best way to organize toiletries is to group them by type or function. Then arrange each group in an organizer and keep them where they're used.

Downsizing Toiletries

The main categories for toiletries are oral care, hair care, bath/body products, skin care, and shaving. Most toiletries are not regulated by the US FDA; therefore, expiration dates are often missing or inaccurate. Every product expires, and most will lose their effectiveness over time. However, some toiletries are classified as drug related because they both cleanse and prevent/treat a condition. Antiperspirants, acne creams, dandruff shampoos, and anything marketed to offer sun protection (certain moisturizers, cosmetics, and sunscreen) have ingredients that classify them as an OTC drug, and the FDA requires these products to have expiration dates.

When it's time to sort and declutter your bathroom toiletries, first discard everything that hasn't been used in a long period of time, because the items have probably expired. Items that no one likes might be repurposed. The internet is a great place to find additional uses for your toiletries. For example, toothpaste is a good cleaning agent for items like jewelry, and many shampoos make good hand soaps or cleaners. Plan to move such articles to other places in the home where they can be used.

The shelf life of any product will be influenced by its ingredients, storage, and handling. Basically, water-based products; those labeled "all natural"; and those containing antioxidants, such as vitamin C or glycolic acid, will break down more rapidly once opened. On the other hand, products that contain preserving agents and alcohol will have a longer shelf life.

Most products in jars, especially those with wide-mouth openings, are more susceptible to bacterial formation from hand use and other elements than pump or spray products are. Common sense is always your best bet when decluttering toiletries; go by the texture, smell, and color. The following is a general guideline for expiration dates of popular toiletries, but contact the manufacturer for exact information:

- Antiaging products and face creams: six months to one year
- Deodorants/antiperspirants: three years
- Hairstyling products: three to five years
- Liquid body wash and bar soap: three years
- Loofahs, exfoliating mitts, and body brushes: one to three months (Note that these items should be rinsed well and air dried completely in between use because they're susceptible to the bacteria and fungus that breeds in wet places. Hooks or vented organizers that attach to a tiled shower wall are perfect. These items can also hang from a shower rod using an additional curtain hook or be stored on a towel rack or hook located in a dry, cool area. Aside from drying out these items completely in between

use, they need to be sanitized weekly. Soak them in a diluted (5%) bleach solution with water or microwave them while damp for two minutes. Soaking them in a few drops of essential oil, such as eucalyptus or lemongrass mixed with warm water, is another antibacterial remedy. Discard these items when they smell musty or have any black spots, which signifies mold.)
- Shampoo and conditioner: two years opened, three years sealed
- Shaving cream: three years
- Toothbrushes: three months. (Note that the American Dental Association recommends that any toothbrush, manual or electric, be replaced every three months, when bristles fray, and after illnesses. Store single toothbrushes upright in an open environment to air drying and not in a community organizer, where brush heads touch and cause cross contamination.)

Generally, toiletries that quickly deplete, such as shampoo, body lotion, deodorant, toothpaste, and the like, are often purchased in larger quantities. While understandable, this often leads to multiple open products at the same time, rather than using one up before opening another. Also, larger quantities of products can lead to disorder. The best solution for combating this problem is to store just one of each product per household member in an accessible bathroom location; then store the remainder in a more remote place, such as a linen closet or overhead shelf not necessarily located in the bathroom.

Plan to use open products completely before retrieving an unopened one. You want to create a surplus storage center that is very organized. Use bins, containers, or baskets on shelves, and divide items by type, such as shampoos/conditioners, face products, oral care, and so on. When buying toiletries in large quantities, record the purchase date on the products. This way you can use the older products first.

Bathroom Paper Products

Most bathroom paper products are used up fairly quickly, so keep a good number of refills near where they're needed. However, these items tend to be space hogs, so keeping an amount that can last a few weeks is sufficient for small spaces. A surplus can reside in locations outside daily used space, such as a nearby hallway closet or overhead compartment.

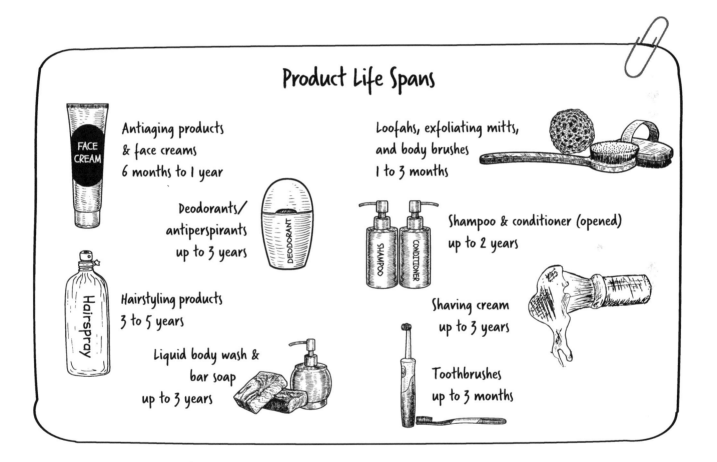

Product Life Spans

Antiaging products & face creams
6 months to 1 year

Deodorants/ antiperspirants
up to 3 years

Hairstyling products
3 to 5 years

Liquid body wash & bar soap
up to 3 years

Loofahs, exfoliating mitts, and body brushes
1 to 3 months

Shampoo & conditioner (opened)
up to 2 years

Shaving cream
up to 3 years

Toothbrushes
up to 3 months

CHAPTER 42

Laundry Rooms

Clothing and linens are washed, dried, and possibly ironed and repaired in a laundry room, depending on the extent of amenities occupying the space. In the past, laundry facilities in a typical house were located in the basement. Therefore, many older homes lack adequate space for bulky washers and dryers in the common living areas. However, consumer demands over the years have created the need for home builders to place laundry rooms on other floors of the home for accessibility and convenience. Today, entire rooms are dedicated to not only laundering clothes but also sewing and ironing them.

For these reasons, there are many different ways laundry rooms or areas are placed in a home. Some laundry rooms are situated in the basement with a laundry chute system that delivers dirty laundry from upper levels. Main-, second-, or third-floor laundry areas can be in a separate, dedicated laundry room; camouflaged in another room, such as the kitchen; hidden in a closet; or openly combined with another room, such as a mudroom or bathroom.

Generally, laundry rooms are hard to organize since they are usually small, busy places which can have numerous activities taking place such as sorting, folding, hanging, stacking, storing and ironing clothing. Another factor that adds to the challenge of organizing the laundry room is that homeowners have a tendency to hide clutter there because it's usually tucked away and out of sight. The goal should be to relocate abandoned articles to a proper storage location or devise a space for them in the laundry area. No matter how small a laundry area may appear, there are ways to utilize the space so it functions well, given the proper design and organizers.

Before starting your laundry-room organizational project, first take into account the most expensive aspects of the space, which are the washer, dryer, sink, and cabinetry, when present in the space. Having to replace or relocate these things within the room will dramatically add to the budget, but it may also increase the overall operation of the room and the value of the home.

Should you plan to replace your appliances or cabinetry or alter plumbing arrangements but can't get to it immediately; you can still set organizational goals for the space. For the time being, seek inexpensive, adjustable storage accessories that could be repurposed elsewhere at a later date, if needed. Organizing the space can generate a solid roadmap for successfully outfitting your laundry facility when the time is right.

The following information offers different ways to arrange appliances, cabinets, and sinks in a laundry room, and detailed information about the various options available given your budget, taste, needs, and space.

Washers and Dryers

The focal point of a laundry room is the washer and dryer since their functions are the sole purpose of the space. Washers and dryers come in four different configurations:

- freestanding front-load washer and dryer;
- freestanding top-load washer and dryer combinations;
- stacked washer/dryer combination; and
- all-in-one washer/dryer.

Front-Load Washers and Dryers

The front-load washer paired with a matching dryer will give you the freedom to create a long countertop above these appliances and design easy-access cabinets above them. The convenient countertop space provides the necessary place to fold, stack, and sort laundry. A front-load washer

has energy- and water-efficient features, but needs particular care to prevent mold formation.

Top-Load Washer and Dryer Combinations

The traditional top-load washer opens from the top of the machine, which can interfere with using the space to fold, sort, and stack, especially when used often. This may bring about a need to create a folding station elsewhere. Organizing space around a top-loading machine calls for more creativity because it requires a vertical clearance, while the dryer mate needs horizontal clearance. If you are unsure whether you want to eventually change from a top- to a front-load washer, you'll not have to change the room's floor pattern since the horizontal dimensions of both machines are roughly the same size.

Therefore, designing and laying out your laundry facility with a top-load washer is not a wasted effort, should you swap it out for a front-load option in the future. The only area that may need an organizational adjustment if you make that change is the space above the washer. A top-load washer needs wall clearance for the door that opens up at the top of the machine, whereas a front-loading one does not.

Stacked Front-Load Washer/ Dryer Combination

A stacking washer and dryer combination is a washing machine with a dryer unit on top. There are stackable laundry sets that are sold together that offer a seamless look. Such units tend to only handle small loads, however. You can also build your own stackable laundry set by selecting your own washer and dryer, and you can pick units with larger capacity. A special kit would then be needed to place the washer and dryer together.

The big advantage to stacking laundry units is that they occupy half the floor space of typical side-by-side units. This type of space savings is necessary in some laundry rooms. It can also be advantageous to use extra floor space for other items, such as folding tables, sewing machines, ironing boards, hanging rods, shelving, or cabinets.

All-in-One Washer/Dryer

When space in your home or apartment is scarce, an all-in-one washer and dryer is a sensible solution. It's basically the size of a single unit appliance, designed to first wash then dry. The advantage to this type of machine is clearly the space-saving feature. However, washing and drying several loads of laundry will stretch out the time of a laundry chore versus using two machines simultaneously. Therefore, these all-in-one machines work best in households with few members or as a secondary laundry machine suitable in places like a master bedroom closet, bathroom, weight room, or spare hallway closet.

Laundry-Room Cabinetry

Although expensive, cabinetry is the neatest, dressiest, and most efficient way to store laundry items. Cabinets add value to your home and keep laundry items accessible when they're built around the machines. Cabinet counters are a great place to sort, stack, and fold laundry.

An extensive number of cabinet organizers are on the market for upper and base cabinets that also include drawers, making it easy to effectively store any laundry item. Some of the best cabinetry

laundry storage accessories are built-in ironing boards, pullout trash bins, pullout hampers, pullout drying racks, and mounted clothing rods.

The only tricky part about cabinets is designing them around your washer and dryer. Technological advancements may change the shape and size of replacement machines. It's a chance you take when incorporating cabinets with current appliances.

Plumbing

In some cases, adding or relocating a washer, dryer, or sink to an existing laundry room may require a plumbing expense. In certain circumstances, it's best to keep plumbing fixtures in a renovation project stationed where they are, to avoid a plumbing relocation expense. A budget is often better spent on swapping out the sink, upgrading a washer or dryer, or adding cabinetry.

However, in some cases, it may be feasible to relocate a washer, dryer, or sink in order to use the space more efficiently, even if an expense is incurred. Adding a utility or floor sink can be a great asset to a laundry room because it can serve other purposes, such as cleaning bulky items like sports equipment, big pots, tools, and even pets. The sink can be used to fill buckets and water plants. And when the laundry room is located near an entry point, a water source can also accommodate outdoor needs, such as cleaning automotive items or filling watering cans.

What Belongs in the Laundry Room?

It's important to determine what is most helpful to keep in your laundry room since everything logical to have in it may not necessarily fit. Everyone has a unique set of laundry items they need in this space, and these belongings must receive priority storage. For example, laundry-related items, such as knitting supplies or clothing art kits, are the types of articles that are important only in households with members who regularly use them in the laundry-room area. In this case, these items would take storage precedence over other items.

The following are the most common items found in a laundry room. Decide which items are the most significant, depending on how you use your laundry space, and rate the others in order of importance. Use a prioritized list to plan your space, offering key placement for the most important items, which means keeping them close to where they're used. Invest in the best organizers for the significant items, and you may opt for more budget-minded storage essentials for the less necessary belongings.

Basic Laundry Items

- Bleach
- Clothes pins
- Clothing dyes
- Dryer sheets
- Garbage can
- Hand soap and lotion
- Hangers
- Iron
- Ironing board
- Laundry markers
- Laundry soaps
- Lint brush
- Loose change container/piggy bank
- Missing sock drawer/container
- Safety pins
- Spray starch
- Stain remover
- Stocked sewing box
- Stool

Extended Laundry Items

- Clothing art, fabric paint, and markers
- Cutting table
- Fabric
- Forms
- Knitting/crocheting supplies
- Sewing desk
- Sewing machine/quilting machine
- Sewing/quilting supplies

Laundry Spaces

No matter how small a laundry area may appear, there are ways to utilize the space so it functions well, given the proper design and organizers.

CHAPTER 43

Organizing Laundry Rooms

There is no one right way to organize a laundry room. The main emphasis should be to concentrate on one item or set of articles at a time. Completely sort, downsize, and rate your belongings in order of importance to arrange your laundry facility in optimal order.

When you begin organizing your laundry space, keep a special binder or notebook with subject partitions to jot down everything involved in your laundry-room organizational project. Each partition can cover a separate topic, such as measurements, merchant websites, organizers, cabinetry lines, and appliances. Make a section for maintenance repairs for any side projects you find while organizing that will eventually need to be addressed. For example, note a leaky faucet or schedule a service call for your appliances. Another idea is to create a shopping list in your notebook for items you want or decide to replace that can be purchased after you are done.

Before you begin the project, complete all the laundry chores so the room is free of daily obligations that can create distractions. That means all the wash, sewing, ironing, and dry cleaning will be done. Then clear and clean the space well. The following is an extensive checklist of reducing strategies for a typical laundry room.

Organizational Checklist

1. Clear out the trash and clutter. Throw out paper garbage, such as old papers, newspapers, magazines, and so on. Go through any drawers, containers, and cabinets and pitch or donate all the unwanted items.
2. Get rid of broken or bent wire clothes hangers.
3. Tackle piles of hopeless clothing that formed in the laundry area, such as those with relentlessly deep stains or that are not worth repairing, such as broken zippers on old pants.
4. Face the missing sock pile and finally toss the ones that have been missing a mate for some time. This may be a good time to check for them behind the laundry machines, under sofas, chairs, and beds one last time. For the more recent orphan socks, attach a piece of paper with a safety pin that records the current date, and then remove them permanently after a month. Keep a bag with safety pins,

paper, and a pen with the sock pile to keep the system going.

5. Evaluate your laundry aids; most have a shelf life, even though some don't have a best-when-used-by date. Store all laundry products in a consistently dry and cool place away from humidity, and plan to use airtight containers.

- As a rule of thumb, powdered laundry detergents may not expire or lose effectiveness, but they'll inevitably become cakey, clumpy, or hard due to moisture present in a typical laundry room. It's best to transfer powdered detergent to an airtight container.

- Liquid detergent usually begins to degrade or separate within six months after opening and one year if unopened. Clumpy detergents, liquid, or bleach can clog washer lines and leave soap deposits on clothes.

- Single-use detergent pods, which are encased in a polyvinyl film, are designed to dissolve in water. These products are also prone to harden in humidity and require airtight storage.

- Most bleach has a manufacturer code marked on the bottle that records the actual year and day of the year it was produced. For example, day fifty-six of a given year would be printed on the bottle. Bleach, whether opened or not, should last up to one year in proper storage, which is in a cool, dark place in temperatures between 50°–70°F. Dryer sheets are also marked with a manufacturer date and last one year unopened. However, once opened, dryer sheets will slowly lose their fragrance, static control, and softening ability.

6. Toss out sewing, knitting, and clothing art supplies or gadgets that won't be used. Test clothing markers and discard the dried-out ones.

Removing or Relocating Laundry-Room Items

Once you have done a thorough job of reducing all the laundry items, start to remove those that don't belong or should be stored elsewhere. Before relocating these items, be sure you really need them. Otherwise, you are wasting time looking for new storage places; it's better to remove them from your home and save the space for items you really need.

Remove items from the laundry room in a systematic manner by keeping like items together. Don't make the mistake of creating a giant pile of them since it will become a chore to break it down and disperse items to different storage spots. Use bags or containers and label them with their contents, plus write what you intend to do with them. For example, a bag of winter hats can be marked for off-season storage, or label sets of clothing art kits to sell at the next garage sale.

Bag donations so they're ready to go, containerize items to be relocated elsewhere, and box and label with contents garage sale items. Quickly snap photos of the items you plan to sell on a resale website like eBay. Keep these items in a designated closet or storage place until they sell.

Certain belongings are harder to place outside the laundry room, which is why they ended up cluttering the laundry room in the first place. For example, light bulbs, bug spray, flashlights, and batteries are the type of random belongings that tend to be displaced. Choose a storage room with the best logical connection to the item. Then search for an organizer to use in a drawer, armoire, cabinet, or closet to carve out the perfect location for them, even if it entails moving things around. Take the time to measure, shop, and plan for organizers for these items so they work well and encourage use.

Storage Solutions

Once the laundry area is reduced and redesigned, you'll have more space to plan and arrange storage for the necessities. If your laundry facility shares space with another room, you'll need to also think about the items you want in the room, as well.

With a budget in place, you can begin to lay out the space and investigate the best storage options that you can afford. Always consider the budget first, then what you need, and, lastly, what you want for the space. Wire shelving, freestanding, or wall-mounted organizers and a basic utility sink work well for smaller budgets.

Moderate budgets can have budget-friendly stock cabinets found at home centers: laminate or wire closet systems and wood or laminate freestanding storage essentials.

An upscale laundry facility might have custom cabinetry built-in features such as pull-out ironing boards and drying racks.

Play around with different grades of storage solutions, fusing them into one space. For examples, you could mix wire shelving above cabinetry or use a wire closet system with laminate components.

Laundry-Room Organizers

It's harder to organize without good storage essentials. They're an expense, and many people don't want to budget for them, but the truth is that storage essentials are one the best household investments you can make because they designate places for things, keep the house neater, and prevent overbuying since they allow you to keep track of items.

Designing, shopping for, and planning a laundry area takes time. When a well-calculated laundry space is devised, the probability of revising the space is dramatically reduced, thus saving time and money on mistakes. A laundry room gathers grime, water, dust, and lint, so select organizers that are rust proof and easy to clean. Choose adjustable organizers to accommodate ever-changing needs.

While searching for laundry storage essentials or organizational systems, make sure to match their sizes to exactly what they'll hold, accounting for situations when you stock up on product. Remember that impulsive shopping for organizers can create frustrating returns and revised space planning time.

Before purchasing any new storage essentials for the laundry room, investigate the potential for using other organizers in the home that are not in use. It's a good practice to have a place where you retire used organizers like crates, bins, baskets, containers, boxes, shelving, brackets, and so on since they're expensive. For example, a particular section of a storage room or closet can become a place to hold used storage organizers. High-quality storage organizers hold up better and are reusable in the future when needs change.

Wall Organizers

Many designated rooms are too small for a complete laundry facility, which needs plenty of room to sort, stack, fold, iron, scrub, sew, and store clothes. The good news is that specific organizational solutions exist to capture untapped wall space.

Some efficient wall organizers for the laundry room are **foldout tables** and **foldaway ironing boards**. A fold-down table hangs from the wall where the table top portion lays perpendicular to the wall when closed, so it becomes compact. When the table is needed, it pulls down from the wall. Similarly, a foldaway ironing board mounts on the wall and opens for use in the same manner.

Many foldaway ironing boards are encased in a frame with a door so it looks like a wall cabinet. Some are made to recess into the wall with built-in electrical outlets for the iron. There is also an **over-the-door ironing board** that takes up space only while in use and folds back on the door when not in use. Both of these ironing board organizers keep clumsy, bulky ironing boards off the floor.

The most important area to outfit with storage essentials is the hub of the room: around the washer and dryer. A **suspended wire-closet system** mounted onto a wall by a track system for different organizers can surround the machines and hold laundry aids and necessities. If you have front-load laundry appliances, take advantage of them by placing countertops above them for sorting, folding, and stacking clothes.

Wall-mounted hanger holder organizers, garment racks, hooks, cubbies, and cabinets can be used to store many laundry items. The wall space above your appliances is perfect for cubbies, shelves, or cabinets to store baskets for unpaired socks, clothespins, dryer sheets, laundry detergent, stain removers, clothing dyes, sewing kits, shoe shine kits, safety pins, and laundry markers. There are also many organizers, like shelving, designed to clamp onto the machines themselves, and you can find rollout, tiered drawer bins designed to slip between the washer and dryer.

Organizational wall systems, like wallboards (i.e., slatwall, gridwall, peg board) that attach baskets and hooks are also perfect for a number of laundry-related essentials.

Functional Laundry-Room Organizers

Your laundry room should reflect the chores you need to do often or enjoy the most. For example, if you don't iron weekly, simply hang an inexpensive folding ironing board from a basic hook inside a closet, and place related articles on a closet shelf. On the other hand, an avid seamstress or quilter will need either a portable or stationary sewing table plus a pressing and cutting area. Cabinets, desks, shelving, and tables should be equipped with organizers to hold a number of different supplies, such as tools, thread, fabric, patterns, and the like.

Space restraints may mean that infrequently used laundry articles need to be moved to other rooms where they can be disguised. For example, a sewing station can be hidden in an armoire or cabinet in a bedroom, study, office, family room, or kitchen. There are also many discrete sewing and quilting desks on the market. Supplies are always easy to hide in closets, cabinets, and drawers.

If you are completely renovating a laundry room, first order the fixed things like appliances, as well as permanent storage solutions, such as organizers produced by the cabinet company and closet system manufacturer. Then after everything is installed, take final measurements and select your removable and freestanding organizers.

Before arranging organizers, make sure to clean, paint, and make any necessary repairs ahead of time. After the organizers are in place and all the laundry articles are put away, review the budget and if there is any extra money, decide whether there is room to enhance the space with an item from a wish list, such as a new faucet.

CHAPTER 44

Laundry-Room Layout and Design

Laundry facilities vary from large, designated rooms to laundry areas that are combined with other spaces or are in closets. When rethinking your laundry arrangements, design and layout can also fall into budget categories like upscale and budget friendly to help you find appliances and other items in your price range. First and foremost, though, the laundry room or area must be designed for optimal functionality, which depends on both the available space and the household needs.

Laundry-Room Layout

The best planning tool for designing your laundry space is a detailed room sketch. A somewhat technical drawing of your laundry facility can be helpful, whether you are modifying an existing laundry facility or performing a complete renovation. In either scenario, it's easiest to navigate any organizational project when you actually see everything on paper.

It's also helpful to document existing features that will not change, such as the location of a sink or appliance. You can take photos and carefully measure every wall, ceiling height, door opening, window location, electrical device locations, and so on. This information can be put into a CAD software as a baseline file for developing the project further by plugging in fixtures and lighting. Look for CAD software that allows you to import your own images or photos of a room and enter exact measurements. A live chat customer service is another thing to look for since there is a learning curve to this software. Most offer 2D and 3D design, which is also great to have. There are a number of interior design software programs on the market for this purpose; most are under one hundred dollars. The best are by Punch! Software and Virtual Architect Home Design Software.

When designing your laundry area, recognize that most laundry chores start at the washer or sink and end in the laundry basket or on a hanging rack. Design your laundry room in a systematic fashion that follows the laundry cycle, so the room functions smoothly. Therefore, counters, hanging racks, and baskets should be strategically arranged near the appliances and sink.

Locate laundry aids and place storage essentials where they're used for convenience. The ironing station requires an electrical outlet and a place to store the iron and spray starch. The dryer needs counter space nearby to fold and stack clothes promptly and reduce wrinkles and creases. For the same reason, place clothes hangers and racks close to the dryer, too.

Upscale Laundry Rooms

In an upscale laundry room, cabinetry can surround the appliances, like the washer, dryer, or even a drying cabinet, which is a luxury appliance that accelerates the drying time for clothes that need to line dry or dry flat. It can also dry

bedspreads, boots, shoes, and coats quickly. A major benefit of laundry-room cabinetry is the counter space, which is ideal for sorting, stacking, and folding clean laundry.

Cabinetry in a laundry room offers more storage options than any other alternative. Tall cabinets can be equipped with a hanging rod to hang garments and hold hangers. Drawers and shelves can stock laundry aids, such as dryer balls, laundry pens, clothing dyes, and lint brushes. Shelving also can hold baskets to collect pocket items left in clothing, like receipts, change, and so on. Baskets can also hold socks missing their mates. Large base shelving can hold portable laundry baskets that need to travel throughout the

Upscale Laundry Room

FIGURE 44.01
Upscale Laundry Room

home. Look for collapsible laundry baskets for space-saving storage strategies.

Cabinets have accessories like pullout hampers to sort laundry. You can also designate one hamper for dry cleaning and another for tailoring. Cabinets also tend to have pullout trash cans, a necessity in a laundry room.

More unique cabinet laundry organizers are built-in, pullout ironing boards that extend from a base-cabinet drawer. There is also an upper cabinet pulldown hanging bar that drops to eye level to hang ironed clothing or dry cleaning. Drying racks are incorporated into cabinetry as pullout drawers commonly placed on the underside of an upper cabinet.

Sewing Center

In a high-end laundry room, one may find a sewing center, in which a sewing machine is stationed on a specialized sewing table equipped with storage drawers for holding tools and accessories. A good sewing table has an adjustable platform that can raise and lower for a wide range of tasks. Many sewing tables have collapsible folding sides to expand the workspace when needed. Wheeled tables with locking casters are great for stability and portability to another storage spot.

The area surrounding a sewing table can also be outfitted with sewing organizers, such as a wall-mounted thread organizer or floor stands that hold rolled fabric. A cutting table with storage below for patterns and folded fabric is another amenity for a more extensive laundry room. Many cutting tables have base shelving to file or stack fabric, patterns, and tools. Baskets on these shelves can hold tools or scrap fabric. An ideal cutting table is accessible from multiple sides and large enough to fit fabrics and use patterns. A cutting table in a laundry room can also serve multiple functions, such as a place to fold and

sort laundry or hold laundry supplies, such as baskets and soaps.

Budget-Friendly Laundry Rooms

An economical way to create order in a laundry room is by using a track-based, suspended wire closet system on the walls surrounding the washer and dryer. These closet systems have accessory components that include pullout baskets, shelves, hooks, drawers, and hanging rods. There are also inexpensive laminate closet systems and wire shelving, which is sold separately at most home centers and can be used to store laundry items. Wire and laminate shelving generally comes in various depths; the deeper shelving can hold bigger items like laundry baskets, and shallow shelves can store smaller items like ironing supplies. An open-storage arrangement, such as a wall-mounted closet system with shelves, is important to keep neat.

Tidy Open-Storage Tips

The following are a few tips to help keep open-storage arrangements tidy yet functional:

- Use bins, canisters, containers, trays, or boxes to divide, organize, and hide articles on shelves. For example, a basic compartmentalized drawer tray can contain smaller items, such as safety pins, laundry markers, scissors, lint brushes, and the like, so they stay orderly.
- Bulky, flimsy cardboard boxes that contain powdered laundry detergents look messy and don't preserve the product properly. It's best to transfer powder into clear airtight canisters with a scooper.
- Contain laundry markers in a cup holder.

Suspended Wire Laundry System

FIGURE 44.02
Budget-Friendly Laundry Room

- A piggy bank is a good organizer to corral loose change.
- All shelving organizers look best when they match in color or material to form a uniform, neat appearance.
- Products placed outside an organizer can form into rows or clusters on shelves, where like items are kept together. For example, line all the spray stain removers in a single-file row. Also, face their labels forward so they're easy to see.
- Keep all the organizers in the laundry room consistent in material or color with that of the closet system as to enhance the overall appearance of the space.

Popular Organizers

The following are the most popular, affordable organizers for a laundry facility:

- Wall-mounted wallboard kits that are marketed to store small laundry items from attachable hooks, shelves, and rods. Similarly, basic sheets of pegboard, slat-wall, or wire grid can be installed to serve the same purpose. Items like lint brushes, laundry pens, scissors, spray starch, stain removers, dryer sheets, sewing supplies, and stain removal tips are good to store on these organizers.

- Slim, tiered-shelf or drawer units designed to slip in between a freestanding washer and dryer will hold large bottles of laundry soap and all related cleaning agents. They come in a hard plastic material for durability and ease of cleaning. The shelf versions of these organizers are wheeled for easy access. These organizers can conveniently store all your laundry supplies out of sight.
- Wall-mounted, retractable valet or hanger storage organizers are inexpensive, space-saving ways to hold hangers or clothing. Many of these organizers are designed to open, retract, or pull down to open into a hanging rod and then close when not in use.
- Drying racks are important in any laundry facility. There are many types of inexpensive drying racks, such as retractable and wall-mounted ones. Others are floor organizers designed to easily collapse and take up little space.
- A freestanding utility sink versus a built-in sink housed in cabinetry is a budget-friendly solution for a necessary soaking tub in a laundry room. These sinks are heavy-duty, one-piece, molded construction and made of polypropylene or stainless steel. They tend to hold over twenty gallons of water and sit on steel legs. It's easy to form storage solutions around these sinks by using tiered drawer carts, hampers, rolling bins, wall-mounted folding tables, laundry carts, or laundry sorters, which are some of the popular economical freestanding organizers.

Laundry Areas in Other Spaces

In many homes, especially townhomes, condominiums, and apartments, closets are used as laundry areas, so they're hidden, convenient, and save space. In a house, a closet is the spot to place a secondary laundry facility on another level. Often, a hallway, bathroom, bedroom, study, or office closet are key places for them.

Laundry Area in a Closet

Generally, a double-size closet is necessary to create a high-functioning space equipped with shelving, hanging rods, counters, hampers and so on. Also, bifold closet doors will be necessary for full access to the space. Louvered doors, which have a series of wooden fins running horizontally to allow for ventilation, as well as privacy, are also necessary for closets that serve as laundry rooms.

The type of laundry appliances selected for a closet space influences storage arrangements. The three main types of laundry appliances are explained, along with how to arrange a laundry facility around them in a double closet space.

Stacked Washer and Dryer

Stacking laundry machines are arranged with the dryer on top of the washer, leaving floor-to-ceiling vertical space on one side of the closet. This open space is flexible for adding shelves, hanging rods, a small countertop, short cabinet, and floor organizers, such as a hamper. Depending on ceiling height, there may be space to add an over shelf or two above the appliances.

Side-by-Side Washer and Dryer

The best way to arrange a closet outfitted with side-by-side appliances that include a front-load washer is to create counter space directly above for folding, sorting, and ironing. You can also capture additional storage space by utilizing the area in between the back of the laundry appliances and the wall. This space runs deep—around seven inches or so—due to the bulky components behind the washer/dryer, such as washer hoses and the dryer vent. A slim wall mounted shelf can occupy this dead space for storing laundry aids.

There is also a specialized over-the-washer storage shelf available that has a cantilevered design and fits most laundry appliances. These organizers are made to just hook onto the laundry machines without installation. In either scenario, overhead hanging rods, cabinets, and shelving can be placed to store laundry supplies.

All-in-One Washer/Dryer

This appliance is the same size as a single washer or dryer. Therefore, only a quarter of a typical double closet is needed, leaving plenty of space left for storage opportunities. Two-in-one machines are front loaders, so a folding and sorting counter can be placed on top that can also extend the full width of the closet. Overhead shelves, cubby compartments, or upper cabinets can sit above the counter.

Another closet design uses the open side of the closet for shelving, a pullout hamper, trash can, hanging rod, laundry baskets, laundry supplies, pullout ironing board, sewing machine, and so on.

Laundry Areas in Shared Rooms

When laundry appliances are shared with other rooms, it can be difficult to keep things organized, separated, and easy to find. Sometimes when a laundry facility resides in a kitchen, family room, office, bathroom, and so on, laundry machines are hidden in the room's closet, and all related products and accessories are collected in a common space, such as an armoire, to disguise everything.

However, it's not always necessary to hide laundry-room components in another room. Relaxed playrooms, art studios, tool rooms, mudrooms, office spaces, and some larger bathrooms are good places for an open laundry facility. In any room that also has a laundry facility, keep all the laundry products and supplies together in their own closet, cabinet, shelf, drawer, or organizer. Otherwise, it becomes easy to lose track of your laundry items amid unrelated belongings.

Laundry Area in the Kitchen

There are many ways to conceal a washer, dryer, and related items in a kitchen, which is a logical larger space to add a laundry area. Base cabinets in a kitchen can disguise laundry appliances behind doors, where upper cabinets or drawers can hold laundry soaps and other items. Kitchen base cabinets can also conceal laundry baskets. The base-cabinet countertop is a great place to fold and sort laundry, if you have the room. The kitchen sink can also be used to hand wash or soak soiled clothing. Upper kitchen cabinets that reach to the ceiling could disguise a laundry chute from an upper level. Clothing can then deposit into a basket located inside the cabinet, making it easy for dirty laundry to enter and hide in the kitchen.

A full-size ironing board organizer can be installed in a base-cabinet drawer, which collapses and hides when the drawer is closed. Above such an organizer in an upper cabinet, a pulldown hanging rod could hold ironed clothing. These hanging rods pull down to eye level and retract back into the cabinet while not in use.

Drying racks are another laundry organizer that are easy to hide in the kitchen. There are many wall-mounted, pullout racks designed to hide in decorative wall cabinets with doors that are perfect for the kitchen.

Laundry Chute from Upstairs

FIGURE 44.03
Hidden Laundry Area Inside the Kitchen

Laundry Area in a Bathroom

A bathroom can be a good place to house a set of laundry machines, whether they're a primary or secondary set, provided there is enough room. The bathroom has the same requirements of a laundry facility, such as a sink, floors, and walls that must withstand moisture. Good ventilation is another feature a bathroom offers that a laundry facility needs. Hampers to hold clothing and towels are common to place in a bathroom and are a natural fit when placed next to laundry appliances. Additionally, a bathroom with a shower or bathtub can use a dryer to warm towels to use after bathing.

There are ways to situate a washer and dryer in a bathroom with the right amount of room. Space-saving, stackable washing machines take up only about thirty square inches of floor space. These units are made with a smaller capacity than standard machines, so they're easier to squeeze into a bathroom closet or nook. Side-by-side laundry machines can be possible in large bathrooms with extensive cabinetry where they can be camouflaged in a base cabinet. Overhead counter space can get used for sorting, folding and stacking laundry. Shower rods and bathroom hanging rods can hold hung clothing. Bathroom cabinets, closets, and drawers can hold laundry essentials such as dryer sheets, detergents, stain fighting agents, and so on.

Laundry Area in a Mudroom

A mudroom is the perfect place to add a laundry facility since both rooms are typically set away from entertaining areas. Mudrooms and laundry rooms are both hardworking places that require similar features, such as a utility sink, durable countertops, good lighting, and easy-to-clean floors and walls.

Another benefit of combining these rooms is that open storage essentials, such as shelving units, wall organizers, and so on, are acceptable, and these organizers are less expensive than concealing cabinetry. A basic utility sink is a must in a combined space, as it will receive use from both laundry and mudroom chores.

One of the best features of this type of room is that messy things, such as sports uniforms, gardening clothes, beach towels, bathing suits, picnic blankets, or muddy belongings that would otherwise track throughout a house, can be washed, soaked, and dried before entering the home.

Laundry Area in an Office

A room or workstation that performs office duties should be combined with a laundry facility only if the washer/dryer noise won't affect the person's concentration. Isolating the machines in an enclosed space, such as a closet, or using the machines at different times may solve the problem. Another factor to consider is that two people could potentially be using the room for different reasons and tasks at the same time, which might be distracting

Generally, a home office is a room not frequented by guests. Some, however, may have an occasional client, which means the washer, dryer, and accessories will need to be disguised. This can be achieved by using cabinets or closets. Otherwise, it's acceptable to expose laundry machines and organizers in an office, especially when it's located in a more private part of the home.

Laundry Area in a Craft Room/Workstation

A craft room or workstation may be a good space to combine with a laundry facility if working on crafting projects isn't affected by the appliances' noise. Some craft room features, such as a crafting table, can be shared with a laundry facility for sewing, folding, and ironing purposes. Additionally, a craft room can benefit from many laundry-room features, such as good lighting, a utility sink, and easy-to-care-for walls and floors.

Laundry Area in a Butler's Pantry

A butler's pantry is a service area, commonly located in a hallway that links the kitchen and dining room. A laundry facility in a butler's pantry is a convenient location just off the kitchen, making any spillover items, such as laundry products or baskets, easy to store in a kitchen cabinet. A butler's pantry is usually equipped with a sink, countertop, base cabinets, and upper cabinets or shelves, making a laundry area easy to integrate here.

This space acts as a serving area for gatherings and is used as a bar or food station. It may also store china, stemware, silver, and liquor. Laundry appliances are easy to disguise in base cabinets, and counters can be used for folding and sorting. A sink located in a butler's pantry or even accessing a nearby kitchen sink is ideal for soaking and handwashing clothing.

PART FIVE

Home Offices and Armoires

CHAPTER 45

The Home Office

Organizing a home office can be a more taxing job than one expects since most office-related belongings, such as files, papers, receipts, and the like, take a long time to sort, read, categorize, or shred. Additionally, designing your office space to operate effectively and efficiently involves careful planning, which also takes time.

One of the hardest parts of organizing a home office is determining where to start. The following list of organizational steps is designed to guide you through the home office organizational process. The best place to begin is organizing your paperwork.

Organize Your Paperwork

Paper proposals, receipts, invoices, schedules, and so on are typically the most important articles in a home office but are challenging to successfully organize. Realize that plenty of time is wasted searching for a piece of paper in disorganization. Money is lost when late fees are accrued due to overlooked bills that were simply misfiled or lost. Neglectful paper management also can lead to identity theft. Therefore, properly organizing your paperwork is the key to saving time, money, and aggravation.

All kinds of papers tend to scatter throughout a home. When you organize a home office, it's important to hunt for all papers around the home that are not currently in a file or organizer. Often, desks, shelves, hutches, credenzas, and sometimes floors are overtaken by piles of papers. Once you tame paper piles at the start—by incorporating a well-managed filing system—you can prevent them from sprouting again. Then, once the floor, desk, and counters are clear of paper, everything else is easier to organize.

As you gather your papers, quickly glance over them and put aside those that need immediate attention, like bills. Likewise, paper that is clearly trash should go in another pile. It's important to move papers that can easily be recreated online to the trash pile. After you have collected all your important papers, unfold them and press out creased corners so they stack neatly.

Get into the habit of filing everything—or at least the important documents—in two different digital formats, such as online storage and an external hard drive backup. All hard-to-replace legal documents should be digitally scanned. Consider using a write-once Blu-ray recordable optical disc, which can last up to 150 years. An optical disc is physical storage that can be secured in a fireproof safe. Then incorporate a digital storage solution since no one storage plan can offer a 100 percent guarantee for the safety of your data.

This also makes it easier to discard useless papers. Successful sorting means attending to the urgent things (like bills) while systematically discarding overwhelming junk. The trash pile should be shredded since you may have overlooked some paper with confidential information. Shredding should be done with a crosscut blade shredder, thus making it impossible to put a piece of paper back together. Personal information is being hunted, so be diligent about destroying yours.

All other papers that need further sorting can then be turned into manageable, medium-size stacks and bound with a binder clip to stay put. Next, determine a place to sort these papers. Large amounts of paper will need a big, flat surface to spread out, like a dining room table or another uninterrupted space.

Create Appropriate Files

Begin sorting papers into *general* piles, which is less overwhelming than trying to make specific classifications right away. Use broad categories, such as bills, auto, receipts, warranties, doctors, and so on, to get the ball rolling.

Next, further break down the general classifications into *subcategories*. When forming these categories, keep them specific enough so they remain exclusive. For instance, just creating an "automobile" file is too general if your household has three cars and the separate insurance

paperwork could all wind up in the same folder. Chances are, when your categories are too vague, you'll wind up with catchall folders that promote misplaced or forgotten papers.

It's best to arrange folders by creating a logical main header file which groups a series of related folders. Therefore, a main subject or umbrella term would encompass several subcategories. For example, a header classification name like insurance would have many subcategory folders that might include: medical, dental, or homeowner's insurance.

When managing many individual client/ business jobs or household projects, it's best to file them individually. Don't categorize them by creating folders pertaining to particulars, such as the project or job's contractors, presentations, spreadsheets, quotes, drawings, graphics, and so on; this makes it more cumbersome to pinpoint specific paperwork. In these cases, it's best to create a general classification, such as "business jobs" and subcategory folders for each client, which can then be filed alphabetically.

It's common for people to create files but not sort and organize the paperwork first. Or they decide that any new paperwork that comes along needs a separate file instead of checking with what files already exist. However, inventing categories with these approaches may generate duplicates, and overall system logic is jeopardized. Before you place papers into their final destination folders, start with piles of papers that are already broken down into their furthest possible point for optimal file accuracy. It's best to set up your file system so the general header classification clearly stands out from the subcategories. All paper organizational file systems on the market are capable of accomplishing this goal.

A good way to make file folders easy to locate is by using different colors of file folders for each subject matter. For example, green file folders could hold investment documents. Color coding files easily leads the eye to the correct file, because the mind associates color quicker than black and white. Most office supply stores carry color-coded hanging file system kits. Arrange labeling tabs in a uniform row, positioned on the left side of folder to make searching easier; it can be harder to scan for a particular file when the tabs are staggered. Using file labels printed from a label maker is often easier to read than most handwriting.

File Classifications

The hardest part about organizing paperwork is choosing the right classifications for the different subjects. The following are common household paperwork categories.

Banking

- All bank accounts and investments documentation and statements
- ATM receipts; store withdrawal and deposit slips separately in a file box
- Mortgage and other loan documents
- Ownership investments like stocks, businesses, real estate, and precious objects

Bills and Papers Involving Credits or Monies Owed

- Claims awaiting payment
- Invoice statements

Decorating

- Designer contact information
- Fabric, furniture, and accessory stores/ websites contact information
- Magazine clippings of decorated rooms
- Room drawings/sketches

Entertainment and Travel

- Airline information and travel agent contacts
- Destination literature and vacation specials and rates
- Dining guides and restaurant brochures
- Sport fields, maps, and game schedules
- Theaters, concerts, comedy clubs, shows, and ticket brokers

Gardening

- Catalogs
- Landscape design drawings and ideas
- Magazine subscription information
- Notes

High-Ticket Items: Individual Folders for Each Product
Appliances/Computers/Jewelry/Furniture

- All product warranty paperwork can be attached to the original receipt
- Authenticity documents/appraisals
- Store product directions, manuals, and service center information

Vehicles/Boats/Motorcycle/Snowmobile/Jet Ski

- Repairs and service agreements
- Service center numbers
- Warranties and manuals

Home Maintenance

- Contractor receipts and service agreements
- Lists of contractors
- Snowplow and landscaper service information

Legal
- Adoption and custody papers
- All titles or deeds
- Birth, death, marriage, and divorce certificates
- Certificates of US naturalization, green card, passports
- Military documents: ID cards (copies) and discharge papers
- Social security cards, copy of driver's license or state ID, and passwords/PIN #s
- Trusts, wills, and burial and medical instructions
- Vehicle registrations

Medical and Dental
- Dental records
- Medical records/allergies/DNA swabs/ record of immunizations
- Medication directions

Organizations/Hobbies/Sports
- Club handbooks, memberships, passes, and rosters
- Pro shops, uniform stores, trainers, and class schedules

Pets
- Medical records
- Ownership papers
- Veterinarian and animal hospital contact information

Retirement and Pension Plans
- 401K, IRAs, and annuities

- Employer/union/government pension plans

Scheduling: Use This File to Record or Check Your Calendars
- Concerts/plays/shows information and tickets
- Copies of work, school, sport, and activity schedules
- Invitations: always respond immediately and then file
- Special events: information on events like seminars, workshops, etc.

Schools: All Schools or Students Have Their Own Folders
- Diplomas
- Placement information and special program literature
- School transcripts, parent handbooks, diplomas, and curriculum guides

Shopping
- Catalogs
- Magazine clippings and ads for items intended to purchase
- Product brochures/pamphlets
- Wish lists

Taxes
- Employment, self-employment and income papers, and homeowner and rental data
- Financial assets and liabilities, automobile deductible expense, deductibles
- Personal records

Filing Systems

Equally important to creating your files is arranging them in the proper organizers. The main filing systems for papers are hanging folders, desktop file totes and crates, project cases, and hanging wall files. Now is the time to either pick new organizers or fine-tune current ones. It's important to look at different filing options and compare them to what is currently working in the home office, as it's common for people to keep using the same system even if it's inefficient.

A factor to consider when choosing a new filing system is finding one that can be physically near the desk so it's reachable. Everyone prefers a certain type filing system, so go with what works for or appeals to you so you'll stick with it.

Systems for Hanging Folders

Hanging folders are pocketed folders with hooks that glide freely along a double track rail. If you already use hanging folders in your home office, recognize that it's worth investigating different ways hanging folders can be utilized in this space. Hanging file folders can be situated in a rolling cart, in file cabinet drawers, or in a desktop crate or portable file box. Some desks have built-in file drawers specifically for hanging folders, but the space is typically limited, so in many cases another organizer is needed to supplement larger file demands. When working with hanging folders, it's important not to overpack them, because they'll become harder to access. Room should be left for new files anyway.

Rolling Carts

A rolling file cart is one good solution for adding file space. Because they're mobile, they can be kept outside the workspace, such as in a closet or spare room, and moved back and forth as needed. They can also be stored underneath the desk, which captures the dead space found between the floor and desktop if the desk has no drawers or cabinets.

File Cabinets

File cabinets also store hanging folders. They generally offer bountiful filing space, but they can be expensive, so it's good if you already have one. However, if your file cabinet is too big for your needs and is hogging space, you can sell it and opt for a more compact file cabinet. An ideal one fits legal and letter size. Also, A4-size folders, to hold the standard letter-size paper throughout the world outside of North America, can also be included.

Desktop File Totes and Crates

Desktop file totes and storage crates are portable, handled, cube-style organizers for hanging folders. They can be accessed at the desk then moved to a storage location, such as a counter, shelf, closet, or bookcase. Don't pack files too tightly, though, because they can be heavy to move around.

Project Cases

A project case is a translucent, heavy-duty plastic case that fits letter-size papers with up to a two-inch depth for holding many documents. These organizers are found at stores that specialize in organizational essentials or office supplies. There are many benefits to using plastic project cases: They have handles for easy transport and usually have a snap closure to prevent accidental opening. Any part of the case is easy to label. Project cases are stable enough to file on a shelf, similar to a binder. They can also lay flat, stack on top of one another, or be filed in deep drawer.

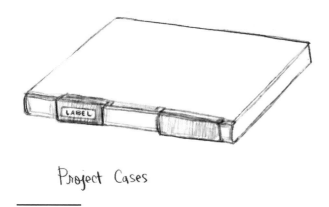

Project Cases

FIGURE 45.01
Plastic project case

There are many uses for project cases in a home office. The following offers some great ways to utilize project cases:

- House temporary papers with pending issues, like insurance claims, bills, receipts, and so on.
- In lieu of a briefcase or tote bag, they can also carry papers that need to travel outside the home.
- Hold art supplies for ongoing scrapbooking, drawing, and collage projects.
- Store homework or research information.
- Store shopping lists, sales flyers, and coupons for the grocery store.
- Keep fabric pieces, pictures, drawings, and paint samples for a decorating project that requires hunting around at various stores.
- Separate photos while organizing albums or gathering photos for a video, montage, presentation, and the like.

Hanging Wall Files

A hanging wall file is yet another way to file paperwork, and there are many different types on the market. One of the biggest benefits of using wall files is that they capture the dead wall space,

leaving more room in your drawers, shelves, or counters. When you plan to acquire them, it's important to know all the options to pick the one that best fits your criteria.

Hanging wall files come in different depth sizes, which is relevant because shallow files cannot hold many papers or file folders. It's better to select expandable wall files, so you can add pockets as you grow. Cheaply made plastic wall files can crack, especially when used daily. There are unbreakable plastic wall files on the market, as well as those made from other materials, such as metal or wood. Consider also the widths of the hanging wall files and select those that fit the folders that you prefer, such as letter, legal, or A4-size files.

There are different ways to arrange papers in a wall file system:

- You could assign each hanging pocket an individual subject, such as decorating, school calendars, or pet papers.
- Each hanging pocket could contain multiple folders that breakdown or divide a general subject further. For example, a hanging pocket that stores the general category of bills would contain individual folders for payables like tuition, car, and so on.

These folders can be alphabetized for optimal efficiency. You can also use color-coded folders for different topics to find them quickly, such as red for "hot-file" pressing matters. Keep hanging pockets tidy, because they're visible in a home office. Also, don't overstuff them, as individual folders are then harder to access. If you already use wall files, it's always a good idea to search for ways to make them better since chances are there is a folder, organizer, or arrangement that may be more efficient.

File System Maintenance

Managing a well-arranged file system is just as important as establishing one. Often, people go from setting up a file system to a paper explosion in no time if no maintenance plan is in place. Filing is often considered a burdensome chore and tends to fall by the wayside in many home offices when there is no procedure for getting the files and paperwork back to where they belong. For this reason, it's easy to put off filing, allowing piles of folders to sprout up everywhere, become buried, or get lost. Just a few good organizational strategies could make a huge difference.

Minimize the need to purchase additional file cabinets or overstuff them by devising daily reduction strategies. First, only create necessary files. Sometimes, we create permanent files for things we don't need or won't use again, such as schedules or program guides that are easy to access elsewhere.

Don't make room for files involving work-in-progress or short-term matters, such as items for review, projects, or incomplete assignments. Rather, store them outside the main file system in a small organizer like a file crate, desktop file holder, or two-pocket wall file. Keep these organizers within arm's reach of the desk for accessibility.

Organizational Strategies for Files

One of the best plans is to use brightly colored file folders so they stand out. Also, pulled files need a temporary storage place while they're in use at the desk. A designated hanging wall pocket or a crate file organizer will make them easy to locate while outside their regular storage location. Label the organizer "Files at Work."

Keep a bin next to the file cabinet to place files that are no longer needed, so they're contained in one place. In your free time, look them over one last time before shredding or disposing them.

Current Paperwork

Urgent paperwork that needs to be addressed in a day or two may be forgotten in a file folder. Instead of creating unnecessary file folders, use a memo board to keep these papers at hand. Once these matters are handled, such papers need to be filed, shredded, or discarded.

Respond to new paperwork immediately and put completed work or copies into their files as soon as possible. For example, answer invitations promptly or get manually paid bills ready in advance. Paperwork procrastination is the leading cause of paper clutter and missed payments.

Filing for Long-Term Storage

When filing paperwork, always put the newest papers in front of the others, so when you need to move them to long-term storage, they'll be in time order. Also, you'll tend to need the more recent papers, so this method quickly allows you to find what you need.

There are two times of the year to reduce or file paperwork for long-term storage: after your tax return has been settled and at year end. You can also keep a bin next to the file cabinet for files that you come across on a daily basis that need to be transferred to long-term storage. Schedule a time, such as weekly or monthly, to move them out of the home office.

Federal and state tax returns need to be kept for up to seven years and can tend to overtake file storage. It's best to electronically file returns, digitally scan all supporting documentation, and save them for at least seven years after the date of filing. However, some states can go back even further. Therefore, before shredding any tax returns, check with your accountant and state tax authorities to know the specifics for your state. After settling your returns, remove them, along with the supporting documents, from your home office and into your long-term storage.

Filing Bound Paper Material

For the most part, items such as books and reference materials, magazines, binders, manuals, handbooks, and notebooks compete for the same storage space. It's best to organize all bound paper material together; therefore, it makes sense to keep these items in one spot so similar bound materials can easily be grouped together. Then, determine their final destinations based on frequency of use and importance.

To begin the process, gather all your books, binders, periodicals, and so on, and sort them by type; separate the personal items from the business ones. Have a few boxes for donation, sale, recycle, trash, business, and personal, plus one to move contents elsewhere in the home. The following sections cover ways to reduce and organize different types of bound paper material.

Books
Many different types of books can be contained in a home office. When you have a diverse collection of books, separate them by type, and then go through each pile and get rid of the ones you'll never pick up again; plan to donate them to the library, sell them to a secondhand bookstore, or

keep them for the next garage sale. After downsizing your different groups of books, decide which should stay in the home office or might be better in another room. For example, children's books would receive more use if they were in a bedroom, playroom, or family room. Cookbooks would be easier to access on a kitchen shelf.

Some books, such as a dictionary, should remain in an office on a special shelf or drawer near the workspace. A desktop binder rack can house reference materials to keep them nearby, like on the desk, hutch, credenza, or overhead shelving. Books read for enjoyment don't necessarily need to be in the home office, but sometimes this is the only space for them. In the home office, collections of books for leisure enjoyment can be stored in bookshelves, armoires, closets, or on shelving. Any shelving for such books should be movable so shelves can adjust in accordance with the height of the books, thus eliminating dead space.

Magazines
In many cases, magazines remain far longer than necessary. Most magazines are issued on a monthly basis, so they can accumulate quickly. It's also possible that as current magazines enter into the home, the likelihood of older magazines being read declines. Should you find you cannot keep up with reading them all, consider canceling some of the subscriptions. It's important to factor in the amount of time available for enjoying magazines, as the average busy person may not have much. Magazines are not built to last, so the longer they stay around, the more likely you'll find missing covers and pages—another reason to stay on top of growing stacks of them.

The best way to control magazine clutter is to rip out all the interesting pictures and articles from those already read. Staple the pages together and create files based on article or picture topics, such as "decorating," or "psychology." Then discard the magazine. To save even more space, you can scan and digitally file all your magazine clippings.

Store magazines you have not yet read or that require more review together in a single location. A desktop bin or individual organizer marked "New Magazines" works well. Divide and categorize those magazines that are important to keep long term. Classifications such as "cooking" or "world news" are sufficient. The best way to contain groups of magazines is to place them into individual magazine organizers by classification.

Many different types of magazine organizers are available, such as wall-mounted pocket organizers, freestanding racks, and desktop magazine file boxes, which are by far the most versatile. File boxes can reside on any flat surface, such as a counter, desk, or shelf, storing the periodicals upright so the spines are easily identified at a glance. Each one can hold a dozen or so magazines and are perfect for dividing classifications; they're also conveniently portable. Clear-plastic magazine covers can be added to individual magazines to protect the most important ones.

Binders

Besides considering the overall importance of an entire binder, it may also be necessary to comb through its contents, pulling out any unnecessary pages. Also, merging more than one binder may also be in order. Shred and recycle the needless paperwork. Empty binders can be stored in a container and reused.

There are several different types of binders: zippered, three ring, data and ledger. Zippered binders are typically used for school and transporting paperwork. These types of binders should be stored near a doorway or inside a carrying device, such as a suitcase or backpack.

Data binders are limited to cabinet storage since they hang from retractable hooks on a rail, similar to a hanging file. Ledger binders can be stacked or filed on a shelf.

Three-ring binders, which are the most common, can be trickier to store. The easiest three-ring binders to store are those stuffed with papers, which makes them a stable rectangular shape versus the pie shape of empty ones. However, there are organizers designed to efficiently store empty or less full binders: A round, spinning carousel-style organizer fits each binder like a piece of an entire pie. Corner shelving and corner desktop organizers in a quarter-pie, triangular shape stores binders in a similar manner.

The best three-ring binders are durable and have a clear vinyl overlay on the front, back, and spine. Underneath the vinyl, you can insert a title page on the cover, and the spine should always have a way to display the contents of the binder, such as a label holder. Some three-ring binders use D-shaped rings mounted on the back cover. This design allows for more paper storage and helps the papers lay flat.

Some three-ring binders have the option of freestanding on a shelf or hanging from a rail, similar to hanging folders. The hanging option incorporates a rail system in which hooks are added to hold hanging binders. These organizers feature retractable hooks that pull out to hang and retract when not needed. The inside pockets are designed to keep loose sheets secure while hanging.

Handbooks, Manuals, and Notebooks

Other bulk-producing bound paper items include product operator manuals, handbooks, and notebooks. Use separate folders to divide different types of items, such as for small appliances, computers, electronic games, and so on. It's a good idea to staple the originals or copies of the receipts, warranties, and service agreements onto the manuals.

All remaining bound paper materials need to be sorted and reduced. In storage, file these items by category. For example, classifications might include "business notebooks" and "industry handbooks." Desktop book stands, magazine file organizers, binder racks, and heavy-duty bookends can divide the different categories. Lightweight, thinner bound items can be housed in common paperwork organizers, such as wall-file pockets, desktop folder file sorters, file crates, or portable file holders.

Common Household Paperwork Categories for Filing System

→ Banking
→ Bills and papers involving credits or monies owed
→ Decorating
→ Entertainment and travel
→ Gardening
→ High-ticket items

→ Home maintenance
→ Legal
→ Medical and dental
→ Organization/hobbies/sports
→ Pets
→ Retirement and pension plans

→ Scheduling
→ School
→ Shopping
→ Taxes

CHAPTER 46

Arranging Office Workspace

When your paperwork, files, and bound paper material are under control, it becomes easier to organize other parts of the office. Before starting, though, make sure all paper-related belongings are properly stored so the office is functional and paper-free. Then organize the rest.

The next logical step is clearing off the clutter that congests your workspace. Have boxes ready for donation, trash, recycle, sale, and items to be relocated into other rooms. For the process to run smoothly, also have a box for the articles you're not quite sure about; after the entire home office is organized, revisit this box and attempt to reduce its contents.

Organizing the Desk

When your desk is cluttered, you may need additional boxes to sort these items out. Stick with broad classifications like office supplies, knick-knacks, computer accessories, and so on. As you remove items from the desk, do away with the things you don't need or like, because a clear desk usually helps one focus better. Everything that

stays should have a purpose, and if it's decorative in nature, it must be cherished.

The type of desk you possess, such as writing, computer, pedestal, armoire, and so on, will dictate how it can be arranged. A desk needs to be organized according to what takes place there. Belongings should receive placement based on their importance and frequency of use. Paper-related materials deserve key placement as, typically, they're the priority articles. Always review your current organizers to make sure they're efficient and situated in the best locations for desk accessibility. A common mistake some people make is sticking with the familiar way the home office ran, even if inefficient, rather than taking the time to investigate changes.

Everything else needed at the desk—pens, staples, and so on—should also follow the same arrangement logic as for paper items. It's best to have everything needed to operate the home office on a daily basis either at the desk or within reach. Therefore, the less often something is used, the farther away from the desk it belongs. It's a good idea to make a list of the things used on a daily basis at the desk. Then, as you put things back, mark them off to ensure they're located in convenient spots. Doing so will also make you aware of the items that now seem unnecessary to place in the desk.

The desktop itself should only have a minimal number of items so it remains clutter-free, ensuring a fit work environment. Also, a clear desktop serves a purpose. Many projects and jobs are managed on a desk. At times, books, files, binders, and paperwork will need to be spread out on it. Plus, the desk can be used for other tasks that require space, such as crafts, homework, gift wrapping, packaging, scrapbooking, and so on.

The following covers common desktop items, along with their storage solutions. It's important to look at the various ways these items can be situated around the desk to make the best decisions based on your personal needs.

Electronics

Every desk will have a variety of electronic devices critical to the office's functionality. Many electronics are vital for communication and information research, which are key operations in a home office. Therefore, such articles need priority placement and access in the desk area; computers, computer peripherals, and mobile and cellular telephones are the main electronic devices used in a home office.

Computer Hardware and Peripheral Equipment

Computer hardware refers to all the physical components of a computer system, such as a hard drive, motherboard, and monitor. Computer peripherals are those external components that provide input and output for the computer. For example, a keyboard and mouse are input peripherals because they're used to enter information, while a monitor and printer are output peripherals because they receive information from a computer. The main types of home office computers

are desktop/workstations and laptops/notebooks. How computer peripherals interact with them varies by computer.

Desktop Computers

A desktop or workstation is appreciated for its powerhouse ability. These computers support gaming/graphics, multiple monitors, multiple USB ports, and larger monitor capability than other computer options. Desktop components are housed in a large computer case, which can also be called a tower, system unit, base unit, or cabinet. The computer tower tends to be bulky and is not portable. In order to save desk space, you can opt for a smaller tower unit, but this can be costly and possibly cut down on power. Large tower units are best secured in a wheeled floor stand, where they're elevated to provide proper air flow.

Portable Computers

Netbooks and notebooks or laptops are computers designed to be slim and portable with a clamshell closure. The netbook is the smallest with the least amount of capability. Notebooks and laptops have almost come to be synonymous with one other, but historically, the notebook is lighter and smaller. These computers are powered by a battery or an AC power cord with little cable and storage space requirements. Unlike desktops, these computers have limited USB ports—usually two.

A "USB hub" is an organizer that furnishes multiple USB ports for charging a number of electronic devices and computer peripherals, such as an external hard drive. A powered hub with its own AC adapter can be placed on the underside of a desk or a wall and be used without the presence of the computer.

Other microcomputers are personal digital assistants (PDAs), tablet PCs, and smartphones, which all operate on touch-screen technology without keyboards and mice. These handheld mobile devices are commonly used in conjunction with a laptop or desktop, where they're able to charge via a USB hub or computer port. They can also plug directly into a dedicated charger. Multiple portable electronics are best stored within a desktop docking charging station. Most docking stations offer many compartments that keep mobile electronics in plain view where their screens are readable while charging, perfect for a desk arrangement.

Monitors

Desktop monitors can be any size; the larger ones are great candidates for wall storage. Depending on certain requirements, a desktop monitor can be wireless, which further increases their storage options. Many other computer peripherals come in a wireless format, which dramatically cuts down on cable clutter and increases storage possibilities for desktop computers. Cordless mice, keyboards, headphones, and speakers have wireless varieties in two types: Bluetooth and radio frequency (RF).

Printers

Wireless printers connect to your Wi-Fi network and have the advantage of allowing multiple printing options, including from devices like a smartphone. An all-in-one wireless printer that scans, copies, and faxes dramatically reduces the number of computer peripherals. Wireless external hard drives can be connected to a smartphone, tablet, desktop, and laptop, making file back up or additional storage effortless. Such a device is good to use in conjunction with another external hard drive or online backup. External hard drives need to be stored in safe places, such as a fire-safe, waterproof data storage chest.

Cellular and Landline Phones

Both landline and mobile telephones can be stationed inside or on top of a desk. Cell phones and cordless landlines are preferred, as they allow multitasking during use. These phones require a charging base or cord; some can collect in a charging station that accommodates several electronic units. A vast range of charging stations is on the market. Some of the best ones for the home office are designed to charge and operate everything, including a computer, clock, radio, or mobile music device. Cell phones can also be charged from the USB port on the computer with an adapter.

Landline telephones or desktop cellular charging stations should be close to your dominant hand. Label all charging and telephone cords to keep them straight. Bind all charging station or cellular cords together, and keep landlines separate. Keep a message pad or sticky notes next to telephones for convenience.

Cord and Cable Management

Managing the many cords and cables is a top priority when organizing the computer hardware and peripheral equipment on and around a desk. Avoid allowing cables and cords to crawl all over the desktop counter space because they take up valuable workspace and look messy. First, bundle like cords together with cable ties, clamp clips, or Velcro wraps. Group the cords by purpose, such as USB devices, speaker wires, and so on. Never bind cords with others if they need to be removed on a regular basis, such as a laptop that travels outside the home office.

The best way to run all desktop cords is by routing them through a hole cut in the desktop's surface. A grommet device, which is a plastic or metal ring, is a protective barrier that lines a cutout hole on a desk's surface that funnels the cords on their way to a power source. Grommets also prevent a disconnected cord from slipping out of reach by catching it before it falls. Some grommets have slits that separate individual cords. Other grommets contain specialized outlets for USB devices. There are also cord-catcher devices that keep detachable, slippery cords from dropping behind the desk or workstation. Some hold one cord, and others hold multiple cords and cables. Mostly, they're suction mounted, requiring no installation.

Label all the cords and cables, especially when they share a common power strip; this dramatically reduces the frustration and confusion associated with cord identification. Create a label from a label maker machine or wrap a piece of masking tape around the cord and use a permanent marker to record the component. Different color markers make it easy to identify the various cords at a glance.

You could also purchase a cord-identifier organizer, which consists of a several different colors of snap-on locking tabs that clamp onto the cord or cable. They usually come with preprinted icons and include blank inserts for making your own labels.

Besides knowing which cord belongs to each device, they also need to be gathered together in an orderly manner. Many cords and cables are too long, so they need to be bound and shortened in order to stay neat. Clean up all your cords by using one or more of the many organizers suitable for the job. There are wire-loom and braided-sleeve organizers that wrap around cords and cables. These organizers are flexible plastic tubing designed to secure bundles of cords and cables. A tried and true cable management solution is the J-Channel raceway, which can hold a bundle of cords and cables. It's an adhesive strip formed into the shape of the letter J that can be mounted vertically or horizontally on the desk sides to carry cables and cords to their power source. Cables and cords enter through the opening of the J shape, where the bottom of the letter curves.

Another cable and cord desk organizer that also holds peripherals is the under-the-desk wire cable tray organizer. This organizer contains a tray with slots for running wires through it to an opening that drops them to the electrical outlet. There are also wire cable baskets that can mount on the side or back of the desk to keep power strips and cords off the ground.

Calendars

There are two main ways to keep a calendar. For the tech savvy, a handheld PDA, smartphone, or online program is the answer. Others may prefer manually writing information on a desk, wall, or engagement calendar. Some people like to keep both. There is no right way; what works is whatever keeps you from not forgetting anything.

Digital

There are several advantages to keeping a digital calendar, and it's an environmentally friendly choice. Digital calendars store information securely, and many digital calendar systems can create texts or email reminders for meetings and other events. Also, sharing calendar information with others is possible, which is important for handling matters like group deadlines, meetings, and appointments. There are usually ways to color-code an electronic digital calendar to differentiate plans or people.

Automation allows you set up recurring appointments, birthdays, or classes without having to manually reenter them. Another good feature is the convenience of being able to access, update, and change a calendar from a mobile electronic device almost anywhere. Lastly, an electronic calendar system eliminates the need to display a calendar or have a particular place to house a physical planner, which conserves office space.

Manual

When a traditional calendar is preferred, it's helpful to follow a few guidelines. First, only use erasable writing instruments, such as pencil, chalk, or dry-erase markers, for entries. Marking up calendars with scratch outs reduces already limited space. Different colors of writing can color-code your calendar. For example, a certain class or person can be identified by a particular color.

Each date slot should have enough room to record all the information that you need. Keep your calendar simple and concise by inputting only scheduled commitments. Any task without a deadline, reminder information, or to-do-list items don't belong on a physical calendar. Such information can be recorded on a piece of paper and clipped to the side of a calendar to be temporary and disposable.

Be selective about which type of calendar to use on the desktop. For example, many promotional calendars or tear-off daily calendars only display a single day rather than a full week and only tend to add to desk clutter. It's best to be able to view an entire month or several months at a time. This can make scheduling and time management easier, because you can see how busy a week is at a glance. Desk pad calendars, wall calendars, and some journal-style calendars can accommodate this requirement.

Desktop Organizers

In lieu of good drawer space, desktop organizers are necessary for items used daily, such as sticky notes, pens, scissors, and so on, nearby. Many desktop organizers come in collections, where you can find a file organizer, letter sorter, stacking bin, and desk tray all in the same design, providing a consistent look to the desk.

You can find longer, narrow organizers that sit on top of the desk, spanning its length, for increased lateral storage. These organizers are removable and offer compartments that can include literature trays, sorting racks, drawers, pencil holders, cubbies, and shelves.

It's best to use desktop organizers that hold many items, as opposed to individual organizers like a business card holder or a cup holder. Single organizers take up more total space and too many of them can offer a cluttered look.

Many all-in-one desktop organizers can store office supplies, as well as paperwork and books. A space-saving spinning carousel organizer typically places a pencil cup in the center with many compartments orbiting around it for holding little things like sticky notes, business cards, binder clips, loose change, rubber bands, index cards, and so on. Miniature staplers, tape dispensers, scissors, and office tools can fit into compact desktop organizers.

Hutches

A desk hutch is a larger, higher set of shelves or cabinets sitting on top of the desk that is secured with hardware. Some are removable; others aren't. A desk hutch dramatically expands desk storage capacity. The only downside is that the desk must be placed against a wall due to the support needs of the hutch.

Hutches come in many configurations and can include drawers, cabinets, shelves, and cubbies. The more options in a hutch, the better for storing a diverse group of items convenient to have at the desk.

Organizing the Desk Drawers

Desk drawers are prime storage space in an office and the most convenient spots to hide belongings. It's important to keep these spaces well organized so items are efficiently stored and easy to locate. Different sizes of desk drawers work better for certain items.

Small Drawers and Pullout Trays

Typically, pullout trays and the small pencil drawers are located in the center of a desk just under the desktop. Computer keyboards are commonly located here. Drawers placed closest to the desktop tend to be the smallest and graduate to large sizes closer to the floor.

Smaller desk drawers are ideal for the small belongings core to all tasks performed at the desk, such as pens, staplers, glue, tape, rulers, and so on. No matter how small your storage space may be, using a compartmentalized organizer will keep it in order. Commonly, shallow desk drawer trays with built-in compartments are a popular option for any smaller drawer space. Also, consider tray organizers marketed for kitchen drawers, such as those that hold cutlery since they're similar.

Measure the space and opt for an organizer tray that best fits the drawer to take full advantage of all the space. These trays come in different sizes: some are expandable with designated compartments to fit writing utensils, keys, wallet, binder clips, and the like. To keep the compartments straight, you can label the bottoms. There are also tray kits that have picture stickers to identify the compartment items, such as keys, coins, sticky notes, paper clips, and so on.

Besides a tray organizer, smaller drawers and pencil drawers can be compartmentalized by using organizers common to a typical lingerie drawer.

There are organizers designed with individual compartments scaled to fit a single pair of socks or undergarment that are perfect for small office supplies. Also, they can have shallow, interlocking plastic strips that snap apart to form custom-sized compartments.

A budget-friendly solution for slim drawer organization is to use common cardboard jewelry boxes in various shapes and sizes to store things. Long necklace jewelry boxes can hold writing instruments. Rectangular and square boxes can hold mechanical pencil lead, erasers, lip balm, clips, and so on. Different sizes of jewelry boxes can puzzle together to form the square or rectangular shape of the drawer. Reinforce jewelry boxes with decorative duct tape so they last.

Medium Drawers

Depending on the depth, a medium-size desk drawer can be tricky to arrange without an appropriate organizer. The deeper the drawer, the more likely it's that items will be buried on top of one another, hard to locate, or even forgotten.

When your drawer needs to hold multiple smaller-size items, a stacking tray organizer specifically designed for drawers is the ideal solution. These organizers have two separate trays that stack on top of one another; a smaller tray rests on top of a larger one. The top tray slides to the side in order to allow access to the bottom tray. The lower tray is deeper to store larger belongings, whereas the top tray is shallow to hold articles such as pens, erasers, stamps, and the like.

Small crates, baskets, boxes, and bins are other organizers well suited for medium drawers. Tall, larger drawer organizers offer more unique storage arrangements, such as holding certain items upright for easier viewing rather than being stacked on top of each other. You can also select portable, handled basket or crate containers. Larger containers can hold items that are not office related but convenient to have in a home office—for example, belongings like electronic supplies, first aid products, grooming supplies, and makeup essentials can be grouped and placed in separate containers. Having items like aspirin, eye drops, lozenges, antibacterial wipes, clothing stain wipes, hand cream, nail files, brushes, and lipstick close by will keep you working at the desk instead of running around the house. Depending on the sizes of your desk drawers, items like computer/office supplies and small electronics can be stored in midsize drawers.

File Drawers

Desks with file drawers are a great place to hold everyday paperwork due to their prime storage location. A desk file drawer is a good place to store a duplicate set of all your keys. There is a key organizer designed to store on a hanging file rail that has inserts for keys. These organizers camouflage with the regular hanging files, so they hide keys and keep them close at hand.

Many file drawers are lockable, making this a great place to secure private information. When you don't necessarily need this drawer for files, consider using it for other items to keep under lock and key, such as personal journals, keepsakes, or anything you don't want small children to find.

Desk Cabinets

Desk cabinet compartments have shelves, and it's best when they're adjustable. Shelving inside a desk can store almost any office item. They can file books, hold containers, and stack anything. Office supplies are key items to keep at this location.

Atypical items are also welcomed in a desk cabinet, especially those that are hard to find storage spots for, such as sewing baskets, first aid kits, shoeshine kits, emergency candles/flashlights, and battery organizers.

A charging station for electronics is a clever, practical arrangement for this space. All that is necessary is a basic notch formed in the back wall of the cabinet for power cords to pass to an outlet and a basic electronic charger.

Don't pass up the opportunity to utilize the backside of a cabinet door for storage possibilities. Use this space to hang hooks for keys, headsets, and desk tools, like scissors. This space can also hold calendars or memo boards. A magnetic board could be stationed here; magnetize small items handy to have at the desk, such a nail file, lip balm, wet wipes, gum, hair ties, and so on.

Modesty Panels

Some desks have a modesty panel, which is a thin board of wood or metal attached to the front and, in some cases, to the sides of a desk. It's intended to shield legs, ankles, and feet from view. A modesty panel can be used to hang or stick organizers. Good items to store from the inside wall of the modesty panel are umbrellas, scissors, headsets, eyewear, bags, keys, lanyards, coffee mugs, and so on. The modesty panel exterior can hold items like wall files, mail holders, calendars, memo boards, and picture frames.

Metal modesty panels can accept magnetic organizers, such as clips, frames, hooks, baskets, notepads, and pencil holders. You can also magnetize anything like mini staplers, tape, key rings, tools, pens, notepads, lip balm, hand cream, pocket tissue, and so on.

CHAPTER 47

Organizing the Desk Area

Space that orbits the desk is challenging to organize when items stored here are needed on a daily basis. Therefore, it's best to situate the areas around the desk according to frequency of use, so everyday articles are the closest for accessibility. Begin to organize the desk areas by deciding which of your current office organizers or furniture pieces are working well. Any organizer or piece of furniture that is flimsy, bulky, clumsy, or not adjustable requires change. Whenever possible, decide if you can make feasible modifications or replace any of the less satisfactory ones.

It's important to gather all the office belongings surrounding the desk to organize them. Sort the belongings by type, reduce what you don't need, and see what remains. Then determine their storage whereabouts. Start with current storage accommodations to determine if they have the capacity and capability to store your belongings efficiently. It may be worthwhile to measure all the various compartments in the organizers or furniture pieces and match them with the belongings that might be stored there.

Consider where the storage organizers or furniture pieces fit well, given their proximities to the work zone. Before situating anything back in place, choose organizers that logically match the belongings so they're easy to see and access. Contained items are far easier to arrange. Otherwise, you can run the risk of wasting time shuffling groups of belongings haphazardly around from place to place while trying to fit things into space.

It's necessary to discover new ways to set up office belongings even with simple alterations or arrangements with existing furniture and organizers. It's common for people to put the things back together the way they were before. If the office didn't operate efficiently in the past, then it's time to make some changes; almost any office can benefit from even simple alterations. The following organizers and furniture are found in a typical home office.

Wall Organizers

The wall space around the desk is often overlooked as a storage opportunity. Utilizing the walls above or next to the desk will greatly free up the desktop and drawer space. There are numerous organizers designed for walls that can hold common desk inventories; they should be in spots that are convenient for accessing what they hold. For example, a wall organizer that houses pens, scissors, and sticky notes should be close to the desktop workspace, whereas seldom-used reference materials can be placed inside a wall cabinet near the desk.

Measure wall organizers to ensure they're the proper size for the allocated wall space. An accurate sketch that details where each wall organizer would go prior to installation is the best plan of action. Otherwise, the risk of placement errors and choosing the wrong size organizers is more likely. Since wall organizers are visible, select ones that are esthetically appealing. Those without doors may need baskets, trays, or bins to contain items so they stay tidy. The following wall organizers are useful for holding office items.

FIGURE 47.01
Space-Saving Office

Wall Files

As discussed in depth earlier, wall files are great for storing papers, file folders, manuals, magazines, and pamphlets.

Wall Shelves and Cubby Compartments

Wall-mounted shelving and cubby organizers are perfect for displaying and holding many items, such as picture frames, knickknacks, coffee mugs, books, magazines, binders, manuals, media, photo albums, papers, clocks, and tiered paper trays.

Key and Mail Organizers

A wall-mounted device designed to hold mail and keys is a good investment since these belongings are easy to misplace. Countless key and mail organizers are on the market, making it easy to find one that suits your taste or decor.

Wall-Mounted Closet Systems

A wall-mounted, suspended, track-based closet system consists of vertical rails in which accessories, such as pullout baskets, shelves, and other organizers, are inserted to create a highly functional workstation. Medium-depth shelves placed at counter height can create a desktop. Deep shelves can be placed toward the base to hold computer peripherals. Overhead shelves can be shallow and store binders, books, or decorative items.

Wall-System Organizers

There are many wall-system organizers consisting of a number of accessories, like hooks, baskets, cups, and so on, that attach to a large wallboard. Some of the more popular wall systems are peg wall, gridwall, and slatwall. Wallboards contain notches, grooves, or wire for hooking accessories. Some wall-mounted workshop tool organizers can be used for home office organization, as well.

Wall-system organizers are designed to house an extensive assortment of items, such as sticky notes, staplers, notepads, pushpins, clipboards, writing instruments, and so on. Some systems are specially reinforced to hold additional weight. These include components such as shelving in order to support the weight of heavier belongings like books. Wall systems are generally simple to clean, operate, and repurpose.

Magnetic, Chalk, Dry-Erase, and Cork Wallboards

It's almost a given that a home office will need some type of board for important reminders, tickets, and scheduled appointments outside of digital notes or calendars. A combination board that incorporates a few different types of surfaces, such as cork, chalk, dry-erase, and magnetic, provides a space-efficient, highly functional organizer.

Magnetic Boards

A magnetic board holds lightweight, magnetized organizers. One of the best magnetic board accessories is the clear-lidded, screw-top, metal canister to visually display small office supplies, like paper clips and binder holders, in plain view. Other magnetic accessories include baskets, shelves, hooks, and actual magnets. Such accessories are perfect for holding common pencil drawer items like pens, keys, sticky notes, stamps, and tape. Regular magnets are useful for holding many types of items from pictures to tickets.

It's easy to create your own magnetic board by framing a piece of magnetic galvanized steel. You can also apply magnetic paint to most surfaces, but it takes many coats to create the right amount of strength.

Chalk and Dry-Erase Boards

Chalkboards are not as office friendly as the dry-erase alternatives. Chalk is messy and harder to write with than a marker. Both chalk and dry-erase boards can be purchased magnetized, where accessories can stick onto the board's surface, which is a space-saving feature since both writing and storing happen on the same board.

Chalkboard paint is actual paint that can be applied to many surfaces to create a writing surface specifically for chalk. However, it's not as easy as it appears to successfully create the final product. The process requires the proper priming procedure and several coats of paint.

Fabric or Cork Boards

Fabric boards have the advantage of being decorative and inexpensive to make: you just need a piece of fabric, cardboard, and a frame. Cork is also affordable, and it's easy to tailor these boards to fit any wall space. The downside is that a cork or fabric boards have limited uses and are hard to clean. The thumbtacks or pushpins necessary for these organizers are sharp and dangerous, especially when small children are present in the home.

Tips for Maintaining Wallboards

Wallboards are convenient, and since these organizers can hold important information visibly, it's important to tame them by keeping papers under control. The following tips will help keep your wallboards organized:

- It's common that papers pertaining to specific events are posted on wallboards. However, this is risky because an important date might be overlooked or lost on a busy memo board. Invitations, schedules, classes, appointments, dates, and meetings should be recorded in a calendar. Create classifications for these papers and place them in an organizer.
- Sticky notes should not be on an office wallboard. First, they can fall off, which is bad if the note is important. Second, they can easily be overused and take over. Quick notes should be logged in a digital device, notebook, ledger pad, or things-to-do chart that resides on the desk. Date every entry on the list and transfer the information at the day's end to a calendar or wherever it needs to go when you have the time to do so.
- Use one magnet or pin per piece of paper. Overlapping can hide some papers and create a cluttered look.
- Separate people and activities by color coding them. A special color marker or folder can be used per individual person or activity.
- Frame and hang the inspirational messages that truly mean something to you, rather than crowding too many on the wallboard space—unless that is the organizer's sole purpose. Likewise, photos remain in better shape when kept off the memo board and into picture frames.
- Buy miniature staplers, calculators, tape dispensers, scissors, and other office tools and stick them onto magnetic boards with magnetic strips. You can also find these tools already magnetized.
- Straighten the memo board weekly; generally, the end of work week, while information is still fresh, is a good time. The more time put into maintaining an important visual organizer, such as wallboard, the more efficient the home office will operate.

Shelving and Bookcases

Open-storage organizers, like shelving and bookcases, can be challenging to arrange because they need to both be functional and neat. Wall-mounted shelves and bookcases are the ones typically found in a home office. Shelving units tend to be a budget-friendly solution for storage, and they use lateral space efficiently. The following covers typical office items and ways to arrange them best on a shelf.

Books

Office-related books should be stored separately from personal or entertainment books in a home office, so place them on separate shelves. Entertainment books are commonly not used on a daily basis. In an office environment, both high and low shelving can hold them, leaving the key eye-level storage shelves for the work-related books used most often.

On the same shelf, split dissimilar books by using book/binder containers. These containers are slim, tall organizers with open tops that commonly have a label holder to identify contents. Bookends can also clearly distinguish various books. In addition, divide different books on the same shelf by standing one group upright and stacking another.

Some people care more about how their books look on the shelf than their order. Visually, one the neatest way to store books is upright by size. The tallest book starts the row, descending in size to the smallest, from left to right. For optimal balance and support, line the bottom shelf with the largest, heaviest books. Then the middle shelves can hold the medium-size books with the smallest, lightest books at the top of the unit.

Arranging books filed upright by the color of their spines is a popular way to display them. It's clearly a decorative statement, and the result is a rainbow-color scheme of many different colors. Some people prefer certain color schemes, like black and white or only neutrals. Realize that choosing fewer colors to display limits the books you can store on your shelves.

When locating a book quickly is more important than the visual arrangement, a system must be in place. First, decide the most logical arrangement for you personally. You might first split books between fiction and nonfiction. These two types of books can further be divided into many different subtypes or genres, such as drama, romance, math, travel, and health. Then further organize books alphabetically according to title, where *the* and *a* don't count, or by the author's last name.

Decorative Items

Shelving offers a great opportunity to decorate the office with keepsakes, art collections, pictures, and the like. Office books, binders, manuals, filing crates, and so on can share shelving space with decorative items. Use bookends, shelf dividers, or filing crates to stabilize office materials so decorative pieces are displayed safely. Another way to share space would be to lay books on top of one another with a decorative object on top of the stack. You can also use ornamental bookends for a decorative touch.

Decorative belongings and office-related items might also be stored on different shelves. To achieve a balanced look, alternate shelving so that one stores office materials and the next holds decorative objects. Keep office-related materials at eye level on the easy-to-reach shelves, and then use the less accessible shelves for decorative items.

Shelf Organizers

Magazine files, storage crates, baskets, photo boxes, containers, and media organizers can be kept on shelving. Such organizers conceal belongings that would otherwise look cluttered on a shelf, such as computer or office supplies. Organizers like file boxes are good for hiding temporary papers that don't require long-term file storage: pamphlets, maps, receipts, stationery, letters, drawings, tickets, schedules, program guides, and so on.

Many things can be containerized on shelves: scrapbooking items, shipping/packing materials, audio/video accessories, flashlights, candles, remotes, batteries, photos, and really just about any household belonging in need of a storage spot. A home office tends to be a good place to stock articles that are hard to place around the home.

A mismatched collection of organizers can look disorganized on the same shelf; therefore, keep them all the same type or color or complementary in some way for consistency and visual harmony.

Electronics and Computer Equipment

Strong, deep shelving can hold items like most computer peripherals, stereos, electronic charging stations, and so on. In many cases, it's best to store such items away from the desk, where they would tend to hog workspace.

Family Memories

Office shelving is a great place to store or display family heirlooms, photos/albums, home videos, trophies, and the like. Using the same type or size organizers for all these possessions is consistent and makes locating things easy.

Office Furniture for Storage

An important feature of good office design is functionality, which always starts with effective and efficient office furniture. After all, office furniture is what holds everything and is the actual working space. A cluttered home office can be transformed into a productive, functional space with the right storage pieces. The following furniture pieces can help combat workspace clutter and keep the home office neat and tidy.

File Cabinets

File cabinets are responsible for storing one of the most important belongings in a home office: paperwork and sometimes even digital disks. They're designed to systematically store paper documents in file folders. However, file cabinets don't necessarily have to be limited to files. Many file cabinets contain deep drawers that are also useful for storing other articles, such as office supplies and computer peripherals. The following information covers the three main types of file cabinets: vertical, lateral, and shelf.

Vertical

A vertical file cabinet is designed to hold letter- or legal-size documents in the conventional front-to-back format. Vertical file cabinets are usually only fifteen inches wide and stack anywhere from two to five drawers high. Due to their narrow width, vertical file cabinets are great for offices with limited floor space. Smaller cabinets like these often come with wheels and are easily movable. This allows freedom to place a vertical file cabinet

anywhere, and when needed, it can easily roll to a workspace for convenience.

Lateral

Lateral file cabinets are mostly designed to hold files in a side-to side-manner although front to back file arrangements are found, as well. They're usually between thirty inches and forty-two inches wide, more than double the width of a vertical file cabinet. They're not space efficient, though, and tend to be rather bulky. However, lateral file cabinets can hold a great deal more than vertical file cabinets, and they can stack up to five drawers high. Counter-height lateral file cabinets make an ideal desktop extension, offering additional space to hold office equipment, desktop organizers, binders, books, and so on.

Shelf

A shelf file cabinet only has shelves, no drawers. Some have doors that retract into the cabinet, but most are open. Such cabinets are commonly found in doctor's offices and law firms, where many client folders exist. Shelf file cabinets are ideal for a small home-based business with many clients, such as a landscaping, roofing, or insurance business.

Shelf file cabinets are designed to hold only file folders stacked on a shelf, positioned perpendicular to the front of the cabinet. Therefore, the file folders need labeling tabs on the side, rather than the top.

Credenza

A credenza is a traditional executive piece of office furniture that is usually placed behind or parallel to a desk. A credenza acts as a desk extension by providing additional counter and cabinet storage space. It comes with or without a hutch for extra storage and usually features shelves and cubbies.

The top of a credenza can accommodate desk spillover, such as lighting, telephones, electronic charging stations, pencil cups, and various desktop organizers. Credenza shelf compartments can be outfitted with pullout shelves so bulky electronic like printers can be easily accessible. Credenza cabinets are good for storing items that are handy to have near the desk, such as office supplies, shipping supplies, work binders, company promotional items, corporate literature, and files.

In lieu of a hutch, wall space above the credenza is ideal for placing office-related wall organizers, such as wallboards, calendars, shelving, and wall files.

Supply Cabinets and Office Closets

A home office is one room in the home that tends to serve multiple purposes, such as for arts/crafts, reading, homework, knitting/sewing, and so on. For this reason, it's acceptable to store some random household items in the cabinets and closets, such as photo albums, shipping supplies, gift-wrapping supplies, home videos, light bulbs, stationery supplies, cleaning supplies, paper goods, and arts and crafts supplies.

A storage unit, such as an armoire or standard office supply cabinet, is the perfect solution for a home office that needs closet space. Similar in structure to that of a closet, a supply cabinet is a great place to store just about anything that needs to be hidden from view. A rod can be installed inside a deep supply cabinet to hang uniforms and outwear, if needed.

Some possible disadvantages to using bulkier storage pieces like a supply cabinet are the amount of space they occupy. Cabinets with deep shelves may be difficult to organize, given that technology has advanced to the point where most office supplies are smaller than ever. This makes tech accessories, such as cartridges, tapes, and so on, compact, and a deep shelves dwarf them.

However, deep shelves do have merit. They can hold bulky electronic equipment, such as a printer, when a nearby power source exists. Keep heavier items on the lower shelves, but not past counter height, so they're easy to operate. Deep shelves are also good to store bulky items, such as reams of paper or rolls of bubble wrap.

Medium-depth shelving is the most versatile spot in a supply cabinet and many closets. Closets can be outfitted with more storage options, such as hanging rods, pullout drawers, baskets, cubbies, and cabinets. Closet and cabinet shelving can also store items by themselves, upright in row order where each aisle represents a given type of item such as air fresheners or light bulbs. Then go by the FIFO, or the first-in, first-out system of

FIGURE 47.02
Home Office Supplies in a Closet

inventory control, meaning taking and using the item in the front completely before taking the next one in line. When you set up a supply cabinet or shelf, create a loose arrangement to leave room for new items. Don't label shelves or sections for designated belongings due to the ever-changing fluctuations in supplies, parts, and so on. Locking in space for certain items may wind up creating empty room on the shelf as groups of belongings deplete and restocking orders grow smaller. It's best to establish a flexible organizational plan. For instance, simply designate each shelf with a certain type of inventory, such as computer/peripheral parts and supplies, so things are easy to find. Then rearrange things as items come and go on a daily basis to keep shelves organized and efficient.

It's a good practice to remove bulk items from their packaging so the individual articles are easy to see and grab. For example, stack reams of paper on shelves and discard the cardboard box. Also, take small loose articles out of hard-to-access packaging and place them in open containers. For instance, remove pens from sealed packages and transfer them loosely in an open bin. Small groups of like supplies can be corralled in handled containers like a caddy or basket. For example, fill one with stationery items like notes, stamps, paper, journals and calligraphy supplies. This way, your supplies are together and easy to transport from the closet to the work zone.

The back wall of a closet or cabinet can be used to mount key boxes, battery racks, hanging files, mail holders, and just about any mountable office organizer. There are a number of mountable organizers on the inside of doors that can securely hold items so they stay put even with plenty of door movement. Pick lightweight organizers, like wire gift-wrapping paper holders that

can store rolls of paper, blueprints, poster board, and so on. This location is also good for hanging calendars, memo boards, schedules, over-the-door organizers, and reminders. Post a clipboard to the inside of the cabinet or closet door that lists all the supplies regularly needed in the home office. When you are running low, mark the item off and use the sheet as a shopping list.

Don't store things on a closet floor unless they have wheels, such as rolling tiered basket carts, file carts, shelves, or dolly type organizers. Wheeled organizers are easy to transport to workstations or wherever they're needed, including wheeled recycling or garbage cans for the closet if your office produces a ton of garbage. Also, they make cleaning the closet floor easy.

Turning a Home Office Closet into a Hardworking Space

Some office closets have the potential to convert into a workstation. The first thing to think about is whether losing closet storage space is a good idea. Then, decide whether the project is worth the effort and money needed to put one together.

To begin a conversion from a closet to a workspace, start with the closet doors. If you keep the doors, you'll maintain a closet, and in real estate, the space can still count as a bedroom. However, if the doors don't allow complete access to the closet, they'll interfere with the workspace. Bifold and pocket doors offer the best access to the inside portion of the closet. When closet doors are removed and the opening is constructed well, the closet can blend well into the rest of the room and not even look as if it were once a closet.

When redesigning an office closet, don't ignore the interior side walls. Use this valuable space to

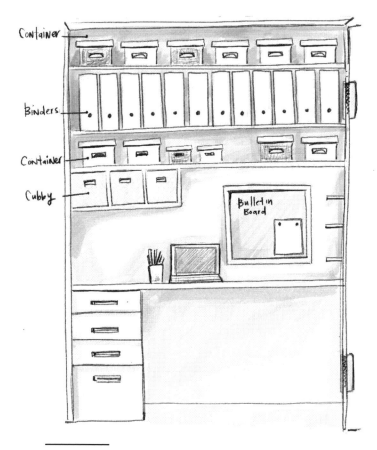

Container

Binders

Container

Cubby

Bulletin
Board

FIGURE 47.03
Office in a Closet

place wall files or wall-mounted corner shelves at these locations.

A suspended counter can be installed along the back wall to use as a workstation. There are several advantages to using a suspended counter rather than a desk. First, there is no dead space because the counter is custom made to fit from one side of the closet to the other. Depending on the material used, a wall-mounted countertop is relatively inexpensive. Mounting brackets suspend the countertop and eliminate the need for support legs. This is important when floor organizers are necessary or if there is little leg room.

You can also create a complete closet office with a closet system. Common wire-based, suspended track rail systems have many add-on accessories to form a high-functioning space. A deep shelf placed at counter height can act as a workstation. Below the counter space, station pullout baskets, drawers, cabinets, and shelves to hold binders, paperwork, and office supplies. Rolling files and drawer carts can also hold these articles. Above the counter, shallow closet shelves can hold manuals, binders, books, discs, and containers of supplies.

A simple closet desk can also be created by using a large piece of material, such as Formica, sized to fit the length of the closet. Then place counter-height, vertical file cabinets at either end of the closet to support the counter.

Plenty of wall-mounted organizers are well suited for closet walls, including magnetic boards, memo boards, cork, hanging folders, and board organizers with attachable accessories, such as cup holders, hooks, shelves, and baskets to hold desk supplies. A basic magnetic board can hold a number of office necessities attached with a piece of magnetic tape. Good items to magnetize are a miniature stapler, tape roll, sticky notes, memo pad, staple remover, nail file, pen, and scissors.

CHAPTER 48

Repurposing Armoires and Wardrobe Closets

An armoire or wardrobe closet is a tall, free-standing furniture piece, usually with two doors at the opening; in the distant past, they were primarily used as closets. Armoires and wardrobe closets are typically around two feet deep and several feet wide, and they're very easy to repurpose for other needs in the home. The interior of these furniture pieces typically have shelves, and the wardrobe versions contain hanging rods for clothes.

Larger pieces of furniture like these can be hard to sell, making secondhand armoires and wardrobe closets easy to find at a bargain. Purchasing one secondhand may also be a good option when you need additional storage or have a particular use for one. There are also many ways to reclaim an empty one currently in your home.

Certain rooms, depending on their locations and functions, will dictate the repurposing of an armoire. For example, a guest-room armoire could be converted into a desk, sewing center, or linen closet. It can sometimes be hard to find the right place to store random belongings, such as stationery, gift-wrapping, shipping supplies,

and arts and crafts items. A single armoire can be converted to a workstation that can also store these items.

Crafts, Stationery, Gift Wrap, and Shipping Armoires

There are a number of ways to construct the interior of a wardrobe closet or armoire to fit these purposes, which are different yet connected in several ways. The following covers detailed storage information for various ways you could convert an armoire or wardrobe closet into a hard-working space.

Arts and Crafts Station

Each type of art or craft usually involves a unique technique that has specialized supplies and tools. For example, scrapbooking can include a craft lever punch, a tool that adds a decorative edge to paper or photo tabs to secure pictures at the corners. Sometimes, specialized organizers or arrangements may be in order to accommodate unusual tools and supplies.

Also, you may choose to separate certain arts and crafts into their own containers for various reasons. Most craft stores carry specialized containers geared toward a particular art or craft; universal containers for general types of supplies, such as paper and groups of small items, like stickers, buttons, or beads, can used, as well.

There are advantages to separating supplies for certain arts and crafts when they're taken out of the home. Carrying totes or compartmentalized plastic, handled art containers are popular options for transportation. However, when many of these supplies are shared with other arts and crafts enjoyed in the home, it may be advantageous to collect them in one common stationery organizer and have empty carry-all containers on hand that can be filled and unloaded as needed. This way, everything stays easy to share.

The following covers different ways to store the more general arts and craft supplies in a typical wardrobe closet or armoire.

Decorative Supplies

Collections of small craft items, such as buttons, feathers, beads, and the like, need to be divided and placed into individual containers or drawers. Make sure that the organizers you select for them are scaled to fit what they hold, with a little leeway in case you need to restock. Generally, inexpensive, stackable plastic containers are good for holding small decorative items, but label their contents when they're not visible. Small, stackable, open-top bins are another option. You can also store decorative craft supplies in easy-to-carry miniature-pail-style buckets. Pails can reside on a shelf or hang by their handles on hooks mounted to the underside of an interior shelf.

Craft stores carry many compartmentalized organizers for specific purposes. Some of the most popular are the round, clear plastic, mini stackable organizers, where each container holds about a cup. The individual screw-top containers nestled inside one large plastic container are marketed for beads. Some also come in the form of dispensed pill boxes, in which each day has a separate flip-top compartment. Another is the compartmentalized, handled carrying case organizer. This organizer features a durable, clear plastic case with a hinged lid that locks at the handle and features many divided compartments to separate supplies. Some of these types of organizers are formed in the shape of satchels or totes.

Since armoires have depth, it's important not to install shelves that are too deep if you store small containers of arts and crafts supplies. Rather, install many shallow shelves that are more proportionate in size for the organizers.

Drawers are another option for storing decorative arts and crafts supplies. For example, an apothecary chest/cabinet with many tiny drawers is perfect for storing craft items like beads, ribbons, bells, feathers, sequins, and so on. Smaller versions of this type of cabinet can fit inside an armoire on a shelf.

Some arts and crafts organizers are almost identical to hardware cabinets and are perfect for small supplies. Both of these organizers come encased in a durable framed housing or shell with several small, clear-plastic pullout drawers suitable for dividing small decorative supplies. Some of these organizers have an option to wall mount, which can be considered for the back wall of a sturdy armoire or wardrobe closet.

Screw-top jars and even recycled condiment containers can store decorative supplies nestled in a drawer so only their tops are exposed, which need to be labeled with their contents.

Essential Arts and Crafts Hand Tools

Basic arts and crafts instruments used to cut, paint, glue, sew, and so on need easy access in an armoire or wardrobe closet. Open organizers like basic pencil cups can divide different tools, such as fabric scissors, craft knives, jewelry pliers, or hole punches. There are also wall-mounted cup organizers that suspend from a rod on an S hook that are perfect to attach to the back wall over a work counter.

A silverware caddy can also separate the different types of arts and crafts hand tools and is a good transportable organizer. There are many different types of wallboard organizers that include accessories like baskets and hooks for holding tools, which are also good to mount to the back wall of an armoire or wardrobe closet.

Infrequently needed hand tools, like specialized jewelry-making tools, can be stored separately in a lidded container in a drawer or on a shelf. Some hand tools are best stored with other articles pertaining to the particular art or craft. For example, a single tote can store yarn in the center compartment and knitting/crochet needles in outside pockets. There are also arts and crafts tool sets sold in specialized, lined tray compartments in their own carry case. Many of the tools contained in such sets can apply to various arts and crafts. Store the kits intact in their carry cases and place in an armoire drawer.

Glues

Extra-strength bonding superglues and many arts and crafts glues are likely to harden quickly and clog nozzles. The problem is caused by how these glues' ingredients negatively react to the humidity in the air. Some preventive measures to minimize glue hardening is to completely seal the opening where the glue is dispensed with a strong tape, like duct tape, and then cover with the cap. Next, place the glues in an airtight container, such as a plastic or glass jar and add a desiccant packet or rice to reduce moisture in the container. Note that desiccant packets are commonly found in medication/ vitamin bottles, dried-fruit packages, beef-jerky packages, shoeboxes, and aspirin bottles. You'll also need to store the glues' container in a dry, cool, and dark place. Therefore, an armoire or wardrobe closet, where the doors are commonly closed, is a good spot. Refrigeration is another option for preventing glue from hardening.

An alternative solution to the hardened-glue problem is purchasing single-use sizes of the glues to minimize storage concerns. Some glue manufactures claim to have perfected the cap by developing precision applicators that cut down on the likelihood of glue hardening, so check consumer reviews before investing in glues.

Basic white glue is generally the least likely to harden, so those glues can be stored in traditional organizers, but place them upright in a caddy, basket, or pencil holder so the glue doesn't rest in the cap, where it's more prone to clog.

Tape

There are many different types of arts and crafts tape, including duct, masking, UV-reactive, tacky, bias, double-sided, washi, transparent, and Stamp Straight tapes. There are a few different ways to store tape in an armoire or wardrobe closet. How you arrange tape in storage will depend on the amount and purpose of each type. For example, large quantities of washi tape may require a specialized container, whereas a few rolls of cellophane tape can stay in a quick-access place such as countertop bin.

Many types of organizers are designed to store rolls of craft tape. A popular one is a multiple-roll dispenser that can hold many varieties and colors of tapes. Large collections of craft tape can be stored in handled, cosmetic-style totes or on the counter or a shelf in a tiered-drawer tape organizer, which has several drawers with curved compartments to accommodate many rolls.

Fabric

Most fabrics can be stored in a number of ways, but the best arrangement is to clamp each fabric onto a hanger and rest it on a rod. Most armoires can accommodate a hanging rod, and wardrobe closets already have one. On the hanger, have the fabric formed in the same size square with the fold face forward so it looks neat. Fabrics look best filed in color order from left to right, lightest to darkest. For example, white, yellow, orange, red, and so on. Color order allows you to keep tabs on amounts, which prevents overbuying.

Another way to organize fabric is to file it in a drawer or container similar to how paper rests in a hanging file. Have the fold of the fabric face up and place in color order. It's never a good idea to stack fabric since it can be damaged in a search and it's hard to see what is at the bottom of a drawer unless the entire pile is taken out. A fabric board found at fabric stores works well for stacking or filing fabric neatly in drawers and on shelves. Fabric simply wraps around the acid-free board and is secured with a straight pin or rubber band. Each fabric is bound to an individual board, so they're all the same size—perfect for uniform stacking or filing.

Fabric also comes in long rolls, which is clumsy and hard to store in smaller spaces like an armoire or wardrobe closet. Rolls have fixed sizes, so whether they store horizontally or vertically, the armoire or wardrobe closet must be able to accommodate the sizes. Rolls of fabric can

be stored upright in tall containers, such as garbage cans, and be placed next to the armoire or wardrobe closet.

Paint

Different paints used for a number of arts and crafts projects can be stored collectively in an armoire or wardrobe cabinet. Assorted sizes of paint bottles or tubes can gather in caddy, basket, or staircase shelf organizer. Paint collections in same-size bottles or jars can stay together in a tiered organizer, such as a wall-mounted shelving unit placed on the back wall of the armoire or inside of the door. Paint sets that come in concealed cases can be stored flat in a drawer organizer, tray, or container. Store like paint colors together. For example, keep all your blue paint in one row on the shelf and the pinks in another.

Construction Paper

Sort construction paper by color and file it in an organizer with multiple slots, like an office desktop or wall-file system. Such organizers can either reside on an armoire shelf or mount on the interior wall of the armoire or wardrobe cabinet. A deep shelf can house a file crate with hanging folders where each one holds a different color of paper. The file tabs can notate the colors.

Spools

String, ribbon, and lace that come on spools can hang from a rod/dowel mounted horizontally on the back wall of the armoire or wardrobe closet. Rods/dowels can also suspend on wallboard organizers from hook accessories, such as a tool shop multiple-holed peg wall or grooved slatwall paneling. Holed-peg wallboards can also support multiple hooks, where each one holds an individual spool.

There are various kinds of portable and free-standing dispensing spool organizers for shelf or workstation placement. These organizers typically hold a number of spools side by side on a dowel encased inside a transparent container. Then each spool of ribbon, lace, or string is placed through an opening for dispensing: you pull the ribbon through the opening and cut off a piece.

Gift-Wrapping and Stationery Supplies

Arts and crafts supplies can be stored compatibly with gift-wrap and stationery supplies. In fact, many arts and crafts supplies can be used to embellish presents or gift cards, such as ribbon, stickers, yarn, paint markers, and other decorative items. Specialized gift-wrapping organizers are designed to hold everything from wrapping paper to note cards. These are ideal for small supplies and spaces like an armoire or wardrobe closet. Many of these organizers are wire based with several compartments, each sized to fit a particular item, such as a roll of wrapping paper. They're designed for wall mounting; the inside of a wardrobe closet or armoire door makes a great spot. These organizers can also hold rolled artwork and poster board.

Also popular are hanging gift-wrap organizers formed in the shape of a garment bag. These organizers have several clear pockets for holding gift wrap, bows, ribbon, and the like. A hook holds the organizer from a closet rod or door hook, making it a flexible storage option for a wardrobe closet or an armoire. Excess wrapping paper, gift bags, and tissue can be kept in a lidded container on an upper closet shelf or under the bed. It's convenient to keep these items at a workstation like a craft armoire since it's also a designated place for the actual wrapping.

Some people may prefer gift bags to wrapping paper or vice versa, so using an all-in-one organizer for gift-wrapping supplies may not be the best option. Rather, it works better for them to store these items in separate places within a craft armoire. The following covers ways to store different gift-wrapping items, such as gift bags, tissue, and wrapping paper, separately.

Wrapping Paper

Folded Sheets: Wall-mounted pocketed folders, hanging file folders, tiered desktop paper sorters, and twelve-by-twelve-inch clear storage scrapbooking cases are perfect for storing folded gift wrap. Wrapping paper can be separated by occasion, like wedding or birthday. Also, wrapping paper can be sorted by color or patterns. Generally, it's both economical and easier to just buy basic, all-occasion paper so you'll not have to sort it or repurchase it as often.

Rolls: There are tall, upright gift-wrap containers, many of which are wheeled, designed to store a number of rolls. There are also long, shallow, lidded containers for holding multiple rolls of gift wrap. These organizers are good for large collections and are especially handy around big gift holidays, like Christmas. Such organizers are better stored on the top of or beside a craft armoire.

Gift Bags: The best way to organize gift bags is to first sort them by size: small, medium, large, and extra-large. You can also divide by type, such as birthday, wedding, and so on. However, like wrapping paper, it's best to purchase universal gift bags like solids, strips or generic patterns like floral. This way your gift bags are easier to stock, organize, and use.

Don't fold gift bags, as they'll be permanently creased. Rather, hang them from mounted or adhesive hooks on the inside walls of the armoire or on the inside of the armoire door. Keep the gift bags in size order, so small bags on one hook and large on another. Since not all the bags will be exactly equal in size, but will fall into a small, medium, or large sizes, keep the smaller bags in front of the larger ones on the hook. Extra-large gift bags that don't fit on an organizer can lay flat on top of the armoire or stacked upright between the armoire and a wall.

Tissue: Gift tissue is commonly sold in layered sheets wrapped in a plastic pouch or bound by a paper sleeve. Gift tissue comes gently folded over on the sides in order to secure the layered sheets, whereas the length remains unfolded. This does not compromise the delicate paper and should remain in this state until used. Therefore, try to store gift tissue without further compacting it in order to prevent creases and tears in a long shallow container, basket, or drawer. Always stack it on top of anything else it's stored with. Cardboard mailing tubes used to hold large rolled papers such as blueprints are ideal for storing delicate tissue. Tissue can also be draped over a pant hanger or towel bar.

Stationery

Stationery items, such as note cards, invitations, gift enclosures, gift tags, greeting cards, and the like, can be kept together in hanging pocketed organizers that contain multiple clear pockets in various sizes. Handheld stationery tools, like wax seal kits, calligraphy pens, paper embossers, inks, and such, can stay together in an under-the-counter pullout tray, drawer, or basket; use drawer dividers to separate them.

Another way to store these items is by corralling them in small stackable bins and placing them on an armoire shelf. When you have specialized cases, containers, or original boxes for these items, keep them there since they're designed perfectly and most are labeled with their contents. Keep them stored alongside other handheld stationery instruments. Stationery items like greeting cards can be filed by occasion in expanding accordion files and photo boxes with tab dividers.

Packing and Shipping Materials

Packing tape, Bubble Wrap, padded envelopes, and boxes mingle well with gift-wrapping essentials. For example, shipping boxes and padded envelopes can be stacked with gift boxes. Packing tape can store with other tape rolls like masking tape. Bubble Wrap and tissue can be stored together since they're both used as packing materials.

Armoires

A single armoire can be converted to a workstation that can store items such as stationery, gift-wrapping, shipping supplies, and arts and crafts.

CHAPTER 49

Different Uses for Armoires

Armoires are versatile and can easily be converted for many different uses, such as into a desk, gardening or sewing center, cocktail bar, or even a diaper-changing area. They may also supplement or emulate an actual closet for storing items like linens, dry goods, or clothing. The benefit of using an armoire or wardrobe closet to create a workstation or storage space is it can hide everything that may otherwise clutter a room. Some additional ideas for armoires follow, but the functionalities and uses for an armoire conversion are limitless.

Desk Armoires

You might find armoires that have already been outfitted as a desk, or you can create your own custom desk in almost any armoire. A desk armoire typically will have a counter-height shelf used as the workstation; a pullout extension shelf can be added to create additional desk space and may be necessary to create legroom when none exists at the base of the armoire.

A home office may have large storage demands that cannot be met in a condensed armoire, but there are many ways to manage the needed space:

- Consider buying compact computers, shredders, scissors, clocks, trash cans, and so on.
- Mount a strip light onto the armoire wall to save desktop space.
- Install a pullout keyboard or pullout tray under the counter to hold common desktop items like staplers, writing instruments, rulers, tape, and so on, in order to conserve space.
- Utilize the interior armoire walls and inside of the armoire doors to mount organizers like memo boards, wall files, pocketed organizers, shelves, baskets, clipboards, and calendars.
- Overhead armoire shelves can hold manuals, check boxes, books, paper, envelopes, label machines, calculators, binders, and computer supplies.
- The base shelves of the armoire can hold bulky or heavy items like copy paper, shipping boxes, file crates, printer, shredder, and a small trash can.

Computer Peripheral

Fold Out table

File Crate   garbage

DESK ARMOIRE

FIGURE 49.01
Office Armoire

Linens Armoires

An armoire is a great option for storing linens in lieu of a linen closet or for excess. Such an armoire can reside in a guest bedroom, hallway, bathroom, office, or any place near where the main linens are stored or used. In a situation where the linens armoire is the secondary storage, use it for the less frequently used items, such as guest towels, blankets, and pillows. Then keep the central linen closet stocked with everyday items like towels and toiletries.

A linens armoire will need good organizers, because linens can easily become jumbled. However, avoid wicker organizers because wicker can snag and rip fabric. It's also important to cover any exposed wood that is not stained or painted, because the oils from the wood will leach into the fabric and create stains.

Shelving is easy to put in an empty armoire by installing an adjustable track rail on the back wall of the armoire for shelving inserts. Since armoires run on the deep side, be careful not to select shelves that have too much depth, because they're harder to arrange. As a general rule, heavy folded blankets need an eighteen-inch-deep shelf; folded towels need twelve-inch- to sixteen-inch-deep shelving, and ten inches is good for sheets or pillowcases.

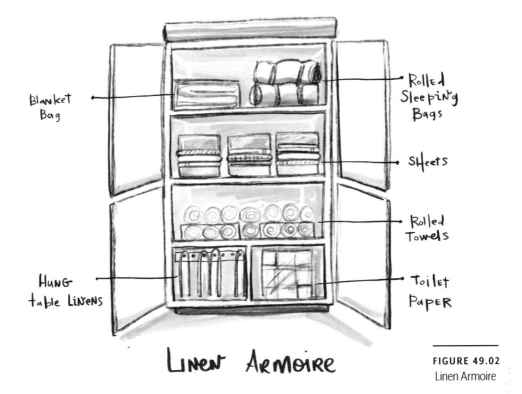

Linen Armoire

FIGURE 49.02
Linen Armoire

If the shelves are not adjustable, use good organizers. Helper shelves, which are raised platforms on legs, create another storage area for linens or toiletries. Helper shelves are found in rectangular sizes; some are pie shaped for corners. Under-the-shelf wire baskets are designed to capture the dead space found in between shelves. These are usually on the small side and are good for storing certain items, such as washcloths, cloth napkins, and placemats.

A hanging bar installed in an armoire can hold linens so they stay wrinkle-free. Hang table-cloths, blankets, throws, runners, and furniture slip covers using open-ended, felt, or plastic gripper hangers.

Sheets and Towels
Separate piles of folded towels and sheets by using shelf dividers, such as those with hooks that insert on the top and bottom of the shelf, where they're held in place by tension. When installed, these organizers resemble bookends, thus forming boundaries between articles that rest side by side on a shelf. Use the front edge of the shelf to label different types of linens, or in the case of wire shelving, simply use a hanging tag label.

Containers are another storage option for linens in an armoire. There are containers specially designed to hold linens that are shaped with a tall back and shallow front so they stack a good amount but the contents are easily seen and accessible. Generally, lidded containers trap air, so the poor air circulation will not keep the linens as fresh.

Always face the sheet or towel with the fold faced forward. Not only does it look neater, but also the fold itself is easy to grip for removal. Rotate linens so they receive equal use. Do this by moving freshly laundered linens to bottom of the stack.

Other Options for a Linens Armoire

Use the linens armoire as a restocking center by keeping bulk quantities of articles used throughout the home, such as toilet paper, cotton balls, cotton swabs, tissue boxes, napkins, paper towels, and toiletries. Certain toiletries, like bottles, jars, and cans, can sit openly on a shelf, but keep like products in single-file rows, as stores do. Place shorter items in the front, graduating to the taller ones in the back.

Handled caddy organizers and open baskets are also good places to store toiletries. Each basket or caddy can hold a separate group of products. As always, label them with their contents in order to promote long-term order. Opt for plastic organizers because they're easy to clean in case of spills.

Other items to consider for storage in a linens armoire are first aid kits, hot water bottles, humidifiers, massagers, neck rolls, foot soakers, manicure and pedicure kits, sound machines, or other bed or bath gadgets rarely used.

Memory Armoires

The most valuable belongings in your home are your photos and home videos, which need a safe and secure spot away from a water source and damaging sunlight. Therefore, an armoire (or wardrobe closet) outfitted with the right organizers is an ideal place to store these belongings. Positioning one in a communal area, like a den, living room, office, dining room, or even a guest room, makes it convenient and accessible for everyone.

It's relatively easy to create photo and video storage in any armoire, but first the photos and videos need to be housed in proper storage essentials to securely hold and keep them intact. The task involved in organizing and arranging individual videos or photos into organizers, such as photo albums, can be a painstakingly long project and is discussed in detail in the "Closets" section of this book.

Ideally, keep your photos in same-size albums or boxes so they fit/stack uniformly and best utilize the space. Likewise, use uniform storage essentials for your videos. Always arrange your photos and videos chronologically. Start with the earliest produced videos and photos and then work your way to the present day, arranging them from left to right as most libraries do.

Shelving in an armoire or wardrobe closet tends to be the best way to store photo albums, cases, and boxes. Open storage, like shelving, allows for easy access and viewing. Since your photos and videos should already be in a photo album or box, you may not have to use additional organizers to pack your shelves tightly. However, stabilize photo albums that can tip sideways in a handled basket or crate, which is also good for moving them around the house. It is best to label containers in date order.

Storing photo albums in a drawer is generally a mistake. Stacking photo albums in a drawer makes accessing those at the bottom hard since you have to remove all the other albums first. Also, those on the bottom can become damaged overtime. Filing them upright in a drawer makes it hard to grasp the binder, and there is no way to know which album is which because you can only view the tops of the albums.

Boxes or containers of photos and videos can be stored in a drawer, but don't stack more than one on top of another because the weight could potentially crush those at the bottom. Photo boxes are also not ideal for drawer storage since they're designed to grab and read from the sides, which are hidden in a drawer. Also, they cannot store sideways in a drawer without their tops falling off.

Home videos can be stored in drawers, but only sideways where the spines of the disc cases are visible. It's also a good idea to keep the disc cases in a stable drawer container so they stay in place from drawer movement.

Games-and-Toys Armoires

There never seems to be enough places to store games and toys. An armoire or wardrobe closet can certainly help contain a good number of them, plus keep them out of sight. A games-and-toys armoire would work well in a den, kitchen, office, basement, playroom, or any bedroom. It's important to think about the best place to situate one, especially when these items belong to small children. For example, a child's bedroom might not always be the best place unless there is enough space in the bedroom and he or she regularly plays there. A child who needs to be monitored while playing with certain toys should not have the temptation of a toys-and-games armoire in their own room.

Arranging a games-and-toys armoire is simple; a set of adjustable shelves and a few basic organizers should do it. Items like board games, art kits, or project kits don't necessarily need organizers if they're boxed. These items can stack on shelves with the smaller boxes on top graduating down to the biggest, but no higher than waist level where they're hard to see. Any boxed game or toy should remain in the original box, which is essentially an organizer labeled with its contents and sometimes a picture of the item. When reorganizing, reinforce worn boxes with clear packing tape.

Loose toys, such as action figures, toy cars, stuffed animals, dolls, balls, and so on, should be separated and stored in their own containers. Large quantities of a particular group of items can be further broken down, divided by size, and then containerized. For example, a large collection of balls can be containerized by size—small, medium, and large—in standard open-top plastic containers. To achieve a uniform appearance, select all medium-size containers that are big enough to store things yet small enough to move and lift. However, the best containers are bins with wide-cutout front openings for easy access, where they don't even have to leave the shelf.

A wardrobe closet should already have a hanging rod, but it's not hard to install one in an armoire. It can hold dress-up clothes or tiered, canvas hanging shelves to separate items. These organizers can store boxed games, electronic games, doll clothes/blankets, stuffed animals, and so on, either loosely or in containers. Some tiered shelves have tabs for labeling, making toy classification easy. Clear-pocket organizers are also designed to hang from a rod. These organizers can accommodate small toys or accessories, like dress-up jewelry, play money, key chains, cards, and more.

Don't overlook the inside of armoire doors for storage opportunities. Provided there is enough space when the door is closed, mount shallow wire baskets on them. Small or thin articles, such as playing cards, flashcards, notebooks, crayon boxes, paint sets, and so on, are easily stored in such baskets. There are also a number of pocketed organizers that can be mounted there. Some have clear plastic pockets and others mesh or canvas; these organizers can hold an array of small toys and games.

Bar Armoires

An armoire can make a great place to serve and house liquor, along with the necessary glasses, ice buckets, condiments, and barware cocktail tool sets. A serving-bar armoire can be placed in any entertainment area, such as a kitchen, den, living room, sunroom, family room, and even an expansive foyer; when closed, it just looks like a handsome piece of furniture.

There are many entertainment-bar armoires sold on the market; most have doors with built-in shelves to hold wine and liquor bottles, which is a great feature. Unfortunately, they can be quite expensive. It's possible to create your own bar armoire. Some of the best ideas are to use wine racks, mirrored backsplash, glass shelves, overhead glass racks, overhead lighting, and tiered liquor shelves. Florescent or LED lighting can be added below a Lucite or glass liquor stand, thus highlighting the bottles and providing a party atmosphere to your bar armoire.

An entertainment-bar armoire has limited space, which can be increased by adding a pull-out shelf to a counter-height shelf also used for serving. To economize space, cut down to just the basic or frequently used barware tools, such as a cocktail shaker, ice bucket, scoop, tongs, strainer, jigger, bar spoon, corkscrew, muddler, and some speed pourers. Keep infrequently needed items in a container located on top of the armoire or in the kitchen. Small barware hand tools can be kept in a compartmentalized utility-tray drawer like those used in the kitchen to separate cooking tools. You can also hang them from a simple peg rack anywhere, including the inside of an armoire door. Barware tools are typically sold in sets that come on a rack stand, which can either be wall

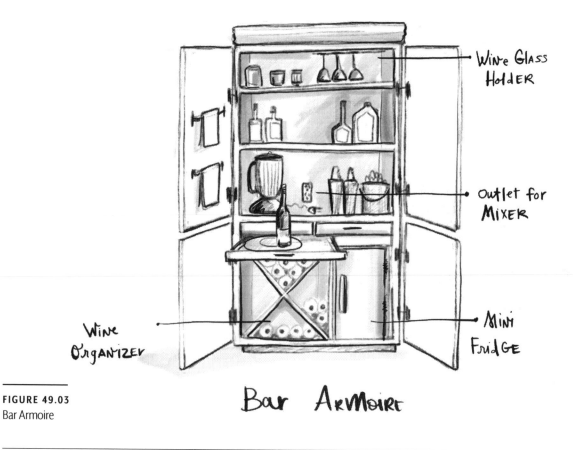

FIGURE 49.03
Bar Armoire

Bar Armoire

mounted inside the armoire or rest on a serving shelf or built-in counter.

Bar linens, such as towels, napkins, and rags, are needed in a bar armoire. Pullout drawers and baskets can be added to a bar armoire to hold the necessary linens. Towel bars or hooks could be added to an interior wall of the armoire or installed on the inside of a door. There is also a combination shelf-and-towel-bar organizer sold as a kitchen aid that can store drink condiments, whiskey stones, tools, and other small bar items. This organizer is designed to be wall mounted; with the proper hardware, it can secure onto the back wall of the armoire's interior.

Due to common space constraints in a bar armoire, it may be possible to stock only your favorites or the main liquors, like vodka, whiskey, gin, scotch, tequila, brandy, and bottled mixers. These bottles are great to line along the back of an armoire shelf or situate on a tiered liquor shelf. Collections of unopened wines are great to lay flat in the base of the armoire on cross-style partitions or cubicle openings. Rolling shelves with slots to hold bottles is another option for storing unopened bottles of hard liquor, mixers, and wines.

Limit your glasses to six or eight per type. Hang stem glasses on overhead stemware racks, which hold them securely upside down in between slots. All other glasses and special decanters should rest on or near eye-level shelving.

Bar gadgets, such as wine chillers, beverage dispensers, red wine aerators, water bottle fruit infusers, and garnish trays, can be held on a lower shelf or inside a cabinet. Similarly, excess alcohol, sodas, water, mixers, and the like can also be stored here.

Keep beverage garnishes, condiments, stirrers, straws, toothpicks, wine rings, cocktail umbrellas, or anything that accompanies a drink nearby.

Cup- or glass-style organizers are great for holding all these items, except for bottled garnishes and condiments that are already self-contained. Arrange these organizers in a row on a shelf or inside a basket. A caddy organizer is another solution for segregating and corralling these items. Plus, you have a handle to carry it back and forth from a lower cabinet or shelf to the serving counter.

A bar armoire can also supplement an existing bar as a storage cabinet for spirits, sodas, water, mixers, condiments, and glasses. A bar armoire that is used only for storage simply requires basic shelves, drawers, or specialized racks to hold glasses, spirits, and beverages.

Laundry Armoires

Using an armoire or wardrobe closet to house laundry supplies is perfect when you don't have cabinets or closets to store them near the laundry appliances. There are ways to convert almost any armoire into a place to fold, sort, and stack clothing or linens. It's rather simple to arrange a basic laundry armoire.

A great advantage to using an armoire or wardrobe closet for laundry items is that related belongings are neatly tucked out of sight. With room to spare, you can store other items in your laundry armoire, like paper products, a waste basket, first aid kits, air fresheners, cleaners, pet toys, lint brushes, stools, a sewing box, and other hard-to-place items.

Laundry items that are used regularly, such as detergents, softeners, stain removers, dryer sheets, and dryer balls, need to be grouped together and stored in the most accessible location within the armoire. A waist-level or eye-level shelf works best. Use a tray or line the shelf so spills or drips are easy to wipe clean.

Ironing supplies like spray bottles, spray starch, wrinkle-removing spray, and hot-iron cleaners can be kept together in a handled caddy. There are wall-mounted organizers that hold the ironing board and iron, plus compartments for supplies. Such organizers can be mounted on the exterior side of an armoire.

Depending on the size, tabletop ironing boards can be stored inside the laundry armoire or even on top of the cabinet. Ironing accessories, like collar points, skirt clips, iron rest, ironing pads, and fasteners, can be kept in a drawer, bin, or caddy. Also, small ironing accessories can be stored in clear-pocketed organizers attached to the inside of an armoire door.

An interior hanging rod placed within a laundry armoire should hold only spare hangers and not clothes, because hanging clothes there leaves little room for storage. For additional hanging clothes storage, install a small hanging rod on the exterior side of the armoire or to an adjacent wall. Use a wall-mounted closet shelf with a rod or wall-mounted coatrack to hang clothes.

Another way to store spare hangers is in a hanger holder. A hanger hamper organizer is a handled canvas container in an elongated triangle that matches the shape of a hanger. The height of the hamper allows for a number of hangers to

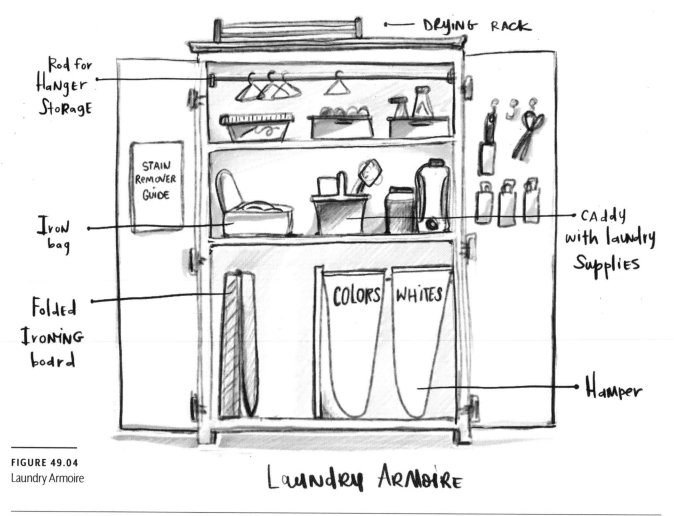

FIGURE 49.04
Laundry Armoire

securely stack inside without tangling together. The handles make the organizer transportable so you can move from closet to closet, collecting hangers. There is also a freestanding hanger storage device, in which hangers fit around and stack onto arched wire metal loops. This organizer is also transportable using the top of the arch as a handle. Both these organizers can rest on a shelf or on the floor of the armoire. Also, you can store one or more of these organizers on the top of your laundry armoire.

Laundry baskets take up a good deal of space. How you use your laundry baskets will determine their role in your laundry armoire. For example, if your laundry baskets fill up at different locations throughout your home and then unload in your laundry room, there is no need to create space for them in your laundry armoire. However, should your laundry baskets start in the laundry room, where they fill with cleaned clothes to disperse to their storage locations, a stack of them could be kept in or on top of your laundry armoire. Alternatively, you may desire to use laundry baskets in your laundry room to hold special-care items or clothes that require dry-cleaning. In these situations, place laundry baskets used for these purposes on the armoire shelves or at the base of the armoire cabinet.

A laundry armoire can conceal hampers that sort dirty laundry into classifications like whites and darks. There are many pullout hamper organizers and wire baskets that can be installed in an armoire or wardrobe closet for this purpose. You can also use a handled tote, mesh laundry bag, or collapsible hampers to sort clothes; these organizers are affordable and easy to arrange on an armoire shelf.

A must-have for any laundry armoire is a pull-out shelf. Installing a counter-height pullout shelf creates additional space for sorting, folding, and even ironing clothes.

A foldable drying rack is a great laundry-room item that is perfect to pack up and hide away in a laundry armoire when not in use. The top of the armoire is good place to keep big drying racks.

Gardening Armoires

An official place to keep gardening supplies is a true benefit for any level of gardener. An armoire is a great organizer for containing a number of gardening supplies, if you don't have outside storage. Dirt left behind on used pots and tools is inevitable, so keep a gardening armoire in an environment where cleanup is easy. Places like a mudroom, kitchen, or garage are the best locations for a gardening armoire.

Key placement needs to be given for the garden tools. Short-handled tools can be stored in a garden bag that travels with you as you work. Keep your garden bag hung on a hook or placed on shelf inside your gardening armoire. Also consider keeping gardening gloves and kneeling pads in your gardening tote, as well.

Wall-mounted magnetic bars, commonly designed to hold metal handyman tools, can also hold metal garden tools like pruning shears or trowels. It's important to know that magnetic bars have weight-bearing capacities, so abide by these weight limitations and plan your space accordingly. Medium- to long-handled tools can hang neatly on a peg or hook rack mounted to the interior back wall. The main idea is for your tools to be easy to see and access.

Lower shelves or base cabinets situated in the armoire can store bigger or heavier items, such as pots, watering cans, seed starting kits, grow lights, fertilizers, mulch, potting soil, and wire plant supports. Composting pails, along with accompanying accessories like liner bags or carbon/charcoal filters, can also be stored in this same area. Secure unsafe items, like weed and pest control supplies, in a drawer or enclosed cabinet within the armoire.

Upper shelves can house gardening books, plant food, bird seeds, soil testers, garden ornaments, or lightweight baskets. Nothing too heavy or big should be kept overhead, for safety reasons. Install an under-mount paper-towel holder beneath a high shelf. Likewise, wire baskets that slide on and hang below the shelf can hold cleaning rags or napkins for quick cleanups, which are to be expected at such a location.

Seeds are important to systematize for certain gardeners. Seeds that need to first grow in seed starting pots should be kept separately in alphabetical order. Arrange all other seeds by the month they need to be planted in the garden. Card file boxes are good organizers for housing packaged seeds. Individual containers marked with a month or a letter of the alphabet is another way to put your seeds in order.

The inside of the armoire door is a good place to mount peg boards, magnetic boards, and even wire shelf racks to hold lightweight garden belongings. Figure out how to display articles so they're easy to see and access. For example, punch holes in your garden gloves and hang them from a peg hook. Any item with a loop, like a gardening tool belt or an apron, can hang from a hook attached to a board. Planting instructions or any important written gardening information can adhere to wall-mounted boards. Wall-mounted wire racks can store cup-style organizers for holding items like plant tags, plant ties, clips, markers, scissors, twine, string, and so on.

A pullout table is a great accessory to add to a gardening armoire, especially when preparing seed starting kits or pots at this location. Also, a pullout table can be used for a number of other purposes, such as reading gardening books, drawing landscape plans, and composting tasks.

Don't overlook the top of the armoire for storage. Infrequently used or off-season items are good for this out-of-the-way location. You can also place related outdoor items on the roof of your armoire. Larger lightweight items, like outdoor cushions and pillows, are good choices.

Armoires for Any Function

Armoires or wardrobe closets have endless storage possibilities, making them useful in almost any home. These furniture pieces are inexpensive and easy to find at most resale stores. Think about your home and decide whether you have rooms or closets where space is running thin. Armoires and wardrobe closets can act as a storage extension to a closet, kitchen cabinet, or dining room china cabinet. They can contain entertainment items for a party or tableware that may otherwise be scattered throughout the home.

Armoires and wardrobe closets make great workstations for almost any hobby, such as photography, metalworking, fishing, model building, and so on. Many personal collections, such as records, statues, action figures, and so, are ideal to place in an armoire by simply removing the doors to create an open show cabinet. Their uses are limited only by your imagination.

PART SIX

Mudrooms and Garages

CHAPTER 50

Mudrooms

A mudroom is commonly located in the rear of a home with its own entrance; it acts as a buffer zone from the outside to contain outdoor grime so the rest of your house stays clean. Mudrooms are places in the home that can serve different duties, such as sports equipment and gear storage, footwear storage, gardening projects, or pet grooming. Being a multipurpose space can, unfortunately, create difficulty in prioritizing what should be stored in the mudroom. The ambiguous nature of the mudroom, coupled with common space limitations, make the room challenging to organize.

Mudrooms tend to lack closets, and many are commonly combined with other rooms, such as a laundry room or kitchen. Mudrooms are atypical rooms since they have two doorways: one entrance from the outside and another leading to other parts of the home. This often shapes these rooms into a tunnel or passageway, which makes them tricky to organize.

The following is a list of the popular items stored in the typical mudroom. It's important to create your priority list of these articles so it's clear what to leave out, should space constraints arise.

Leftover items can be relocated to areas such as the garage, attic, shed, basement, or storage closet:

- Art and crafts items
- Backpacks, tote bags, health club bags, briefcases, and purses
- Cleaning tools and household cleaners
- Clock
- Daily worn footwear, outerwear, and accessories (e.g., eyewear, gloves, hats)
- Doormats and boot trays
- Electronic devices, audio/video equipment, and charging stations
- Fire extinguishers, flashlights, and emergency candles
- First aid kit: poison ivy lotion, insect repellant, burn ointments, sunscreen
- Freezer or second refrigerator
- Gardening tote/supplies
- Message station: corkboards, writing boards, key organizers, and mail sorters
- Pet supplies: leashes, litter box, pet dishes, cage, and pet toys
- Picnic baskets, blankets, and coolers

- School textbooks, library books, reference manuals, and maps
- Shoe cleaning supplies
- Sitting bench
- Sporting goods
- Tool box with basics and combination locks
- Umbrellas and stands
- Wastebasket and recycling bins
- Water cooler, water bottles, and bottled water

The Mudroom Organizational Process

It's best to follow certain steps when you organize a mudroom, in order to stay on track and decrease the risk of becoming overwhelmed. Each step is designed to handle a distinct part of the mudroom that needs to be completed in its entirety before moving on to the next one.

Step One: Optional

Purchase a notebook with pockets to store information about the organizational project. Use your notebook to create lists, ideas, and space measurements and gather information on storage organizers. Make a list of all home-maintenance repairs you discover while organizing, like a loose hinge. Such repairs tend to be a distraction and by writing them down, you are able to stay on track with an organizing project.

Create a shopping list for items that require replacement or are just needed. The most important list to create when you organize a mudroom is one ranking the belongings that need to occupy the space, in order of importance. Since every household prioritizes a unique set of items to store in a mudroom, clarifying them in a list is beneficial. This is also necessary when dealing with small spaces or in mudrooms that share space with another room, such as a laundry room.

Step Two: Removing Items That Don't Belong

The mudroom is a notorious dumping ground for everything, so it's important to return things back to their original storage places. There may be those items that don't have a home anywhere, including a designated spot in the mudroom. Now is the time to determine whether they qualify for mudroom storage or need to be stored elsewhere.

Often, the mudroom fills with articles that seek only temporary storage, such as gifts, library books, returns, dry cleaning, and donations. These items usually find themselves left on countertops or floors, which crowds space. To avoid this problem, consider transferring such items to your automobile, which is where they tend to end up anyway. You can also plan a spot for them in a mudroom that gets them off the floor and other surfaces, such as a wall-mounted shelf or a designated cabinet compartment.

It's common to make the mudroom a place to store household items that need repair, like a broken picture frame or camera since it's a visible location where you'll not forget about them. If you have such items that have not left the mudroom for months, it may be worthwhile to have them repaired by someone else, provided the cost does not exceed the item's value. Getting into the habit of immediately determining whether a repair is worthwhile can get them in route to a repair center or stop them from collecting in the first place. For now, it's important to label and box the DIY repairs and move all others off to a repair center.

Step Three: Start Decluttering Everything Else

Use bins or cardboard boxes and label them with the following classifications: "Donate," "Sell," "Relocate," and "Trash" for sorting items. Start reducing by first removing the trash, such as old papers, expired sunscreen, or broken flashlights. Consider relocating or removing items that are not working in the space to another location. For example, a water cooler may have been more of an inconvenience and a space hog with all the hefty refillable bottle storage requirements. It could be time to get rid of that water cooler and opt for refrigerated bottles to reclaim space.

Step Four: Downsizing Outerwear and Footwear

Outerwear and footwear are popular articles to store in the mudroom since it's next to an exterior door. The problem with many mudrooms, though, is that it's easy to allow too many coats, jackets, shoes, and boots to pile up and congest this space. Most often, the average mudroom is incapable of accommodating such storage demands, thus turning the space into a disorganized mess. The best way to manage outerwear and footwear in a mudroom is by only keeping articles used daily in the space. Also, limit each household member to just a few coats, jackets, or pairs of footwear.

When your mudroom is currently overstuffed with footwear and outwear, sort and declutter it in the same way as a bedroom closet. That means grouping all like items together and then downsizing them. Since a mudroom is a community space, you'll be dealing with outerwear and footwear that belong to others; consult with household members before repairing or moving their items elsewhere. Generally, it's best to pack away off-season outerwear and footwear and move infrequently used

articles into better places, such as bedroom closets, front hallway closets, guest-room closets, or storage rooms.

Footwear is commonly easier for people to part with because wear is evident, and shoes usually dictate current fashion. Outerwear, on the other hand, tends to be more classically designed and stays in style longer; articles also hold their shapes well. Jackets and coats are often perceived to be more valuable because they tend to cost more and are necessity items. For these reasons, reducing collections of outerwear can be trying, but it's important to keep only what has been actually receiving use in the past two years.

Step Five: Storing Remaining Mudroom Items

Many different types of belongings can occupy a mudroom. The following items are commonly stored in a mudroom, and detailed storage options are included.

Sporting Goods

A mudroom is an ideal place to store sporting goods, especially in lieu of a garage. Sheds and garages that receive extreme humid, hot, or cold temperatures are not always suitable places for sporting goods made from wood, leather, and certain metals. Mudrooms outfitted with a bench are convenient for putting on difficult sport shoes. Storage lockers are great for uniforms and sporting goods. A sink in a mudroom, if it's possible to have one, makes for a convenient place to clean dirty sports equipment.

Decluttering Sports Equipment

Before you establish a place for sporting goods in the mudroom, make certain to declutter all the current equipment so you are only storing what is actually used and enjoyed. Gather containers to collect items: Donation, Sale, Trash, Off-Season, or Relocate. Sort sporting equipment by type and then go through the various piles and get rid of items that are broken, worn, or no longer used. It's easy to see wear and access damage on sports equipment, which makes the decluttering process easier than with other types of articles. All retired sports gear, plus older equipment that has been replaced with new, should be tossed into the Donation or Sell container.

It's necessary to decide which sporting goods should go where in the home when they all cannot fit in one location like the mudroom or garage. Just eyeballing your storage options should offer insight into storage solutions. Most mudrooms are not large enough to handle the storage demands of sporting goods belonging to a family of sport enthusiasts. Even a single household member engaged in a few different sports can accumulate a number of sporting goods that cannot ever squeeze into the best-designed mudrooms. Under such circumstances, you may need to devise a plan or system to handle large quantities of sporting goods. The following options can be helpful:

Option One
Store in your mudroom only those sporting goods that are used all year round. Plan to keep in-season sporting goods in the garage, shed, basement, or personal closet space. Off-season sporting goods should be packed away in overhead garage compartments, closets, the attic, or the basement. A sport that is played year round should have its own or specialized organizational system that can hold everything. For example, for a sport like tennis, use a wall-mounted storage device in your mudroom that can hold a racket, tennis balls, and a pair of tennis shoes.

Option Two
Rotate sporting goods storage according to seasons. Store the off-season sporting goods outside the mudroom and keep only in-season and year-round equipment in the mudroom. In this storage arrangement, seasonal items will require an adjustable storage essential since sporting goods will share it, rotating from season to season.

The main drawback to switching out sports equipment in storage from season to season is the work involved in adjusting and arranging.

Option Three
Store only certain items in the mudroom or bedrooms and the rest somewhere else. Divide sports-related items and keep the bigger and bulkier items, like balls, rackets, sticks, pads, bats, cages, helmets, bags, golf clubs, and so on in the garage or shed. Store smaller items, such as cleats, shoes, gloves, goggles, uniforms, mouth guards, and so on, in the mudroom or bedrooms. You may also want to keep favorite sports equipment in the mudroom and everything else in garage.

It's also a good idea to keep in the mudroom or bedrooms only expensive sporting goods or items that can degrade from harsh climatic conditions in the garage and store everything else in the garage or shed. Once you decide which sporting goods you desire in the mudroom, set them aside until the entire room is thoroughly decluttered.

Pet Supplies
It's often hard to find the right place for pet supplies since they don't logically fit in a particular room as dishes do in a kitchen. However, a mudroom with a sink is an ideal place to fill and prepare dishes and clean all pet belongings. Also, pets may use the mudroom door on a daily basis, making it a convenient spot for outdoor toys, clothes, leashes,

and so on. However, where your pet plays, rests, and eats will have the biggest impact of where pet items should go.

Begin organizing pet items by categorizing them into groups—for example, toys, food, leashes, medications, and so on. Use bags or containers and label them Donate, Trash, Sell, and Relocate when you sort through your pet items. How to organize each category of pet belongings follows.

Pet Toys

It should be obvious which pet toys need to be thrown away since these will be the ones that are broken or worn to threads. The toys that never get played with should be donated or sold at the next garage sale. All the toys that you want to keep should store in easy-to-access open containers in places where they're visible, so they receive use. It may be necessary to divide toys between different locations. For instance, toys taken outside the home can be stored in the mudroom and those played indoors can be housed near the pets' beds.

Pet Food, Treats, Medicines, Vitamins, and Dishes

Food and treats your pets won't eat need to go. Store open bags of dry pet food in airtight containers for optimal freshness. Bulk quantities of these foods benefit from organizers designed especially for them, such as the large wheeled pet food containers. These organizers are designed for floor storage, which may be a good option in your mudroom. Treats can be kept in canisters and jars in cabinets or on shelves or countertops.

It's important to keep only a couple sets of pet dishes and water bowls since it's easy to form a collection through the years. Store pet food dishes with the food near where the pets are fed. If the mudroom has a sink, any location near the sink is perfect for these items.

All medications and vitamins can be stored in a separate container like a compartmentalized caddy. Lazy Susan turntable organizers that spin around are also great for holding medications and vitamins. These organizers can rest on a shelf. Make certain to follow storage instructions for medications.

Leash, Harness, Muzzle, and Collar

Go through all the leashes, harnesses, muzzles, and collars and get rid of those that are never used or are broken. No more than two of each of these items is necessary to keep on hand per pet. When your pet travels outside the home, it's good to keep a leash and collar inside the glove box of the car in case you forget to bring one or they break while you are out.

All these items are best stored in the mudroom when pets enter and exit the home from this location. Leashes, collars, muzzles, and harnesses can be stored on a wall-mounted peg or coat organizer. They can also be placed in a divided drawer organizer, where each item can be rolled up, bound, and placed in a separate compartment to prevent tangling.

Grooming Supplies

Mudrooms are common places to groom pets when the room provides a sink or pet washing station. In lieu of a sink, shaving and brushing can be performed in a mudroom designed to handle mess.

Begin organizing grooming supplies by sorting everything into categories, such as brushes, powders, shampoos, electronic gadgets, dental care, and towels. Then go through each pile, getting rid of the broken or expired items and those that are never used. In general, one of each of the following can accommodate a certain type of pet:

- Shaving kit with trimmer, clipper, scissors, and combs
- Two bottles pet shampoo, one powder
- Two brushes
- Two to three towels
- One toothbrush, one tube of toothpaste, and one oral care powder or rinse

Store all grooming supplies in a single compartmentalized, handled caddy kept in a mudroom closet, cabinet, or shelf. Portable organizers like caddies are good to use when grooming duties are taken to a different room. Grooming supplies can also be divided between daily and occasional use. For example, daily-used brushes and oral care products can be stored in a drawer tray, while infrequently used shaving tools, shampoos, and towels can be stored in an overhead compartment or under the sink.

Waste-Disposal Items and Litter

Pet-waste-disposal items, like dog-waste bags, can keep in a couple places, such as the car plus a mudroom location next to the leashes. Store dispensing roll refills along with other pet litter supplies, such as training pads, kitty litter, cage bedding, and the like. Always contain loose waste bags by compacting them into a dispensing device or pouch. A recycled tissue box works well.

Transfer litter products that come in flimsy packaging to plastic containers. Bulky containers can be housed in base cabinets or on lower shelving. Certain hampers, trash cans, and wheeled pet-food containers can successfully contain bulk quantities of litter and work well in mudrooms. Litter tools, such as scoopers, should reside near

the cage or litter box. Place them on a wall hook or attach them to the cage or litter box.

Pet Carriers, Bags, and Cages

Keep only the pet carriers, cages, and pet-carrying bags that are used and get rid of those that have been outgrown or belonged to past animals. Most often, pet carriers and bags are seldom needed. For this reason, it's not necessary to store them with other pet supplies that may require key placement in the mudroom. Such items can be stored in overhead compartments in the mudroom or in other places like sheds, basements, and storage rooms.

Pet Clothing/Accessories

It's important to first recognize whether your pets are actually wearing clothing and accessories on a regular basis. Cold weather, rain, or holidays should bring about a need to use many of these items. When your pet seldom uses clothing and accessories, it's important to retain just a few, keeping only the best.

Begin organizing your pet clothing and accessories by sorting them into categories like hats, jackets, T-shirts, bows, costumes, and so on. Go through the piles, eliminating items that are never worn, are ruined, or don't fit. Keep clothing and accessories categorized by type in storage containers. Use open baskets or bins for frequently used items. Infrequently used items can be stored in stackable containers.

Pet Paperwork

Store any significant paperwork pertaining to your pet, such as medical records, licenses, and the like, in a digital or manual file. Make a separate file for each pet. Set up reminders in your calendar system for pet checkups and vaccinations. Actual documents can be kept with other household papers, such as landscaping or home appliances. Translucent hard plastic project cases are designed to hold and protect papers. These organizers can stack with others, creating a file system, or by themselves. Such organizers are perfect for containing pet papers, and they can store in a mudroom drawer or on a shelf.

Electronic Devices

A mudroom is a convenient location to store and charge mobile electronic devices, such as cellular phones, e-readers, gaming devices, cameras, and tablets. A great idea is to install an outlet inside an upper cabinet, cubby, drawer, or closet to create an electronic charging station. You can use an integrated charging station or one with interchangeable connector tips to store and charge multiple electronic devices in a contained area.

Backpacks, Totes, Purses, and Briefcases/Satchels

School backpacks, gym bags, grocery totes, work briefcases, and handbags are convenient to store in a mudroom, where they're easy to grab on the way out the door. It's important to store only the currently used gym bags, totes, and the like in the mudroom. Collections of briefcases, satchels, handbags, and purses are often stored in bedroom closets, whereas groups of backpacks, totes, and sports bags are typically housed in common areas of the home, such as a mudroom or hall closet.

It's important to downsize these belongings when they reside in the mudroom. When organizing backpacks, totes, and sports bags, lay them all out and check for wear on zippers, straps, Velcro closures, and so on. Some may need cleaning, which can usually be handled with a damp towel and dish soap. It's important to consult with household members before getting rid of their

bags. However, make sure they know how many they have of each type beforehand since generally no more than two of each is necessary.

Storage Arrangements

Larger lidded, labeled containers can store excess totes, backpacks, gym bags, and the like—in the mudroom closets or overhead locations are best. Currently used handbags, satchels, briefcases, totes and sports bags require easy access since they're typically grabbed on the way out the door. Open storage arrangements, like wall hooks, cubby organizers, shelving units, and locker-style organizers, are the best ways to situate these items in the mudroom.

Keys and Mail

Keys are probably one of the most critical household items. It's important to organize them well since they start cars and open safes, doors, sheds, locks, and so on. Begin organizing your keys by dividing them into categories like house, office, cars, parents, neighbors, and so on. Make sure to investigate the "mystery" keys that tend to accumulate over the years. Go through these keys and match them up to others or test them in doors, on locks, and so on until you determine where they all belong. Definitely discard the ones you cannot figure out.

Obtaining a key box to house spare or infrequently used keys is a great investment. Key chains that have identification tags for labeling are perfect for storing spares. The color-coded varieties can classify keys into groups: house, office, shed, safes, and so on. You can also color-code keys by using different nail polish colors.

It's a good plan to have one main key box that holds one or two sets of each key. This key box should be stored in a private location, like inside a cabinet, closet, or drawer since you'll want to keep people from making a habit out of grabbing these keys, which should only be used when a set is permanently lost. A locking key box can add controls.

For everyday needed keys, a wall-mounted combination mail and key holder is perfect next to the entrance door in a mudroom. It's a good place to keep unread mail until you are able to sort through it.

Gardening Equipment

A gardening shed or garage is the ideal location to keep gardening equipment. However, it may be necessary to use the mudroom for some or all of these items due to space constraints. Decluttering gardening items starts with sorting everything into categories, such as clothes, tools, pots, seeds, fertilizer, and so on. Go through the different groups of items, getting rid of ripped gloves, cracked pots, or tools that don't work. Each household gardener will need one or two (at the most) of each tool; a single apron, hat, tool belt, pair of gardening shoes, and pair of gloves are sufficient.

A dedicated gardener needs a workable and organized space. If there is room, plan a counter space in the mudroom where all the necessary gardening supplies are within reach, near a sink, if available. Wall shelves are great for holding supplies over a gardening station for pots, plant foods, pesticides, seed starter kits, gardening ornaments, and so on. A well-equipped gardening tote with compartments for everything—one that is lightweight to travel outside—is a good organizer to stash in the mudroom.

In some homes, it makes sense to store certain items in the garage or shed and others in the mudroom. For instance, gardening hats, aprons, tool belts, shoes, and gardening totes can be stored in the mudroom, whereas soil, fertilizer, carts, seeds, and large tools can be kept in a shed or garage.

Musical Instruments

An actively played instrument that travels in and out of the home on a regular basis is convenient to store in the mudroom, where it needs to remain in its protective carrying case. It can be stored in an individual locker or next to where the backpacks, briefcases, purses, totes, and the like are kept.

Recycling Bins

It's convenient to place recycling bins in the mudroom, especially when there is a door leading to the curbside recycling containers. Select the appropriate size bins for what you need them to hold in between pickups so you are efficient with your space.

Thermoses, Coolers, Water Bottles, and Picnic Baskets

Generally, where your thermos, water bottle, cooler, and picnic basket are filled should also be the place to store them. Kitchens are common places for this activity; however, the mudroom is a good spot for certain water bottles or thermoses that go to school, work, sporting events, and the gym. These types of items can be placed right inside the cubby, locker, backpack, briefcase, or gym bag stationed in the mudroom so they'll not be forgotten at home

Typically, items like picnic baskets, larger thermoses, and coolers take up too much valuable space in a kitchen, making them more suitable to store in a mudroom, shed, garage, or basement. As seldom-needed items, store them in overhead storage compartments or in base cabinets located in the mudroom.

Eyewear

Eyewear collections, especially sunglasses, are convenient to store in a mudroom. However, certain pairs of eyewear are also convenient to keep in a car, desk, nightstand, briefcase, satchel, or purse. Each household member's eyewear can be stored in a personal locker, drawer, cubby, or basket designated for them in the mudroom. It's necessary that household members be responsible for decluttering his or her own eyewear, which entails discarding broken, out-of-style, and no longer needed or liked pairs. Every pair of eyewear needs its own case or should be stored in an organizer designed especially for it.

There are all types of eyewear organizers. Drawer organizers are made with individual compartments to separate each pair so they don't touch. Countertop and wall organizers for eyewear are similar in design to how they're showcased in stores. Usually, these organizers are tiered and the lenses face forward so each pair is easy to see. A multipurpose wall organizer that holds a number of common mudroom articles, like keys, notepads, eyewear, pens, and the like, is another storage solution when limited pairs are involved.

Household Message Board

Given that a mudroom is a place most household members frequent, a community message board makes for an effective central communication station. You can post reminders about parties, schedules, birthdays, appointments, errands, and so on. A message board can also occupy untapped wall space.

Rain Gear

Every member of the household needs one umbrella or a rain poncho, if they wear one. A few golf umbrellas are also convenient to stock since they're larger and useful for many sports and outdoor events.

When your umbrella collection resides in the mudroom, declutter it. Go through all the umbrellas and open them up, checking for damage. Discard the broken umbrellas and count the number left to see if you have enough for everyone. An excess of umbrellas is not a bad thing since they're easy to lose and break; plus, they don't take up that much storage space, especially the compact ones, which are always advisable to buy.

Each automobile should have one to two umbrellas or ponchos. The large golf umbrellas can be stored near the golf clubs or in the car, as well. When they're closed and bound, several umbrellas can collect in an umbrella stand or a single pullout basket, bin, or drawer in the mudroom. Individual umbrellas can hang from wall-mounted coat hooks or pegs, or in each personal compartment like a cubby or locker.

Wastebasket/Hamper

Every mudroom needs a wastebasket. A freestanding lidded model can reside on the floor next to a sink, recycling bin, or door. A pullout wastebasket can be mounted in a base cabinet, and many closet systems have trash can accessory organizers.

A hamper is a useful addition to a mudroom for messy items, like beach towels, rags, or messy sports uniforms, so they don't track dirt through a clean house. Like trash cans, hampers come in freestanding models and as a cabinet or closet-system pullout organizer.

Benches

A place to sit while putting on and removing footwear is a welcome addition to any mudroom. A bench designed with storage compartments beneath the seat can contain a number of mudroom items; those designed with shelves can hold footwear, sporting goods, and baskets for smaller articles like hats and gloves. Some storage benches are designed with shoe cubbies and pullout baskets beneath the seat. It's easy to create storage below an existing bench that does not have anything.

Countless floor footwear organizers, primarily designed for closets, are available that could fit beneath a bench. Many are formed with shelves and cubby compartments; some are even wheeled for added convenience. You can also place a boot tray beneath a bench. Place cleaning tools, such as boot scrapers and brushes, inside the tray so it's convenient to clean messy sports cleats and muddy boots.

A multiple purpose room such as the mudroom can store many different items. Therefore, smart storage planning is required given space limitations.

It is best to create a priority list of the most important articles to store in the mudroom in case they cannot all fit.

CHAPTER 51

Organizing a Mudroom

Only when all the mudroom belongings are downsized can you successfully arrange the room. At this point, you know which items will remain in the room, so it's easier to determine the amount of space needed. You'll also be able to select the appropriate storage organizers sized in proportion to what they're intended to hold.

Depending upon the amount of work necessary to complete your mudroom organizational project, using a notebook to record measurements and draw room sketches can help plan your space accurately. Good measurements to take are room dimensions, accounting for doors, windows, or any obstructions. Same goes for any closets. Then sketch a diagram of the room, figuring that any fixed organizers are staying, such as a closet system or shelving. Before shopping for anything, settle on a budget.

When you need to purchase new organizers or a closet system, do some research first, because there are many to choose from. Search online or in specialty storage and organization stores. Make a list of the organizers that appeal to you and their dimensions. Check prices so you can make the best choice given a budget.

Thoroughly clean and paint the entire mudroom, if desired. Whether you plan your mudroom in your head or on paper, purchase any needed organizers or closet systems and begin to put the room together. The following illustrations show many ways a mudroom can be arranged, given different budgets, which will dictate the types of organizational essentials or closet systems chosen. Recognize the option to mix high-end, middle ground, and budget-friendly organizers in the same mudroom.

Upscale Mudroom

There are many things to include in an upgraded mudroom. First and foremost, good quality cabinetry marks a high-end mudroom. Since a mudroom typically takes a beating, it's important that your cabinets are solid and come with heavy-duty hardware that can handle abuse. Investing in mudroom cabinetry is a good choice when the room is viewed from entertainment areas like a kitchen or family room.

Cabinetry is the ultimate organizer since it can be outfitted with many accessories that contain items perfectly. It also hides everything. A pantry cabinet may be a good option, if space allows. Standard heights for pantry cabinets are eighty-four inches, ninety inches, and ninety-six inches. Standard pantry cabinet widths vary more than height, ranging between nine inches and thirty-six inches, typically in three-inch increments (nine inches, twelve inches, fifteen inches, eighteen inches, etc.).

A pantry cabinet can resemble a closet and be equipped with multiple pullout shelves for footwear, sports equipment, totes, sports bags, backpacks, briefcases, pet supplies, picnic baskets, audio/video equipment, and so on. Basic stationary shelving placed in a pantry needs to be adjustable to respond changing storage needs. Cleaning supplies and tools are also perfect items for cabinet pantry storage. Mount stationary pegs or retractable hook organizers onto the inside walls of the pantry for holding items like brooms, mops, dustpans, dusters, and the like. Add overhead shelving and use the floor to place cleaners, hand tools, buckets, and organizers to transport cleaners to other rooms of the home.

Upper cabinets in a storage room can store everyday articles, such as trash liners, flashlights, light bulbs, insect repellant, first aid kits, air deodorizers, lighters, shipping supplies,

Upscale Mudroom

FIGURE 51.01
Upscale Mudroom

gift-wrapping supplies, batteries, and so on. When arranging articles in the cabinets, keep items of similar nature grouped together in a designated area on the shelf to help you remember where things are located. For example, a tool box, hardware oil lubricants, glue, tape measure, light bulbs, and picture-hanging supplies can be stored next to each other. Many articles can file or stand in rows on the shelves, like cans and bottles of insect repellent. Groups of small articles are best stored in open stacking bins. However, such belongings are good to contain in handled containers for portability when these items are taken out of the mudroom.

Although a more expensive feature, upper cabinets can include common dead space by extending them to the ceiling for added cabinet storage space. Higher placed cabinet shelving can store infrequently used or off-season articles, such as coolers, picnic baskets, beach towels, sand toys, and so on.

Many different organizers can be installed in the base cabinets, such as pullout shelves, trash cans, hampers, and recycling containers. One of the most useful aspects of cabinetry is drawer storage. Little odds and ends, such as rubber bands, safety pins, and lighters are great to stash in compartmentalized drawer trays or divider containers.

A custom built-in locker system is another high-end feature to add to a mudroom. The main advantage to using lockers in a home is they perfectly separate household members' personal items, such as a coat, backpack, purse, shoes, and so on. Inside the locker door, a personal chalkboard or corkboard can be placed, which is useful for individual reminders or for posting personal documents. A custom locker setup can have an attached built-in bench with pullout drawers beneath the seat for additional storage.

If space allows, a floor sink is a big upgrade to any mudroom. Not only useful to bathe the family pet, but also it's big enough to clean large items like sporting goods, pots, boots, mops, buckets, and bulky garage items.

Semicustom Mudroom

A semicustom mudroom can easily mimic an upscale one simply by using well-designed, moderately priced organizers. Many cabinet distributors and home centers carry stock cabinetry that costs significantly less than custom or special order. With the right design, a mudroom outfitted with such cabinets adds significant storage capacity and increases the home's value.

A good selection of cabinet organizers is sold separately outside a cabinet line and is easy to find at specialty storage and organization stores, as well as many home centers. There are rollout shelves, pullout baskets, trash cans, or hampers that will fit most standard cabinets. Also, many loose organizers, such as baskets, trays, and containers, can compartmentalize items.

Freestanding lockers are another type of organizer that can fall into the moderately priced budget. However, there are many types of freestanding lockers designed to outfit a mudroom, and some can be costlier. Classic ventilated steel lockers, which are found in schools, break rooms, gyms, or fitness centers, can be found at stores that sell industrial products and also at many home centers. Many furniture stores carry mudroom furniture in the form of semicustom, entryway lockers, which are commonly featured in a solid wood construction designed for the home. These

Cabinet Closet

Bench with Cushion on Cubby Organizer

Pull out Wire Baskets

Semi-Custom Mudroom

FIGURE 51.02
Semicustom Mudroom

entry systems typically have a top cubby compartment and an open locker with coat hooks and are finished with a bench seat. Sides of the lockers are flush, so you can line up as many lockers as needed, which creates a cohesive, custom look.

A sink is an expensive upgrade for a mudroom due to plumbing costs, but the benefits are endless. When you already have a sink or plan to install one, prepare a highly functional space. There are two types of sinks: a utility or traditional counter sink. A utility sink will require wall-mounted organizers and perhaps a floor organizer to contain sink items in lieu of cabinets. A counter sink will have a base-cabinet storage compartment and matching upper cabinets—always the best way to obtain wall storage.

In a mudroom, a sink is called to perform cleaning duties. Therefore, a wall-mounted, counter, or cabinet paper-towel dispenser is needed. Cleaning soaps should be easy to access from a wall-mounted or counter dispenser.

Budget-Friendly Mudroom

An economical way to furnish a mudroom is to install an inexpensive DIY, wire-based closet system right onto the mudroom wall. Most home centers carry off-the-shelf closet systems that come in kits with basic shelving and hanging rods. These kits are helpful for those who struggle with organizing, because the manufacturers do the basic thinking for the consumer by including ready-made layouts from which to choose. Most closet kits offer additional organizers that can be purchased separately, such as pullout baskets, hampers, hooks, and the like, so it's to your advantage to select a system that has many such organizer accessory add-ons.

A closet system becomes an open-storage arrangement when mounted onto a mudroom wall, so it should be arranged neatly since it's so visible. If needed, add extra storage essentials to help maintain order. For example, add baskets to divide and contain many groups of different belongings.

There are many ways to configure a wire closet system in the mudroom, given different accessories. A hanging rod can be added to hang outwear or sports uniforms. Attach S hooks to the hanging rod for all looped belongings, such as backpacks, totes, handbags, and certain sporting goods.

Shoe organizers or shelving can hold footwear. For an open space, opt for wire shelving since solid varieties are prone to dust in such settings. Slanted or pullout shoe organizers are easiest to view and access. Pullout baskets can contain many items, such as outwear accessories, sporting goods, pet items, drawstrings, backpacks, water bottles, trash liners, and so on. Pullout hampers, recycling bins, and trash cans are other common closet-system organizers that work nicely in a mudroom.

Mudroom Equipped for Children

The mudroom is a great place to teach children responsibility by having them put all their things away upon entering the home. Also, a mudroom can stop their belongings from becoming scattered throughout the home.

In order to successfully contain children's belongings in the mudroom, organizers must be scaled to their size so they're easy to use. Lockers, cubbies, and benches are primary children's organizers they're comfortable with since they're used at school.

It's a good idea to use either picture or worded labels on organizers for children. It's also helpful to have a bulletin board for children's papers, notes, calendars, and so on for their use, which fosters responsibility.

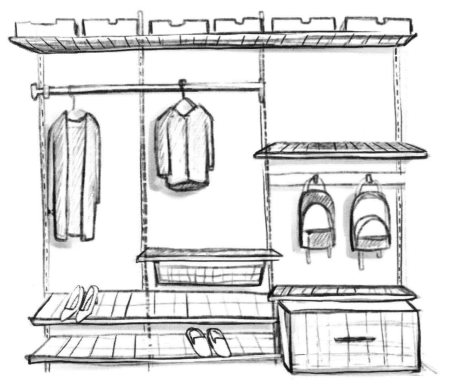

FIGURE 51.03
Budget-Friendly Mudroom

A Garage with Mudroom Duties

Some homes don't have a separate mudroom space; therefore, an attached garage can take on mudroom duties when organizers can be arranged around the doorway to the home. A great advantage to using the garage for this purpose is being able to clean or leave messy, wet belongings in the garage, as opposed to ever having them enter the home. Another benefit's being able to use less expensive or heavy-duty commercial grade storage organizers that would otherwise not look as appropriate inside the home.

Almost any traditional mudroom organizer, such as benches, cubby organizers, or lockers, work in a garage space. There are commercial-grade, heavy-gauge steel garage organizers that are formed into racks or lockers that are durable and practical for mudroom items, such as footwear, back packs, sporting goods, and so on. Many home centers and specialty garage organizational storage companies sell cabinetry designed to store tools, automotive and gardening supplies, and outdoor items. These cabinet lines are also good for storing mudroom belongings. Other garage organizers, such as the commonly marketed wall systems that come with attachable organizers, can also be used for mudroom items.

The problems with using the garage for mudroom belongings are the fluctuating temperatures of seasonal climates and common garage debris or dust. A good way to combat some of the problem is to choose organizers that are enclosed, such as cabinets and lockers.

FIGURE 51.04
Garage with Mudroom Duties

GARAGE MUDROOM

CHAPTER 52

Garages

A garage is a great place to store many articles that would otherwise crowd the home. Most of the time, a garage's size and location will influence what should be stored in the space. For example, an attached garage is the perfect location to store household overflow, like totes, beach gear, back packs, footwear, outerwear, beverages, pet items, holiday decorations, and so on. Detached garages are often limited to more traditional inventories, like lawn and garden essentials, especially if they're a good distance from the house.

Households with carports or limited garage space can benefit from an outdoor shed in order to protect and secure items like snowblowers, lawn mowers, patio furniture, bicycles, and the like. A shed may be a wiser investment than an extensive line of garage cabinets or organizers, which may be more expensive and store less.

A household member's hobbies and interests can dictate what is housed in the garage. Gardeners, mechanics, hunters, sports enthusiasts, and the like may need to store their tools and gear in the garage. It can be advantageous or necessary to carve out a workspace for certain activities, such as a tool station to fix things, should the space be available.

It's necessary to establish a budget for garage organizers since there are huge differences in the types available. High-end organizers feature wheeled cabinets, tool tables, and motorized lifts. Alternatively, standard, more affordable organizers come wall mounted or are designed as floor organizers. Once you have a budget in place, prioritize your needs so you are allocating the most money toward the important items to store.

Since there are countless items that can be stored either in the home or garage, such as Christmas decorations or sports equipment, it's best to make a list of such items in order of importance. Then, in the event not everything fits, leave out those at the bottom of the list. The most significant items should be those that are hardest to find adequate storage space inside the house or those you really don't want in the house, like messy sports equipment or footwear. Also, place items at the top of the list that are most convenient to store in the garage because they'll be transported outside, such as picnic baskets, coolers, or gardening pots. Pin this list on the garage wall and start sorting and reducing current garage belongings.

It's common to become overwhelmed, sidetracked, and lost while organizing big spaces. Therefore, it's recommended to organize the garage in logical steps to stay focused and on task. The following steps are designed to move an organizational project along so the process clearly progresses.

Sorting and Downsizing Garage Items

The first thing to do before you start organizing your garage is to determine an amount of time it's going to take to finish the entire job. When it has been several years since you have last performed a clean sweep of the garage, many articles may have accumulated since then, so allow yourself a few days to complete the project, allocating a few hours at a time. Garages with minimal inventories may require just an afternoon.

Schedule your garage organizational time on a day when the weather is good so you have plenty of sunshine for good lighting. Also, you want to be able to move things outside to clean them. Get boxes or bags to mark garage items: Sort, Donate, Sell, Trash, Repair, and Relocate. Make sure you have extra-large-size boxes to hold large, bulky garage belongings. While you sort, first decide whether something is even worth keeping before tossing it in a box with the intention of holding onto the article. Belongings that are hard to determine what to do with can be placed in a box designated for the next garage sale for the time being. There is peace of mind knowing that such

items are still in your possession and not yet gone, buying you time to think them over. You do want to discard anything that is expired, broken, or useless, so valuable space isn't wasted.

As you come across items to keep, create categories for them and label the boxes accordingly. You can have boxes already labeled for common garage inventories, like gardening, tools, auto, and the like. If you have room, keep your boxes in the center of the garage where it's convenient to sort things while you work.

Once you are done sorting your garage belongings, count assorted items that you have in each box and mark these amounts on the outside. For example, within a box that collects tools, add up the number of each kind of tool, such as five hammers, two screwdrivers, one power drill, and so on. This way when it's time to put everything back, you can easily determine how big or small an organizer needs to be. Also, such information will help you further downsize your items since you may realize that you have too many of a certain item—in which case, keep the well-made items in working order and donate or sell the excess.

Reclaiming Floor Space

Take a hard look at all of the large garage items, like your snowblower, lawn mower, bicycles, and like, and make certain that these items are really needed, wanted, and used. It makes no sense to keep bikes that the children have outgrown or lawn mowers when you use a landscaping service. Such items are space hogs, and when they're old, they have lost considerable value, so keeping them for their "value" can be a mistake. When these items are in need of repair, such as an inoperable snowblower, now is the time to fix them. Find out whether their repairs are feasible then decide to fix or junk them and reclaim your garage space.

Make sure that you are not using your garage space as a storage center. Old furniture, television sets, or boxes of outgrown toys and clothes should not occupy garage floor space any longer. Make decisions on whether to donate or sell them. Plan a date for the garage sale or list these items on a resale website. Label these boxes or items and remove them from the garage.

Evaluating Current Organizational Accessories

Review the storage arrangements or essentials that currently hold your garage belongings. Decide whether your items are presently easy to find and access in their storage places or organizers. Take notes and make plans to keep or change them.

You'll also need to inspect any current storage essentials for safety and stability. Check for wobbly legs, crooked drawers, and loose brackets or shelves. No organizer should be hard to open or inoperable in any regard. Garage organizers also need to be durable in order to withstand the ravages of outdoor elements since the garage takes in climatic conditions. Therefore, any organizers that are waterproof, rustproof, and moldproof (or -resistant) are preferred.

Make sure to have organizers with locks for storing flammable or poisonous items, especially when small children are present in the home. Overhead storage compartments, high shelves, or upper cabinets can also work well to move anything combustible out of children's reach.

Planning and Arranging Garage Space

No two garages will have the same belongings to house, nor will they have identical dimensions. For this reason, there is no one set formula for arranging them. In order to best utilize your garage space, it's important to understand your household members' needs, given their skills, hobbies, or interests. Then establish specific purposes for your garage space, so you can make the best storage plan.

Before you begin putting your garage back in order, get it in good shape. First, discard, disassemble, or dismount any ineffective or poorly located organizers. Then patch, paint, clean, and make necessary repairs so that doors, windows, electrical items, and the like are in good working order.

Allow plenty of planning time for your garage layout. First, draw a diagram of your garage using its length, width, and height dimensions. Note all obstructions, windows, and doors. Additionally, mark off locations where switches, outlets, sprinkler systems, attic openings, garage door openers, lights, and other permanent fixtures are placed. Take into account the needed walking space surrounding the automobiles when they're present to allow for room to open car doors, trunks, and the like.

Make a list of your current garage organizers: their sizes and what they can be used to hold. If you already made a list of all your different garage items, see which items can go with which organizers. Don't get stuck using the same organizer for same thing as before when it could be used in a more effective way for something else. It's common to revert back to old storage habits, but it's important to think differently, which is why to take down organizers that were not working;

create a blank canvas in order to see the space more objectively.

Decide how to make your garage belongings easy to access and visible while using your space in the most efficient way. Knowing which items are most important will allow you to decide where to place them since these articles would receive storage priority. Also, search for the most logical places for your garage items. For example, a set of shelves next to a garage entrance that leads to the home would be an ideal location to place footwear.

As you plan and arrange your garage, remember that learning to live with less will save you a bundle on costly organizers and space. You also want things to stay off the garage floor whenever possible. Not only will the garage look better, but also it's a safety measure since you'll avoid tripping hazards, plus it will keep dangerous tools and chemicals out of harm's way.

There are many different ways to store your garage inventories. You can invest in a garage system, use individual storage accessories, or a combination of the two. The following information details different garage organizational systems and organizers. It's important to investigate many options before you put everything back together.

Slatwall Garage Systems

Slatwall goes by other names: Slatboard, slotwall, grooved board—but the basic system is comprised of paneling with horizontal grooves designed to accept a variety of attachable organizers. It is sold in sheets and installs over the wall. You can cut slatwall to shape around every inch of an entire wall. Slatwall can also be installed over a small section, so it can meet certain budgets or design preferences. It's sold in starter kits with small slatwall sections and particular storage

accessories tailored to a need, like sports or lawn care. Organizational accessories are hung from grooves that are formed on the slatwall.

There are different varieties and grades of slatwall on the market. A garage-grade slatwall panel should be heavy duty, waterproof, and scratch resistant. Select a slatwall that is compatible with standard accessories so you are not limited to a particular manufacturer's line.

Slatwall has many advantages because it's an adjustable system. It's strong, easy to clean, and insulates the garage. It's attractive and looks high end. The problem with slatwall is the high costs associated with the system, such as requiring professional installation. Although you can limit the amount of slatwall used in the garage, wall-to-wall coverage looks best.

Track Rail Systems

A simple track organizational garage system is basically a horizontal rail that runs along a solid surface, like a wall. Organizational accessories attach to the rail. You can place two tracks or rails parallel to one another in order to gain more wall storage space. The storage accessories are designed to hold just about every garage inventory with the use of hooks, baskets, rods, cubby organizers, shelves, and even cabinets.

These systems are adjustable and easy to install and arrange. The downside to these systems is that your wall surface is mostly exposed, and if you have drywall, scuff marks and dents are bound to happen.

Gridwall Systems

Gridwall is a rugged hanging system made from either a steel wire construction or epoxy-coated wire. Most are rust proof and built to withstand extreme heat, cold, and humidity. Gridwall is a framework of crisscrossed or parallel wire bars formed into a panel that holds items. Gridwall organizers are sold in particular sizes, like three-by-four feet, and are installed on walls.

There are gridwall systems that accept slatwall organizers, thereby broadening your accessory options outside what is offered. Gridwall systems are relatively affordable. These organizers are flexible and can easily transfer to other locations, making them good investments. The only downside to using a gridwall system is that it's not designed to cover the entire wall so it requires more planning and imagination to lay out.

Pegboard Systems

Pegboard systems have been around for a long time, proving that they have merit; they're also one of the most affordable garage organizing systems. Pegboard is mostly manufactured with perforated holes that run in parallel rows across an entire sheet of material. Standard pegboard holes are quarter inch in diameter and evenly spaced one inch apart. It's best to select a standard hole size since you want to be able to acquire a large assortment of accompanying storage accessories, like bins, hooks, baskets, and shelves. The storage accessories are easy to rearrange to meet changing needs. Pegboard is commonly sold in sheets and often sold in kits that serve a particular function, like gardening, tools, and sports.

Pegboard is manufactured in a variety of materials, such as tempered hardboard, plastic, and metal. Each type of material has different characteristics that affect the range of possible uses. It's important to note that added thickness to any pegboard will increase weight capacity.

Hardboard Pegboard

Hardboard pegboard is the least expensive type of pegboard. You can say that you get what you pay for when it comes to pegboard material. The main problem with hardboard is that it's a wood product mainly consisting of wood fibers, so it's prone to warping or bending under certain conditions. This softer material is why the peg holes eventually wear out, causing the hooks to fall out. Hardboard does have a high tensile strength, but it's prone to sag when not enough mounting points are properly positioned to hold proportionate weight. Therefore, hardboard pegboard can be tricky to install. Hardboard cannot hold heavy garage items, so it's limited to storing only light things, such as small hand tools, accessories, small hoses, garden tools, brushes, cords, rope, chains, and the like.

Plastic and Metal Pegboards

Plastic pegboard is more durable than hardboard, but nothing surpasses metal in terms of strength. In addition to the peg holes, many heavy-duty metal pegboard systems have vertical slots for added support, which reinforces storage organizers and holds more weight. Items like bicycles, wheelbarrows, and ladders can be stored on many metal pegboard systems.

Both plastic and metal pegboards are also sold in strips. Peg strips are long, narrow pieces of pegboard, rather than large square or rectangular sheets. They're more economically sold in strip form and can hold a number of heavier garage items that take up vertical space, such as shovels, ladders, spectator chairs, and the like.

The downside to plastic and metal pegboard systems is that they're not designed to be cut, so you cannot customize them to fit on your wall. However, you can puzzle together many individual plastic or metal pegboard sheets to increase wall coverage.

Utilizing Overhead Garage Space

Probably the most overlooked storage space in the garage is overhead. In most garages you have to tap into this space in order to successfully get the majority of the stuff off the ground. The best items to stow away overhead are infrequently needed items, like holiday decorations (both indoor/outdoor), spare tires, canoes, skis, fishing poles, tents, outdoor cushions, snowboards, sleds, camping gear, coolers, firewood, pots, off-season sporting goods, and so on. The following organizers are designed to capture overhead garage space.

Ceiling-Mounted Platforms

The overhead organizer offering the most storage space is the ceiling-suspended platform. This type of organizer is a large, raised structure with a flat surface, such as a rack, that is mounted from the ceiling. It can mount in the center of the garage ceiling over parked cars. Proper installation is needed, because mounting points rely on ceiling joists for support and strength. You must investigate load capacities for ceiling-mounted organizers since they vary, and that will determine what can be stored on them.

It's ideal to select an industrial wire material for such organizers to ensure optimal strength and high visibility so belongings can be seen from below. Wire also does not collect dust like solid platforms do. Choose a wire that has a powder-coated paint finish to protect against corrosion and rust. The disadvantage to platform storage is the inconvenience in accessing items stored in the center.

Ceiling- and Wall-Mounted Lifts

A ceiling- or wall-mounted lift organizer is one that loads belongings at ground level and is then hoisted either manually or by using an electrical pulley device to an overhead or wall storage location. There are platform or roped lifts specifically designed to store items, such as bicycles, canoes, ladders, kayaks, fishing poles, containers, and the like in this way. The main drawback to these organizers is that they can be dangerous since they bear heavy weight; if mishandled, they could crash to the ground and cause damage.

Wall- and Ceiling-Mounted Shelves

Shelving or racks placed on the garage walls close to the ceiling is another way to capture overhead space. Shelving depth can be selected to match the size of the articles or containers stored on them. This avoids the problem of belongings becoming too hard see and retrieve when placed behind each other, as is the case of deep storage compartments, like suspended platforms. Wall or overhead shelves commonly can suspend hooks to hold many garage items, like brooms. shovels, umbrellas, tools, ladders, bicycles, and so on.

The biggest downside to fixed overhead shelving is the inconvenience of needing a ladder or stool to retrieve the belongings. It can also be dangerous to unload heavy containers or objects from an overhead location. Therefore, it's best to limit the weight of a container by using several smaller ones to occupy a given inventory, as opposed to one large one.

Garage Cabinetry

Garage cabinets should be industrial strength, plus waterproof, moldproof, and rustproof due to their exposure to the outdoor elements. Cabinets constructed of powder-coated steel, thermofused melamine, or heavy-duty plastic are recommended for garages.

Cabinets marketed for garage installation can be found online, at many cabinet shops, and in most home centers where many garage cabinets are in stock, with individual pieces sold separately. Some are sold as sets or as starter kits that belong to an extensive line of cabinetry, so adding to them is possible. It's also common to find garage cabinet sets that include storage organizers, like slatwall components and preplanned organizers.

Garage cabinetry is often featured with the base cabinets raised off the floor, either mounted on the wall or on wheels, which creates mobility—especially convenient for components like tool chests or workbenches. This is so base cabinets don't get wet and damaged by water associated with blowing rain or hose cleanings.

Individual Garage Organizers

There is an individual organizer that can be used for every garage belonging. Some organizers are specific in that they hold a certain item, such as a hose or skateboard; others are universal and can hold a number of different articles. Multipurpose organizers include baskets, bins, chests, racks, cans, drawers, cabinets, shelving, and pocketed organizers. An entire garage can be successfully organized with individual organizers, or they can supplement an actual system.

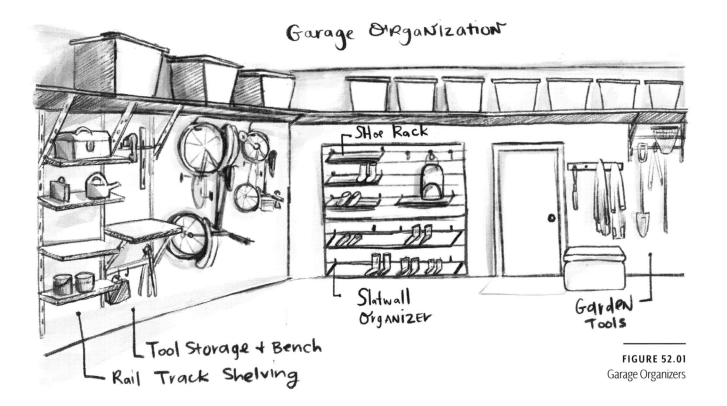

FIGURE 52.01
Garage Organizers

CHAPTER 53

Storing Specific Garage Items

Many garage items are neglectfully stored in hard-to-access or find locations. Most often, homeowners are unaware of better storage options for even the most common garage articles, such as ladders and extension cords. The following information can help you organize some of the more popular articles to store effectively in a garage.

Ladders

Every home needs a ladder or maybe even a few, like an easy-to-carry folding stepladder and an extension type for reaching high places. Ladders are easy to store. They can be situated on a relatively inexpensive ladder rack that places them in a vertical position on a garage wall. However, in such a position, a large ladder can fall and either dent a car or harm someone.

It may be safest to store a ladder horizontally low on a wall where there is additional support with the use of multiple hooks holding the ladder in more than one location. Hanging them close to the ground is not only safer, but also leaves you more space to situate daily used items at eye level on the wall. All garage organizational systems, such as slatwall, gridwall, and the like, have storage accessories designed to accommodate ladder storage.

Ladders can also be stored on an overhead platform or ceiling. However, they can be dangerous to lift from overhead platforms or shelves. You can use rack lifts designed to hoist heavy items from the floor to the ceiling for ladder storage, especially larger ones that reach to a second level of the home. Rack lifts can operate manually with a pulley system or electrically.

Workbench

A workbench is a strong, heavy-duty, usually rectangular-shaped table where manual work is performed. Workbenches are made of sturdy material, such as dense woods, metals, composites, and stone, depending on the work done at the table. They come in all sizes and configurations, such as tool compartments, hutches, base cabinets, and so on.

In order for a workbench to be a value-added fixture in the garage, it must receive frequent use for its intended purpose or serve multiple uses. A workbench will benefit the auto mechanic, craftsman, artist, gardener, or the weekend warrior. When no such persons exist in your home, a workbench may become the catchall table where piles of junk form. Therefore, in these cases, it's best to donate or sell it. A seldom-used workbench table that is taking up a good deal of space can be replaced with a space-saving portable folding table that can be tucked away when not in use. Another option would be to install a wall-mounted foldout table that occupies space only when in use.

A regularly used workbench table needs to be organized well so that tools and related accessories are easily accessible. A wall-mounted tool organizer, table hutch, base cabinet, or mobile cart is the perfect solution for storing tools and supplies. There are many specialized wall-mounted organizers specifically designed to hold work tools, cleaners, supplies, bottles, and so on, making it easy to create a highly organized workstation.

Pegboard, slatwall, gridwall, shelves, cabinets, rail and track organizers are some of the most popular wall-mounted storage solutions to place above a workbench. The goal is to create places to store belongings used on the workbench nearby but off the work surface. Other accessories that complement a regularly used workbench are trash cans, vacuum cleaners, task lighting, power receptacles, and a static-controlled surface.

Power and Extension Cords

Power and extension cords need to stay properly organized since they're necessity items that need to be easily located in the right size quickly without the time-consuming untangling a spaghetti mess of them. You want to carefully store them

so they stay protected, especially certain indoor extension cords that can deteriorate from elements like sunlight, moisture, and kinks.

The first step to organizing extension cords is to put them in order by length and type, such as indoor or outdoor use. Usually, all this information is recorded on the extension cord, but it may be a good idea to attach a large separate label with that information on it to save time. Record the cord's length, its power rating (which is the maximum current the cord can handle), and the number of prongs in the plug.

Divide extension cords by length—such as short, medium, and long—so you know how many you have of each. You want to have an assortment of extension cord lengths because they should exactly stretch the distance from the outlet to where they'll be used for optimal safety. Usually, a few extension cords in each length or size category are sufficient.

Make sure that the extension cord is approved by Underwriters Laboratories (UL) so it's certified as safe and well constructed. Look over your extension cords and make sure they're safe to use: no loose plugs or exposed wire should be seen through the insulation.

Once you have decluttered and sorted your extension cords, plan how to arrange them. There are a few different ways to contain extension cords so they stay tangle-free. You can even create a makeshift extension cord organizer by curling the cord around a cylindrical object, such as metal coffee can or a flat object like a block of wood. There are many versions of a retractable or nonretractable reel organizer that loops the extension cord around a reel so it does not tangle. You'll find that these extension cord organizers come spring loaded or operate with the assistance of a hand crank. Such organizers come in wall-mounted, handled, or freestanding models for all cord lengths and are suitable for most garage compartments and walls.

There are many workshop extension cord organizers designed to be used for a garage workbench. They're commonly wall mounted and contain cords, hooks, or baskets. Also, many garage organizational systems, like pegboard, gridwall, or slatwall, have organizational accessories to house extension cords. It's most convenient to locate your extension cord organizer near an outlet. Extension cords can also be stored in a container or basket that resides on a garage shelf or overhead compartment. In a container, they need to be wrapped in a bundle and bound by a clip, tie, or Velcro strip. They can also be individually bagged.

Pet Items

Many pet supplies are not needed on a daily basis: carriers, grooming supplies, seasonal toys, aquarium supplies, sand, litter, cage liners, pet bedding, filter cartridges, gravel, seeds, training pads, gates, costumes, sprays and so on. For this reason, these items can be containerized and stored in an overhead shelf or compartment in the garage to free space in the home.

However, there are some items, such as foods, medications, shampoos, deodorizers, and so on, that may be dangerous, damaging, or harmful to store in a garage location with insects and dramatic temperature fluctuations. Most importantly, pet foods should not be kept in the garage unless they can be contained in a garage freezer or refrigerator. It's worth noting that many garage items, like insecticides, gasoline, and other chemicals that are stored in porous containers or become exposed to the air, can leach into the pet foods

or medications. Even canned food will spoil in extreme heat, and water can cause the can to rust, which is not food safe.

Different storage containers are good for certain items. For example, an open-handled caddy organizer is good for holding bottled items, such as grooming supplies, pet sprays, aquarium supplies, and pet cleaners. Bulky items like gravel, seeds, sand, and litter can be stored in heavy-duty wheeled cans on the ground or in bins located on a base-cabinet shelf.

Store regularly used items, like pet strollers, leashes, muzzles, harnesses, scoopers, bags, brushes, and the like, in easy-to-access locations. A wall-mounted, peg-style coatrack is a perfect organizer for storing many of these types of items, or you can simply place some wall hooks beside the garage door for them. Organizational garage systems, such as slatwall or gridwall, have hooks that can contain these items at eye level.

Camping Gear

The checklist of items needed for a camping trip is somewhat extensive. The type and amount of camping gear you have will determine where to store it. Big items, like tents, tarps, stoves, grills, heaters, and the like, can be kept in overhead garage rafters. Also, any bulky sporting goods that accompany a camping trip, like fishing poles, canoes, kayaks, or water skies, should also be stored in overhead garage locations to free up wall and floor space. There are many specialized organizers, such as pulley lifts and wall-mounted fishing pole organizers, for such articles.

All smaller specialized camping cooking gear, like aluminum or stainless steel cookware and dinnerware, can be stored in stackable lidded containers in the garage so they stay clean. Keep these items together in storage along with related items, such as candles, tablecloths, thermoses, coolers, canteens, or any outdoor cooking gadgets.

Many camping accessories, such as cookware and coolers, tend to be chunky and can easily weigh down a container and make it heavy to move. Therefore, it's best to divide these things among several smaller containers, grouping like items together. Then, keep these containers next to one another on shelf or overhead platform. Label the containers with headings like Camping Cookware, Tent Accessories, and so on.

Instead of containers, you can also store your items in duffel bags that are commonly used as luggage when you camp. Simply use tags and place them on the handles of these bags to record their contents. It's important to always clean everything off well before you pack away camping gear, especially eating utensils, and always remove batteries from electronics to prevent corrosion.

First aid kits are an essential camping item, and they need a compartmentalized container so the many pieces, such as Band-Aids, gauze, finger splints, and the like, stay in place. These containers should be well stocked before they're stored away to avoid future work. Keep first aid kits on a garage shelf or in an overhead container with other miscellaneous camping gear like flashlights, radios, compasses, and so on.

Outdoor bedding, including sleeping bags, air mattresses, pads, and the like, should be stored indoors in a dry, stable temperature where there is ventilation. Many of these items should be stored loosely or gently stuffed in the ventilated cotton sacks they're often sold in since tightly rolled or compressed fabric can degrade fibers overtime. Airtight packing or plastic wrap that would be necessary to ward off rodents and insects for garage storage can trap moisture and encourage mold, mildew, or bacterial growth. Any miscellaneous camping bedding items like plastic tarps, air mattress pumps, or repair kits can stay in the garage next to other camping items.

Large Wheeled Items

Most of your large items with wheels, such as motorcycles, yard tractors, bikes, and snowblowers, are space hogs that usually wind up taking a good amount of garage floor space. It's important to focus on getting these items off the floor since they're usually the reason your automobiles are parked in the driveway. The good news is that there are a plenty of organizers designed to get a number of them off the floor and onto the walls or ceiling locations.

Wheeled items that have connected or looped handles, like wagons, wheelbarrows, and coolers, can hang on a single wall hook or from a storage accessory belonging to a slatwall, gridwall, or pegboard wall system.

Bicycles

Bicycles are known to damage vehicles from car doors crashing into them or bikes tipping over onto them. For this reason, prioritize moving bikes up and off the ground; avoid freestanding bike racks that take up floor space. Bikes are one the easiest items to get off the garage floor because there are so many different types of bike organizers that fit almost any garage or budget. Bikes can easily suspend upside by the tires from a track rail ceiling organize, which is a long anchored strip with multiple hanging hooks.

There are also pulley-style systems that can hoist bikes to the ceiling either manually or electrically, which makes retrieving the bikes effortless. These storage devices are especially useful in garages with high ceilings. There are also many wall-mounted rack and hook bike organizers that can either hold bikes parallel or perpendicular to the wall. Most garage organizational systems have storage accessories for bikes.

Smaller Wheeled Items

Smaller wheeled items, including scooters, power toys, tricycles, skateboards, push cars, and so on, tend to be harder to store in the garage since they can roll off elevated surfaces like shelves or platforms. Some of these items are hard to store on wall organizers due to their bulkiness or awkward shapes. Given the appropriate space, such items can be tucked beneath a deep garage shelf, staircase, or some alcove where they're out of the way and not a tripping hazard, yet are easy to access.

Large Wheeled Tools

Heavy bulky items, like lawn mowers or snowblowers, have the most limited storage choices in your garage. You may have to resort to your floor space or a specialized lift platform that can bear the weight and securely carry your item to the ceiling. Both manual and electronic-pulley-style platforms are available. In the event your garage is extremely small, consider an outdoor shed to house items like lawn mowers or snowblowers.

Footwear, Backpacks, Outerwear, and Accessories

Some of the best, but often overlooked, items to store in an attached garage are footwear, outerwear, and backpacks, especially if your home doesn't have a mudroom. Housing these items, which are needed on a daily basis, in the garage keeps the home entrance floors clear, and hanging storage is less congested. Another advantage is the opportunity to use economical storage essentials that would otherwise be too casual for the interior of the home. Namely, basic wall-mounted wire shelving, tower shelving units, or stackable plastic shelving organizers. These are commonly hidden in closet spaces, but can work well in the garage for this purpose.

Sporting Goods

Many specialty organizers are designed to hold individual sports equipment, and they're typically of the wall-mounted or freestanding varieties. Most garage systems also carry accessories to hold sporting equipment. Prioritize key storage placement for sporting goods that are played throughout the year. You may only want to invest in a specialized organizer for a particular sport when it's played often. For example, a regular tennis player would benefit from an organizer that holds the racket, balls, and shoes. Pack away off-season sporting goods in labeled containers and store them in overhead garage compartments, sheds, or garage attics.

Use adjustable, basic organizers for seasonal sporting goods so that the incoming season's items are easy to load when it's time to rotate them. There are countless garage organizers that can house seasonal sporting goods, such as those that contain hooks, bins, baskets, racks, shelves, baskets, cubbies, and the like. For example, baskets or bins can hold balls, goggles, knee pads, and so on. Also, shelving can openly display sports shoes, helmets, and sports bags, making them easy to find and access.

It's a good practice to create ready-to-go bags for each sport or person. Fill them with the necessary items for a particular sport like a clean uniform, water bottle, mouth-guard, stick, ball, shoes, and socks. This bag can hang from a hook or rest on a shelf.

Cleaning Tools and Supplies

It's best to keep cleaning agents inside the home because garage temperature fluctuations may degrade their solutions and effectiveness. Also, many cleaning products are combustibles so they need to store in a cool, dry place. Cleaning wipes, rags, sponges, or paper towels should also store inside the home. Moisture, insects, and rodents can ruin these items.

However, you can store mops, brooms, dustpans, squeegees, buckets, gloves, brushes, wet-dry shop vacs (vacuums), and the like in the garage. These items get drippy and grimy, so the garage is the perfect place for them, especially if you don't have a mudroom. It's best to hang these items on a peg rack, wall hooks, or specialized organizer on a wall where they can drip dry onto a tray, mat, or concrete floor.

The best mop-and-broom holder is one that can hang long-poled cleaning tools without looped handles by using a friction-grip or spring-activated clip mechanism. Buckets should be nested together and stored on a shelf or in a cabinet. Keep gloves, scrubbers, and brushes inside buckets. Trash supplies like bags and liners can also be kept in the garage. These items can rest on a shelf with the buckets.

Recycling and Trash Cans

Trash cans and recycling receptacles should be stationed close to door where they most frequently move in and out of the garage. Your community's recycling procedures will dictate how many containers you possess and their sizes. For example, areas with recycling facilities that have automated sorting and processing equipment will offer one large receptacle for all recyclables. Some towns need their residents to partially sort and separate into midsize bins: one for paper and the other for cans, jars, and plastic. Recycling materials outside your curbside recycling program would require additional containers.

Recycling bins, such as city- or town-issued containers, are logical to store next to one another. One large wheeled recycling receptacle should sit beside your regular trash container. When you need to perform a good amount of sorting yourself, stackable recycling bins are efficient. There are many wall-mounted recycling bin solutions that allow you to easily take them down to unload. Many garage systems, such as slatwall, have recycling bins and trash organizational accessories.

Holiday Decorations

In certain homes, the garage is the only storage option for holiday decorations, although some people prefer to house holiday decorations in their garages. Since the garage attracts bugs and animals, it's important to safeguard your holiday decorations. Reduce bug and animal invasion by using proper storage organizers, such as plastic airtight totes that also perform pest control.

In the garage, ceiling platforms, overhead shelves, or any out-of-the-way spot is the best place to store holiday decorations that are only needed once a year. Make sure to keep containers light and manageable to lift when placed overhead. Stackable plastic, lidded containers are best for preserving decorations in the garage versus porous cardboard boxes. Color-coded containers, like orange for Halloween, are easy to locate in a crowded garage. Also, label holiday containers in big, easy-to-read letters so you can see their contents from a distance.

Organize as you pack your holiday containers. Toss broken items, test lights, remove batteries, and divide everything so like items are together. There are many ways to organize holiday decorations so things are easy to set up for the next year. For instance, you can separate decorations by room or keep all the ornaments for a particular Christmas tree in one container, when you have more than one. Coffee cans, plastic baggies, garage liners, and so on can safely compartmentalize holiday items inside larger organizers.

There are several containers designed specifically for holiday items that are airtight, durable and good for garage storage, such as plastic stackable wreath containers, string light/garland storage reels, wheeled tree storage bags, ornament containers, and so on. Most of these types of organizers can be found in home centers and stores that provide seasonal items.

Lawn and Garden Supplies

Sheds, mudrooms, and garages are the most convenient places for lawn and garden supplies. In warm-weather climates, outdoor potting benches can be used to store garden supplies. These organizers consist of a workstation table attached to a hutch with open shelving for supplies and accessories. In addition, potting benches have hooks for hanging tools and towel racks.

Generally, it's best to keep all these items in one central location so everything is easy to find. Large collections of these articles may force you to divide them into different storage spots, but make certain to do so on in logical manner so locating them is easy. For example, place the belongings that relate to the lawn together, such as lawn mowers, sprinklers, trimmers, edgers, mulchers, and leaf blowers, in the garage. Then, store gardening items, such as potting soil, pots, gardening bags, small tools, plant food, gloves, and so on, in a mudroom or shed, if available.

Store hand tools in a dry area of the garage since moisture can damage the metal and wood of most tools. Before you put away your gardening tools, make sure to properly clean and dry them, because metal surfaces are prone to rust. Using tool oils can prevent this problem, and it's important to apply them before long-term storage. Tools with wooden handles can also be coated with special oils that will prevent them from splitting in subzero temperatures.

Gas-powered tools need special attention, especially before they rest between seasonal uses. Tasks like lubricating, cleaning, draining, sharpening, and replacing filters are necessary to perform on certain tools before extended storage. Likewise, remove batteries from tools that take a break from use.

Proper arrangement of your gardening tools is another way to keep them in good shape. Tools can break or scratch when recklessly tossed in a pile with others. When arranging your gardening tools, make sure they're not stacked or hung too closely together; this prevents them from potentially damaging one another. It's best to separate your long tools from the short, handheld ones since this makes it easier to store them on the same organizer. However, small collections of tools and certain organizers make storing them all together more logical. For example, many wheeled, mobile tool organizers are intended to travel from the garage to the outdoors and can store both long and short tools.

Long tools, like gardening shovels, rakes, hoes, and so on, should hang next to each other on a wall without touching. They also need to stay off the floor where they can be damaged or create a tripping hazard. Hook- and rack-style organizers and all garage organizational systems, like track, gridwall, or slatwall organizers, can hang long tools. Many of these organizers carry different-sized storage accessories made to store small, medium, and large items.

Drawers

Drawer storage for smaller hand tools should have individual compartments for gardening tools due to safety reasons and also to make them easy to find. Additionally, you don't want gardening tools colliding into one another from drawer movement, which can cause breakage or scratches. In drawer storage, arrange gardening tools by keeping like tools together; therefore, place gardening cutting instruments in one section of the drawer and digging tools in another. Small handled gardening tools with metal components can also be stored on magnetic strips attached to the garage wall. All wall-mounted garage systems, like pegboard or slatwall, have hooks and organizers to hold this type of tool.

Garden pocketed pouches or bags are also good carry organizers for short-handled tools on a shelf or hanging by the straps on a hook.

Shelving

Standard shelving is the best universal organizer for holding a number of lawn and garden items, such as buckets, pots, baskets, containers, soil, fertilizers, pest controls, boots, watering cans, hoses, seeds, and knee pads. Wire shelving is a good choice because the dirt and debris from lawn and garden items will fall in between the wires, making cleanup easy.

There are different ways to incorporate shelving in a garage. Shelving is included as an accessory with most organizational systems, such as pegboard, slatwall, and so on. Or you can use shelves with brackets that hook into an adjustable track. A freestanding shelving unit's another option. Utility cabinets contain shelves, and their doors hide their contents, offering a neat appearance in a garage.

When storing items on a shelf, keep good order and use the space efficiently. Nest all your buckets and pots in order to conserve shelf space. It's important to containerize small items and groups of things. Baskets, bins, and containers work great—and as always, label them. To house small tools on shelving, use a tool caddy that has dividers. Similarly, a bucket organizer is designed with pocketed tool dividers that wrap around it for holding tools and gloves.

Pesticides and other hazardous lawn and garden chemicals should be kept on high shelves, especially when pets and children reside in the home. A locking utility cabinet is another option. Keep all combustible chemicals away from any heat source.

Heavy bags of soil, mulch, grass seed, and the like are best kept on the lower shelves; they're also convenient to place on rolling carts that can slip under a shelf or worktable. Any storage organizer that can roll these bags out to your work area will be worthwhile.

Pool/Hot Tub Accessories

The first thing to think about when it comes to organizing pool or hot tub supplies and accessories is locating the best storage spot, given the proximity to the pool or hot tub. It may be necessary to split pool or hot tub articles between a few storage locations, such as the garage, shed, or outdoor location, depending on the climate and space.

Pools or hot tubs that are in use only part of the year must be broken down, and everything related to them must be put away for a period of time. Draining, packing, cleaning, covering, deflating, and winterizing are among the necessary chores. If you have the space, an outdoor shed is an ideal place to store pool toys, loungers, slides, pool covers, ladders, swim vests, goggles, and so on, whether all year round or off-season. A conveniently located shed encourages items to seek regular covered storage, which keeps the yard neat and shields damaging sunlight that fades articles. You can even set up a shelf to store towels and use the shed as a changing room. Whenever possible, let the sun dry pool accessories before storing them inside a shed or garage. There are outdoor poolside and fence organizers designed to line dry wet items. Choose indoor pool organizers that prevent water from standing. Wire shelves are great for wet items so puddles don't form and warp shelving material. Containers used to hold wet items, like swim masks, flippers, goggles, water guns, pool toys, and so on, should have slots or hole openings so water can drain, preventing mold. Pool items need organizers that are mold or mildew resistant, like PVC plastic since you are storing items that have been in the water. Plastic is also easy to clean.

Mesh nylon drawstring laundry bags can hold both pool and beach items; specialized beach totes are made similarly. These types of bags are designed to shake out the sand through the mesh, making them easy to hose down and hang dry. You can also use ventilated laundry baskets and hampers designed for air circulation for these items. Laundry hampers can rest on the garage floor and store tall pool accessories, like noodles, kickboards, and rafts. Cut out additional holes at the base of a laundry basket to allow for water drainage. Specialized mesh ventilated poolside storage bins on casters are also made for this purpose and are sold at many lawn and garden centers. Wheeled hampers are convenient for moving items back and forth from the pool to the garage.

In the off-season you can stow pool skimmers, rescue tubes, life jackets, preservers, poolside coolers, basketball hoops, floating volleyball nets, slides, and golf games in the garage's overhead compartments. Always deflate, clean, dry, fold, and pack these items away in their original packages or containers before storing. You can quickly deflate pool items with an electric air pump.

Pool chemicals need special storage attention since they can be dangerous. Inhaling harmful fumes or improper handling can lead to serious problems. They should, first and foremost, be stored out of the reach of children and pets in a cool, dry place and away from sunlight. Never store them next to fertilizers, gasoline, grease, paints, herbicides, turpentine, tile cleaners, or flammable materials.

This really narrows storage choices for pool chemicals and makes storing them in congested garages, sheds, or spaces tricky. Refrain from storing chemicals overhead since they could spill onto a person or animal and cause bodily harm. Make sure caps are screwed tightly, and don't transfer chemicals into different containers because you never know the reaction they could have with another material. To avoid spills, don't stack chemical containers. Know which chemicals can store safely with others. A locking, vented chest placed on the ground is a good storage option.

Beach/Boating Items

Beach gear, like outdoor games, coolers, picnic baskets, folding tables, chairs, and sand toys are logical to store with pool and hot tub belongings. However, if a shed is not an option, the garage is the next best storage space for these items. Shelving units, utility cabinets, and wall hook organizers are good storage solutions for housing these belongings in the garage.

Bulky beach items, like sand umbrellas, tents, canopies, and shelters, can be stored in overhead compartments in the garage. They can also hang sideways on the garage wall from large hooks. These items should be kept in an outer case to protect them from tears and dirt in between use. Beach chairs can hang on a wall rack with lawn and spectator chairs since they're often interchangeable. Many organizational systems, like slatwall, have several sizes of hook accessories that can hold these items.

Water companions, like rafts, water trampolines, inflatable boats, kayaks/canoes, and all body or surfboards, do require specific garage-storage arrangements. Specialized dowel-based organizers are designed to separate and secure many of these types of items. There are lift systems that can store the larger, heavy items, like canoes. An overhead platform is another storage idea for large bulky items. Many related accessories, such as fishing poles, oars, and water skis, can be stored on wall-mounted hooks or brackets. There are also specialized racks for accessories. All these items are good to store near sporting goods.

Reduce beach toys every season or once a year, like before the summer. Remove all the worn, broken, and outgrown toys. With a permanent marker, label each sand toy with your last name. Clean all your sand toys well before packing them when the season is over.

Patio Furniture and Accessories

In seasonal climates, you can store your patio furniture and cushions in the garage, provided you have ample space. Otherwise, it's best to invest in well-made patio furniture covers and keep the furniture outside during the off-season. Cushions need to be bagged and stored in overhead compartments or even taken into the home during the off-season. Consider stacking chairs on top of tables, provided you can do so safely, and nest outdoor tables and chairs whenever possible. Table umbrellas can be stored in overhead compartments alongside beach umbrellas or other long and narrow belongings. They can also be stored lengthwise on the garage wall from wall hooks. Umbrella covers are necessary to protect them from tears and dirt.

Automotive Supplies

Every household has a unique collection of automotive belongings, and some have none. For example, a household mechanic will have an extensive line of automotive tools and parts, whereas many homes will just have the basics. The most popular automotive items stored in the average home are tools, car care items, roadside emergency items, engine oils, fluids, and chemicals. The following information details how to organize and arrange them in a garage.

Basic auto tools and mechanic repair gadgets need a work zone in a garage where the service work is performed. Larger vehicle repair-related items, such as work lights, hoists, and jacks, need to be stored openly so they're easy to access in the garage stall where service is provided. Since many of these types of items are heavy and bulky, floor space should be carved out for them.

Handheld Tools

First, group all your handheld auto tools by type, such as wrenches, screwdrivers, and so on. It's important to discard tools that are rusted, broken, or ineffective. Any tools not used should also be removed. After decluttering, count how many you have of each type and make sure to end up with a quantity that satisfies your work routine.

Store your smaller auto tools openly above a workbench on a wall-mounted organizational system, such as slatwall, gridwall, or pegboard, where they can suspend from hooks or pegs. Magnetic strips can hold metal tools. Hand tools can also keep in a portable tool box when they need to be mobile. The most popular place to store a large collection of smaller automotive tools is in a rolling tool cabinet, commonly made of steel. Such organizers contain several compartmentalized

pullout drawers in small, medium, and large sizes. Use drawer compartments to divide tools by type. Usually, laying tools in opposite directions, so the top of one meets the bottom of the other, will condense storage space.

Automotive Liquids

Oils, fluids, and chemicals account for one of biggest categories of automotive items stored in the garage. There are numerous types of liquid items since there are so many working parts to the engine that require a different oil, fluid, or chemical. How many varieties of these products are stocked in the garage will depend on the depth of work a household mechanic performs on a vehicle.

There are a few good ways to situate these products in a garage; for the most part, store them together in a single tower cabinet with multiple shelves where each shelf holds a certain type of product. Such items can also be stored inside garage cabinetry or closets. Many automotive liquids are flammable or combustible. Dust, moisture, and temperature conditions can degrade some of these products, so it's important to read all labels or contact the manufacturer for storage recommendations if they're not provided.

All of these products are recommended to stay in their original containers to avoid contamination and product confusion. Leaky containers and poorly screwed on enclosure caps can cause hazards, so it's important to be diligent about proper handling. The following are the most popular automotive products, along with the best storage and handling information for each.

Motor Oil

Motor oil has a shelf life of approximately five years. However, improper storage conditions affect shelf life. After opening, motor oil must be well sealed since any moisture, dust, and other airborne chemicals introduced to it degrade the quality, causing sludge or deterioration. Extreme temperatures—below 40°F or above 85°F—affect the oil quality. Motor oil is also flammable, so don't store it near high heat or fire. For these reasons, garage storage can be a tricky place to store motor oil.

Coolants

Antifreeze, or coolant, keeps car radiators from freezing or overheating, which makes it a temperature-stable product to store in a hot or cold garage. Although coolants are not flammable, it's best to store them as combustibles, meaning away from high heat and fire. The biggest concern with antifreeze and coolant is the toxicity levels in the key ingredient, ethylene glycol, which is a big concern with pets and small children. Some antifreeze and coolants are marketed as less toxic but are still classified as "hazardous when ingested." Therefore, high shelves or locked cabinets are best for these products.

Wiper Fluid

Windshield wiper fluid can be stored in fluctuating garage temperatures, but keep it in its original container with a childproof cap for a good reason: it's highly toxic. The chemical methanol is in the solution and can be fatal if ingested. Store this product in a locking garage cabinet or on a high shelf.

Power Steering and Brake Fluids

Both power steering fluid and brake fluid should remain in their original containers and stored in a dry area away from dampness, dust, and air. Since they're classified as combustible, don't store them near heat, sparks, open flames, or any source of ignition. Always reference the product's labeling for safe storage procedures.

For the most part, brake fluid is recommended as a single-use product since it easily absorbs moisture from the atmosphere once opened, which quickly degrades its quality. However, it can store up to a year, provided it's immediately resealed. Unopened brake fluid can last up to five years in optimal storage conditions.

Gasoline

Gasoline must be kept in an approved container; check the fire codes in your area for how much can be kept on your property. For safety reasons, gasoline must be stored fifty feet away from heat sources, such as pilot lights or any ignition source. Always store it away from puncturing tools and high off the ground where only adults have access. Gasoline can remain usable for three to five months. An added fuel stabilizer extends its shelf life a few more months.

Car Cleaning and Detailing Products

Vehicle detailing or cleaning products, such as wax, polish, protectants, and shampoos, are typically safe to store in the garage. However, a storage problem arises in extreme temperature hikes and drops, like from 30°–70°F, because dramatic temperature fluctuations can cause many cleaning products—namely oil-based waxes, compounds, sealants, polishes, and such—to separate. Eventually, repeated occurrences can permanently alter the composition of the product to the point that the separation is irreversible. This is less likely to occur with liquid soaps, degreasers, and glass cleaners. Generally, most auto detailing products have a three- to five-year shelf life, which is shortened by great temperature changes.

It's convenient to store detailing cleaners in handled caddy organizers for easy transport back and forth to the vehicle. It's best to separate exterior and interior cleaners. Storage containers can house corresponding cleaning tools, such as rags, buffers, brushes, and so on. Shop towels and rags can also be stored in towel-dispensing organizers on a wall, where they're easy to access for many garage uses.

Paints and Primers

Automotive paints and primers come in many forms, such as aerosols cans, regular metal cans, and touch-up pens. Similar to other types of paint, these products require storage in a warm, dry place. The cold dramatically and permanently affects their viscosity, which can lead to a host of problems with your vehicle's painting process and the results. Therefore, store these products in the garage only when temperatures remain constant between 60°F and 80°F, which is the optimal condition and should keep paints usable for up to five years.

Acknowledgments

When I was about twelve, my strong and selfless mother, Marilyn Costello, exposed my sister, Kathy, and me to an act of kindness that was so powerful I still remember nearly every detail of the event. I am fortunate to have a large extended family that looked out for one another. At that time, an elderly relative's landlord was going to evict her if she didn't clear out the tremendous clutter in her apartment, so my mother recruited us to help her keep her home. I can remember moving through the apartment on a narrow path in between mounds of belongings that towered over our heads. My mother helped us through that massive decluttering process that resulted in a wonderful person keeping her apartment, which was now a more peaceful place.

During that experience, I vividly remember that I innately knew how to reduce the enormous amounts of clutter without feeling overwhelmed or stumped. That experience has always stayed with me and eventually led me to form my residential home organizing company, Organizing Interiors. I am truly just one of those oddballs obsessed with order and born to organize. It's great how life can work out to allow a person to form a career out of a passion and help others at the same time.

With the help of a highly skilled developmental editor, Jill Welsh, and an extraordinarily passionate copy editor, Kim Bookless, I was able to pull off this all-encompassing book. Both of these editors showed me how my knowledge of home organizing ultimately could become a reference guide for readers who want to get their own homes in order. Illustrator Katie Erickson visually transferred my home organizing concepts perfectly. Polishing off the act was Jera Publishing. This incredible organization artfully and effectively brought this book to the world.

About the Author

Caralyn Kempner is a professional home organizer and an active member of the National Association of Productivity and Organizing Professionals (NAPO). She specializes in residential organizing. Nothing is more rewarding for Caralyn than less stressed clients after she's helped them manage their home clutter with customized storage arrangements that fit their lifestyles and personalities. *Top-to-Bottom Home Organizing* is her first book.

Caralyn lives in the Chicago suburb of Northbrook with her husband, three children, and two small dogs. Before becoming a professional home organizer, Caralyn was the president of a successful telecommunications business, but now she is the happiest doing what comes naturally: planning and organizing home storage spaces.

If you find *Top-to-Bottom Home Organizing* helpful for organizing your home, stay tuned because there is more, including a new product in development! Visit Caralyn's website, www.organizinginteriors.com, and her blog at www.organizinginteriors.blog for unfolding details and even more home organizing advice and photos of her projects. You can contact Caralyn at caralyn@organizinginteriors.com and also find her on the following:

www.caralynkempner.com
www.facebook.com/caralynkempner
www.instagram.com/caralynkempner
www.pinterest.com/caralynkempner
www.twitter.com/caralynkempner

Made in the USA
San Bernardino, CA
13 May 2020